A Fuego y Sangre:
Early Zapotec Imperialism
in the Cuicatlán Cañada, Oaxaca

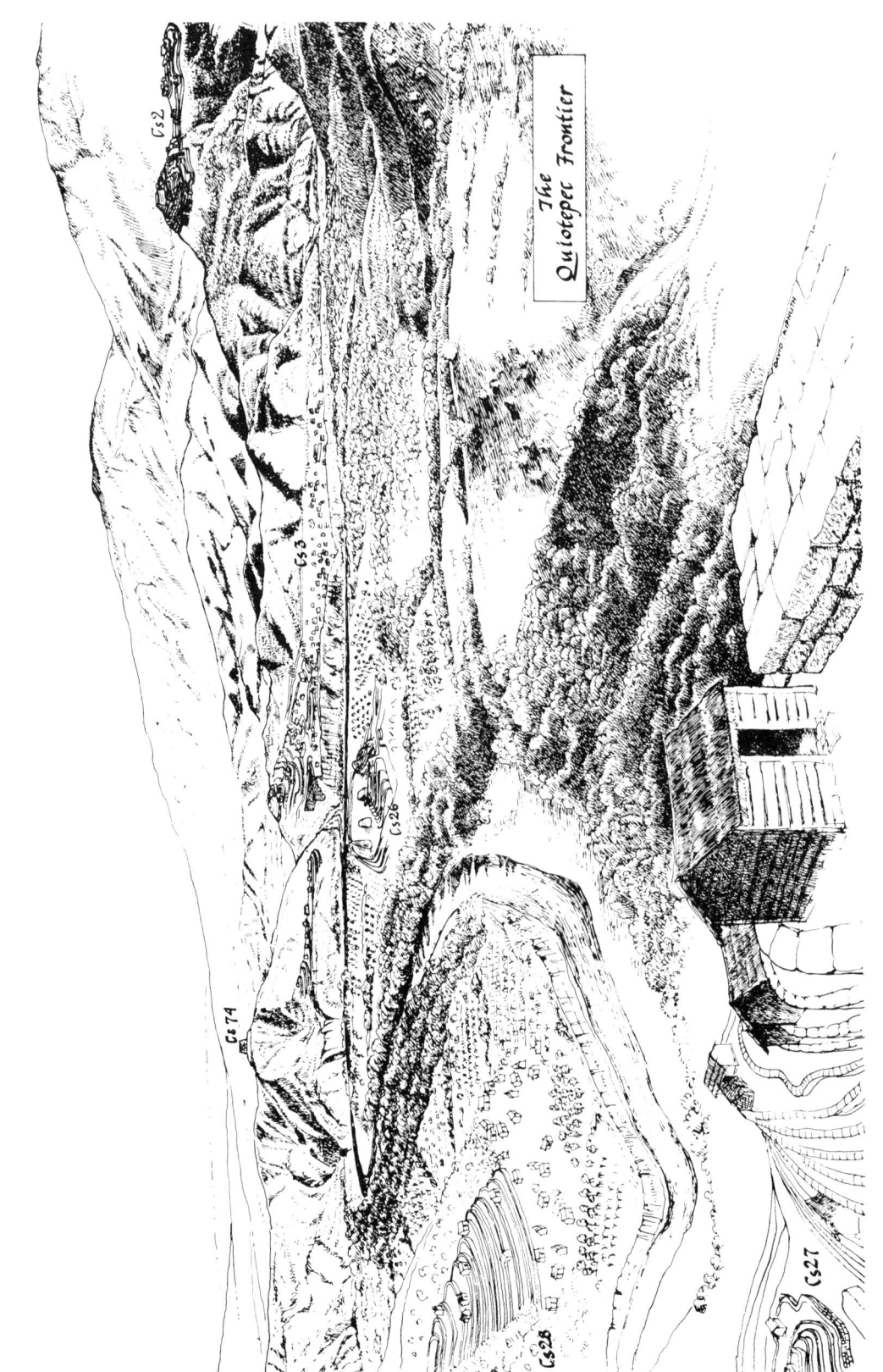

Frontispiece. The Quiotepec frontier. Sites Cs2, Cs3, and Cs74 guarded the narrow pass through the mountain ridge at the Cañada's northern boundary. Opposite the pass lay the open plaza of Cs26, and the associated communities of Cs28 and Cs27 extended farther to the south.

MEMOIRS OF THE MUSEUM OF ANTHROPOLOGY
UNIVERSITY OF MICHIGAN
NUMBER 16

**Studies in Latin American
Ethnohistory & Archaeology**

Joyce Marcus, General Editor

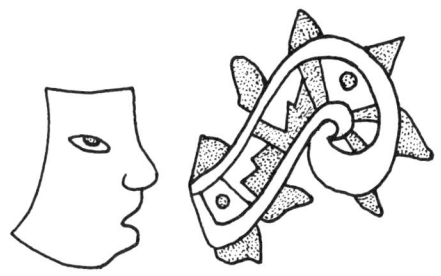

Volume I

A Fuego y Sangre:
Early Zapotec Imperialism
in the Cuicatlán Cañada, Oaxaca

by

Elsa M. Redmond

ANN ARBOR
1983

This series is partially supported by a grant-in-aid No. 4453 from the Wenner-Gren Foundation for Anthropological Research, whose Director of Research, Lita Osmundsen, offered both encouragement and help during the preparation of the grant proposal. Generous funds were also supplied by the Museum of Anthropology, University of Michigan, through the efforts of former Director Richard I. Ford.

© Regents of the University of Michigan
The Museum of Anthropology
All Rights Reserved

Printed in the
United States of America

ISBN 0-932206-97-2

An Introduction to the Series and to Volume 1

by
Joyce Marcus

With this *Memoir*, the Museum of Anthropology at the University of Michigan begins publication of a new series of monographs entitled "Studies in Latin American Ethnohistory and Archaeology." For some time since coming to the University of Michigan, I have felt that investigators who combined archival and documentary research with archaeological data needed an outlet for their monograph-length studies. Ethnohistory and archaeology can be used as two independent lines of primary research; the results from these two lines of information may agree, may conflict, or may not even overlap. However, when ethnohistory and archaeology are well integrated, these two sub-disciplines can produce results that are more powerful and impressive than either, alone, could have contributed.

Some scholars consider ethnohistory "documentary ethnology" or the collection of sixteenth- and seventeenth-century "ethnographic" data obtained through the efforts of the first European eyewitnesses (e.g., Spores 1973:25). In the New World, ethnohistory is our bridge to the past (Marcus 1978:173). For a whole series of topics—including religion, ritual, political strategies in warfare and alliance, ancient place names, meaning of iconographic elements in ancient writing systems, tribute quotas—the ethnohistoric record serves as our interpretive key.

Ethnohistory's strength is that it often permits a detailed synchronic reconstruction involving the interplay of multiple events and factors at one point in time, or over a short period of time. On the other hand, the strength of archaeology is that it allows us to document process, change, and evolution over very long spans of time. If we combine ethnohistory's detailed view of synchronic developments with archaeology's diachronic record, we are often in a better position to weigh, interpret, and explain the various transformations that we can detect in the evolution of ancient societies.

Ethnohistory may be used to develop testable models about past behavior. Just how far back these ethnohistoric patterns and models can be projected or extended will vary significantly from region to region and from ethnic group to ethnic group. There are certainly some areas of Latin America where ethnic and linguistic groups show long-term stability in their geographical location and in boundary maintenance. In such areas, it seems likely that certain beliefs, customs, and practices recorded in sixteenth-century dictionaries of indigenous languages and in ethnohistoric documents constitute long-term adaptations that over time may have been readapted or modified in degree, rather than in kind. In other words, ethnohistory may sometimes record strategies, beliefs, and practices that are legacies from earlier epochs.

The first volume in this series is an example of model-building from the ethnohistoric sources, and it is also an example of how various models can be evaluated against archaeologically-derived (survey and excavation) data. The degree of "fit" between two epochs—archaeological and ethnohistorical—and two data sets can then be assessed. Oaxaca is a very good place to attempt such integration and such evaluation of degree of "fit," because we have reason to believe that many Otomanguean populations have been in the southern Mexican highlands for several thousand years, occupying virtually the same territories in the sixteenth century as they did in Prehispanic times.

In her study of the Cuicatlán Cañada, Elsa Redmond seeks to evaluate the applicability of a sixteenth-century model from ethnohistorical sources—based on Zapotec militaristic strategies, presence of military "orders," use of frontier garrisons, exaction of tribute after subjugation—to earlier times. One of her conclusions is that the ethnohistoric model of Late Postclassic Zapotec expansion into *tierra caliente* for the purpose of exacting tribute in the form of tropical fruits and nuts also fits the archaeologically-documented expansion of the Zapotec state centered at Monte Albán during Period II, around the birth of Christ. At that time Monte Albán apparently sought to expand its territory by implementing a strategy of raiding, conquest, and subjugation of localities outside the Valley of Oaxaca. Evidence for this model comes from the Zapotec capital, Monte Albán, in the form of more than 40 inscribed slabs set in the walls of Building J, slabs which record the names of those regions or locales dominated by Monte Albán. While we do not know all the motives behind this expansion, Redmond believes that the subjugated peoples supplied some of the goods, services, and labor that were necessary to maintain Zapotec garrisons and fortified sites on the frontier. So far all of the places tentatively identified among the "subjugated places" lie outside the Valley of Oaxaca proper, and one of these subjugated places is believed to be Cuicatlán (Marcus 1976, 1980).

Redmond's model views some of the sixteenth-century militaristic practices of the expansionist Zapotec as analogous to militaristic practices of the earlier Monte Albán II state. Her perspective was to view the strategy of the state's center from its frontier. The focus of Redmond's attention is the Cuicatlán Cañada, a narrow canyon that serves as the main corridor linking the Valley of Oaxaca with the Valley of Tehuacán. At the time of the Spanish Conquest, the Cañada was inhabited by Cuicatec speakers who were closely related to the highland Mixtec, and more distantly related to the Chocho-Popolocan speakers of the Tehuacán Valley (Hunt 1972:166-176).

After developing an ethnohistorically-derived model delineating some of the causes, preconditions, and consequences of a Zapotec conquest of the Cuicatlán Cañada, Redmond begins her archaeological story with settlement pattern data from the Middle Formative (ca. 650-300 B.C.). Redmond reconstructs Middle Formative society in the Cañada as a series of small, autonomous, ranked societies whose chiefly elites were participating in interregional exchange networks, linking the elites of neighboring or adjacent polities over much of southern Mesoamerica. Redmond's systematic survey recovered 12 Middle Formative sites, two of these being chiefly centers. All sites at this time were located in close proximity to the low alluvium; the sites were all on high alluvial terraces except in areas with no high alluvium, where they were situated on the lower part of the piedmont slope. The sites display a two-level size hierarchy that may represent a simple chiefdom composed of a senior lineage at the chiefly center, with lower-ranking cadet lineages at the smaller, newer sites. Her proposed chiefly centers were larger, with more public architecture, more imported Valley of Oaxaca pottery, more marine shell, and more obsidian than the smaller communities. In exchange for these imported items, the Cañada chiefs may have been sending tropical fruits and nuts (e.g., black zapote, coyol nuts, ciruela) to the Valley of Oaxaca.

In the succeeding period (Lomas phase, ca. 300 B.C.-A.D. 200), the Valley Zapotec expanded into the Cañada region (as well as other regions outside the valley). Twenty-one newly-established settlements were now located on the piedmont spurs and on ridges that overlooked the canyon floor. The largest settlements were established in the Quiotepec region, with sites so large that the population could not have been supported exclusively with the yields available from the Quiotepec alluvial fan. Redmond presents convincing evidence that this sudden concentration of settlement in the Quiotepec region represents the location of military forces in fortified sites on both sides of the critical mountain pass along the northern boundary of the Cañada; here on the Quiotepec frontier, the Zapotec state stationed its troops to guard and defend the state's frontier, and to regulate the flow of goods and people across those boundaries. Significantly, Quiotepec is the northern limit of both local Lomas phase pottery and imported Monte Albán Ic-II pottery.

If the Zapotec state was interested in controlling the Quiotepec pass and extracting tropical goods from the region, they would have placed military personnel in the Quiotepec area and relocated the local people away from their alluvial sites so that that land could be devoted exclusively to orchards and fields. In support of this reconstruction Redmond presents the following evidence: (1) all 12 of the Middle Formative Perdido phase sites (all located close to the low alluvium) were abandoned by Late Formative times; the new Lomas phase communities were located on piedmont spurs, thereby freeing the high-quality alluvial land for extensive fields of desired agricultural products; (2) during the Lomas phase the high alluvium was brought under canal irrigation for the first time; (3) a disproportionate number of people were concentrated in fortified sites in the northern frontier zone, presumably placed there to control the pass connecting the limits of the Zapotec state with the Tehuacán Valley; and (4) a significant amount of the Cañada agricultural produce may have been used to provision the Zapotec troops at the Quiotepec frontier.

Perhaps the most dramatic physical evidence for the Zapotec subjugation of this area was the discovery of a toppled-over skull rack, composed of 61 skulls, in the main plaza atop Loma de la Coyotera (Spencer 1982:236-239). The presence of this skull rack agrees well with the "terror tactics" practiced by the Postclassic Zapotec in newly-subjugated regions.

In the succeeding Trujano phase (A.D. 200-1000) the Zapotec apparently withdrew their forces from the Cañada and turned their attention to the Valley of Oaxaca proper, as well as to long-distance diplomatic relationships with major centers such as Teotihuacán. The Trujano phase had a two or three-level hierarchy of settlement size; each of the four alluvial fans in the Cañada had one large settlement (8-12 ha) with smaller sites around it. Redmond suggests that the autonomous *cacicazgo* may have arisen in the Cañada at this time and endured until the Spaniards arrived in the sixteenth century.

At the time of the Spanish Conquest, each alluvial fan supported a *cacicazgo*. The three major Cuicatec *cacicazgos* were focused on the Atlatlauca, Dominguillo, and Cuicatlán fans; a Mazatec *cacicazgo* was located on the Quiotepec alluvial fan (Hunt 1972:167). Each *cacicazgo* delimited its territory with natural landmarks such as painted boulders, barrancas, and so forth. These *cacicazgos* were linked by an exchange network as well as strategic marriage alliances between ruling elites.

Redmond discovers that the fit between sixteenth-century ethnohistoric data on the Cuicatec *cacicazgos* and archaeological data from the Trujano (A.D. 200-1000) and Iglesia Vieja (A.D. 1000-1520) phases is close. Near each alluvial fan she found a major settlement on a hilltop with sizable public buildings, surrounded by residential terraces. These hilltop centers presumably correspond to the *cabeceras* the Spaniards described.

The autonomous *cacicazgo* was apparently the most stable and long-term adaptation made in the Cuicatlán Cañada. Without the temporary Zapotec takeover, however, the story of the Cañada probably would have been one of slower evolution from simple ranked society to complex chiefdom. In Redmond's study, therefore, the ethnohistoric data on the Zapotec provide us with a description of the strategies of the expansionist state, while the ethnohistoric data on the Cuicatec provide us with local integrative strategies such as exchange and marriage alliances between members of chiefly lineages.

Bibliography

Hunt, Eva V.
    1972   Irrigation and the Socio-Political Organization of Cuicatec Cacicazgos. In *The Prehistory of the Tehuacan Valley*, Vol. 4: Chronology and Irrigation, edited by Frederick Johnson, pp. 162-259. Austin: University of Texas Press.

Marcus, Joyce
    1976   The Iconography of Militarism at Monte Albán and Neighboring Sites in the Valley of Oaxaca. In *The Origins of Religious Art and Iconography in Preclassic Mesoamerica*, edited by Henry B. Nicholson, pp. 123-139. Los Angeles: Latin American Center, University of California at Los Angeles.
    1978   Archaeology and Religion: A Comparison of the Zapotec and Maya. *World Archaeology* 10(2):172-191.
    1980   Zapotec Writing. *Scientific American* 242:50-64.

Spencer, Charles S.
    1982   *The Cuicatlán Cañada and Monte Albán: A Study of Primary State Formation*. New York: Academic Press.

Spores, Ronald M.
    1973   Special Problems in Methodology. In *Research in Mexican History*, edited by Richard E. Greenleaf and Michael C. Meyer, pp. 25-48. Lincoln: University of Nebraska Press.

Contents

Tables xi
Figures xiii
Plates xv
Acknowledgments xvii

1. Introduction 1
    Monte Albán as a Militaristic State 1
    The Role of Militarism in Early State Development 10
    Toward an Interregional Perspective on Militarism and the Monte Albán State 14

2. The Cuicatlán Cañada: A Model of its Proposed Subjugation by Monte Albán 17
    The Cuicatlán Cañada 17
    Selecting the Cuicatlán Cañada for Study 23
    The Proposed Subjugation of the Cuicatlán Cañada by Monte Albán 26
        Selection of the Conquest Hypothesis 26
        Zapotec Militarism and Frontier Administration 26
        Framework for Evaluating the Conquest Hypothesis 29
        Preconditions of Conquest in the Cuicatlán Cañada 30
        The Transformation of the Cuicatlán Cañada into a Frontier Tributary Region 32
        Effects of the Conquest Strategy upon the Emerging Zapotec State 34
    The 1977-78 Cuicatlán Cañada Project 36
        The Cuicatlán Cañada Survey 36
        A Catchment Analysis of the Cuicatlán Cañada 39
        A Ceramic Chronology for the Cuicatlán Cañada 41
        The Dating of Surface Collections 50
        Neutron-Activation Analysis of Ceramics from the Oaxaca Valley and the Cuicatlán Cañada 60

3. The Cuicatlán Cañada During the Perdido Phase 63
    Perdido Phase Settlements and Regional Organization 63
    Perdido Phase Settlements and their Highland Neighbors 73

4. The Cuicatlán Cañada During the Lomas Phase 83
    Transition 83
    The Structure of a Frontier Region 87
    The Quiotepec Frontier 91
    Military Control and Administration at the Quiotepec Frontier 107
    Civil Administration of the Central and Southern Cañada 120

	A Port of Trade Beyond the Frontier	130
	Summary	142
5.	**The Cuicatlán Cañada During the Trujano Phase**	145
	Transition	145
	Classic Period Developments in Highland Mesoamerica	149
	Ethnohistory and Postclassic Period Developments in the Cuicatlán Cañada	154
	The Emergence of Autonomous *Cacicazgos* in the Cuicatlán Cañada	163
6.	**Summary and Conclusion**	169
	Summary	169
	Conclusion	170
	Establishment of a Permanent Military Organization	171
	Administration of a Tributary Network	176
	New Interregional Exchange Mechanisms	180
	Political Ascendance of the Military	182

Appendix I. Neutron-Activation Analysis of Ceramics from the Valley of Oaxaca and the Cuicatlán Cañada, by Elsa M. Redmond and Garman Harbottle 185

Bibliography 207

Resumen en Español 213

Tables

1.	Differing Irrigated Maize Yields in Physiographic Zones of the Cuicatlán Cañada	39
2.	Corrected Maize Yields for Pre-Conquest Cob Lengths and Higher Average Maize Productivity in the Cuicatlán Cañada	40
3.	Area of Low Alluvium and High Alluvium on the Cañada's Alluvial Fans	40
4.	The Sizes of Perdido Phase Settlements	64
5.	Estimated Carrying Capacity of the Cañada's Low Alluvium and Perdido Phase Settlement	64
6.	Distribution of Perdido Gray Incised Outleaned-Wall Bowl Motifs 5 and 6 at 12 Late Middle Formative Settlements	75
7.	Distribution of Late Middle Formative Ceramics Imported from Oaxaca at 12 Perdido Phase Settlements	75
8.	Distribution of Late Middle Formative Ceramics Imported from Tehuacán at 12 Perdido Phase Settlements	77
9.	Distribution of Obsidian at 12 Perdido Phase Settlements	79
10.	Distribution of Obsidian and Late Middle Formative Ceramics Imported from Oaxaca at 9 Perdido Phase Settlements	80
11.	The Sizes of Lomas Phase Settlements	85
12.	Comparison of Perdido and Lomas Phase Settlement on the Cañada's Alluvial Fans	86
13.	Distribution of Late Formative Ceramics Imported from Oaxaca at 17 Lomas Phase Settlements	86
14.	Distribution of Monte Albán Ic-II Ceramics Within and Beyond the Cuicatlán Cañada	87
15.	Distribution of Chipped Stone at 13 Lomas Phase Settlements	88
16.	Estimators of Population at Lomas Phase Settlements in the Quiotepec Area	96
17.	Distribution of Ground Stone Tools at Lomas Phase Settlements in the Quiotepec Area	96
18.	Estimated Carrying Capacity of the Cañada's Alluvium during the Lomas Phase	106
19.	Distribution of Projectile Points in the Survey Area during the Lomas Phase	110
20.	Distribution of Stone Labrets at Settlements in the Quiotepec Area	110
21.	Distribution of Craft-Related Artifacts at Settlements in the Quiotepec Area	112
22.	Dimensions of Clay Spindle Whorls Recovered from the Cuicatlán Cañada Survey	114
23.	Distribution of Obsidian Artifacts at Settlements in the Quiotepec Area	115
24.	Distribution of Lomas Plain Imitations of Monte Albán Ic-II Cremas at 17 Lomas Phase Settlements	117
25.	Estimated Labor Requirements for Farming the Cañada's Alluvium during the Lomas Phase	117
26.	Estimators of Population at Lomas Phase Settlements in the Central and Southern Cañada	129
27.	Distribution of Ground Stone Tools and Comales at Llano de los Mogotes	137
28.	Density of Sherds in the Ceramic Workshop	138
29.	Craft-Related Artifacts in the Ceramic Workshop	139
30.	Distribution of Thin Orange Ceramics and Green Obsidian at Llano de los Mogotes	141
31.	Distribution of Foreign Ceramics at Llano de los Mogotes	141
32.	Distribution of El Riego Gray Decorated Ceramics at 17 Lomas Phase Settlements	142
33.	The Sizes of Trujano Phase Settlements in the Cuicatlán Cañada	146
34.	Comparison of Lomas and Trujano Phase Settlement on the Cañada's Alluvial Fans	146
35.	Estimators of Population at Trujano Phase Settlements in the Cuicatlán Cañada	147
36.	Estimated Carrying Capacity of the Cañada's Alluvium and Trujano Phase Settlement	147
37.	Ranking of Largest Trujano Phase Settlements and the Cañada's Four Alluvial Fans	149
38.	Public Sectors of Trujano Phase Settlements in the Cuicatlán Cañada	149
39.	Population Estimates for the *Cacicazgo* Centers in the Cuicatlán Cañada	153
40.	The Sizes of Iglesia Vieja Phase Settlements in the Cuicatlán Cañada	158
41.	Comparison of Trujano and Iglesia Vieja Phase Settlement on the Cañada's Alluvial Fans	160
42.	Estimators of Population for Three Iglesia Vieja Phase Centers in the Cuicatlán Cañada	161
43.	Estimated Carrying Capacity of the Cañada's Alluvium and Iglesia Vieja Phase Settlement	162
44.	Distribution of Chipped Stone at 10 Trujano Phase Settlements	165
45.	Distribution of Thin Orange Ceramics at 14 Trujano Phase Settlements	165
46.	Distribution of Ceramic Urn Fragments at 10 Trujano Phase Settlements	166

Figures

Frontispiece.	The Quiotepec Frontier	ii
1.	The Oaxaca Valley, with locations of archaeological sites mentioned in text.	2
2.	Plan of the Main Plaza at Monte Albán.	3
3.	Conquest-slab inscriptions from Building J at Monte Albán.	11
4.	The Cuicatlán place glyph in the Codex Mendoza.	12
5.	The Cuicatlán Cañada, Valley of Oaxaca, and Valley of Tehuacán.	18
6.	The Cuicatlán Cañada, with the locations of all modern communities	19
7.	The Cuicatlán Cañada Survey area	37
8.	Correspondence of ceramic phases in the Valley of Oaxaca, the Cuicatlán Cañada, and the Valley of Tehuacán	43
9.	Perdido Gray outleaned-wall bowls	44
10.	Perdido Gray outleaned-wall bowl rims	45
11.	Perdido Gray outleaned-wall bowl rims	46
12.	Perdido Plain olla rims	47
13.	Perdido Plain tecomate rims and bottles	48
14.	Perdido Plain tripod plate rims; hollow foot	49
15.	Lomas Gray convex-wall bowl rim; outleaned-wall bowls; shallow cylindrical bowls with basal bulges	51
16.	Lomas Gray outleaned-wall bowl rims with incised decoration	52
17.	Lomas Plain olla rims	53
18.	Lomas Plain outleaned-wall bowl and convex-wall bowl sherds with post-firing scratching	54
19.	Lomas Plain outleaned-wall bowl sherds with post-firing scratching.	55
20.	Trujano Gray outleaned-wall bowl rims	56
21.	Trujano Gray convex-wall bowl rims; solid feet	57
22.	Trujano Gray convex-wall bowl with groove below rim; S-shaped rims; molcajete rim	58
23.	Histogram of Lomas phase diagnostic ceramic densities in the surface collections	60
24.	Perdido phase regional settlement pattern map	62
25.	Scatter plot of low alluvium and Perdido phase settlement on the Cañada's four alluvial fans.	65
26.	Histogram of Perdido phase settlement sizes.	66
27.	El Mirador site map (Cs10)	67
28.	Hacienda Tecomaxtlahua site map (Cs19).	69
29.	Plan of the Perdido phase residential compound (Area A/B) at La Coyotera.	71
30.	Diagram of the regional organization of the Cuicatlán Cañada during the Perdido phase	73
31.	Two decorative motifs commonly incised on Perdido Gray bowls	74
32.	Scatter plot of the ratio of total Oaxaca imports/total diagnostics and distance from Monte Albán	76
33.	Diagram of the exchange of Oaxaca ceramics in the Cuicatlán Cañada and beyond during the late Middle Formative period	81
34.	Lomas phase regional settlement pattern map	82
35.	Histogram of Lomas phase settlement sizes in the Cuicatlán Cañada	84
36.	Histogram of Lomas phase settlement sizes in the central and southern Cañada.	85
37.	Distribution of Monte Albán Ic-II phase ceramics within and beyond the Cuicatlán Cañada.	87
38.	Scatter plot of obsidian at 13 Lomas phase settlements and distance from Monte Albán.	88
39.	Lattimore's model for the structure of a frontier region.	89
40.	Quiotepec glyph in the Codex Fernando Leal	91
41.	Paso de Quiotepec site map (Cs3)	94
42.	Martín Bazán's map of La Ciudad Vieja de Quiotepec.	98
43.	Cerro de Quiotepec site map (Cs2)	100
44.	Campo del Panteón site map (Cs26).	107
45.	El Campanario site map (Cs27)	109
46.	Cuba Libre site map (Cs6)	121
47.	Loma Grande site map (Cs13)	122
48.	La Coyotera site map (Cs25)	124
49.	An artist's reconstruction of the skull rack at Loma de la Coyotera.	132

50.	Llano de los Mogotes site map (Cs1).	134
51.	Trujano phase regional settlement pattern map.	144
52.	Histogram of Trujano phase settlement sizes.	148
53.	Loma Larga site map (Cs14).	150
54.	Sitio Entre Dos Ríos map (Cs16).	151
55.	Loma del Llano Chiquito site map (Cs11).	152
56.	Solid ceramic slab-foot support with bas-relief depiction of the central Mexican fire-serpent, Quetzalcoatl, recovered in the ballcourt of Cerro de Quiotepec (Cs2).	153
57.	Iglesia Vieja phase regional settlement pattern map.	157
58.	Histogram of Iglesia Vieja phase settlement sizes.	160
59.	Profile of an anthropomorphic ceramic urn from Monte Albán that displays many of the insignia associated with warriors.	172
60.	Ceramic jaguar statue from Suchilquitongo.	174
61.	Lápida de Bazán.	175
62.	Perdido Gray outleaned-wall bowl rims.	189
63.	Monte Albán I Crema ware in the Cañada.	190
64.	Lomas Gray outleaned-wall bowl rims and bases.	191
65.	Monte Albán Ic-II Crema ware in the Cañada.	192
66.	Lomas Plain ware imitations of Monte Albán Ic-II Cremas.	193
67.	Lomas Plain ware.	194
68.	Rosario Gray outleaned-wall bowl rims.	195
69.	Monte Albán I Gray ware.	196
70.	Monte Albán I Crema ware.	197
71.	Monte Albán Ic-II Gray outleaned-wall bowl rims and bases.	198
72.	Monte Albán Ic-II Crema ware.	199
73.	Monte Albán I-II Café ware.	200
74.	Monte Albán IIIb Gray ware.	201
75.	Dendrogram of ceramic samples submitted to neutron activation.	202

Plates

1.	Period Early I Building L at Monte Albán. Individual *danzante* relief	5
2.	The Main Plaza at Monte Albán	8
3.	Park bench in the main square of present-day San Juan Bautista Cuicatlán with the ancient toponym for Cuicatlán	13
4.	Narrow stretch of the Cuicatlán Cañada between Santiago Quiotepec and Guadalupe Obos	20
5.	Northern end of Cuicatlán alluvial fan, near Guadalupe Obos, where canyon floor widens	21
6.	Cuicatlán alluvial fan	22
7.	El Chilar alluvial fan	23
8.	A simple diversionary dam diverts water from the main river onto the flanking low alluvium in the background	24
9.	Modern irrigation facilities in the Cuicatlán Cañada: Matamba dam and Matamba canal	25
10.	Aerial view of the site of El Mirador (Cs10) on the Cuicatlán alluvial fan	68
11.	Oblique aerial view of the northern half of the site of Hacienda Tecomaxtlahua (Cs19)	70
12.	Aerial view of the Perdido phase residential compound (Area A/B) at La Coyotera	72
13.	General view of the Quiotepec alluvial fan	90
14.	View of the Quiotepec alluvium and of the natural pass through the Quiotepec mountain ridge	92
15.	Distant view of Cerro de Quiotepec (Cs2) from where the natural pass meets the Río Grande	97
16.	View of the public sector of Cerro de Quiotepec (Cs2)	99
17.	Cut stone slab and mortar retaining wall at Cerro de Quiotepec (Cs2)	102
18.	View of stone fortifications along sheer western slope of Cerro de Quiotepec (Cs2)	103
19.	Stone monuments in the ballcourt at Cerro de Quiotepec (Cs2)	104
20.	Single entryway to Cerro de Quiotepec (Cs2)	105
21.	Aerial view of the natural pass through the Quiotepec mountain ridge, the ford on the Río Grande, and the site of Campo del Panteón (Cs26) on the Quiotepec alluvium	106
22.	Two views of the large plaza at Campo del Panteón (Cs26)	108
23.	Stone projectile points found at settlements on the Quiotepec frontier	110
24.	Stone labrets found at settlements on the Quiotepec frontier	112
25.	Clay spindle whorls found at settlements on the Quiotepec alluvial fan	113
26.	Notched stones collected at El Campanario (Cs27)	114
27.	Polished-stone artifacts collected at settlements on the Quiotepec alluvial fan: adzes and a celt	115
28.	Entrance to Monte Albán-style tomb at Cerro de Quiotepec (Cs2)	118
29.	View of hilltop site of Cuba Libre (Cs6) from across the Río Grande	126
30.	Eastern face of mound at Cuba Libre (Cs6)	127
31.	View of site of Loma Grande (Cs13) on piedmont ridge rising above high alluvium	128
32.	Main aqueduct of irrigation facility associated with Loma de la Coyotera (Cs25)	130
33.	Mound A at Loma de la Coyotera (Cs25)	131
34.	Ceramic jaguar-paw urn fragments recovered from plaza areas of two Lomas phase sites in the Cuicatlán Cañada	133
35.	View of site of Llano de los Mogotes (Cs1) on high alluvium and low piedmont from opposite side of Río Salado, facing east	136
36.	View of central civic-ceremonial area of Llano de los Mogotes (Cs1)	137
37.	Misfired sherds from the ceramic workshop at Llano de los Mogotes (Cs1)	138
38.	Polished stone bark-beater from the ceramic workshop at Llano de los Mogotes (Cs1)	139
39.	Ceramic urn fragments from Trujano phase centers	167
40.	Jaguar paws on the inset panels that flank the staircase of Mound X at Monte Albán	173
41.	Period II site of Suchilquitongo, Oaxaca Valley	178
42.	Building J conquest slab with palm-fronds place glyph	179

Acknowledgments

The regional settlement pattern survey that I conducted in the Cuicatlán Cañada constituted the first phase of a collaborative research project with Charles Spencer, who later selected one of the Formative sites found during our survey for extensive excavation. My survey was supported by the Wenner-Gren Foundation for Anthropological Research (Grant No. 3211). Travel funds were provided by two Josef Albers Fellowships from Yale University. Our fieldwork in the Cañada began in May of 1977, and the ensuing period of laboratory analysis in Mexico came to an end in November of 1978.

There are two individuals without whose assistance we would never have been able to bring our field research to a successful conclusion. The first is Dr. Robert D. Drennan, who kindly offered to include our investigations in the Cuicatlán Cañada as part of his Palo Blanco Project centered in the Tehuacán Valley, and who gained the necessary permission from the Mexican authorities for our work. I have enjoyed the many scholarly and friendly benefits of my collaboration with Dr. Drennan. We are also indebted to Rafael Vásquez Cruz of Telixtlahuaca, Oaxaca, who has long been the federal archaeological inspector for the Cuicatlán Cañada. Sr. Vásquez first introduced me to the Cañada in 1974 and piqued my interest in the region and its prehistory. Upon our return in 1977, Sr. Vásquez took it upon himself to lead us on a preliminary archaeological survey of the Cañada and to assist us in our dealings with townspeople and local officials. In fact, it is thanks to Sr. Vásquez that I was able to collect information pertaining to the productivity of maize grown on the region's alluvial fans today. Sr. Vásquez's immense enthusiasm for the archaeology and natural history of Oaxaca is matched only by his own colorful storytelling.

Among the I.N.A.H. anthropologists in Mexico City who were most helpful during the months of fieldwork were Arqo. Eduardo Matos Moctezuma and Prof. José Luis Lorenzo. At the I.N.A.H. regional center in Oaxaca, Manuel Esparza and Dr. Marcus Winter assisted us in a variety of ways. I thank Dr. Winter especially for his help in selecting the sample of sherds from Monte Albán and other sites in the Oaxaca Valley for the neutron-activation analysis. Tolentino Orozco of Quiotepec, Oaxaca, facilitated our work in that wild and woolly area.

My assistants on the regional survey were Glenda Sánchez, Charles Spencer, and Pedro Carvajal and Irineo Jiménez of Cuicatlán. Their effort and goodwill in spite of the very high temperatures are greatly appreciated. Chuck deserves special credit for masterminding most of the individual site maps and for recognizing the potential significance of the natural pass at Quiotepec, even before we discovered the site of Campo del Panteón on the Quiotepec alluvium opposite the pass (see Frontispiece).

Manuel Hernández Bravo, of Coxcatlán, Puebla, contributed a variety of services to the project during the period of laboratory analysis in Tehuacán, and Laura Schlageter de Krause offered her artistic expertise. Further analysis of the survey data was conducted at the University of Michigan in Ann Arbor, where thanks to Dr. Richard Ford, Director of the Museum of Anthropology, I obtained office and laboratory space. I am also grateful to Dr. Robert Whallon and Dr. John Speth, who made it possible for me to carry out the computer analysis of my survey data there.

Dr. Garman Harbottle, of the Department of Chemistry at Brookhaven National Laboratory, performed the trace-element analysis of pottery from the Valley of Oaxaca and the Cuicatlán Cañada, the results of which are presented in Appendix I. I gratefully acknowledge the assistance of the U.S. Department of Energy for this analysis.

The dissertation upon which this volume is based assumed its final form at Yale University. I thank the members of my dissertation committee—Dr. Michael D. Coe, Dr. Kwang-chih Chang, and Dr. Frank Hole—for their criticisms and suggestions. My advisor, Dr. Coe, has been an unflagging supporter and a fountainhead of ideas and inspiration. I also wish to thank Dr. Joyce Marcus, who offered many useful corrections after carefully reading the manuscript. Dr. Marcus spurred my investigation of Zapotec militarism by introducing me to the appropriate ethnohistorical sources on the Zapotec. Dr. Robert D. Drennan and Dr. Robert Dewar also read the manuscript and contributed valuable comments. David Kiphuth, of the Yale Peabody Museum, rendered the frontispiece, among other illustrations, and Chuck Blankmeyer drafted the final versions of the artifact drawings.

As the study takes the shape of a manuscript between two covers, I remember some advice given me by a former professor: avoid reworking already published data; instead, go out and pursue your own regional settlement pattern survey. The advice was heeded, and, as a matter of fact, I already look forward to the next opportunity to carry out a similar research project.

Chapter 1

Introduction

The early Spanish friar, Francisco de Burgoa, described the Zapotec state as:

> . . . so great and so much more powerful than the nations on its horizons, that its ambitious kings proceeded to expand beyond its borders and ferociously and bravely entered the regions inhabited by Chontals and Mijes, as well as the coastal regions to the south and north, wounding, killing, and defeating until they commanded the fertile plains of Tehuantepec. [Burgoa 1674a:412, my translation]

In the present study, I hope to show that Burgoa's characterization of the protohistoric Zapotec nation is equally applicable to the earliest Zapotec state, which arose in the Valley of Oaxaca around the time of Christ. The capital of this early state was the hilltop center known to us today as Monte Albán. Accordingly, Monte Albán is the starting point for my study of Zapotec militarism and the rise of the early Zapotec state. Evidence from the site of Monte Albán suggests that the emergence of the Zapotec state during the Late Formative period was concurrent with a campaign of Zapotec military conquests in regions outside the Valley of Oaxaca. One of the regions that was apparently taken over by the polity centered at Monte Albán was the Cuicatlán Cañada, and it is in this narrow semi-tropical canyon north of the Oaxaca Valley that my investigation is based.

I will approach the study of early Zapotec imperialism by first constructing a model of the Cañada's proposed subjugation in the Late Formative period. With the aid of ethnohistorical information about the militaristic practices and imperial policies of the Valley Zapotec during the Postclassic period, I will attempt to relate the determinants and consequences of such a conquest strategy. The conquest model embraces an interregional perspective, one that weighs the effects of an early Zapotec imperial policy upon a target region like the Cuicatlán Cañada and upon the expanding polity centered at Monte Albán in the Oaxaca Valley.

I will then evaluate the conquest model with archaeological data that Charles Spencer and I recovered during our joint project in the Cuicatlán Cañada, as well as with the published data of many researchers who have investigated Monte Albán and its origins. The evaluation of the conquest model is intended to elucidate not only the sequence of prehistoric development in the Cuicatlán Cañada, but also the role that Monte Albán's conquest strategy might have played in the development of the early Zapotec state.

Monte Albán as a Militaristic State

The site of Monte Albán covers a group of five hills that preside over the junction of the three arms of the Oaxaca Valley (Fig. 1). These hills rise 300 to 400 m above the valley floor, and offer a commanding view of the entire region. Our understanding of the founding and development of Monte Albán derives from the work of a number of Mexican and American archaeologists. Alfonso Caso initiated the first large-scale explorations at the site in 1931. Over the following 27 years, Caso and his collaborators, Ignacio Bernal and Jorge R. Acosta, conducted 18 seasons of fieldwork at Monte Albán (Caso 1932, 1935, 1938, 1942; Acosta 1958). During this time they cleared and reconstructed many of the major buildings and residences in the area of the Main Plaza, and they conducted stratigraphic excavations in the central portion of the site. Their monumental endeavors produced a well-documented ceramic sequence (Caso, Bernal, and Acosta 1967), and provided a history of the construction of the platforms and buildings in and around the Main Plaza (Acosta 1965; Marquina 1964). Moreover, their research included studies of Monte Albán's inscribed stone monuments (Caso 1928, 1947), a study of Zapotec ceramic urns and figurines (Caso and Bernal 1952), and a detailed report on the tombs discovered during the first field season at Monte Albán (Caso 1970).

Within the last decade, research at Monte Albán has continued through the efforts of a number of American archaeologists. Richard Blanton directed the surface survey and mapping of the ancient city The corresponding ceramic phase is the Monte Al-

Figure 1. The Oaxaca Valley, with the locations of archaeological sites mentioned in text.

(Blanton 1976a, 1976b, 1978, 1980) as part of the ongoing Valley of Oaxaca Settlement Pattern Project (Varner 1974; Kowalewski 1976, 1980; Blanton et al. 1979). Marcus Winter conducted excavations at a group of residential terraces on the northern slope of Monte Albán (Winter 1974). Joyce Marcus is currently involved in a study of the inscribed stone monuments from the Valley of Oaxaca, and has already contributed important syntheses on the nature of the inscriptions at Monte Albán (Marcus 1974, 1976, 1980).

Monte Albán was established towards the end of the Middle Formative Period, at about 500 B.C. bán Ia phase (Caso, Bernal, and Acosta 1967:96), which Blanton designates Period Early I (500-300 B.C.) (Blanton 1978:26-29). Blanton has defined a 69-ha core area of relatively dense Early Monte Albán I occupation at Monte Albán, and a peripheral zone of light Early Monte Albán I occupation that covers an additional 255-ha area. On the basis of the distribution of Early Monte Albán I pottery within the core area of the site, Blanton proposes that the initial settlement of Monte Albán consisted of three discrete residential areas or *barrios* (Blanton 1978:33, 37-39). Blanton estimates

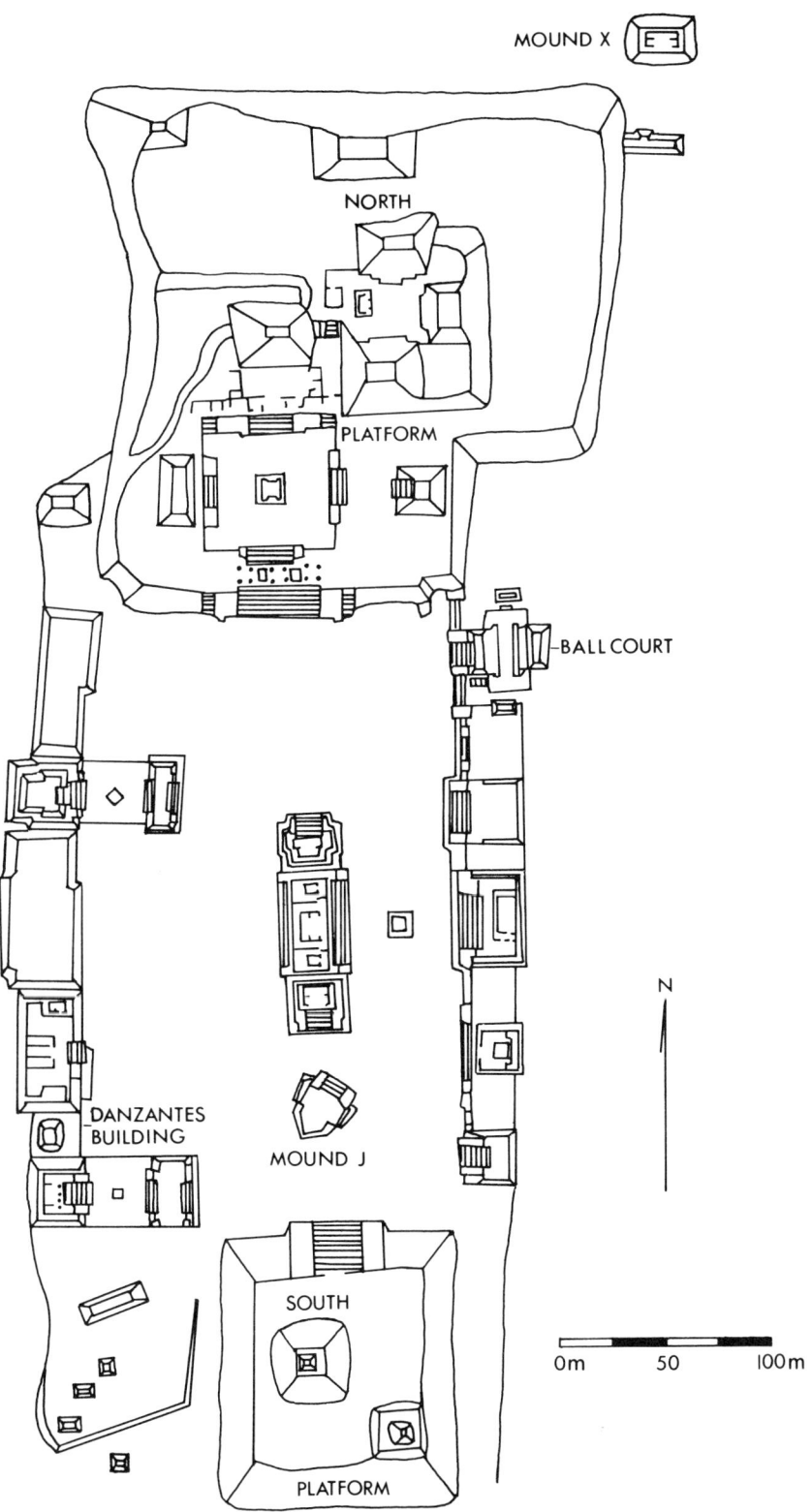

Figure 2. Plan of the Main Plaza at Monte Albán (redrawn from Marcus 1980:54).

Monte Albán's founding population in Early Monte Albán I to have been between 3500 and 7000 persons, and suggests that the figure was probably around 5000 (Blanton 1978:35; Blanton et al. 1979:377). Monte Albán was by far the largest settlement in the Valley of Oaxaca at this time (Blanton 1978:36). Monte Albán (Fig. 1) clearly formed the apex of an administrative hierarchy, which Blanton and his associates believe consisted of three distinct administrative levels (Blanton et al. 1979:377).

The Monte Albán I architects erected a small number of public buildings, at least two of which occurred in the area which later became the Main Plaza. A 2.5-2.75 m tall platform with a sloping or *talud* base and a plaster surface lay directly above bedrock on what was later the north side of the plaza. Only a small section of this building was exposed in the "P.S.A." excavations that Caso and his assistants conducted in the southeast corner of the North Platform (Caso, Bernal, and Acosta 1967:95-96). A subsequent building project succeeded in raising the platform to 3.5 m, and in decorating its façade with elaborate serpentine motifs modelled in stucco (Caso, Bernal, and Acosta 1967:814; Flannery and Marcus 1983a: Fig. 4.3).

Another Monte Albán Ia public building was Building L (Marcus 1976:125), which lay at the southwest side of what in Monte Albán II times became the Main Plaza (Fig. 2; Pl. 1). Unfortunately, the original Monte Albán Ia platform erected here has been largely altered and buried under later building stages, and its dimensions are unknown. But the Mexican archaeologists discovered that the front of this building originally featured hundreds of stone slabs with bas-relief representations of naked human figures, or *danzantes*. These nude, grimacing male figures display a variety of distorted poses, and their eyes are closed. Many wear distinctive hair styles—including hair knots and braids—as well as earplugs and necklaces; in a few instances flowery scrolls depict bleeding wounds and possibly mutilated genitalia. According to Marcus (1980:54, 56-57), the 310 or more surviving stone figures, many of which were removed and reused in buildings of later periods, were arranged originally in four rows along the east face of Building L. The figures in the lowest row were upright and faced to our right, while the second-row figures were displayed horizontally. The figures of the third row were again upright, but faced to our left. In the top row the figures were again arranged horizontally.

Furthermore Marcus notes that the figures in the bottom row at ground level were the most elaborately adorned; a few of them were even accompanied by name glyphs (Pl. 1).

Through the years since their discovery, the *danzantes* have been the subject of wide-ranging interpretations. Michael Coe (1962:95) proposed that these nude, mutilated, and lifeless figures represented slain captives. Marcus agrees with Coe's interpretation of the *danzantes*, and has attempted to understand this display of slain captives in the context of Monte Albán's political history (Marcus 1974, 1976). Marcus suggests that while a number of the distinctively adorned prisoners depicted on the east face of Building L might represent rival chiefs, "the majority of the *danzantes* probably portray lesser villagemen taken in *raids* and *skirmishes*" (Marcus 1976:126-127, emphasis added). Moreover, she believes that the *danzantes* may not necessarily be portraits of actual slain captives; instead, "they may only be symbols of 'potential' or 'attained' power" (Marcus 1976:127). Marcus' discovery that the 310 or more Monte Albán I *danzantes* constitute 80% of the total inscribed stone monuments from Monte Albán lends support to this interpretation.

> This early effort probably coincides with the time when the rulers of Monte Albán would have felt the greatest need to legitimize their power and sanctify their position. Perhaps by creating a large gallery of prisoners, they were able to convince both their enemies and their own population of their power, although it was not yet institutionalized or completely effective. [Marcus 1974:90]

In sum, Monte Albán was founded by a sizable population during Monte Albán I. At least two public buildings were erected on the north and west side of what later became the Main Plaza, on the highest point of the hill above the residential areas. One of these buildings presented an awesome display of prisoners, which leads Marcus (1974, 1976, 1980) to infer that as early as Monte Albán Ia, the monuments displayed in the Main Plaza show militaristic themes. Blanton (1976a:230-231) suggests that Monte Albán's founders were representatives drawn from previously autonomous societies on the valley floor and that Monte Albán was established as a community of specialists involved in regional decision-making matters. He believes that the three discrete residential areas surrounding the Main Plaza reflect the different groups of people—perhaps one group from each of the valley's three branches—who founded Monte Albán (Blanton 1978:37-40). But Blanton is quick to point out that

Plate 1. Monte Albán Ia "Building of the *Danzantes*" at Monte Albán. *Above*, Building L, with remaining *danzantes* reliefs, facing northwest. *Below*, individual *danzante* relief.

the establishment of Monte Albán in Period Early I may not represent the integration of the Valley of Oaxaca into a single sociopolitical unit.

> I do not necessarily mean to imply that Monte Albán was, at that time, a regional capital. Decision-making and intermediation on a regional level can occur in the absence of centralization of power at the center where the intermediation takes place. [Blanton 1976a:228]

The absence of fully centralized power at Monte Albán in Monte Albán Ia which Blanton discusses is entirely consistent with Marcus' (1974:90) interpretation of the *danzantes* as a ritual and symbolic display of potential power—intended by Monte Albán's newly-founded elite as a way of legitimizing their as yet uninstitutionalized power.

I believe that it was not until the end of Monte Albán I or the beginning of Monte Albán II (ca. 100 B.C.-A.D. 200) that the administrative community atop Monte Albán achieved fully centralized, institutionalized power. The institutionalization of power is considered by many anthropologists to be an essential ingredient of the state, and it is implemented and maintained by the use of force (Service 1975:14-15; Fried 1967:229-230). As Henry Wright has pointed out (1977:380-381), however, definitions of the state that revolve around the use of force are difficult to operationalize. Consequently, many researchers working on the origins of primary states in various developmental sequences have found it difficult to determine the point of actual state emergence.

Wright believes that states can be recognized by other characteristics besides those related to the use of force. States differ from chiefdoms in a number of ways, and these differences are archaeologically detectable, and hence, operational (Wright 1977:381, 385). Wright defines the state as:

> a cultural development with a centralized decision-making process which is both externally specialized with regard to the local process which it regulates, and internally specialized in that the central process is divisible into separate activities which can be performed in different places at different times. [Wright 1977:383]

A state's internally-specialized decision-making process differs from the central decision-making activities of a chiefdom, which can be recognized as:

> a cultural development whose central decision-making activity is differentiated from, though it ultimately regulates, decision-making regarding local production and local social process; but it is not itself internally differentiated. It is thus externally but not internally specialized. [Wright 1977:381]

The dominant political strategy of the central decision-maker in a chiefdom is to avoid the emergence of intermediary decision-makers by fostering only two levels of actual decision-making in the regional administrative hierarchy. Local community level decision-making would concern itself with local matters alone, while regional level decision-making occurs at the regional center. Since chiefly organization lacks internal specialization, any delegation of authority by the central decision-maker would be complete delegation, and the central decision-maker would run the risk of political usurpation. Local units are therefore encouraged to remain as independent and economically self-sufficient as possible, thereby placing few administrative demands on the central decision-maker (Wright 1977:381).

By contrast, the optimal organizational strategy of the central decision-maker in a state will be to encourage as much hierarchy and specialization as possible. Because state organizations are internally specialized, the central decision-maker is able to delegate certain aspects of regional level decision-making without running the risk of subordinate insurrection. Consequently, higher-order decision-makers can intervene directly into local affairs, and thereby undermine the autonomy of local decision-makers (Wright 1977:383; Flannery 1972:413).

How can archaeologists detect the changes in decision-making organization—in terms of hierarchical structure and optimal political strategy—that accompany the transition from chiefdoms to states? One way of detecting the internally-specialized administrative organization of a state is through its regional settlement pattern. Gregory Johnson (1973:15) argues that a state will exhibit at least a three-level settlement-size hierarchy. But since "such a settlement hierarchy alone implies little about administrative organization" (Wright and Johnson 1975:270), it is important to determine that the three (or more) levels of the settlement hierarchy manifest administrative functions. Researchers in the Near East are able to examine the regional distribution of a variety of "administrative artifacts" to this end. If the internally-specialized administrative organization of the state encourages decision-making "in different places at different times" (Wright 1977:383), evidence of regional level decision-making ought to occur at other sites besides the state capital. For example, some of the administrative facilities erected by the state and their associated artifacts should appear at other communities within its boundaries (e.g., Morris 1972:393-396).

A state's internally-specialized administrative organization will also be reflected in its public architecture. This approach derives from the view that the major differences between states and simpler societies lie in the area of decision-making and its hierarchical organization (Flannery 1972:412). Flannery sees the generation of new sociopolitical institutions—particularly those which process information—and their transformations as major phenomena of evolutionary advance. New institutions will arise when a critical threshold in the need for information-processing is reached; through time, some of the institutions that are among the specific lower-order controls of a society's decision-making hierarchy will assume higher-order, more general control functions (Flannery 1972:411, 423). The internally-specialized administrative organization of a state will exhibit a variety of new sociopolitical institutions that arise to process increasingly greater quantities of information. Since public buildings are assumed to be the loci of decision-making, the numerous and varied institutions characteristic of a state will be reflected in its public architecture (Flannery and Marcus 1976a:206).

Archaeologists view the sizes of public buildings, the diversity of their structural types, and their formal layout at sites as important indicators of a society's administrative institutions (Sanders 1974:98; Fox 1978:173, 290). Thus, the internally specialized administrative organization of a state will be manifested at the state capital by the appearance of a variety of large-scale buildings. But because state level decision-making can occur at other localities besides the state capital, public buildings that serve as administrative facilities of the state might also be found at certain subsidiary settlements.

Finally, the emergence of the state will also be reflected in changing patterns of residential architecture. Because chiefly authority is based largely upon ideological sanctions, chiefs can summon labor for the construction of public buildings—such as temples and tombs—but they cannot easily amass manpower for the construction of residences for themselves (Sanders 1974:109). Rulers of state societies can, of course, amass the corvée labor needed to construct not only public buildings, but also their elaborate residences or palaces. Thus, the appearance of palaces in the archaeological record in the form of large, multi-component walled compounds containing a variety of residential and public structures will signal the emergence of such a professional ruling class, which is another characteristic of state societies (Adams 1966:142-145).

In view of the above considerations, let us examine the evidence associated with Monte Albán's ascension to statehood at the end of Monte Albán I or the beginning of Monte Albán II. During Monte Albán Ic or Late I (ca. 300-100 B.C.) and Monte Albán II (ca. 100 B.C.-A.D. 200), Monte Albán's population grew to over three times its original size. Blanton estimates the Monte Albán Ic population of Monte Albán at 10,200 to 20,400. This population size was maintained during Monte Albán II, which Blanton estimates to have been between 9,650 and 19,300 (Blanton 1978:41). Settlement expanded over much of Monte Albán proper at this time, and the city was apparently subdivided into a number of separate neighborhoods or *barrios*. At the center of each subdivision stood a cluster of public buildings and elite residences (e.g., Blanton 1978:Fig. A.X.-30).

Major building projects occurred in the Main Plaza, particularly during Period II. The plaza was leveled and formally laid out at this time. This involved the leveling of massive rock outcrops in places and the filling in of deep hollows. Some of the outcrops were used as nuclei for the major constructions bordering the plaza (Acosta 1965:818). Excavations have revealed that large public buildings atop platforms lined the western, northern, and eastern edges of the Main Plaza; we must await excavated evidence pertaining to the history of construction along the southern edge of the plaza, which I suspect was also defined by Period II. The magnitude of construction is exemplified by the volume of Monte Albán Ic and II construction exposed in the "P.S.A." excavations conducted in the southeast corner of the North Platform (Caso, Bernal, and Acosta 1967:90-106, Plano I). Blanton (1978:46) has measured the volume of Monte Albán Ic and II construction exposed in the "P.S.A." excavations and estimates that 77% of the construction in this portion of the North Platform was carried out in Periods Ic and II. Furthermore, on the basis of evidence from other excavations near the center of the North Platform, in Montículo I Romano (Caso, Bernal, and Acosta 1967:137-141), Blanton proposes that the North Platform was greatly enlarged

Plate 2. The Main Plaza at Monte Albán, facing northeast. Building J is the arrowhead-shaped building in the foreground.

in Period II. The Mexican excavators reported Period II materials lying on bedrock here; in fact, Blanton estimates that 40% of the construction exposed here belongs to Period II (Blanton 1978:46).

The Monte Albán Ic and II building projects, centered on the Main Plaza, were not only large-scale, but also diverse (Acosta 1965:818-824; Flannery and Marcus 1976a:217-221). A variety of new public building types appeared at Monte Albán during Period II. One of these building types is the rectangular, two-room temple, the best-known example of which lay within Mound X (Fig. 2). This temple sat atop a platform located northeast of the Main Plaza and contained a main chamber, a vestibule, and columns on either side of the doorway (Acosta 1965:822, Fig. 8; Marquina 1964:334, Lámina 93; Flannery and Marcus 1976a:217, Fig. 10.8). The I-shaped ballcourt is another type of public building that was erected for the first time in Period II (Acosta 1965:824). The Period II ballcourt at the northeast corner of the Main Plaza had a north-south orientation, and its dimensions were probably similar to those of the Period III version that overlies it (Flannery and Marcus 1976a:219).

The most unusual Period II public building erected in the Main Plaza was Building J, located at the southern end of the central spine (Fig. 2, Pl. 2). Building J has an arrowhead-shaped ground plan, with a staircase on the widest side and a narrow covered tunnel or gallery (Acosta 1965:823-824, Figs. 10, 11). Its outer walls exhibit a series of 40 or more carved stone slabs, which I will return to describe shortly.

The elaborate palace on the East Platform of the Main Plaza also appears to have been built originally during Period II (Caso, Bernal, and Acosta 1967:443, Plano X). The palace or royal residence is another type of structure that appears for the first time in Period II, "distinct from the multifamily apartment complexes occupied by other persons of high rank" (Flannery and Marcus 1976a:217). Blanton reports that the subdivision of the city that was associated with the Main Plaza had the greatest number of elite residences, and he suggests that it was an elite residential district in the Late Formative period (Blanton 1978:47). His interpretation on the basis of intensive surface survey is partially corroborated by the excavation of one of these elite residences (System Y), which was occupied originally during Monte Albán Ic and II (Caso, Bernal, and Acosta 1967:106-137). Period II also marks the introduction of new styles of funerary architecture at Monte Albán. In addition to the use of simple, rectangular-shaped tombs having horizontally-laid stone slab roofs that were known already from Period I, many Period II tombs had antechambers and wall recesses, vaulted roofs, and paintings in fresco (Acosta 1965:818; Caso 1965a:863-864).

Finally, it is during Monte Albán Ic and/or II that a massive defensive wall was built along the north and northwest boundaries of Monte Albán. The wall is approximately 20 m wide, and is generally 5 m high, though in some places atop natural outcrops the wall reaches 9 m in height (Blanton 1978:52). Blanton suggests that the wall was built along Monte Albán's gradual northern slope for defensive purposes, but that where it crossed a deep *cañada* the wall also created a sizable reservoir. Blanton also reports the presence of a strategically located platform at a point along the wall where four major ancient roads converged and crossed the wall, which he argues was a gatelike feature that served to regulate the flow of traffic in and out of the city. Directly upslope along one of the main roads entering the city lay a large mound group cluster (Blanton 1978:45, 87), which may have had a related function. Two smaller walls enclosed the southern boundary of Monte Albán, and one of them exhibited an entry point similar to the one piercing the principal defensive wall on the site's northern slope (Blanton 1978:53-54).

The scale and diverse nature of the building projects at Monte Albán during Monte Albán Ic and II constitute abundant evidence for the appearance of an internally-specialized administrative organization at that time. It is clear that specialized components of the emergent state's decision-making process underlay the need for temples, ballcourts, defensive walls, and arrowhead-shaped buildings.

> Clearly, the activities carried on in these buildings must have been very different, presumably reflecting different sociopolitical institutions and different sets of personnel. Such architectural complexity is one archaeological manifestation of state organization. [Flannery and Marcus 1976a:221]

The growing population at the state capital was internally differentiated into subdivisions or neighborhoods, each centered upon a complex of public buildings and elite residences. While a great number of elite residences were found in the subdivision associated with the Main Plaza, the appearance of a true palace on the Main Plaza further signals the rise of a professional ruling elite to new levels of authority and involvement with state institutions.

In line with Wright's discussion of the state's centralized decision-making process, "divisible into separate activities which can be performed in different places at different times" (Wright 1977:383), is the appearance of state-level institutions at secondary centers on the valley floor in Period II (Flannery and Marcus 1976a:216-219; Wright 1977:389-390). At that time, ceremonial plazas modeled after the Main Plaza at Monte Albán were laid out at secondary centers such as San José Mogote (Fig. 1). Moreover, some of the new types of public buildings erected in the Main Plaza of Monte Albán have counterparts at certain subsidiary centers. For example, Flannery and Marcus (1983:111-112) have discovered several two-room temples at San José Mogote that closely resemble the aforementioned Period II temple atop Mound X at Monte Albán. The earliest ballcourt at San José Mogote also dates to Period II, and its orientation and dimensions match those of the ballcourt on the Main Plaza of Monte Albán. Finally, an arrowhead-shaped building similar in plan and orientation to Building J at Monte Albán is found at the site of Caballito Blanco in the Tlacolula branch of the valley (see Fig. 1; Paddock 1966:Fig. 89; Flannery and Marcus 1976a:217-219). The appearance of these specialized public buildings at secondary centers on the valley floor probably reflects their role in the internally-specialized administrative organization of the emergent Monte Albán state. The preliminary results of the surveyed portions of the valley floor reported by Blanton and his collaborators lend support to the above interpretation. They report the rapid growth of administrative centers in the valley and an expansion of the regional administrative hierarchy in Period Late I. In the succeeding Period II, a number of these secondary administrative centers actually increased in size (Blanton et al. 1979:379).

It seems clear that the early Zapotec state arose with its capital at Monte Albán by the end of Monte Albán I or the beginning of Period II. One group of carved stone monuments from Monte Albán provides us with an intriguing insight into the character of the newly-formed state. The carved stone slabs in question are those set into the walls of Building J, the arrowhead-shaped structure that was erected in the Main Plaza during Period II. Alfonso Caso studied the more than 40 carved stone slabs from Building J and concluded that they refer to places conquered by Monte Albán (Caso 1947:27-28). Each conquest slab typically includes the following elements: (1) an upside-down human head with closed eyes, wearing distinctive headgear, and sometimes adorned with facial painting; (2) a "hill" glyph that signifies "place"; (3) a combination of glyphs above the "hill" glyph that refers to the name of the place; and (4) a glyphic text that can include year signs, month signs and day signs, together with some unknown noncalendric glyphs (Fig. 3a; Caso 1947:21-28). Caso interpreted the upside-down human head as a representation of the dead ruler of a conquered place; thus each conquest slab records one of Monte Albán's military conquests. The accompanying text probably lists the date of that particular place's subjugation by the Monte Albán state (Caso 1947:27-28).

More recently, the Building J conquest slabs have figured importantly in Joyce Marcus' ongoing study of the stone inscriptions from the Valley of Oaxaca. Marcus notes the fact that the 40+ conquest slabs on Building J are the only known Period II stone inscriptions at Monte Albán, a marked decrease from the 310 or more *danzantes* known for Period I. She suggests that as Monte Albán's power became more institutionalized and more effective—which I have proposed was the case by the beginning of Period II—the need to erect stone monuments to reinforce that power would have declined (Marcus 1974:90). While the Period II stone monuments on Building J are far fewer in number than those of Period I, their commemoration of specific military victories is more informative than the Period I *danzantes* gallery. Indeed, Marcus believes that the Building J conquest slabs describe the limits of Monte Albán's territorial expansion in Period II and record the newly-conquered, tributary places within its expanded frontiers (Marcus 1976:137, 1980:55-56, 1983a:106-108).

The focus of Marcus' study of the conquest slabs has been the identification of places that were conquered by Monte Albán. Her intent is to determine the limits of Monte Albán's political and tributary territory. With the aid of the Codex Mendoza, a sixteenth-century Aztec tribute roll, Marcus has identified the names of at least four conquered places (Marcus 1976:128-131, 1980:56), all of which lie *outside* the Valley of Oaxaca proper. One of the place signs on Building J consists of a head in profile from which emanates an elaborate speech scroll (Fig. 3b). On the basis of its close resemblance to a known place glyph listed in the Codex Mendoza (Fig. 4), Marcus (1976:130-131, 1980:56) has proposed that the designated "Place of Song" corresponds to Cuicatlán in the Cañada, the region in which my investigation of early Zapotec imperialism was based (Pl. 3).

The Building J conquest slabs underscore the militaristic character of the emergent Monte Albán state. The evidence presented here suggests that Monte Albán's ascension to statehood was concurrent with a campaign of military conquests in regions outside the Valley of Oaxaca. The role of militarism in the development of the early Zapotec state might well have been significant and is worthy of further examination.

The Role of Militarism in Early State Development

Warfare has long been considered an important factor in the formation of early states. But views on the precise causal significance of warfare in state origins have changed over the years. One of the earliest proponents on the subject was Herbert Spencer, who was convinced that habitual warfare led directly to the emergence of state societies. Spencer believed that the centralized regulating system that is the state develops in response to war with other societies. Spencer's evolutionary formula was straightforward:

> In primitive headless groups temporary chieftainship results from temporary war; chronic hostilities generate permanent chieftainship; and gradually from the military control results the civil control. Habitual war, requiring prompt combination in the action of parts, necessitates subordination. Societies in which there is little subordination disappear, and leave outstanding those in which subordination is great, and so there are produced societies in which the habit fostered by war and surviving in peace brings about permanent submission to a government. [Spencer 1967:215]

A century later, Carneiro also identified war as the *mechanism* of state formation, but proposed a set of specific *conditions* under which war gave rise to the state (Carneiro 1970:734-738). One particularly compelling condition was the growth of popu-

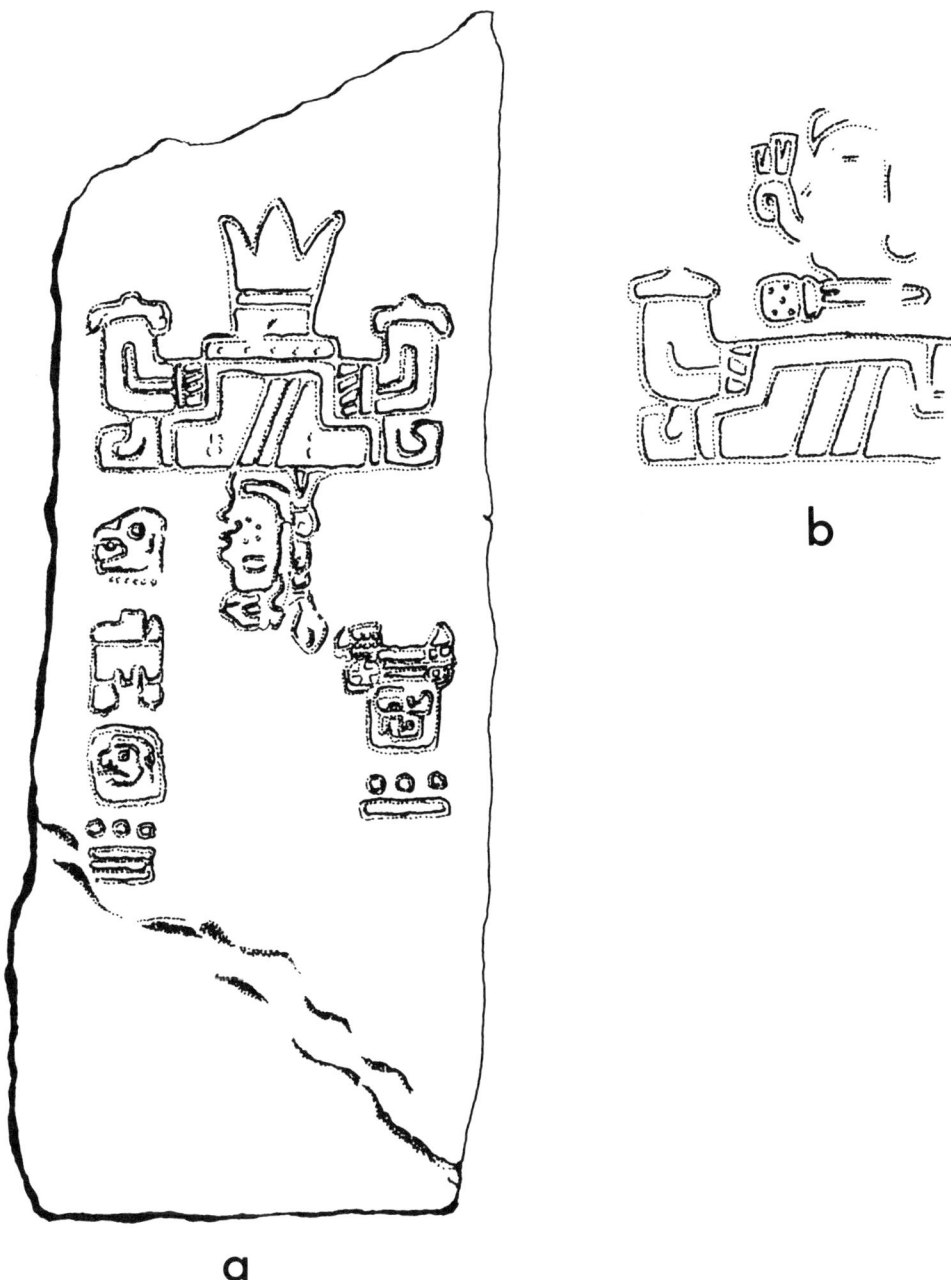

Figure 3. Conquest-slab inscriptions from Building J at Monte Albán: *a*, a completely preserved conquest slab (redrawn from Caso 1947:78); *b*, Cuicatlán place glyph (redrawn from Marcus 1980:50).

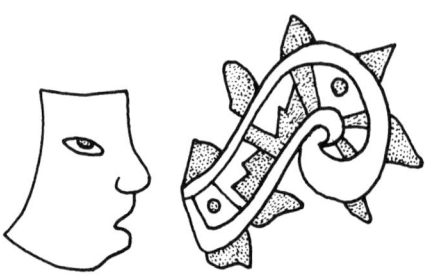

Figure 4. The Cuicatlán place glyph in the Codex Mendoza (redrawn from Marcus 1980:59).

lation within areas of circumscribed agricultural land, which would eventually lead to warfare, territorial expansion, and the incorporation of previously autonomous societies into a centralized state polity.

Adherents of multivariate causality (Adams 1966; Flannery 1972; Wright and Johnson 1975:284-287) continue to consider warfare an important factor in the rise of the state. But they regard warfare as only one of a series of consequential variables characterized by complex interrelationships. Flannery's model for the rise of the state is based upon the evolutionary principles of living systems in general. His explanatory scheme distinguishes between the evolutionary *mechanisms* whereby processes of state development take place, and the *socioenvironmental stresses* that select for those mechanisms. Flannery considers warfare—along with other variables such as population pressure, trade, and irrigation—as one of the many socioenvironmental stresses that will trigger the evolutionary mechanisms. Warfare is seen not as *the* mechanism of state formation, but as an external socioenvironmental condition that might select for certain mechanisms of evolutionary development. In Flannery's scheme, warfare is one of the socioenvironmental variables that in the control hierarchies of complex societies are regulated directly by specific, lower-order institutions, and indirectly by higher-order, more general institutions (Flannery 1972:409-411).

Both of the mechanisms of evolutionary change outlined by Flannery can be triggered by warfare. The mechanism labeled *promotion* involves the rise of a specific, lower-order institution to a more general, higher-level position in the control hierarchy. Another example of promotion is the creation of a new institution out of what was previously a multi-purpose institution. In the mechanism Flannery calls *linearization*, the regulating functions of lower-order institutions in the control hierarchy are taken over directly by higher-order institutions. Countless promotions and linearizations, which are set off by stressful socioenvironmental conditions, will produce the internally-specialized administrative organization that is characteristic of the state (Flannery 1972:412-414). Warfare might be among the specific socioenvironmental conditions present in particular regions where early states arose, and its role in the formation of the state will be to initiate these mechanisms that are responsible for changes in the hierarchy of decision making.

Militarism is a particular form of warfare, one which has been defined as follows:

> Militarism is the effective institutionalization of warfare and its accoutrements in the social organization, ideology, and symbolism of complex societies. [Webster 1977:363]

Among the characteristics that distinguish militarism from simpler forms of warfare are the groups of specialized warriors that are led by military strategists, the specialized weaponry and military facilities that are introduced, and the increased scale of warfare, wherein new territory and populations are consolidated (Webster 1977:363-364). Consequently, before we can evaluate the role of militarism in the administrative transformation and change in political strategy that characterize the transition from chiefdoms to states, we must outline how warfare becomes effectively institutionalized in the first place.

While warfare and conflict are known to exist at all levels of pre-state societies, warfare is especially frequent in chiefdoms (Wright 1977:382; Flannery 1972:412). In his ethnographic survey of warfare, Fried (1961) discovered that among ranked societies warfare generally occurs on a small scale and is of short duration. The military body is drawn from the pre-existing kinship and community organization for the specific war party. Moreover, the poor development of military command ensures that wartime statuses will not affect the normal sociopolitical organization of these societies (Fried 1961:142-144).

I believe that the military organization of Cherokee villages during the first half of the eighteenth century was such an ephemeral, multi-purpose institution. The village war organization convened

Plate 3. Park benches in the main square of present-day San Juan Bautista Cuicatlán sport the ancient toponym for Cuicatlán.

only when the village's decision-making body, known as the village council, decided on war (Gearing 1962:47). Four respected elders were elected to head the military operation, and they in turn appointed eight junior officers to direct the various war-related activities. A war council that consisted of a prominent warrior from each of the village's seven clans was also assembled. Below these officials, the military body was hierarchically organized into five warrior ranks, which were earned through war deeds. At the bottom of the hierarchy lay one unranked class of young, undistinguished warriors (Gearing 1962:26). Winter was the season of warfare, during which time the war organization convened for a total duration of 10 to 20 weeks. This same body of warriors regrouped for negotiations at other times of the year, and for inter-village ball games in the non-warring summer months. The military organization of Cherokee villages was thus temporary and multi-functional. In fact, upon the return of war parties to the village, the warriors participated in rituals of purification, which can be seen "as a device which insisted that the young men lay down their unrestraint with fellow warriors, and assume the proper deferential relations with their families, clans, and with villagers at large" (Gearing 1962:69). Analogous rituals of purification were performed after the summer ball games.

In response to stresses produced by the increasing colonial encroachments of the 1750s, however, the Cherokee war organization became a separate and permanent institution. War statuses became institutionalized and for the first time prominent warriors joined the decision-making council in their capacity as warriors. This shift in the stature of the war organization "marked warring as a fully acceptable avenue of the good life; conditions were now set for the institutionalization of coercive sanctions" (Gearing 1962:104). The permanent military organization of the Cherokee arose by *promotion* from one of three roles assumed by the previously ephemeral war organization, in response to external stresses (Flannery 1972:412-413).

The military can play a power-seeking role in the administrative transformation of chiefly societies into states. Webster's model for evaluating the role of militarism in the rise of the state is useful because it begins with a consideration of the internal constraints on the evolutionary potential of chiefdoms, which remain integrated through the kinship mode, and whose leaders lack the ability to impose coercive sanctions (Webster 1975:465-466). Militarism, according to Webster, can provide the socioenvironmental conditions that favor the administrative transformation of a chiefdom by overcoming the inherent weaknesses of chiefly administration.

First of all, while the expansionistic tendencies of chiefdoms can result in military successes, they can also generate internal power struggles due to political and territorial overextension. Both the external conflict and internal factionalism produced by expanding chiefdoms will place great adaptive value upon stable military leadership. The increased political authority that accrues to a successful warring chief can then enable him to circumvent any internal challenges to his position (Webster 1975:467). Successful military expansion might also place external resources—acquired through warfare with other polities—in the hands of the chief. The chief can then manipulate these external sources of wealth to his advantage, by rewarding his supporters and thereby fostering the emergence of special-interest groups (Webster 1975:468). The role of militarism in the transition from chiefdoms to states is to provide conditions that support the emergence of a permanent military organization, and to place external sources of wealth in the hands of the chief.

Militarism can therefore lay the foundation for an administrative transformation by nurturing the "manpower, resources, and organization" (Rappaport 1974:65) necessary for the support of an internally-specialized administrative organization. Changes in the decision-making organization will be accompanied by new coercive sanctions, which are absent in chiefly societies. According to Rappaport, the switch from the sanctity devices that maintain a chiefly administrative hierarchy to the coercive powers of the state occurs when the central decision-making subsystem possesses sufficient manpower, resources, and organization to secure compliance through force. The decision makers are then in a position to shed their sanctified authority and to claim that their *own* purposes are sacred (Rappaport 1974:65). The role of militarism in the emergence of the state is perhaps best summarized by Adams:

> The emergence of the political and economic organs of the state cannot be understood exclusively as a series of internal processes within even the largest urban communities. Both the perils and the rewards of militarism lay beyond the immediately adjoining, more or less permanently attached and dependent, territories. The increasing concentration of political authority in dynastic institutions at the expense of older communal and religious bodies obviously took place in a setting in which both the perils and the rewards of militaristic contention were fully and deeply understood. Successful conquest brought political prestige in its wake, not uniformly enriching the community but, instead, increasing the stratification within it and permitting the consolidation of an independent power base by forces whose initial role had merely been that of leading elements in a common enterprise. In these and many other ways, the consolidation of the institutional structures of the newly-developed urban polities must be seen as an internal adjustment to a steadily widening and sharpening context of intercommunity, and even interregional, hostilities. [Adams 1966:152-153]

A final point that needs to be introduced in this discussion of militarism and early state development is the potential for a special-purpose institution like the military to assume higher-order, general-purpose functions in decision-making hierarchies. Under certain conditions, the military arm of a state organization may take on a share of the state's centralized decision-making functions. In the process, the military organization passes from being a system-serving institution to one that can be characterized as self-serving (Flannery 1972:411-413). I will return to this point in the final chapter.

Toward an Interregional Perspective on Militarism and the Monte Albán State

As Adams (1966:152-153) has suggested, the emergence of the state can be profitably viewed in the context of external conditions created by intercommunity and interregional hostilities. The need to expand our framework for investigating early state development is clearly justifiable in the case of the early Zapotec state. The iconographic evidence presented in this chapter suggests that Monte Albán became the center of the militaristic state, bent on a policy of territorial expansion and political subjugation. Moreover, the inscriptions from Monte Albán suggest that the expansionistic strategy pursued by the emergent Zapotec state involved the conquest of regions *outside* the Valley of Oaxaca proper. Accordingly, in the present investigation of militarism and the rise of the Monte Albán state I have adopted an *interregional* perspective, one which considers separate topographic and sociopolitical units—such as valleys or drainage basins in Mesoamerica—in a single framework.

The following chapters will attempt to outline the role of Monte Albán's proposed conquest strategy in the emergence of the early Zapotec state. What function, if any, did an interregional conquest strategy have in the appearance of an internally-specialized administrative organization centered at Monte Albán by Period II? As part of this interregional perspective, we will consider the effects of such a conquest strategy upon the Cuicatlán Cañada, one of the regions possibly listed as a conquered place on Building J at Monte Albán.

Chapter 2

The Cuicatlán Cañada: A Model of Its Proposed Subjugation by Monte Albán

The Cuicatlán Cañada

The Cuicatlán Cañada is a narrow canyon in the southern Mexican highlands that serves as a corridor linking the Valley of Oaxaca with the Tehuacán Valley. At the time of the Spanish Conquest, the Cañada was inhabited by Cuicatec speakers who were ethnically distinct from the Zapotec speakers of Oaxaca and the Chocho-Popolocan speakers of Tehuacán (Hunt 1972:166). The Río Grande, originating in the mountains north of the Oaxaca Valley, flows north along the canyon floor to Quiotepec where it joins the Río Salado, flowing south from the Valley of Tehuacán (Fig. 5). This river junction and the resulting deep gorge of the Río Santo Domingo, which cuts steeply through the Sierra Madre Oriental to feed the Río Papaloapan, form the northern boundary of the Cuicatlán Cañada. The 3200 m high Llano Español plateau borders the canyon to the east; to the south and west rise the Almoloyas and other 2000 to 2500 m mountain ranges of the Mixteca Alta. These mountains are the sources of the Río de las Vueltas, the Río Tomellín, and the Río Apoala, major tributaries of the Río Grande.

The canyon provides a major route of communication through the highlands of Central Mexico and, during the Colonial period, formed a segment of the Camino Real. We know that the Camino Real was also used in pre-Conquest times, for several early Spanish travelers and historians have described how Motecuhzoma II's troops passed through the Cuicatlán Cañada en route to the Valley of Oaxaca (Hopkins 1974:81). A Oaxaca-bound traveler following the Camino Real from Tehuacán would have journeyed through Tecomavaca, crossed the Río Salado, and entered the Cañada after traversing a narrow mountain pass and fording the Río Grande at Quiotepec (Fig. 6). From here the Camino Real wound to the east, climbing above the canyon floor because just south of Quiotepec the canyon of the Río Grande becomes narrow (Pl. 4). During the dry season an alternate route from Quiotepec along the banks of the Río Grande could be taken to Cuicatlán. Proceeding from Cuicatlán along the canyon floor, the Camino Real reached Dominguillo at the southern end of the Cañada. Here the traveler could choose betwen two alternate routes to Oaxaca: one route followed the Río de las Vueltas to Jayacatlán and on to San Juan del Estado at the entrance to the Valley of Oaxaca; a second route climbed the mountains south of Dominguillo to Cotahuixtla and proceeded to Huitzo, at the north end of the Valley of Oaxaca (Hopkins 1974:81-85).

Today, the Mexican railroad system links the nation's capital with Oaxaca City via the Cañada. The railroad follows the path of the Camino Real for most of its route, though it connects the Cañada with Oaxaca by way of the Río Tomellín canyon (Fig. 6). A recently paved highway also transits the Cañada to Dominguillo where it climbs up into the mountains bordering the Oaxaca Valley, and constitutes the shortest route from Tehuacán to Oaxaca.

In contrast to the 1500 to 1700 m elevations of the Oaxaca and Tehuacán valleys, the floor of the Cuicatlán Cañada varies between 500 and 700 m above sea level. Thus, the region falls squarely within the zone of *tierra caliente,* well below the surrounding *tierra templada* and *tierra fría* mountain valleys (Sanders and Price 1968:104). In the Cañada the average annual temperature is 24.5° C, but maximum recordings over 40° C are not uncommon, particularly during the months of April and May (Hopkins 1974:48).

The massive Sierra Madre Oriental rising to the east of the Cañada creates an effective rainshadow in the canyon, where the annual rainfall averages less than 300 mm (Hopkins 1974:47). When evapotranspiration rates are taken into account, the total amount of useful rainfall per year drops to 130-140 mm (Hunt and Hunt 1974:136-137). Consequently, this hot semi-arid region supports a natural xerophytic vegetation characterized by mixed thorny trees (*Prosopis juliflora, Acacia unijuga, Cercidium praecox*) and cacti (*Lemaireocereus weberi, L. pru-*

Figure 5. The Cuicatlán Cañada, Valley of Oaxaca, and Valley of Tehuacán.

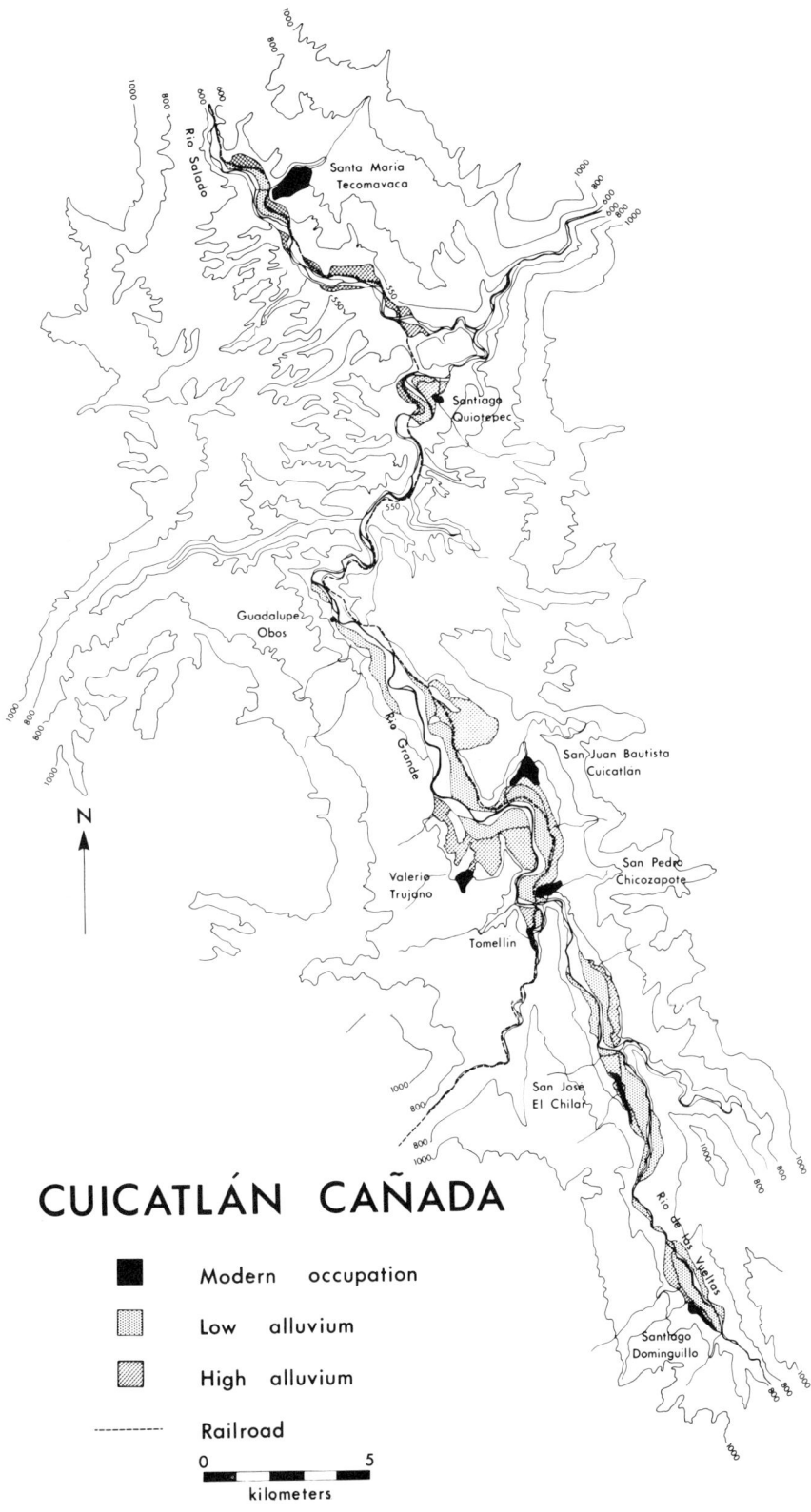

Figure 6. The Cuicatlán Cañada, with the locations of all modern communities.

Plate 4. A narrow stretch of the Cuicatlán Cañada between Santiago Quiotepec and Guadalupe Obos.

inosus, Opuntia sp.). Down on the sand and gravel bars flanking the Río Grande the natural vegetation includes willow (*Salix chilensis*), willow-like trees (*Asianthus viminalis*), and stands of river cane (Spanish *carrizo*) (Hopkins 1974:48-49).

In general, the terrain is mountainous and uncultivable; all agriculture is confined to segments of the region where the canyon floor widens and where the major tributaries join the Río Grande to produce large, relatively flat alluvial fans (Pl. 5). There are four of these alluvial fans in the Cuicatlán Cañada, separated by narrow constrictions of the canyon walls. Each alluvial fan comprises strips of low alluvium flanking both sides of the river as well as zones of high alluvium on remnant river terraces above the low alluvium (Pls. 6, 7). Although there is too little rainfall in the Cañada for successful dry farming, these alluvial fans are intensively cultivated using various methods of irrigation. Simple techniques of floodwater farming (Kirkby 1973:36-41) are practiced on some stretches of the low alluvium along the Río Grande and the Río de las Vueltas. These involve the construction of temporary diversionary dams from brush and river cobbles in order to divert and channel water from the major river flows onto the flanking low alluvium (Pl. 8). The higher alluvium is irrigated using feeder canals (*upuntles*) that draw water from the numerous tributaries and streams of the Río Grande and direct it onto the available alluvium by means of a vast network of ditches (see Pl. 9; Hunt 1972:188). The complete dependence upon the alluvial fans and upon irrigation techniques for their cultivation is reflected in the distribution of settlement in the region today. All the modern settlements are situated on the Cañada's four alluvial fans, here named for the towns marking them (Quiotepec, Cuicatlán, El Chilar, Dominguillo) (Fig. 6). As E. Hunt (1972:168) quite accurately states, "Elsewhere the terrain is rough, non-irrigable, and uninhabitable."

The agricultural potential of the irrigated alluvial fans is enormous. We acquired firsthand information pertaining to the agricultural productivity of these alluvial fans through direct interviews with elders and municipal authorities residing in Dominguillo, El Chilar, and Valerio Trujano. The irrigated

Plate 5. The northern end of the Cuicatlán alluvial fan, near Guadalupe Obos, where the canyon floor widens, facing south.

maize yields reported to us for the low alluvium (*tierra de primera*) and the high alluvium (*tierra de segunda*) farmed by inhabitants of the representative towns are listed in Table 1. Because the Cañada features a frost-free climate, two plantings are possible every year, and as a result these figures can be further doubled. The productivity of maize agriculture in the Cuicatlán Cañada is high and compares favorably with the yields of maize planted on the most productive land in the adjacent highland valleys of Oaxaca and Tehuacán (Kirkby 1973:61-62; Spencer 1979:65; Kowalewski 1980:153).

During the course of our interviews we learned that, in years of greater rainfall, marginal unirrigated piedmont plots of land are planted in maize (*tierra de tercera*). This sporadic and limited amount of rainfall agriculture constitutes a high-risk, low-return strategy, since reported yields never exceed 250 to 500 kg of shelled maize for every hectare planted. In general, rainfall farming is not feasible and is rarely practiced in the semi-arid canyon.

Along with the productive cultivation of maize and other Mesoamerican staples such as beans and squash, many varieties of indigenous tropical fruits flourish in the Cuicatlán Cañada. The most notable fruits cultivated are the chicozapote (*Achras zapota*), the black zapote (*Diospyros digyna*), and the ciruela (*Spondius purpurea*), none of which can grow in the higher elevations of the surrounding mountain valleys. Today, however, much of the Cañada's alluvium is under cultivation in post-Hispanic cash crops, the most important of which are sugar cane and the more recently introduced mango. A handful of Colonial period sugar cane plantations (*haciendas*) still dot the canyon floor; a similar pattern of large, private landholdings devoted primarily to mango cultivation exists in the region today. Today limes and papayas are also commercially grown there.

In sum, the Cuicatlán Cañada is an important corridor for communication between the highland valleys of Central Mexico. Its strategic location with respect to travel between the valleys of Tehuacán and Oaxaca has been recognized and recorded since the sixteenth century. This narrow canyon is, in

Plate 6. The Cuicatlán alluvial fan, facing east. High alluvial terraces overlook strips of low alluvium flanking the Río Grande.

Plate 7. El Chilar alluvial fan, facing south. Today much of the alluvium here is used to cultivate tropical fruits, principally mangos and limes.

effect, a pocket of *tierra caliente* surrounded on all sides by the high semi-arid mountains and mountain valleys of the southern highlands. Maize agriculture is practiced on the Cañada's alluvial fans using various irrigation techniques, and the resulting yields compare favorably to those reported for the most productive lands in the adjacent highland valleys. The Cañada today is a region that specializes in the production of lowland tropical fruits for export to neighboring highland markets. Because these tropical fruits cannot be grown in the higher elevations of the surrounding regions, they are greatly desired and highly priced in highland markets. Aside from the Cuicatlán Cañada's strategic location, we will see how the agricultural potential of this lowland region has figured importantly in its relationship with its highland neighbors, particularly with the ancient Zapotec state that emerged during the Late Formative period in the Oaxaca Valley.

Selecting the Cuicatlán Cañada for Study

To the north and south of the Cuicatlán Cañada, respectively, are the Tehuacán Valley and Oaxaca Valley, regions that have seen a substantial amount of archaeological research within the past two decades. The Tehuacán Archaeological-Botanical Project (MacNeish 1964; Byers 1967; MacNeish et al. 1967, 1970, 1972; Johnson 1972) and the Oaxaca Valley Prehistory and Human Ecology Project (Flannery et al. 1967, 1970; Flannery 1976a; Flannery and Marcus 1976a, 1976b; Blanton 1976a, 1978; Flannery, Marcus, and Kowalewski 1981) have outlined clear developmental sequences for the two semi-arid mountain valleys. They begin with the earliest known settlements in the preceramic era and proceed through the origins of domestication, the appearance of sedentary villages, and the emergence of ranking. Where the two developmental sequences diverge is in the period following the

Plate 8. A simple diversionary dam diverts water from the main river onto the flanking low alluvium in the background.

emergence of ranked societies. In the Valley of Oaxaca we have already seen how Monte Albán, established around 500 B.C., became the capital of the early Zapotec state that arose there sometime during the Late Formative period (ca. 300 B.C. to A.D. 200). For the Tehuacán Valley, however, it is now recognized that no centrally-administered state emerged there during the Late Formative or Classic periods. Instead, Terminal Formative and Classic period society in Tehuacán was characterized by a series of small autonomous polities with no higher-order administrative center or capital (MacNeish et al. 1972; Drennan 1979).

A developmental sequence comparable in detail to those recovered for Oaxaca and Tehuacán has been lacking for the intervening Cuicatlán Cañada. MacNeish and Peterson's regional reconnaissance of the Tehuacán Valley brought them as far south as Tecomavaca (see Fig. 6; MacNeish et al. 1972:343, 410). Drennan and Vásquez had surveyed the mountains bordering the Valley of Oaxaca to the north and had advanced as far north as Jayacatlán (Drennan and Vásquez n.d.). Therefore, as part of the continuing Tehuacán-based Palo Blanco Project (Drennan 1977, 1978, 1979), Charles Spencer and I selected the Cuicatlán Cañada for archaeological investigation. One goal of our project was simply to close the gap in archaeological coverage that existed between the well-studied valleys of Tehuacán and Oaxaca.

Although the archaeology of the region was largely unknown except for brief travel reports (Rickards 1926; Bernal 1966) and a few short-term salvage projects (Bazán 1928; Pareyón 1960; Winter, Gaxiola, and Hernández 1977), a considerable amount of ethnohistorical and ethnographic information about the Cuicatlán Cañada was available (Hunt 1972; Hunt and Hunt 1974, 1976; Hopkins 1974). The Hunts' study of the role of irrigation in intercommunity relationships within the Cuicatlán Cañada included a vast amount of geographic and ethnographic information dealing with modern systems of water control, land use, land tenure, and settlement. Furthermore, Eva Hunt's detailed analysis of the Colonial and pre-Colonial period documents provided an excellent reconstruction of the

Plate 9. Modern irrigation facilities in the Cuicatlán Cañada. *Above*, the Matamba dam taps the higher Río Grande. *Below*, the ensuing Matamba canal to the left of the main river carries water over great distances to large expanses of the region's high alluvium.

Cuicatec *cacicazgos* present in the region during Postclassic times (Hunt 1972). Joseph Hopkins' study of the Cuicatec region also presented an enormous amount of ethnographic and ethnohistorical information about the lowland Cuicatec in the Cuicatlán Cañada. In addition, Hopkins had surveyed the Cuicatlán alluvial fan for archaeological sites and prehistoric irrigation canals and had briefly visited and recorded other archaeological sites in the southern Cañada (Hopkins 1973, 1974:301-312).

The Proposed Subjugation of the Cuicatlán Cañada by Monte Albán

Selection of the Conquest Hypothesis

In addition to providing a developmental sequence for the Cuicatlán Cañada, Spencer and I wished to explore the relationship between the Cañada and the Valley of Oaxaca during the Late Formative, the period when the Zapotec state was emerging with its capital at Monte Albán. At the outset, our investigation of the Cuicatlán Cañada's relationship to the Valley of Oaxaca during the period of Zapotec state formation was tempered by the well-documented sequence of developments at Monte Albán itself (Chapter 1). Although we initially considered and constructed several alternative hypotheses with which to assess the nature of the relationship that existed between the Cuicatlán Cañada and Monte Albán, each hypothesized interregional relationship having its particular set of general expectations and predicted archaeological correlates, the evidence from Monte Albán succeeded in narrowing the range of alternative hypotheses examined. The sequence of developments outlined for Monte Albán during the Late Formative period provided the independent and prior plausibility considerations (Smith 1977:605-606) deemed necessary in the process of selecting a suitable working hypothesis to evaluate the relationship between the Monte Albán state and an adjacent region.

The most specific prior consideration stemming from the site of Monte Albán involved the 40 inscribed stone slabs set into the sides of Building J, which referred to places conquered or in a tributary relationship to Monte Albán. One of the conquest slabs identified by Marcus referred to Cuicatlán, leading her to propose that during the Late Formative period the Cuicatlán region—among other places—assumed a subordinate tributary relationship to Monte Albán (Marcus 1976:130, 137, 1980:56). This reading of the Period II inscriptions on Building J, while it had obvious implications for our investigation of interregional relationships during the time of Zapotec state formation, nevertheless had the status of an untested hypothesis.

In light of the sequence of developments seen at Monte Albán during the Late Formative period, and specifically in light of the possible Zapotec military victories recorded on Building J, the hypothesis we selected for assessing the relationship of a hinterland region like the Cuicatlán Cañada to the emerging state in the Valley of Oaxaca was one of conquest. The conquest hypothesis—involving the subjugation of the Cuicatlán Cañada by the Monte Albán state in the Late Formative period—was the hypothesis having the highest prior plausibility; consequently, it is the conquest hypothesis that I will formally state here and later will evaluate with separate and independently-derived archaeological evidence from the Cuicatlán Cañada.

Zapotec Militarism and Frontier Administration

If the Building J conquest slabs do in fact record Monte Albán's policy of military expansion into neighboring regions, we must first take up the subject of Zapotec militarism in order to derive suitable patterns of conquest and subjugation for one of the regions involved, the Cuicatlán Cañada. Much information about Zapotec militarism can be culled from the writings of Fray Juan de Córdova and Fray Francisco de Burgoa, two Dominican friars who lived among the Valley Zapotec in the early Colonial period. Fray Juan de Córdova came to the Valley of Oaxaca soon after the Spanish Conquest and compiled a dictionary and a grammar of the Zapotec language, both of which were published in 1578. Fray Francisco de Burgoa was born in Oaxaca in 1605, and his accounts of the Dominican mission there include firsthand information about Zapotec life and history (Burgoa 1670, 1674a, 1674b). According to Burgoa, the Zapotec nation was powerful and expansionistic, and at one time it controlled most of the southern Mexican highlands and adjacent coasts (Burgoa 1674a:412). From Burgoa's writings and Córdova's compilation of the Zapotec language I am able to present a relatively complete picture of Postclassic Zapotec militarism and

Zapotec administrative policies in frontier regions.

It should be pointed out that hundreds of years separate the sixteenth-century Valley Zapotec from their early forerunners who founded the Monte Albán state. Many of the policies associated with the Postclassic Zapotec might have been considerably different from those pursued in earlier times. Furthermore, these firsthand accounts of Zapotec culture, while they are rich in detail, were written by foreign missionaries, who no doubt held certain preconceptions concerning native Indian practices, and whose interpretations were sometimes clouded by their own European culture.

Despite these limitations, I believe that this ethnohistoric information concerning the military organization and imperial strategies of the Zapotec nation during the Postclassic period can be brought to bear upon the question of earlier and undocumented instances of Valley Zapotec expansionism. This detailed information can be profitably integrated into a general model of Monte Albán's supposed subjugation of regions like the Cuicatlán Cañada in the Late Formative period, a model which will of course be subjected to independent archaeological verification. Many continuities have been found to link the culture and language of the modern Zapotec with their predecessors of the historic and prehistoric past (Whitecotton 1977; Flannery and Marcus 1976b; Marcus 1978; Marcus and Flannery 1978). We should therefore not be surprised if *some* of the characteristics of military organization and frontier administration that are known to have been practiced by the Postclassic Zapotec were legacies from earlier times.

According to Burgoa, there were two basic motivations for Zapotec imperialism: (1) the taking of captives for sacrificial or commercial purposes, and (2) the collection of tribute. The taking of sacrificial victims in warfare was important for sustaining the Zapotec supernatural being named the *Príncipe de las Tinieblas*; as part of ceremonies honoring him the victims' hearts were torn out and pressed against the lips of his stone image (Burgoa 1674b:10). If spared from that fate, some war captives became slaves to be bought and sold in Zapotec markets (Whitecotton 1977:152). Warfare was also conducted in order to subjugate towns and entire foreign regions for the purpose of extracting tribute from them (Burgoa 1674b:341), and the Zapotec had a special term for these conquered places (*tiàquiqueche*) (Córdova 1578:88).

Burgoa's descriptions of Zapotec military campaigns are as rich in detail as the corresponding terms in Zapotec listed in Córdova's dictionary. First, there was an enormous amount of preparation for war (Burgoa 1674b:341, 345; Córdova 1578:33). Civilian forces were mobilized and underwent training, trenches and fortifications were repaired and in places expanded, and military equipment and provisions were garnered. We know that they had scouts or spies who acted as advance-men by gathering information in enemy territory (Burgoa 1674b:265; Córdova 1578:186). Armies consisted of captains who led squadrons of warriors; there were separate titles for novices, general warriors, bowmen, and great warriors (Burgoa 1674b:341, 345; Córdova 1578:183, 211, 285, 292, 308, 384, 409). Warriors wore padded cotton armor, body painting to represent jaguar skins, and insignia of their rank and lineage. Those warriors singled out for bravery wore a special hair knot on the crown of their heads as a badge of courage (Córdova 1578:38, 45, 316, 409). Chosen warriors became knights of wild beast orders such as the order of the jaguar; these warrior-knights donned the elaborate costumes of their orders (Burgoa 1674a:412).

Certain aspects of warfare were clearly ideological since war captives were sought for ritual sacrifices. The Zapotec are known to have consulted with their supernatural beings before carrying out their military campaigns. Idols were even carried into battle to ensure victory (Burgoa 1674a:393; Whitecotton 1977:142). Sometimes the warriors sang to the beat of a wooden drum as they marched into battle (Whitecotton 1977:142).

The Zapotec armies employed a variety of weapons and warfare tactics. One method was to march into enemy territory in overwhelming numbers, carrying shields and meeting the opposing forces with clubs, broadswords studded with obsidian blades, spears, dart-throwers, and arrows (Burgoa 1674b:123, 235-236, 339-340, 345; Córdova 1578: 37-38, 159, 214, 252, 403). Some of the spearheads and arrowheads used in war were treated with a strong poison. In some instances they proceeded to subjugate communities "*a fuego y sangre*" by setting them on fire and by massacring any inhabitants who resisted (Burgoa 1674b:189, 328, 341). The Zapotec executed war signals, shouted and whistled battle cries, and thus were inspired to commit acts of bravery on the battlefield (Córdova 1578:29, 377, 380). In this way they advanced through enemy territory, leaving special garrison troops to guard defeated towns, which were transformed into way stations to provide food and shelter for the conquering armies (Burgoa 1674b:235-236; Córdova 1578:205).

Another warfare tactic—exemplified by the Zapotec campaign against the Mexican armies in Tehuantepec—involved erecting massive stone slab and boulder fortifications on mountaintops situated at strategic points overlooking major communication routes. These war forts were reinforced with warriors and supplied with equipment and provisions in order to await quietly the arrival of the unsuspecting enemy forces. Scouts brought information as to the enemy's position, and at the appropriate moment after dark, a surprise attack was launched. The Zapotec warriors silently descended upon the enemy troops from different directions and succeeded in cornering them and stifling any resistance. It is known that the Zapotec armies carried out a number of these military stratagems in order to confuse and encircle the enemy forces (Burgoa 1674a:394, 1674b:340, 344-345, 235-236; Córdova 1578:202, 413).

Following a region's defeat and surrender to the Zapotec forces, the Zapotec state seized control over the previously autonomous region (Burgoa 1674a: 412, 1674b:265, 272). Those towns that had formerly paid tribute to their own rulers, now became tributary to the Zapotec state. In order to ensure the allegiance of the newly-tributary populations, the Zapotec ruler established fortified garrisons in all the conquered regions. Chosen Zapotec military captains and garrison troops manned these frontier installations, under the supervision of a designated frontier administrator. This frontier administrator was either a member of the ruling elite or a distinguished military captain. In two cases recorded by Burgoa, the person administering the frontier region was a member of the Zapotec ruler's lineage (Burgoa 1674a:412, 1674b:341, 265, 235-236, 242, 272, 330; Córdova 1578:205).

The administration of a subjugated region included both military and civil functions. Zapotec military might was concentrated in fortified garrisons, for the purpose of defending the frontier region from external threats and controlling the subject population. Although these frontier forts quartered Zapotec military captains and garrison troops from the Valley of Oaxaca, they were *locally* supplied with manpower, food, and equipment (Burgoa 1674a:236). In one case a previous community situated along the banks of a river was re-settled on top of an adjacent ridge, and transformed into a Zapotec garrison (Burgoa 1674b:265). One important role of the local subject population, therefore, was to provision the Zapotec military installations in that region. Not only did the elaborate hilltop fortifications require abundant manpower for their construction and maintenance, but the military retinue guarding them needed personnel to make weapons, to produce food and other supplies, to draw water, to act as spies, and so on (Burgoa 1674b:236, 342, 345, 265). In Córdova's dictionary we find names for some of the officials (*copayóhopije*), troops (*coopèetòaquelayè*), and craft specialists (*copeeche tozàa xipequitequiba quelayè*) who served these Zapotec frontier facilities (Córdova 1578:20, 38, 205, 421).

If part of the subject region's tribute went to provision the Zapotec military installations in that region, the remaining tribute was sent to the Zapotec rulers in the Valley of Oaxaca. Unfortunately, the early Spanish sources did not record the precise mechanism underlying the collection and shipment of tribute from the conquered regions to the Oaxaca Valley. Burgoa did, however, describe the local collection of tribute in Nejapa, one *tierra caliente* region that was taken over by the expanding Valley Zapotec; tribute here was paid in prickly pear fruit, vanilla, cochineal, and mantles (Burgoa 1674b:240, 251-252). One of the duties of the administrator of each tributary region was to enforce the exaction, collection, and shipment of this tribute, an expression for which can be found in Córdova's dictionary (*tocociñaya quelachiña*) (Córdova 1578:33, 412).

In sum, there was a variety of Zapotec military and civil servants sent from the Valley of Oaxaca to defend and administer the tributary regions. When Burgoa visited two of these regions in the 1600s, he noted the lingering but dwindling presence of descendants of the original Zapotec military captains and civil administrators stationed there (Burgoa 1674b:263, 338).

The administration of conquered regions constituted a reign of terror for the subject populations. The favored terror tactics ranged from various kinds of torture to punitive executions; the victims were butchered and their skulls and bones were used to construct skull racks. These terror tactics were practiced immediately after the surrender of a region to the Zapotec forces as a symbol of conquest, and were repeated in the event of any lack of compliance on the part of the subject population (Burgoa 1674b:11-12, 342; Córdova 1578:368, 403). Such practices were committed by the Zapotec in frontier regions in order to terrorize the subjugated population to the point of total submission.

Some wars the Zapotec armies fought resulted in temporary truces with the enemy; these peace treaties were marked by the formation of marriage alliances between sons and daughters of the two opposing rulers (Burgoa 1674b:343-345; Córdova 1578:411). We also know of the existence of Zapotec ambassadors or messengers who were sent into enemy territory to announce the Zapotec plans for expansion into that region, and to suggest that the enemy avoid mounting opposition (Burgoa 1674a:394; Córdova 1578:153).

Another function of the Zapotec military organization was to defend the Valley of Oaxaca from any attacks by external powers. For this purpose a garrison of chosen military captains and warriors was founded on a hilltop at the northern end of the valley and named *Huijazoo*, which signifies military watchtower. This fortified installation guarded two natural passes or entrances into the Oaxaca Valley from the north (Burgoa 1674b:11). The modern counterpart of this installation, the town of San Pablo Huitzo, lies at the northern end of the valley (see Fig. 1).

Military achievements were highly sought because they resulted in the bestowal of awards and privileges. Warriors who excelled in battle thereafter wore a special hair knot on the crown of their heads (Córdova 1578:409). The Zapotec term *tàcaxillàaya* means "to earn salary in war" and "to deserve" (Córdova 1578:390). All great warriors, military captains, and frontier administrators were honored at death: great warriors and military captains who died in battle in faraway places were returned to the Valley of Oaxaca for burial; one notable frontier administrator was elaborately entombed with sacrificial retainers, feather-work, incense burners, braziers, and urns in the region he administered during his lifetime so that he could continue to watch over that province in death (Burgoa 1674b:124, 242, 246). Through brave deeds there was always the possibility of being promoted not only to higher positions within the military organization but also to positions in other spheres of power. In this way the Zapotec ruler maintained a daring military force ready to implement his expansionistic policies (Burgoa 1674b:236).

There were close ties between the military and political institutions in sixteenth-century Zapotec society. Throughout the ethnohistoric sources, the terms for lords and military captains are found side by side; we know, for example, that lords and military captains shared a special room in the palace at Mitla (Burgoa 1674b:124). In the general divisions of Zapotec society given to us by Córdova, the military leaders were considered part of the noble lineage (*tijajoàna, tijajoanahuini*). Although the military leaders ranked below the ruling lineage, (*tijacoquij*), they were nonetheless differentiated from the lineage of commoners (*tijapèniquéche*) (Córdova 1578:246; Whitecotton 1977:142-144). Regardless of their social position at birth, military leaders were considered part of the nobility and were entitled to many of the same privileges and sumptuary rules of dress and diet enjoyed by the Zapotec ruling elite. The military organization was one institution in Zapotec society through which social mobility could occur. The Zapotec rulers themselves carried two military accouterments as symbols of their power: in their left hand they carried a shield, and in their right hand they carried a spear (Burgoa 1674b:123).

*Framework
for Evaluating the
Conquest Hypothesis*

By choosing to assess whether or not the Cuicatlán Cañada's relationship to the emerging Zapotec state centered at Monte Albán was one of conquest and subjugation, I needed to consider a set of interrelated determinants and consequences of such a conquest strategy, in the form of a conquest model. By *conquest*, I mean not simply an isolated military victory, but rather the complete political usurpation of foreign territory, marked by a newly-imposed relationship of subjugation and tribute exaction, which we have seen was a major characteristic of Postclassic Zapotec imperialism (cf. Brown 1977:290). Such a conquest in the Late Formative period obviously would have disrupted any previous relationships between the neighboring regions and would have brought significant changes in its wake.

Taking up part of Hill's (1977:90) discussion on a suitable framework for explaining prehistoric change, certain requirements would have to be met by the conquest model in order to explain this change successfully. One of these requirements involves describing a given system of interest *prior* to the occurrence of change, and also describing its operation *after* change has occurred. Accordingly, for the present investigation of the Cañada's relationship to the Valley of Oaxaca during the Late Formative period, I would have to begin by describing the Cuicatlán Cañada, its regional organization, and its relationship to the Oaxaca Valley prior to the proposed period of subjugation, that is, during the Middle Formative period. Moreover, the model would have to describe the Cuicatlán Cañada, its regional organization, and its relationship to the Oaxaca Valley in the period following its proposed conquest by Monte Albán.

In keeping with the definition of conquest as the complete political usurpation of foreign territory, I needed to consider those aspects of the Cuicatlán Cañada that might have attracted the Zapotec in the first place, perhaps inducing them to expend the effort required to subjugate and control the region. Certain environmental and/or sociopolitical preconditions in the Cuicatlán Cañada during the Middle Formative period might have influenced the Zapotec's decision to disrupt the previous relationship maintained with the Cañada by pursuing a military conquest there. Furthermore, considerations about the Cañada's environment, economic potential, and existing sociopolitical organization, for example, might have had a great bearing upon the nature of Zapotec domination of the region (Morris 1972:400-401; Lattimore 1962:475-477).

Likewise, the effects of the proposed conquest occurring sometime during the Late Formative period (ca. 300 B.C.-A.D. 200) would have to be monitored both in the region conquered, that is, in the Cuicatlán Cañada, and at the center of the expanding polity, Monte Albán. In the case of the newly-subjugated Cañada, the effects of such a conquest might have included a major reorganization of the conquered region's administrative hierarchy by the expanding Zapotec polity. New demands might have been imposed upon the subject region's population in response to the expanding polity's interests. Back at the administrative center of the expanding polity, at Monte Albán, the consequences of the conquest strategy should also have been felt, initially in response to the military operation required to subjugate regions like the Cuicatlán Cañada, and later through the growing administrative apparatus needed to manage one of many far-flung tributary regions.

Aside from establishing whether a Zapotec conquest of the Cuicatlán Cañada did in fact occur sometime during the Late Formative period, the conquest model sought to relate the following determinants and consequences of the proposed subjugation:

1. Preconditions in the Cuicatlán Cañada prior to the proposed Zapotec take-over, and the nature of interregional relationships at this time.
2. The transformation of the Cuicatlán Cañada into a frontier tributary region of the Monte Albán state.
3. The effects of the conquest strategy upon the emerging Zapotec state centered at Monte Albán.

The theoretical underpinnings of these related aspects of the conquest model will be discussed together with their derivable expectations, and where possible, their archaeological correlates.

Preconditions of Conquest in the Cuicatlán Cañada

There are certain characteristics of the Cuicatlán Cañada that might have figured prominently in the Zapotec's decision to subjugate this region. We have seen how the Cuicatlán Cañada is strategically located between the Oaxaca and Tehuacán valleys, and how it forms a major artery of inter-valley travel and communication. The Colonial period Camino Real, which is known to have been used before the Conquest, transited the Cañada to link the Basin of Mexico with the Oaxaca Valley. Most travelers, trade items, and information moving between these highland valleys would have necessarily passed through the Cañada. For example, certain raw materials such as obsidian that are not indigenous to the Valley of Oaxaca would probably have been procured by means of long-distance trade networks with the Basin of Mexico; obsidian artifacts fashioned from the known obsidian sources in that region are present in Middle Formative deposits in the Valley of Oaxaca (Pires-Ferreira 1975). The proposed obsidian trade networks between the two highland valleys would probably have involved the conveyance of obsidian through the Cañada. Control over this segment of the highland trade route might have been in the vital interests of an emerging polity in the Valley of Oaxaca (Webb 1975:190-191), especially if it depended upon the regular delivery of trade items such as obsidian. We do know that the sixteenth-century Valley Zapotec were interested in gaining control over major communication routes.

In addition to the Cañada's strategic location, a major consideration of the expanding Zapotec might have been the region's agricultural potential. We have seen how productive maize agriculture is here due to the canyon's fertile alluvium, its potential for irrigation, and its lowland climate. Aside from the Cañada's potential with respect to maize agriculture, today the region is famed for the other tropical products grown there. The Cañada's productive specialization in the cultivation of tropical fruits has a long history inasmuch as it was recorded by the earliest European travelers who passed through the region (Burgoa 1674a:387). Among the fruits recorded by these travelers were chicozapotes, zapotes, and ciruelas, many of which were traded and sold in neighboring highland markets. The tropical fruits from the Cañada were regarded as the best in New Spain, for the *Relación de Cuicatlán* noted: "... *como es tierra caliente ay en el muchas frutas de la tierra y muy buenas, que se tiene por çierto son las mejores de la nueva España* ..." (Gallego 1580:187). In pre-Colonial times, we know that the Valley Zapotec elite desired these tropical fruits, and imbibed fermented fruit drinks made from some of them (Burgoa 1674b:125). Cotton was also grown in the Cañada at the time of the Conquest and was woven into cloth for mantles (Hunt 1972:195; Hopkins 1974:77-80). We know that cotton was greatly desired by the Valley Zapotec at this time (Spores 1965:967, 969); Zapotec warriors wore padded cotton armor (Córdova 1578:38), and cotton mantles were part of the Zapotec elite's distinctive attire (Whitecotton 1977:143). Furthermore, we have seen how the *tierra caliente* region of Nejapa paid part of its tribute to the Valley Zapotec in cotton mantles (Burgoa 1674b:240, 251-252).

If these tropical products were also cultivated in the Cuicatlán Cañada during the Middle Formative period and formed part of an existing interregional exchange system between the Cañada and the surrounding highland valleys, one factor in the Zapotec's decision to subjugate this tropical region might have been the desire to regulate the production of these *tierra caliente* items according to their own needs, instead of relying upon exchange with the Cañada to provide them with the desired products (see Spencer 1982:65-67). We might, therefore, expect to find evidence of the cultivation of these tropical products at Middle Formative communities in the Cuicatlán Cañada. The economic potential of the region during the Middle Formative period, particularly with regard to the cultivation of tropical items, might then have constituted a precondition of conquest, and might have figured in the extractive considerations of the expanding Zapotec.

Before deciding to pursue a conquest strategy in the Cuicatlán Cañada, the Zapotec would need to weigh the nature of the local forces present in this region that would resist such a conquest. A consideration of the existing sociopolitical organization in the region would be important in a subjugation involving the region's complete political usurpation by the Monte Albán state. Thus, if the proposed conquest were to occur, we might expect the existing sociopolitical conditions in the Cañada to be suitable for conquest from the Zapotec's point of view. We should not be surprised to find evidence of a relatively small Middle Formative population inhabiting the canyon. Compared to the political situation in the Valley of Oaxaca during the late Middle Formative period, which featured the establishment of a large center at Monte Albán, we might expect the Cuicatlán Cañada to exhibit a simpler, less centralized administrative hierarchy, one that could not easily mobilize the necessary military strength in the face of a Zapotec advance.

Related to the existing sociopolitical organization in the Cuicatlán Cañada would be the nature of the existing relationship between the two regions—and for that matter, between the Cañada and other regions—prior to the proposed subjugation. It is widely believed that during the Middle Formative period the elites of certain neighboring regions of Mesoamerica were participating in interregional exchange networks (Flannery 1968; Pires-Ferreira 1975; Pires-Ferreira and Flannery 1976). If the elites of the Cañada participated in exchange relationships with the Oaxaca Valley elites, such exchange might form a significant precondition for conquest. An exchange relationship between the Valley of Oaxaca and the Cuicatlán Cañada would relay those precious native resources from each region to the other, and thereby form the initial supplying mechanism. Such exchange networks between the elites of the two regions might be manifested archaeologically by the occurrence of items from the Oaxaca Valley at Middle Formative sites in the Cañada, and by the occurrence of items imported to the Oaxaca Valley from the Cañada.

With the establishment of a major ceremonial center at Monte Albán in the Valley of Oaxaca, an imbalance might have developed between the growing desire on the part of the Zapotec elite for the resources of the Cañada, and the Cañada's ability to supply enough of the desired resources (see Spencer 1982:54-62). Spencer examines the destabilizing effects of asymmetric regional political growth in the Oaxaca Valley upon the interregional system of exchange which linked the Valley with the Cañada and other regions during the Middle Formative period. If the Cañada was not growing politically as rapidly as the Oaxaca Valley, the increasing demands by the Zapotec elite for imported goods from the Cañada would not have been matched by an increase in the Cañada elite's demand for goods imported from the Oaxaca Valley. Consequently, the Zapotec might well have embarked upon a conquest of the region in order to secure the traded resources according to their growing needs (Webb 1975:185, 190). The existing reciprocal exchange relationship between the elites of the two regions would have been disrupted and likely replaced by an entirely different kind of interregional relationship, one characterized by the extraction of tribute from the Cañada to Monte Albán.

In sum, among the conditions in the Cuicatlán Cañada during the Middle Formative period suitable for a take-over of the region by Monte Albán would be the canyon's strategic location with respect to inter-valley travel and trade routes, the region's agricultural potential especially in regard to the cultivation of exotic tropical products, the size and complexity of the sociopolitical unit(s) present in the Cañada that would have resisted this imperial expansion, and the nature of the existing relationship between the two regions that would have been altered by the proposed Zapotec subjugation. We might expect that there would have been resources in the Cañada during the Middle Formative period of interest to the Valley Zapotec, and that the existing sociopolitical conditions in the region would not have presented much of a threat to the expansionistic Zapotec.

The Transformation of the Cuicatlán Cañada into a Frontier Tributary Region

If the Valley Zapotec proceeded to subjugate the Cuicatlán Cañada sometime during the Late Formative period, we might expect the effects of such a conquest strategy to be detected archaeologically in the target region. Given what we know about Zapotec militarism and imperial policies prior to the Spanish Conquest, we would expect the impact of the proposed Zapotec conquest to have been clearly manifested in the Cuicatlán Cañada. The effects of the conquest strategy upon this region would derive, on the one hand, from the Zapotec military campaign directed here for the purpose of subjugating and maintaining control over the local population, and from the transformation of this previously autonomous region into a tributary province of the Monte Albán state on the other.

As the Zapotec armies swept through the Cañada, they would probably have left signs of war and violence. The Zapotec stratagems for gaining control over a region, which included the open advance into enemy territory and the erection of fortifications on strategically located mountaintops, likely would have resulted in major observable changes on both the regional and community levels of analysis. We might expect to find abrupt discontinuities in the regional settlement pattern in response to the Zapotec attack, including the sudden establishment of hilltop fortifications at strategic points overlooking major communication routes. Individual communities might have suffered the destructive effects of a Zapotec attack *"a fuego y sangre"* (Burgoa 1674b:189, 328), and survivors might have been forcibly resettled by their new Zapotec overlords.

Following the Cuicatlán Cañada's defeat and surrender to the Zapotec forces sometime during the Late Formative period, the conquered territory might witness the establishment of Zapotec frontier installations manned by chosen Zapotec military captains and garrison troops. The functions of these military outposts might include defending the incorporated region from external threats (Rowlands 1972:457), regulating the movement of people and goods in and out of the canyon (cf. Frere 1974:158), and effectively ensuring the subject population's allegiance to the Zapotec state. These installations might include elaborate hilltop stone fortifications like those described for the later Zapotec by the earliest Spanish sources. Aside from the strong Zapotec military presence here, we might also expect to find evidence for a variety of associated personnel in charge of servicing such facilities.

A major implication of the Zapotec conquest for the Cuicatlán Cañada would be the virtual elimination of the native political institutions there (Andrzejewski 1954:134) and the incorporation of that region as a subordinate and tributary province of the Monte Albán state. The local inhabitants of the previously autonomous region would be governed by a Zapotec frontier administrator, one of whose principal duties would be to enforce the collection of tribute from the Cañada. This political reorganization of the Cuicatlán Cañada at the hand of the Monte Albán state might be reflected on the regional level of analysis by the curtailment of local political institutions associated with the native ruling elite, and by the overlay of a single centralized Zapotec administrative hierarchy in this frontier region. This might be manifested archaeologically by a new hierarchy of settlement sizes in the Cañada and by the introduction of Zapotec-inspired public architecture here (Sanders and Price 1968:166).

Under the direct intervention of the conquering Zapotec, local native administrators residing at individual communities would probably be either eliminated or redirected to enforce Zapotec imperial policies. Within an individual community we might expect to find evidence of this Zapotec political intervention, in the form of a change in the nature and organization of public architecture here (Cheek 1977:163-166), and in the appearance of Zapotec symbols of imperial power (cf. Frere 1974:364; Fox 1978:72).

If a major function of the Zapotec conquest of the Cuicatlán Cañada was to collect tribute from this *tierra caliente* region, the proposed conquest would have obvious implications for the local economy of the Cañada. If the region's local economy prior to the Zapotec conquest was not capable of meeting large-scale tribute demands, we might expect to find evidence for a reorganization of the Cañada's productive regime. Given the Cañada's lowland climate, its long history as a region specializing in the production of tropical fruits, and the fact that other *tierra caliente* regions paid tribute to the sixteenth-century Valley Zapotec with native tropical products, we might expect that the Cañada supplied the Zapotec state with some of the indigenous tropical products that were grown there at the time of the Spanish Conquest (chicozapotes, black zapotes, ciruelas, and cotton). If previous to the Zapotec conquest the Cañada communities were cultivating these items in amounts considered only supplementary to the basic Mesoamerican staples, upon the region's incorporation into the Monte Albán state, the Zapotec might have increased the production of the desired tribute items. The Cañada's agricultural regime might then have been expanded and manipulated in the interests of the Monte Albán state.

On the regional level of analysis, we might expect to find evidence of such a reorganization and expansion of the local productive regime. Such policies might be manifested by changes in the general location and distribution of the region's settlements with respect to the available farmland. For example, we might observe a changing relationship between the amount of cultivable land on each of the Cañada's alluvial fans and the sizes of the settlements. The Zapotec might also have introduced new forms of agricultural technology into the region with the aim of improving or expanding the Cañada's existing agricultural base (cf. Frere 1974:315). At the level of the individual community, the Zapotec reorganization of the local economy might have resulted in the increased production of certain tribute items and in the consequent reduction of other economic activities carried out by this previously self-sufficient commuity.

With the Zapotec overthrow of the Cañada's ruling elite and the region's transformation into a subordinate frontier region, tributary to Monte Albán, any previous interregional exchange relationships maintained by the native ruling elite would have been disrupted abruptly and discarded by the conquering Zapotec (Rowlands 1972:460). In the first place, with the realignment of the Cañada as a tributary province of the Zapotec state, any previous reciprocal exchange ties between the two regions would have been replaced by a one-way flow of tribute from the Cañada to the Valley of Oaxaca. Under this new relationship, those items from the Cañada that had previously reached the Valley of Oaxaca by means of a reciprocal exchange agreement, but that now formed items paid in tribute, no longer needed to be repaid with trade items from the Valley of Oaxaca. Thus, we might expect to find a certain decrease in the relative frequency of imported items from the Oaxaca Valley to the Cañada. The importation of any Oaxaca products into the Cañada after the Zapotec take-over would probably be directed as provisions or rewards to the Zapotec military and civil servants stationed in the region and not to the local tributary population. Thus, the regional distribution of imported Oaxaca goods in the Cañada after the Zapotec subjugation might reflect the

Zapotec administration of this frontier region, and might constitute a different regional distribution from that obtained in the Cañada during the time period prior to the conquest, when a reciprocal exchange relationship probably existed between the adjacent autonomous regions. After the subjugation we might expect to find a discontinuous distribution of imported Oaxaca products in the Cañada, with the highest frequencies of these items associated with the loci of Zapotec military and civil administration here (Morris 1972:394-395).

In addition to disrupting the previous exchange relationship between the Cuicatlán Cañada and the Valley of Oaxaca, it is likely that a Zapotec subjugation of the Cañada would have halted ongoing exchanges between the Cañada and *other* regions. Inside the conquered territory guarded by the Zapotec, we might expect to find an absence of imported goods from areas like the Tehuacán Valley that lay beyond this frontier region. Once again, any imported items entering the Cañada from other regions at this time would probably be controlled by the Zapotec state for the purpose of provisioning the Zapotec military and civil servants stationed there, and would probably not be generally available to the subject population at large.

In sum, the transformation of the Cuicatlán Cañada into a frontier tributary region of the Monte Albán state would likely feature a strong Zapotec frontier administration and a reduction in importance of the region's previous sociopolitical institutions. We might expect to find signs of the war and violence accompanying the initial Zapotec military campaign, and the establishment of military outposts for guarding the conquered territory and controlling the subject population. In accordance with the imperial practices of the later Zapotec described in the early Spanish sources, we might expect to find evidence in the Cañada for the Zapotec practice of extracting tribute from conquered regions. Depending upon the scale of the tribute demands and the nature of the region's local economy prior to the subjugation, this might have necessitated a reorganization of the Cañada's local economy. Previous reciprocal exchange relationships maintained between the Cañada and adjacent regions would probably have been disrupted; while any previous reciprocal exchange relationship between the Cañada and the Oaxaca Valley would probably have been replaced with a non-reciprocal relationship characterized by the one-way flow of tribute from the Cañada to Monte Albán, additional exchange ties maintained by the Cañada with other adjacent regions might have been eliminated under Zapotec rule.

Effects of the Conquest Strategy upon the Emerging Zapotec State

In the introductory chapter we saw how the evidence at Monte Albán for the proposed Zapotec conquest strategy is concurrent with the evidence for Monte Albán's ascension to statehood. If the Zapotec did pursue an interregional conquest strategy during the Late Formative period, the effects of such a strategy should also have been felt back at Monte Albán, the center of the expanding Zapotec polity. By determining what the consequences of such a conquest strategy might have been for the emerging Zapotec state, we might then be in a position to evaluate a long-debated topic: the role of militarism and conquest in the formation of early states.

To begin with, in order for the Valley Zapotec to have embarked upon a conquest strategy, they would have needed to establish a strong military operation, especially if previously there was no such permanent institution. We have seen how vast the military preparations for war were among the sixteenth-century Zapotec: civilian forces were mobilized and trained; military equipment and provisions were stockpiled; and trenches and fortifications were repaired and expanded. If prior to the Late Formative period there existed no permanent body of military specialists and warriors, we might expect that such an institution would have arisen at this time.

Gearing's study of eighteenth-century Cherokee politics delineates the socioenvironmental conditions under which such a military organization would arise and describes the processes of institutional metamorphosis. Gearing documents the permanent institutionalization of the Cherokee military organization, which arose from a previously ephemeral war organization in response to Colonial period encroachments. The previous war organization convened for the varied tasks of conducting warfare in the winter months, negotiating with other tribes, and playing ball games in the non-warring summer months (see Chapter 1; Gearing 1962:26-27). Thus the permanent Cherokee military organization arose from one of three roles assumed by their previously ephemeral war organization.

There is evidence to suggest the existence of "dance societies" in the Valley of Oaxaca during the late Middle Formative period, prior to the proposed Zapotec conquest of neighboring regions (Flannery 1976d:336-340). The archaeological contexts of certain ritual artifacts in villages of this time period suggest the possibility that these societies or sodalities drew members from many different households and that dancing was only one of the activities performed by these cross-cutting sodalities. Another activity performed by these probably all-male societies might have been small-scale warfare or raiding, similar to the multiple-purpose war organization of the Cherokee. We do have evidence of Zapotec warfare in the time period prior to the proposed conquest strategy; the *danzante* reliefs found on Building L at Monte Albán have been interpreted as representations of captives taken in *raids and skirmishes* by the founders of Monte Albán (see Chapter 1; Marcus 1976:126-127). Thus, minor warring and raiding might have constituted another role for such an all-male institution in Middle Formative Oaxaca. Out of this multi-purpose institution for dancing and warfare might have emerged the true military organization that was required in order to embark upon the conquest of neighboring regions during the Late Formative period.

Given what we know about Postclassic Zapotec militarism, Monte Albán's early military organization might have consisted of warriors, led by professional military captains, and differentiated into ranked warrior orders. Evidence of these warrior orders might be traced in the archaeological record by means of their known association with jaguars and other wild animals (Burgoa 1674a:412). We would also expect to find archaeological correlates of Zapotec militarism resulting from the body of activities performed by this new institution. Permanent offensive and defensive military facilities might have been constructed by the Zapotec at this time, not only outside the valley in the conquered regions, but also within the valley and at Monte Albán itself.

The effects of the conquest strategy would probably have been significant for Monte Albán's administrative apparatus. Aside from the burgeoning military organization required to subjugate neighboring regions, the known Zapotec practice of replacing the native ruling elites of conquered regions with Zapotec administrators for the purpose of enforcing the collection of tribute might have necessitated an elaboration of Monte Albán's administrative organization. The management of such a vast imperial network would have included coordinating an increasing number of activities and integrating new administrative units. Due to the variety of new information sources to be integrated, we might expect to find an increasing amount of horizontal specialization in Monte Albán's administrative body; we might further expect the emergence of higher-order vertical control units, termed vertical specialization, for achieving system integration (Johnson 1978:87-100). Among the new horizontal units to be integrated would have been the military and civil administrative units established at critical nodes in the tributary network. Higher-order vertical control units at Monte Albán would probably have been needed to integrate this proliferation of organizational units. We might therefore expect to find evidence of an increase in the complexity of Monte Albán's decision-making organization concurrent with the proposed conquest strategy. We have seen how one measure of the elaboration of Monte Albán's administrative apparatus might be an increase in the amount and variety of public architecture erected at the capital (Flannery and Marcus 1976a:206).

A large part of the new information to be processed as a result of the conquest strategy probably would have derived from the exaction and collection of tribute. Administrative units in the foreign territories probably would have been responsible for the local collection of tribute. As we have seen for the Postclassic Zapotec, while part of this tribute went to provision Zapotec garrisons in the conquered regions, the remaining due was forwarded to the Valley of Oaxaca. We might therefore expect to find evidence for the construction of administrative and storage facilities at key nodes in such a tributary network during the Late Formative period. We might expect also to find evidence at Monte Albán for the eventual receipt of tribute items from regions like the Cuicatlán Cañada.

If tribute items were moving in one direction from the conquered regions, military equipment and official remunerations presumably would have been sent in turn from the Valley of Oaxaca to the military and civil servants stationed in the conquered regions. The Zapotec elite at Monte Albán likely would have favored a centrally-administered policy for equipping and remunerating its military and civil administrators in the subjugated regions, for this would ensure against any break in their allegiance (Andrzejewski 1954:87).

With Monte Albán's imperial expansion into surrounding regions, new exchange mechanisms might have arisen in order for the Valley Zapotec to maintain long-distance trade relationships *beyond* their frontier regions. For example, if certain raw materials such as obsidian, which probably formed an important part of Zapotec military equipment, were not available within Zapotec-controlled territory, the Zapotec would have had to maintain their previous trade relations with the obsidian suppliers located beyond the frontier. Furthermore, since one way for a state to ensure command over its troops stationed in foreign regions is by controlling the supply of raw materials used in the production of military equipment (Andrzejewski 1954:87), Monte Albán probably would have sought to control the trade relations governing the importation of these raw materials into its expanded territory. Any new long-distance trade mechanisms fostered by the Monte Albán state in the aftermath of its conquest strategy necessarily would have entailed a further elaboration of its administrative apparatus.

A final possible implication of the proposed conquest strategy for the Monte Albán state might have involved the growth in political prominence of the military organization. We know that in Postclassic Zapotec society the military organization served as a vehicle for social mobility. The proposed conquest strategy during the Late Formative period might have also resulted in the emergence of a privileged group of warriors (Andrzejewski 1954:39, 134). Equipped with manpower, resources, and organization, the Zapotec military institution, born in order to subjugate neighboring regions, in time could have grown to assume many of the decision-making functions of the ruling Zapotec elite. The conquest strategy might have nurtured the rise to political prominence of war leaders and enabled the military institution to assume a higher-order, more general-purpose position in the state's administrative hierarchy (Flannery 1972:412-413; Adams 1966:139, 152).

The 1977-78 Cuicatlán Cañada Project

Charles Spencer and I conducted an archaeological research project in the Cuicatlán Cañada from May 1977 until April 1978 that was designed to collect the necessary information with which to evaluate the previously presented model of the Cañada's subjugation by Monte Albán during the Late Formative period. An evaluation of this model called for information pertaining to both regional and community level organization in the Cañada beginning in the Middle Formative period and continuing through to the Late Formative and Classic periods. In building our research design we relied upon the model presented by Flannery (1976a) and set out to collect data on several analytical levels: from the level of the region's settlement pattern to that of the individual community, the household, and down to the individual feature or activity area. I directed the first part of the project involving the regional survey of the Cuicatlán Cañada; subsequently, Spencer selected one of the region's Formative and Classic period sites, La Coyotera (Cs25), and directed a program of excavations there. The regional settlement pattern survey was expected to provide information on changes in the nature of regional organization in the Cañada over time, but particularly during the transition from the Middle Formative to the Late Formative period. The excavations at the site of La Coyotera were designed to investigate the nature of local economy and sociopolitical organization at this community before and after the proposed Zapotec subjugation of the Cañada.

The Cuicatlán Cañada Survey

We began the Cuicatlán Cañada Survey in May 1977. As indicated in Figure 7, the regional survey extended from the modern towns of Santiago Dominguillo north to Santa María Tecomavaca in the state of Oaxaca. We borrowed our regional survey methods from the Basin of Mexico and Valley of Oaxaca settlement pattern projects (Parsons 1971; Sanders, Parsons, and Santley 1979; Blanton et al. 1982), with some modifications to suit the Cañada's particular terrain and vegetation. Using 1:10,000 scale aerial photographs of the region supplied by the *Compañía Mexicana de Aerofotos*, we carried out a 100% field-by-field coverage of the canyon floor (sand and gravel zones, low alluvium, high alluvium, reclaimed piedmont). Our survey team included me, Charles Spencer, a student assistant, and two Mexican workmen. Together we traversed a given section of terrain designated on the aerial photograph,

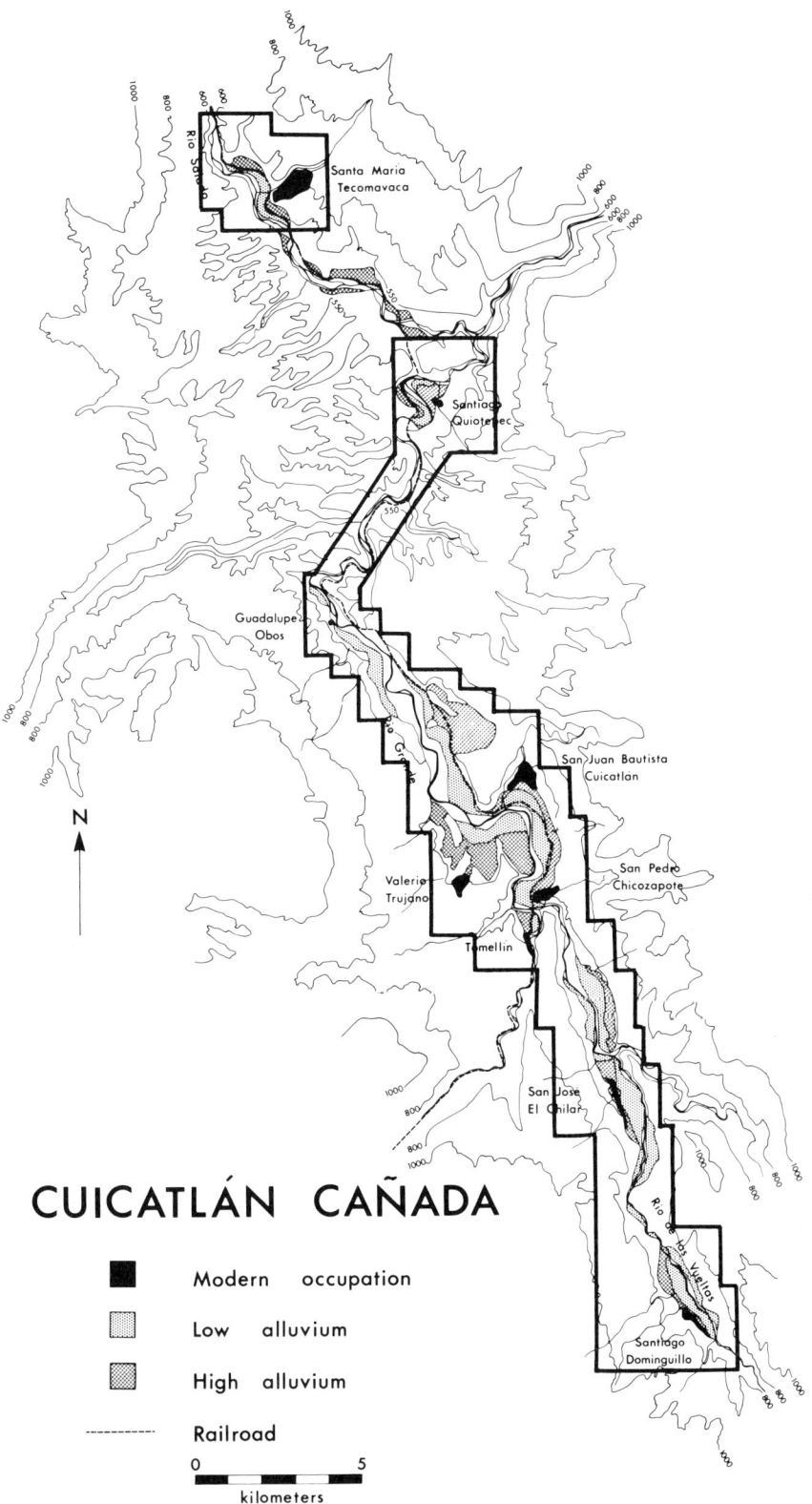

Figure 7. The Cuicatlán Cañada Survey area.

spaced at intervals ranging from 20 to 30 m apart. This field-by-field survey of the canyon floor was combined with systematic coverage of all eminences and piedmont ridges overlooking the canyon floor. Due to the rather dense natural xerophytic vegetation covering these eminences and ridges, we chose to follow the numerous trails used by goatherders and firewood collectors that crisscross these foothills. We proceeded to cover the survey area employing both the field-by-field method of survey and the systematic survey of all eminences and piedmont ridges.

The only location where we did not survey every field was the area around Tecomavaca, north of the junction of the Río Grande and Río Salado. This was due principally to the fact that this area had already been surveyed by MacNeish and Peterson (MacNeish et al. 1972:341-344). Here our survey began with the aid of MacNeish and Peterson's original survey forms, as well as with the help of local guides. Our main interest here was to return to map and to surface collect the site of Llano de los Mogotes (Cs1/Tr19).

Each archaeological site found on regional survey was assigned a Cañada site number (Cs__). Each site was assigned only one number, regardless of the multiple occupations it might feature. Back in the laboratory, however, when the successive occupations at those multiple component sites had been assigned, each occupation was referred to using the site number followed by a dash and an abbreviation for that particular phase: -P for Perdido phase occupation; -L for Lomas phase occupation; -T for Trujano phase occupation; and -IV for Iglesia Vieja phase occupation. After an extensive reconnaissance of a site to determine its occupation(s) and its size, the outlines of the site were drawn in on the pertinent aerial photograph. A site report with details of the site's name, location, vegetation, any sources of disturbance, size, periodization, and a description of its public and residential architecture was filled out at this time. During the course of the Cuicatlán Cañada Survey we located and described a total of 93 sites with occupations ranging from the Middle Formative to the Late Postclassic period.

A second stage of the Cuicatlán Cañada Survey involved returning to all the Formative and Classic period sites in order to collect more precise information on their internal structure by means of intensive mapping and controlled surface-collecting techniques (Redman and Watson 1970; Flannery 1976a; Spencer 1979). Individual site maps were drawn at a 1:1000 scale using an alidade and plane table in combination with a tape measure and Brunton compass in places where the vegetation was too dense to permit accurate sighting with the alidade. Arbitrary datum points were independently established for mapping each site; consequently, contour intervals are internally consistent within, but not between, sites. The site maps indicate the precise areal extent of the sites and, in the cases of multiple component sites, the outlines of the separate occupations. All the civic-ceremonial architecture, housemounds, house foundations, and any other associated features such as defensive walls and irrigation canals evident on the surface were drawn on the site maps. The site maps also indicate the locations of the surface collection units.

Although it might have been desirable to map each site completely before deciding where to locate surface collection units by means of some random sampling procedure, limitations of time and personnel required us to map and surface collect in tandem as we moved across a site. We used the following criteria in selecting locations for surface collections: (1) we tried to locate collection units so that they could be directly associated with nearby architectural units (e.g. civic-ceremonial structure, housemound); and (2) we tried to sample the various sectors of a site more or less evenly. The surface collection units consisted of squares measuring either 5 m but usually 10 m on a side laid out with a tape measure and temporary stakes or rocks. The actual surface collecting involved the removal of all sherds, chipped stone, and other artifacts from the designated area. When the collection was completed, the material was resorted into the following categories: rims and diagnostic body sherds; chipped stone; other small artifacts; gray paste body sherds; plain paste body sherds; other body sherds. The first three categories of material were bagged and labeled for future laboratory analysis, but the gray paste, plain paste, and other body sherds were simply counted and left in their respective piles in the vicinity of the area collected.

Each collection square received a provenience number consisting of the particular site number followed by a slash and the collection number (e.g. Cs25/228). We used a continuous numbering system for the collection squares in order to ensure that no two collection squares from different sites could ever have the same collection square number. In addition to filling out a lot card detailing the provenience and size of each collection square as well as the kind of material collected, a surface collection form was completed for each collection square. Although this form repeated some of the information recorded on the lot card, it provided the information associating the collection square to a particular architectural feature and to a particular sector of a site. We also used the surface collection form to record any material collected in the square that was not removed for laboratory analysis, such as body sherds, mano and metate fragments, and any Colonial period or modern artifacts.

In sum, the Cuicatlán Cañada Survey was designed to provide general information concerning the changes in settlement patterns and regional organization in the Cañada from the Middle Formative period right through to the Late Postclassic period. The supplementary program of returning to map and surface collect the Formative and Classic period sites was aimed at gaining more precise information on the internal structure of these communities and on the artifactual variability between and within them. The artifact samples from the controlled surface collections could be used to make meaningful comparisons between sites or between different sectors of individual sites on the basis of the varying densities of particular artifact types. Due principally to the relatively small survey area it was possible to accomplish both the general regional survey and the program of intensive mapping and surface collecting the Formative and Classic period sites by the end of October 1977.

A Catchment Analysis of the Cuicatlán Cañada

Aside from outlining the sequence of settlement patterns in the Cuicatlán Cañada from the Middle Formative period on, I wished to examine the relationship between the sizes of these settlements and the agricultural potential of their catchment areas (Vita-Finzi and Higgs 1970; Flannery 1976a:91-95; Sanders 1976:136-159; Roper 1979). Given my research problem, it was important to consider the possible implications of the proposed Zapotec subjugation upon the relationship between the sizes of settlements and the available agricultural resources in the Cañada. The catchment analysis that I undertook in order to measure this relationship involved the following procedure: (1) an ethnographic inquiry of the agricultural practices and yields in the region today; (2) estimating the carrying capacity of the available farmland on each of the Cañada's alluvial fans through time; and (3) estimating the actual site populations that occupied the Cañada's alluvial fans through time. In this section I will present the results of the modern ethnographic inquiry and will describe the ways in which I arrived at my carrying capacity estimates and my population estimates. The results and interpretations of the catchment analysis are embedded in the following chapters that deal with the Cuicatlán Cañada before, during, and after the proposed Zapotec subjugation.

As we saw in a previous section of this chapter, the cultivation of maize in the Cuicatlán Cañada is confined to the strips of low and high alluvium found on each of the canyon's four alluvial fans and is dependent upon irrigation techniques. The low alluvium (or *tierra de primera*) flanking the river can be irrigated using simple floodwater-farming techniques, but the higher alluvium (or *tierra de segunda*) is irrigated by drawing water from the tributaries and streams of the Río Grande in the form of canal irrigation. With irrigation techniques the zones of low and high alluvium on each of the Cañada's alluvial fans are enormously productive; furthermore, the Cañada's frost-free climate permits two growing seasons each year.

We acquired information on local agricultural practices and maize yields through direct interviews with elders and municipal authorities residing in Dominguillo, El Chilar, and Valerio Trujano. Table 1 lists the irrigated maize yields (in terms of kilograms of shelled maize per hectare per planting) reported to us for the low alluvium and high alluvium of the three alluvial fans farmed by inhabitants of these towns. As a result of the Cañada's two growing seasons each year, these figures can be doubled to calculate the annual maize yields per hectare of low and high alluvium on these three

Table 1. Differing Irrigated Maize Yields† in Physiographic Zones of the Cuicatlán Cañada

Alluvial Fan	Low Alluvium	High Alluvium
Dominguillo	1800	1000
El Chilar	1000	500
Cuicatlán	2000	1000

†in terms of kilograms of shelled maize per hectare per planting.

alluvial fans. These maize yields for the only two environmental zones amenable to irrigation agriculture constitute the basic data needed to measure the agricultural potential of the Cañada's alluvial fans. Rainfall farming on marginal piedmont plots of land (or *tierra de tercera*) is rarely practiced in the semi-arid Cañada where the years 1944 and 1969 are remembered as the most notable for rainfall agriculture in recent times. Furthermore, the reported yields for these unirrigated piedmont plots never exceed 250-500 kg of shelled maize for every hectare planted. Rainfall farming will therefore not be considered in the present analysis of the agricultural potential of the Cañada's alluvial fans.

hectare planted (Kirkby 1973:61, Table 3), they must be further corrected in order to account for the higher average maize productivity in the Cuicatlán Cañada. Using the maize yield figures reported to us for the Dominguillo, El Chilar, and Cuicatlán alluvial fans, the average maize yield for the Cañada's low alluvium is 1600 kg of shelled maize per hectare planted, and the average maize yield for the Cañada's high alluvium is 830 kg of shelled maize per hectare planted. For the Valley of Oaxaca's alluvium, Kirkby reports an average yield of 1260 kg of shelled maize per hectare planted (Kirkby

Table 2. Corrected Maize Yields for Pre-Conquest Cob Lengths and for Higher Average Maize Productivity in the Cuicatlán Cañada

Phase	Average Cob Length (cm)	Average Valley of Oaxaca Yields (kg/ha)	Average Cañada Low Alluvium Yields (kg/ha)	Average Cañada High Alluvium Yields (kg/ha)
Perdido	7.5	450	$450 \times \frac{1600}{1260} = 571$	$450 \times \frac{830}{1260} = 296$
Lomas	8.0	550	$550 \times \frac{1600}{1260} = 698$	$550 \times \frac{830}{1260} = 362$
Trujano	9.0	700	$700 \times \frac{1600}{1260} = 889$	$700 \times \frac{830}{1260} = 461$
Iglesia Vieja	11.0	1200	$1200 \times \frac{1600}{1260} = 1524$	$1200 \times \frac{830}{1260} = 790$

The figures pertaining to the yields of maize grown in the Cañada today cannot be directly applied to the Middle Formative, Late Formative, and Classic periods since, as Flannery (1973:297-300) and Kirkby (1973:124-127) have demonstrated, the productivity of maize has grown remarkably over the past several thousand years due to selective intervention by man. Using pre-Conquest archaeological corn-cob specimens from the Valleys of Tehuacán and Oaxaca, Kirkby reconstructed the average productivity of maize for the sequence of prehistoric time periods (Kirkby 1973: Fig. 48). The modern maize yield figures from the Cañada can be corrected for a smaller corn-cob length and a resultingly smaller yield during these earlier time periods using Kirkby's set of graphs (Table 2). Since Kirkby's figures deal with prehistoric maize yields in the Valley of Oaxaca where maize yields obtained by means of dry farming in all the physiographic zones today average 800 kg of shelled maize per hec-

1973:61, Table 3). Kirkby's reconstructed maize yields for the four time periods in question can then be applied to the Cuicatlán Cañada using a time-corrected ratio of the average maize yields on the two regions' alluvial zones (see Table 2). The resulting figures for the four phases listed would need to be doubled in order to calculate the annual maize yield per hectare of low or high alluvium planted.

The next step towards estimating the carrying capacity of the Cañada's alluvial fans involves measuring the amount of cultivable land on each of the region's four alluvial fans. As part of our regional

Table 3. Area of Low Alluvium and High Alluvium on the Cañada's Alluvial Fans

Alluvial Fan	Low Alluvium (ha)	High Alluvium (ha)
Dominguillo	142.65	59.20
El Chilar	297.43	118.20
Cuicatlán	523.60	514.77
Quiotepec	32.85	59.55
Tecomavaca	60.50	151.83

survey methodology, we drew the outlines of the low alluvium and high alluvium zones on our aerial photographs of the region, including the area around Tecomavaca. The zones of low and high alluvium on the Dominguillo, El Chilar, Cuicatlán, Quiotepec, and Tecomavaca alluvial fans were later measured using a compensating polar planimeter (K&E 620005); the resulting areas are presented in Table 3.

The final procedure for estimating the carrying capacity of the Cañada's alluvium is to determine the average annual maize consumption of an individual or household. In a comprehensive carrying capacity analysis of the Basin of Mexico, Sanders proposed two models of prehispanic dietary habits based on either 80% or 65% dependence upon maize (Sanders 1976:109-110). Under the 80% maize dependence plan, an individual's average annual maize consumption would be 160 kg, while under the 65% maize dependence plan an individual's average annual maize consumption would be 128 kg. In his study of the Chalco-Xochimilco chinampa district, Parsons increased Sanders' highest average annual per capita maize consumption figure to 200 kg of maize in order to account for the production or exchange of other subsistence items (Parsons 1976a:244). For estimating the carrying capacity of the Cañada's alluvial fans I will use this 200 kg estimate of the average annual maize consumption of an individual, and the resulting carrying capacity estimates will be expressed in terms of the number of people that could have been supported on a given amount of low or high alluvium.

The final component of the catchment analysis involves deriving population estimates for the Middle Formative, Late Formative, and Classic period settlements in the Cuicatlán Cañada. The procedure most commonly followed for making population estimates from archaeological surface remains involves measuring the area over which the surface remains are distributed (in hectares) and multiplying this area by a density figure (people per hectare). The actual density figure used usually depends upon a visual appraisal of the surface sherd density, which is assumed to correspond to the varying densities of occupation (Parsons 1971:21-24; Blanton 1972:18-21; Sanders, Parsons, and Santley 1979: 34-40). In view of the number of external factors that can affect surface sherd densities, and the limitations of relating refuse densities to actual occupational densities, varying surface sherd densities will not be used for making population estimates here.

In the present analysis, I will derive the population estimate of a site by measuring its surface area (in hectares) with a compensating polar planimeter and multiplying this area by the constant density figure of 10-25 persons per hectare (Blanton et al. 1979:372), which is the figure given for contemporary compact low-density Mexican villages (Sanders 1965:50). Where possible, this admittedly simplistic method for calculating the population estimate of sites will be supplemented with other ways of estimating population. Spencer's extensive excavations at the Middle Formative community of La Coyotera uncovered a number of residential structures from which Spencer projects an average population density of 63.3 persons per hectare (Spencer 1982:129-130). We can apply this population density figure from La Coyotera to other Middle Formative communities in the Cuicatlán Cañada known only from the surface. At those Late Formative and Classic period hilltop sites where housemounds, house foundations, and residential terraces are evident on the surface, and where the date of occupation is unambiguous, population estimates will also be generated by counting the number of households and multiplying this figure with an estimate of the average household size (5 persons per household) (Spencer 1979; Kirkby 1973:127). In all those cases where more than one population estimate can be generated for a site, these independently-derived population estimates will be listed together.

A Ceramic Chronology for the Cuicatlán Cañada

One of the tasks of the Cuicatlán Cañada Project was to establish a local ceramic sequence for the region, since the only published report on the subject (Hopkins 1973) was largely restricted to a description of Postclassic period ceramics. Although we discovered a number of stylistic similarities between the ceramics of the Cañada and those already known from the Oaxaca and Tehuacán valleys, there was a body of local ceramics within the Cañada that was not encompassed by the published sequences of either Oaxaca or Tehuacán. Furthermore, the stylistic similarities between the Cañada and these two adjacent regions shifted in orientation and varied in intensity over time, making the application of the Oaxaca or Tehuacán Valley ceramic sequences to the Cuicatlán Cañada somewhat difficult.

Spencer and I established a local ceramic sequence for the Cañada using ceramic samples recovered from primary excavated deposits at La Coyotera, occupied from Middle Formative times through the Classic period. Contemporaneity among deposits was established principally through stratigraphic association, and less frequently, through seriation techniques. Some material from the surface survey collections was later added to these primary ceramic samples with the aim of accounting for any variability within the region. The ceramic phases we constructed for the Cuicatlán Cañada were then correlated with the Oaxaca and Tehuacán sequences by cross-dating certain ceramic traits from the three regions (Michels 1973:99-111). Figure 8 presents the chronological sequence we established for the Cuicatlán Cañada together with the corresponding portions of the ceramic sequences of Oaxaca and Tehuacán. Here I will briefly describe the three phases that will be of greatest concern in the present study. A more detailed description of the chronological sequence for the Cañada appears in Spencer and Redmond (1982).

PERDIDO PHASE. The Perdido phase is a late Middle Formative manifestation that dates from about 650 B.C. to 300 B.C. It features a strong grayware tradition referred to as Perdido Gray. Perdido Gray ceramics are generally well burnished and evenly fired. Outleaned-wall bowls constitute the most common Perdido Gray vessel forms, which include a variety of rim forms. The interior walls and rims of these bowls are usually decorated with a range of incised motifs (Figs. 9-11). Another common Perdido Gray vessel form is the vaso, with flared or everted rims, S-shaped walls and flat to slightly rounded bases. Their exterior surfaces are usually decorated with incising and sporadic applications of red pigment. Less commonly found are incurved-rim bowls, ollas, composite silhouette bowls, ovate pinched-rim bowls, and potstand bases.

A second major Perdido phase ware consists of a group of plain paste ceramics called Perdido Plain. These sand-tempered ceramics feature large ollas (Fig. 12) and thick-walled comales, made from a coarse paste, as well as smaller vessel forms (such as bottles and tripod plates) fashioned from a finer paste. Only the latter Perdido Plain vessel forms tend to be burnished and decorated with red paint and zones of incised dashes or punctations (Figs. 13-14). Less common Perdido Plain forms include braziers, *apaxtles*, and tecomates.

Many similarities exist between these Perdido phase ceramics and contemporaneous gray and plain paste wares of neighboring regions. Perdido Gray is reminiscent of Quachilco Gray and Quachilco Brown of the Late Santa María phase in Tehuacán (MacNeish, Peterson, and Flannery 1970:114-134) and Socorro Fine Gray and Period Early I grayware in Oaxaca (see Drennan 1976a:21-45; Caso, Bernal, and Acosta 1967:23-33, 146-195). Perdido Plain ceramics resemble in many respects the plain wares of the Rosario and Period Early I (Monte Albán Ia) phases of Oaxaca (see Drennan 1976a:21-45; Caso, Bernal, and Acosta 1967:44-51, 201-209). We have therefore aligned the Perdido phase with the Late Santa María phase in Tehuacán and with the Rosario and Period Early I phases in the Oaxaca Valley (Fig. 8). Perdido phase is named for the field, Llano Perdido, where we excavated the largest sample of material dating to this time period.

LOMAS PHASE. The Lomas phase pertains to the Late and Terminal Formative periods, here referred to inclusively as the Late Formative period. The Lomas phase probably lasts from about 300 B.C. until approximately A.D. 200. A dominant ware in the Cañada at this time is Lomas Gray, which exhibits a more porous paste than Perdido Gray, and less well burnished surfaces. Outleaned-wall bowls continue to be the principal grayware vessel form during the Lomas phase, with flared rims (Figs. 15b-c, 16). But unlike their Perdido Gray counterparts, fewer than 50% of them are decorated. Decorated outleaned-wall bowls commonly have two parallel horizontal lines incised on the interior surface of their rims, but some have additional incised lines (Fig. 16). Another form of decoration seen on some of these bowls consists of "combed" designs on the interior surface of their bases. They strongly resemble those outleaned-wall bowls belonging to the G.12 ceramic type defined by Caso, Bernal, and Acosta (1967:25-26, 214) for the Oaxaca Valley, which appear during Monte Albán Ic and continue into Period II. Pattern burnishing occurs on the interior surface of some outleaned-wall bowl bases.

Shallow cylindrical bowls with slightly flaring

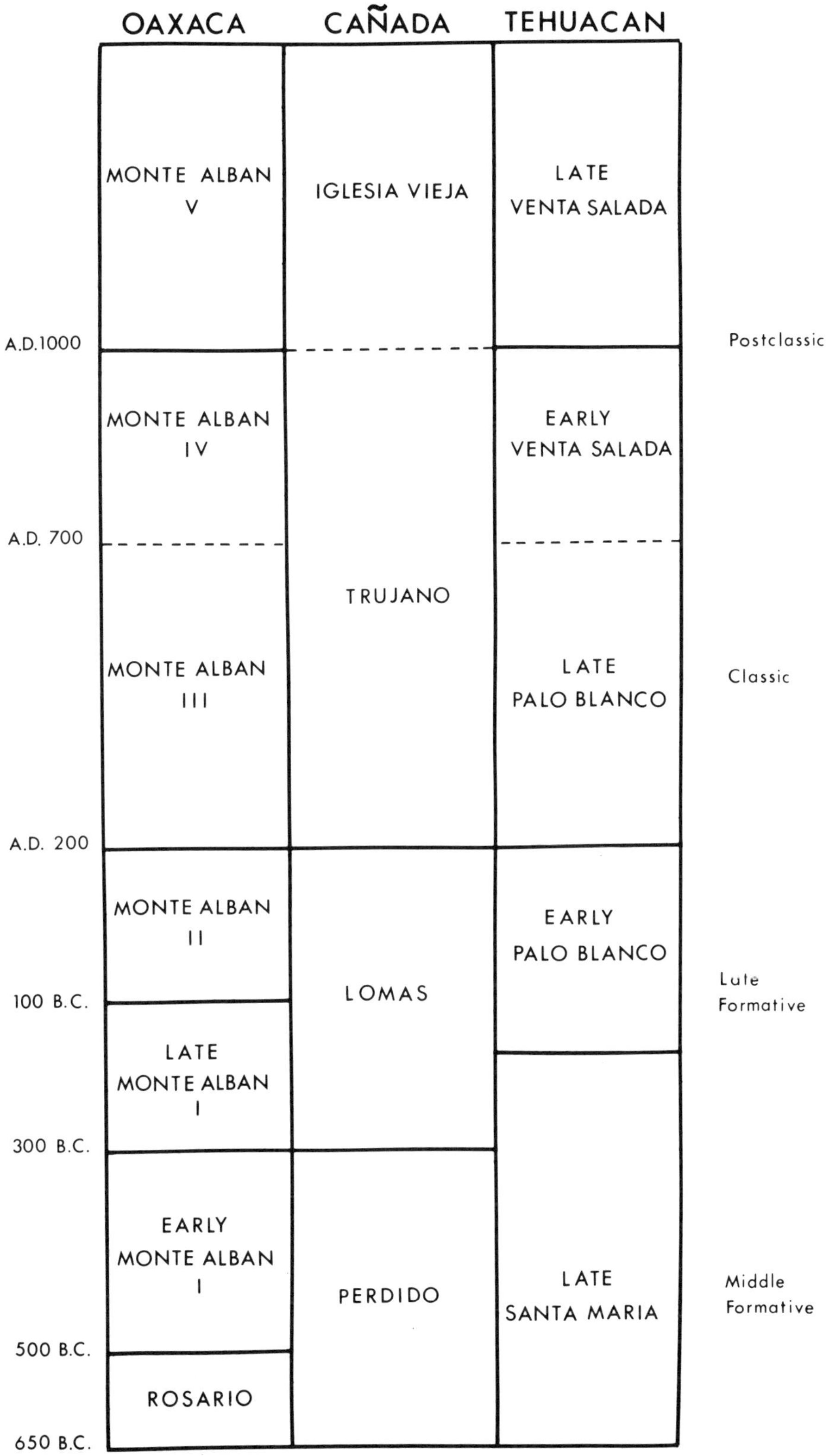

THE CUICATLÁN CAÑADA

OAXACA	CAÑADA	TEHUACAN	
MONTE ALBAN V	IGLESIA VIEJA	LATE VENTA SALADA	
— A.D. 1000 —	- - - - - -	- - - - - -	Postclassic
MONTE ALBAN IV		EARLY VENTA SALADA	
— A.D. 700 — - - - -	TRUJANO	- - - - - -	
MONTE ALBAN III		LATE PALO BLANCO	Classic
— A.D. 200 —			
MONTE ALBAN II	LOMAS	EARLY PALO BLANCO	Late Formative
— 100 B.C. —			
LATE MONTE ALBAN I			
— 300 B.C. —			
EARLY MONTE ALBAN I	PERDIDO	LATE SANTA MARIA	Middle Formative
— 500 B.C. —			
ROSARIO			
— 650 B.C. —			

Figure 8. Correspondence of ceramic phases in the Valley of Oaxaca, the Cuicatlán Cañada, and the Valley of Tehuacán.

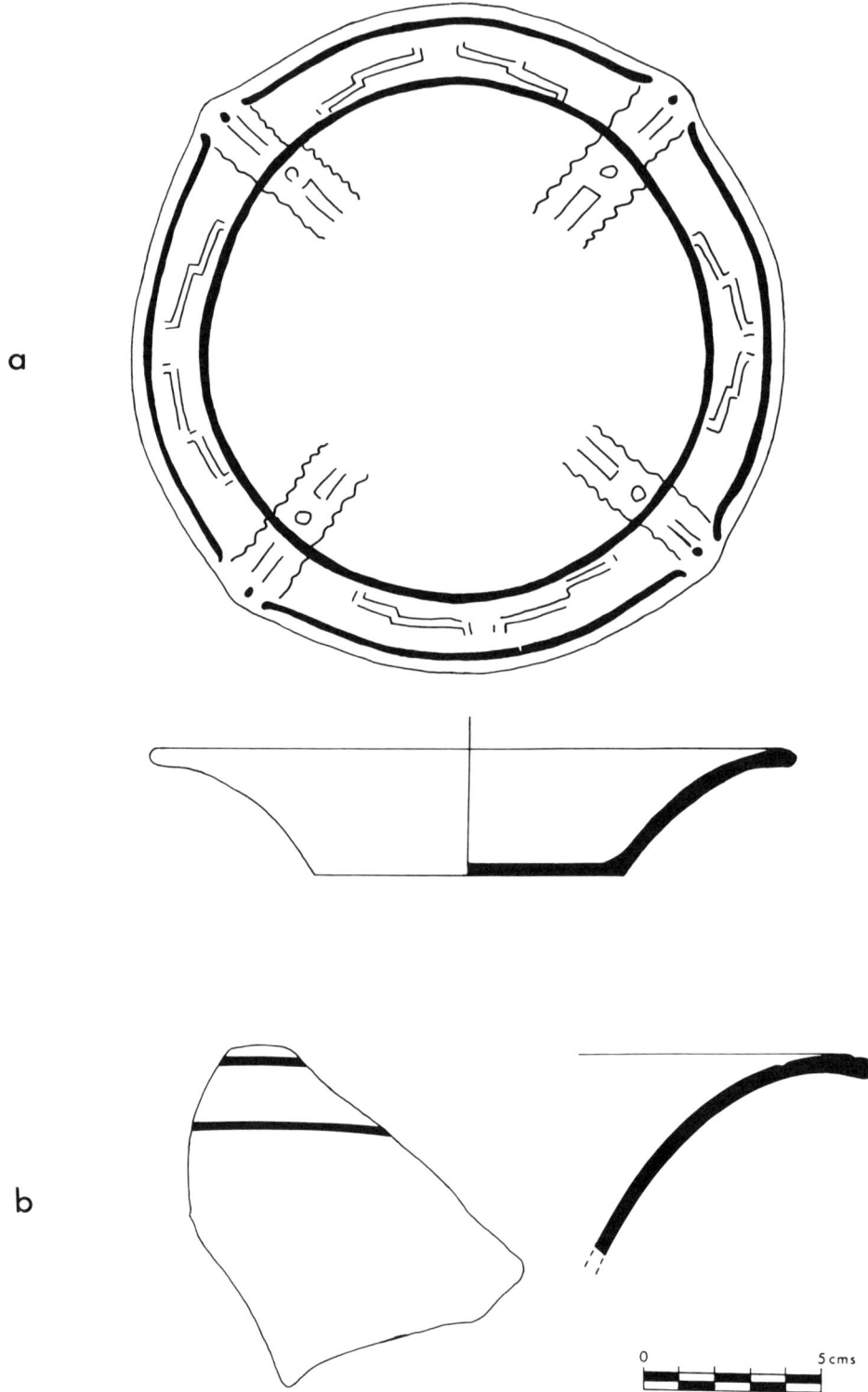

Figure 9. Perdido Gray outleaned-wall bowls.

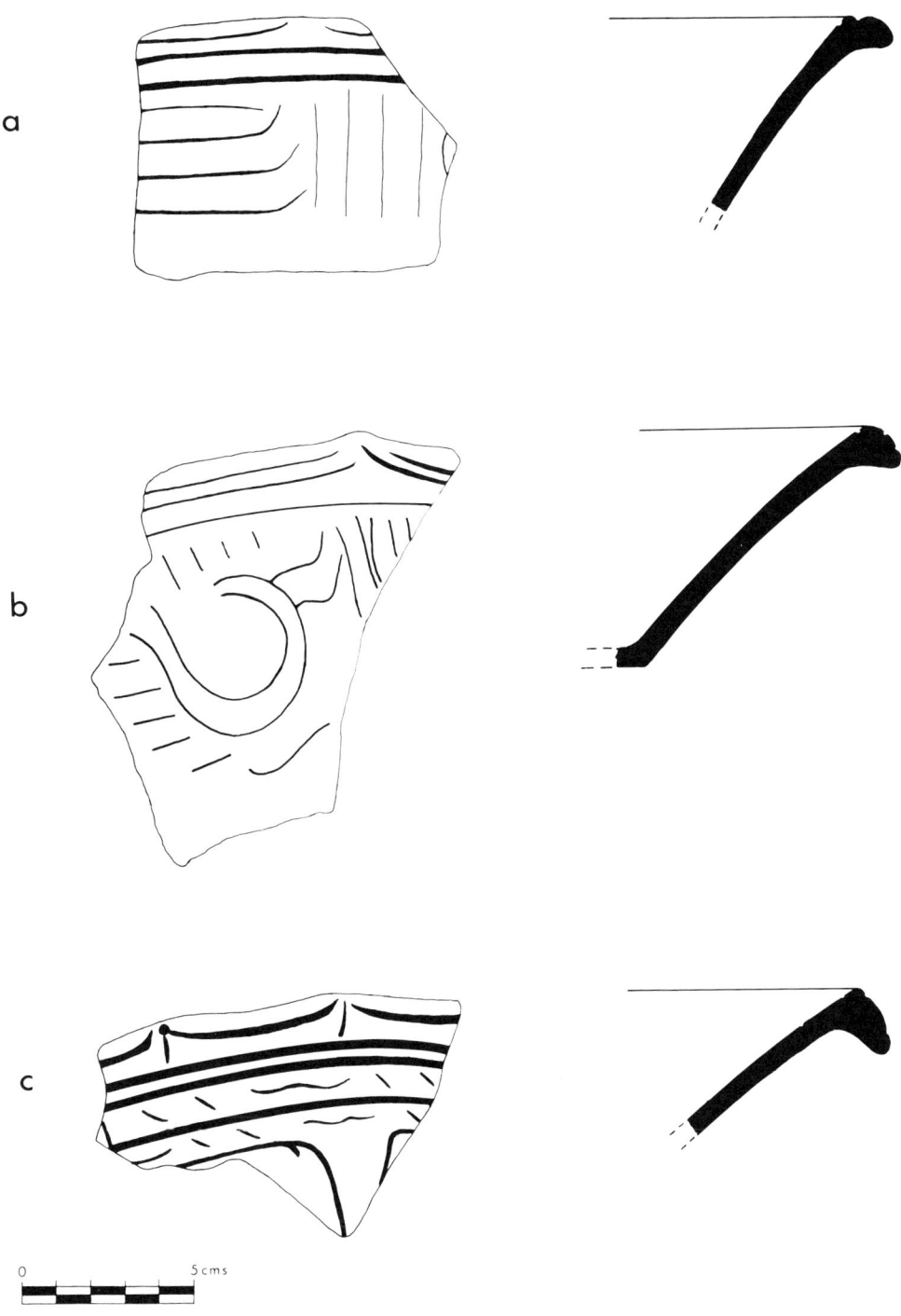

Figure 10. Perdido Gray outleaned-wall bowl rims.

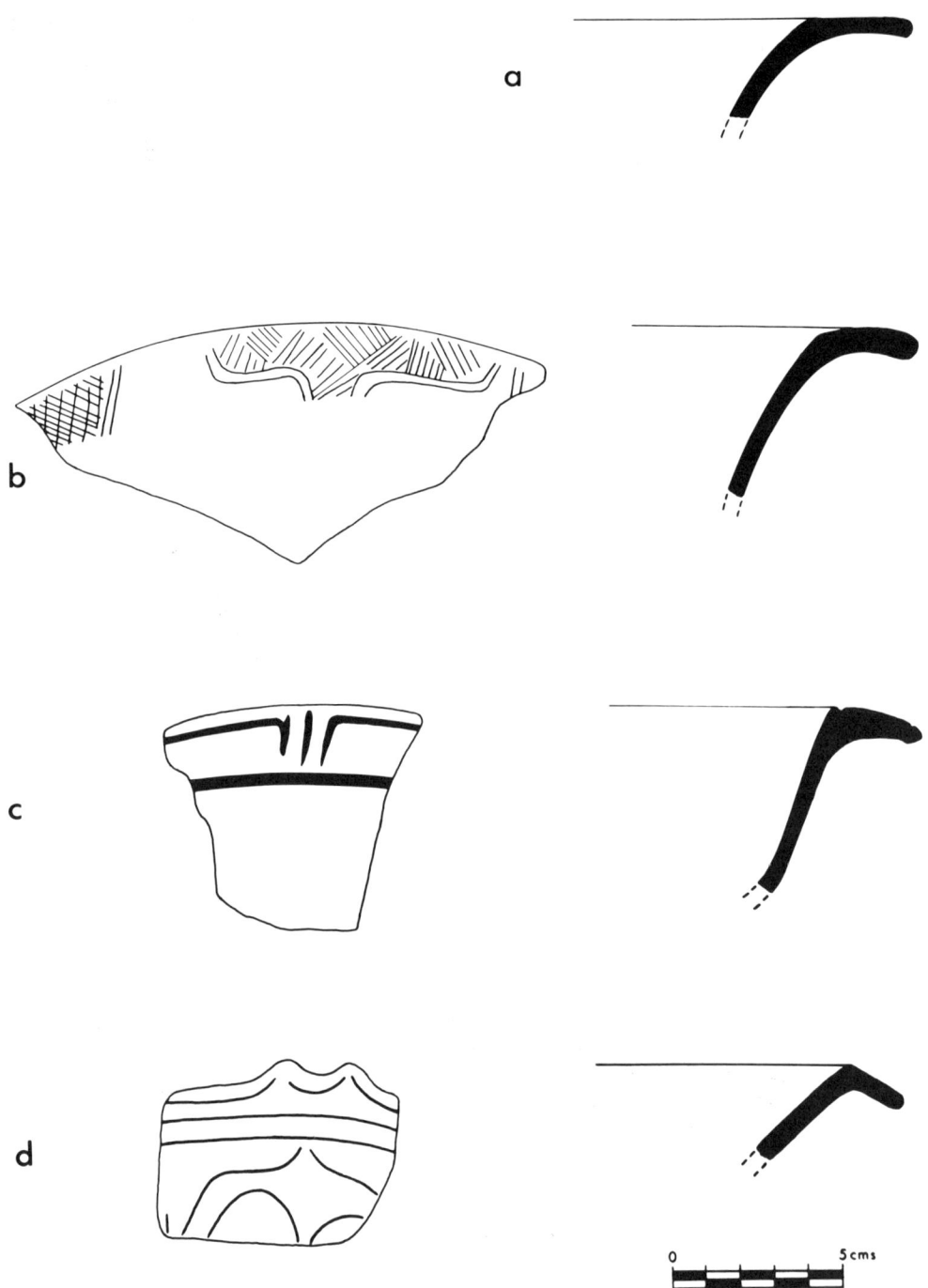

Figure 11. Perdido Gray outleaned-wall bowl rims.

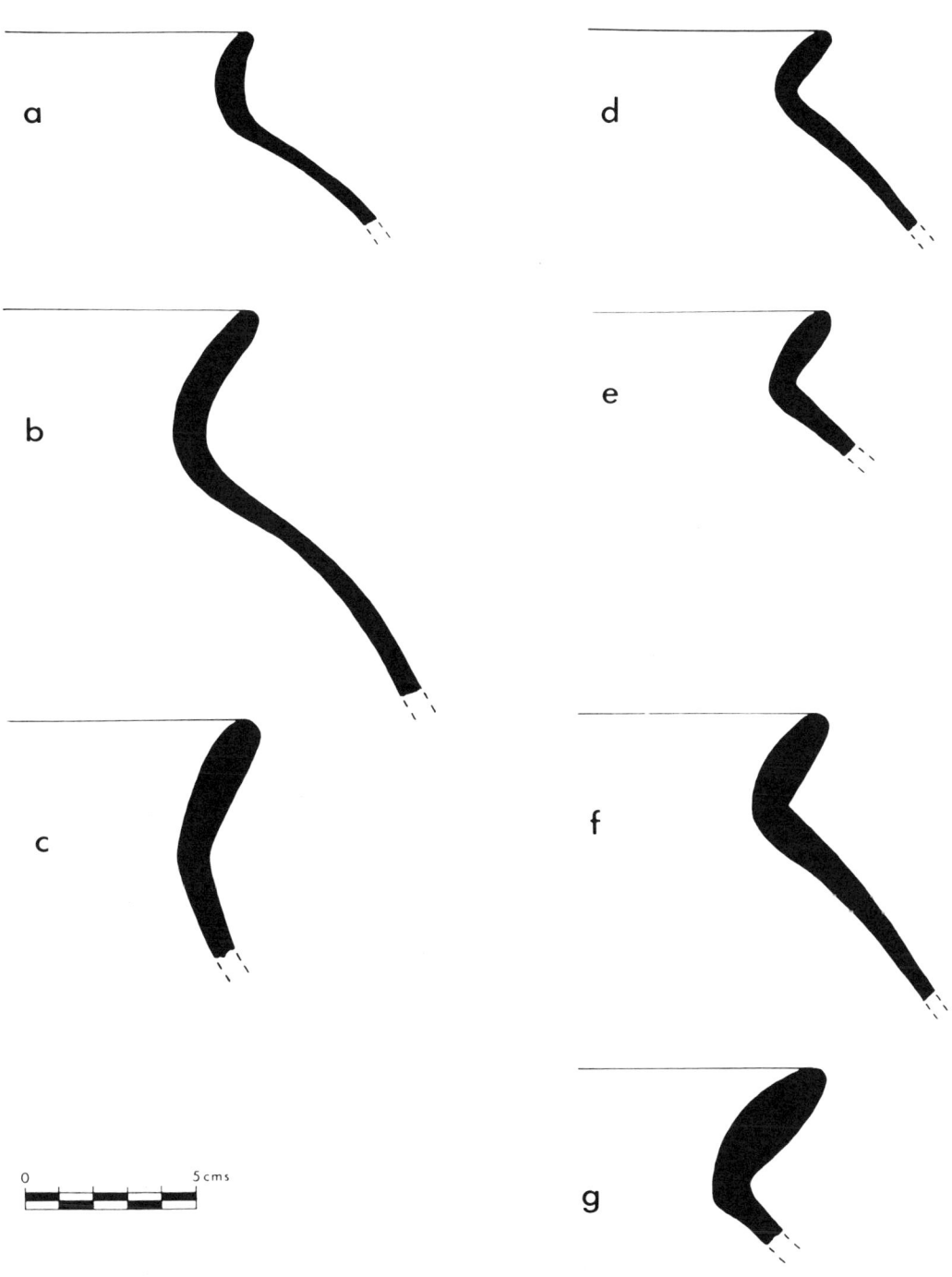

Figure 12. Perdido Plain olla rims.

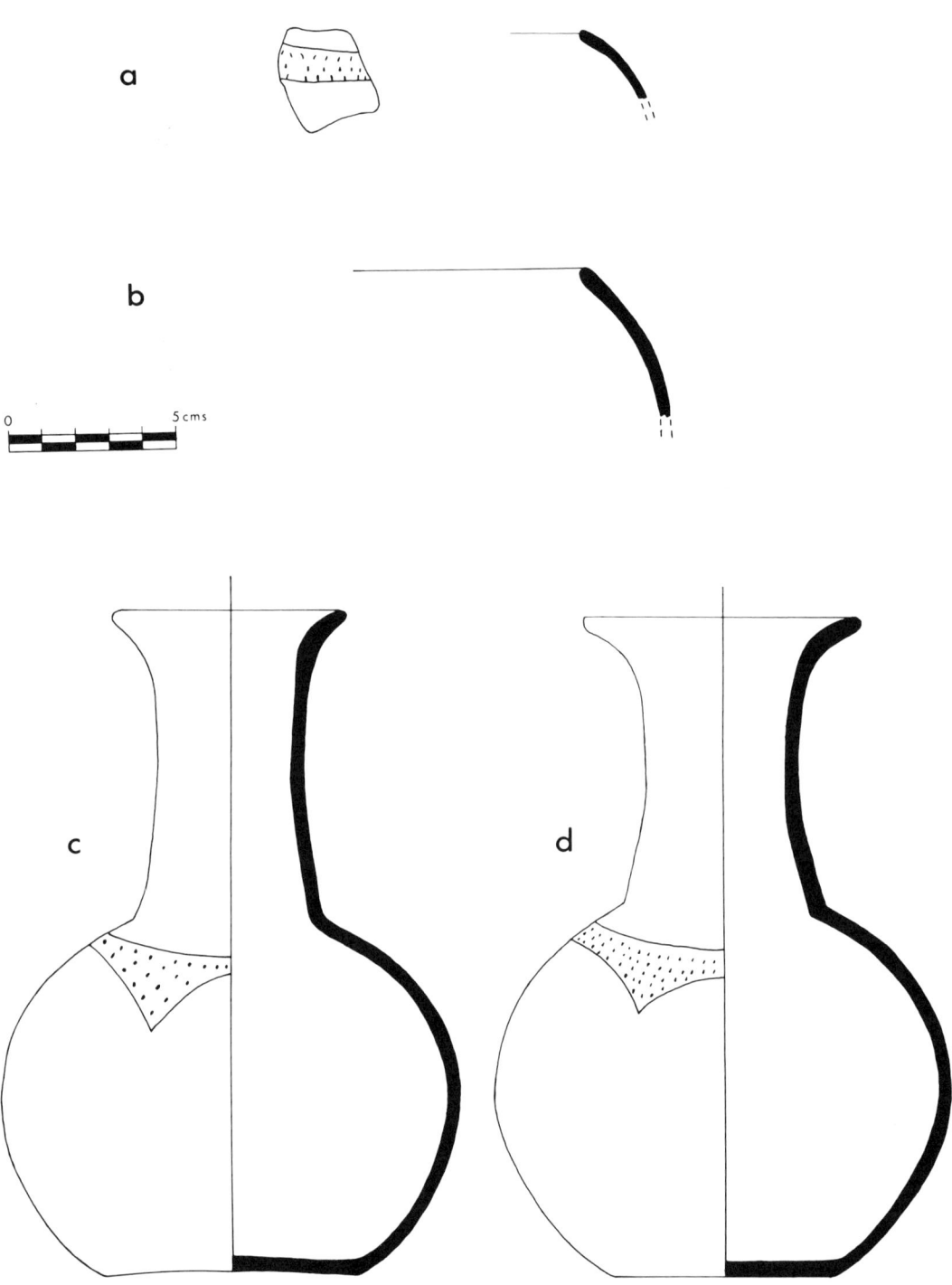

Figure 13. Perdido Plain tecomate rims (*a,b*) and bottles (*c,d*).

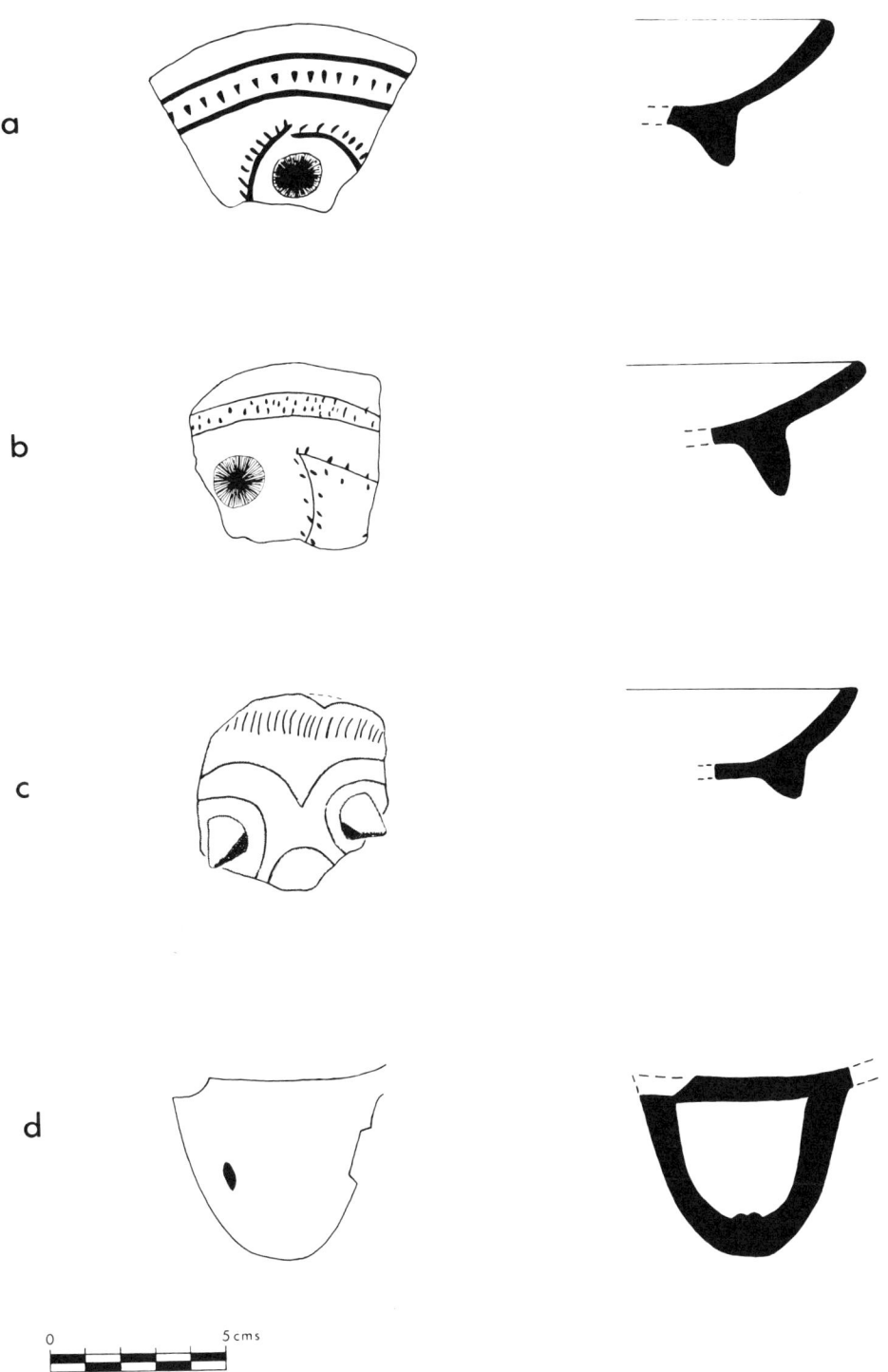

Figure 14. Perdido Plain tripod plate rims (*a-c*); hollow foot (*d*).

rims and basal bulges are also a common Lomas Gray vessel form (Fig. 15 d,e). They tend to be made from a coarser, more porous paste, and to exhibit smoothed, undecorated surfaces. Other Lomas Gray vessel forms include convex-wall bowls (Fig. 15a), cylindrical bowls, short and tall-necked ollas (many of which have strap handles), bridge-spouted jars and sahumadores.

A second broadly defined ceramic ware of the Lomas phase is Lomas Plain. Like Perdido Plain, these sand-tempered ceramics consist mainly of utilitarian forms such as ollas (Fig. 17) and thinner-walled comales, which often show signs of uneven firing, including firing clouds on their undecorated surfaces. Lomas Plain encompasses a series of decorated thin-walled vessels that are made of a finer paste; they include outleaned-wall bowls, cylindrical bowls, convex-wall bowls, and bridge-spouted jars. Their rims and exterior surfaces have been burnished, and decorated with red or streaky reddish-orange paint and post-firing incisions scratched through the painted surface (Figs. 18-19). They bear a strong resemblance to the waxy crema ceramics (C.7 and C.11) reported for Late Period I and Period II in the Valley of Oaxaca by Caso, Bernal, and Acosta (1967:47-68).

The ceramics of the Lomas phase are most similar to the Period Late I and Period II ceramics in the Oaxaca Valley. Consequently, we have aligned the Lomas phase with Periods Late I and II in Oaxaca, and by extension, with the contemporaneous Early Palo Blanco phase in the Tehuacán Valley (MacNeish, Peterson, and Flannery 1970:145-161). Lomas phase is named after Loma de la Coyotera, one of many hilltop sites in the Cañada that date to this time period.

TRUJANO PHASE. Because the excavated samples of Trujano phase ceramics are limited, the present assessment of this ceramic phase should be considered preliminary and subject to future revision. The Trujano phase is a manifestation of the Classic period; while it is clear that Trujano phase begins at the end of Lomas phase, around A.D. 200, I am less certain about when Trujano phase gives way to the Postclassic Iglesia Vieja phase, which is described by Hopkins (1973), and which is closely related to the Venta Salada phase in the Tehuacán Valley (MacNeish, Peterson, and Flannery 1970:177-237).

The grayware of this phase, Trujano Gray, has a relatively fine, compact paste. The paste and surface colors of these gray ceramics range from very light gray or white to very dark gray. They also exhibit a variety of surface treatments, which include smoothing, wiping, scraping and burnishing techniques. Outleaned-wall bowls continue to be the dominant grayware vessel form, with a variety of rim forms (see Fig. 20), and occasionally, with nubbin supports (Fig. 20e). But convex-wall bowls become much more common in the Trujano phase; among their most frequent rim forms are direct rims (Fig. 21a,b), S-shaped rims (Fig. 22b-e), and rims that have a groove on the exterior surface below the rim (Fig. 22a). Solid conical supports appear on many convex-wall bowls toward the end of the Trujano phase (Fig. 21e,f). Other Trujano Gray vessel forms include vasos, tall-necked ollas, tecomates, molcajetes (Fig. 22f), and braziers. Only a few vasos exhibited carved or *raspada* decoration on their exterior surfaces.

The plainware of the Trujano phase, Trujano Plain, is difficult to distinguish from Lomas Plain. The most common Trujano Plain vessel forms are flaring-rim ollas and thin-walled comales. None of the Trujano Plain ceramics exhibited any decoration.

These Trujano phase ceramics bear certain resemblances to the Classic period pottery of both the Oaxaca and Tehuacán valleys. In particular, the numerous Trujano Gray outleaned-wall bowls with scraped exterior surfaces are similar to the G.35 bowls commonly found in the Oaxaca Valley in Period III (Caso, Bernal, and Acosta 1967:80-82). Drennan's ongoing analysis of a large body of Late Palo Blanco ceramics from the Tehuacán Valley (Drennan 1977:31-34; Drennan 1979:169-195) will eventually enable us to make a detailed comparison between the Classic-period pottery from these two regions (see MacNeish, Peterson, and Flannery 1970:146-157, 168-170). Trujano phase is named for the present-day town of Valerio Trujano, which marks the area of greatest settlement in the Cañada during this time period.

The Dating of Surface Collections

The surface collections from the Cuicatlán Cañada Survey were intended to provide the artifactual

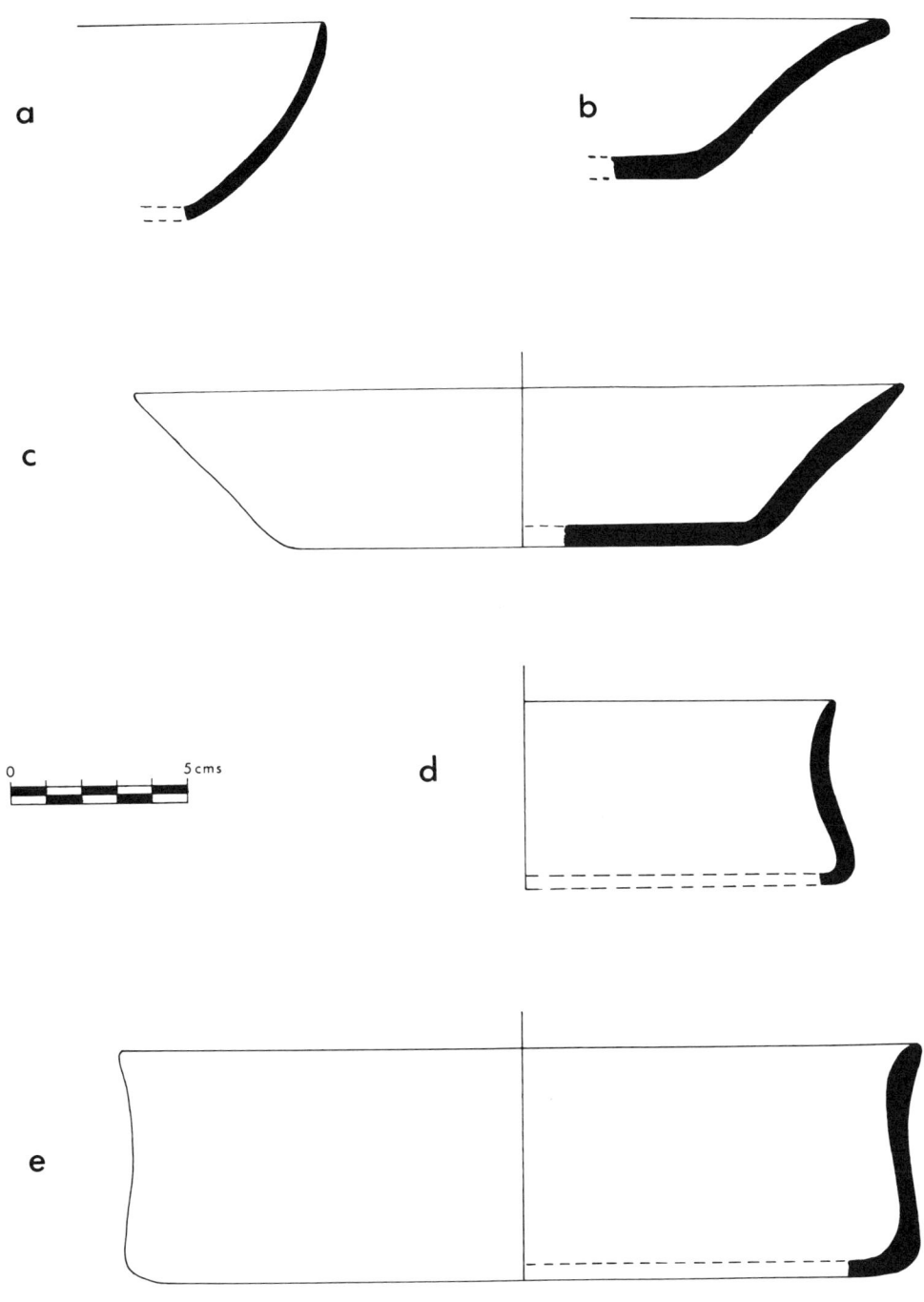

Figure 15. Lomas Gray convex-wall bowl rim (*a*); outleaned-wall bowls (*b,c*); shallow cylindrical bowls with basal bulges (*d,e*).

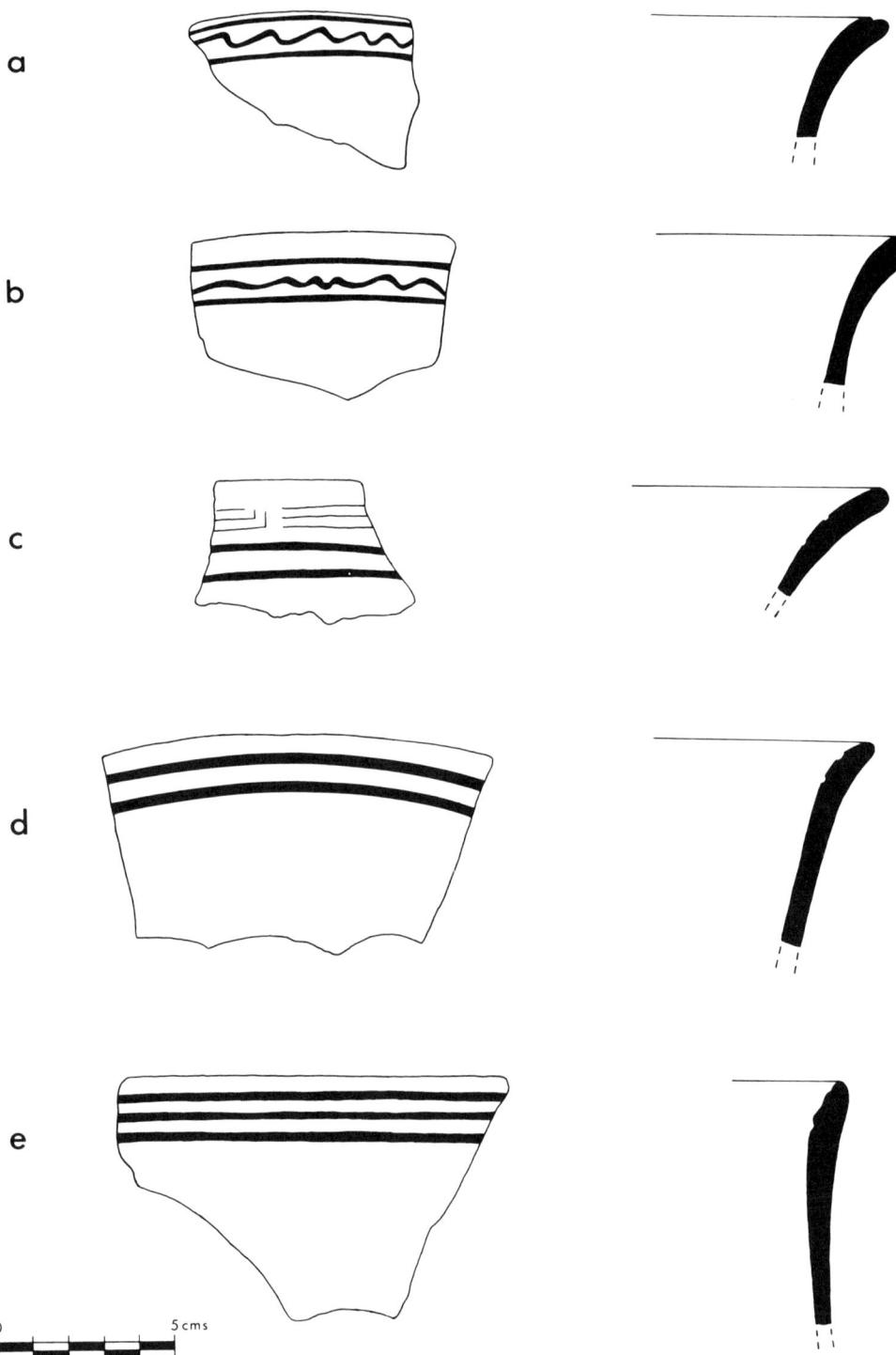

Figure 16. Lomas Gray outleaned-wall bowl rims with incised decoration.

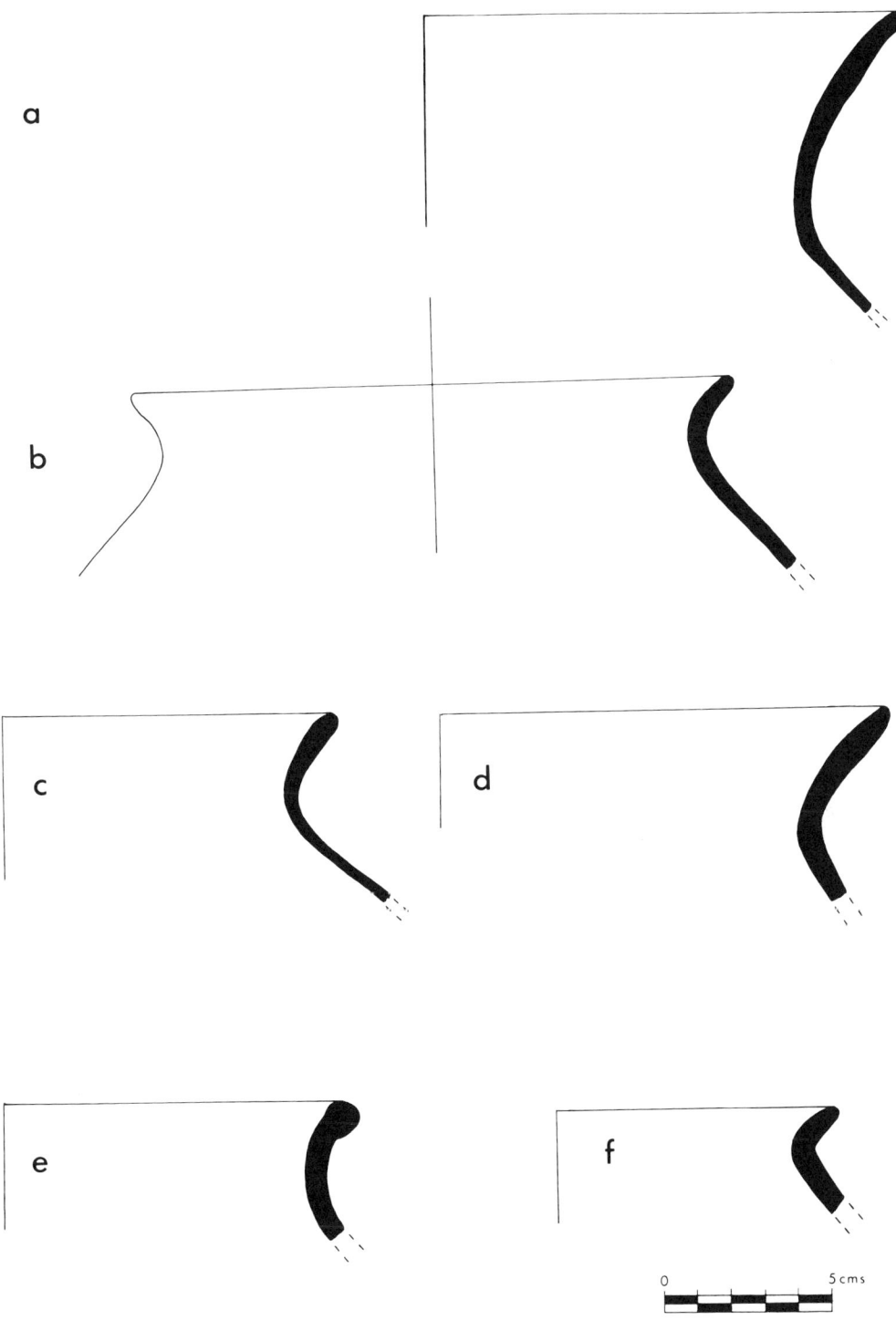

Figure 17. Lomas Plain olla rims.

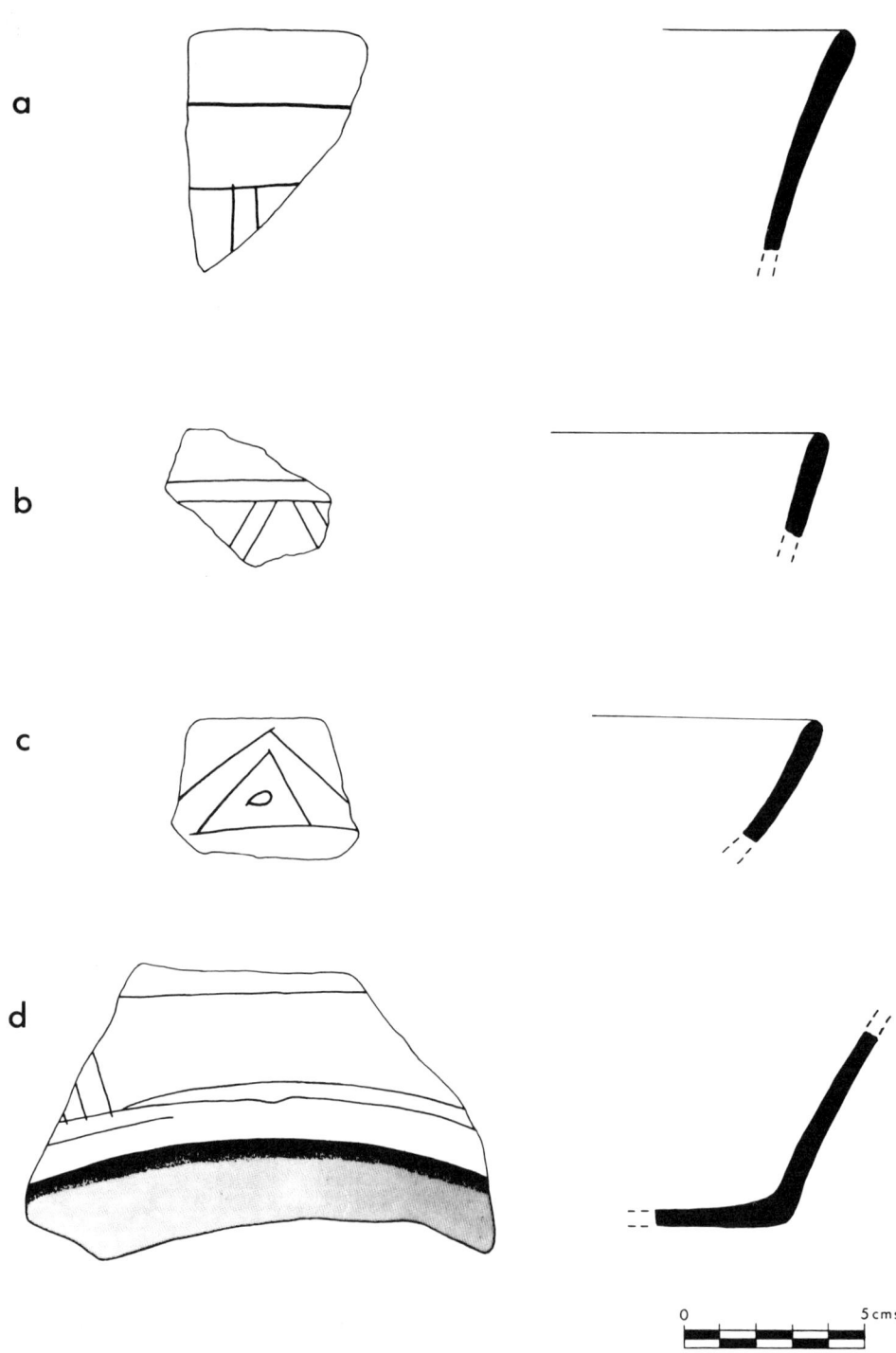

Figure 18. Lomas Plain outleaned-wall bowl (*a,b,d*) and convex-wall bowl (*c*) sherds with post-firing scratching.

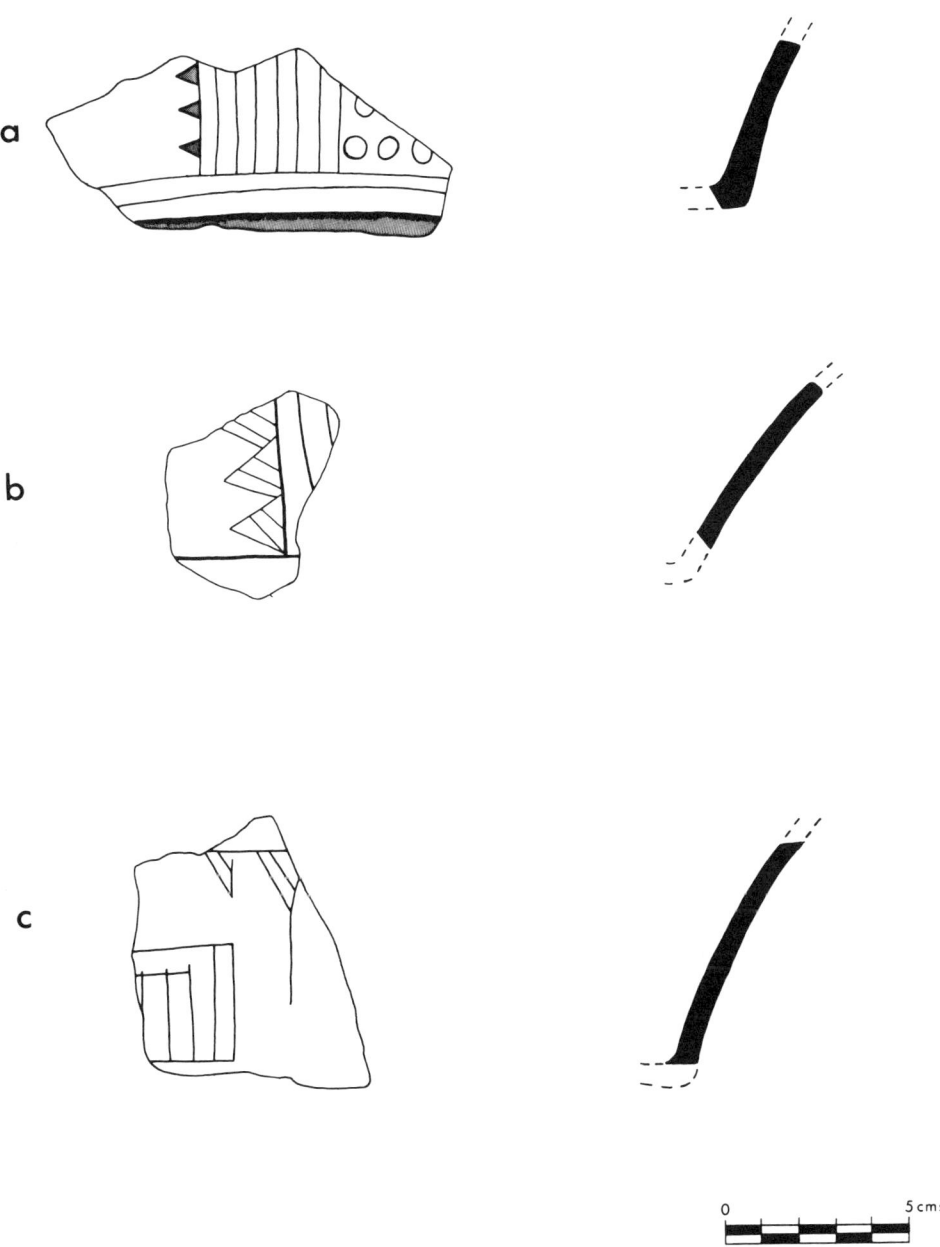

Figure 19. Lomas Plain outleaned-wall bowl sherds with post-firing scratching.

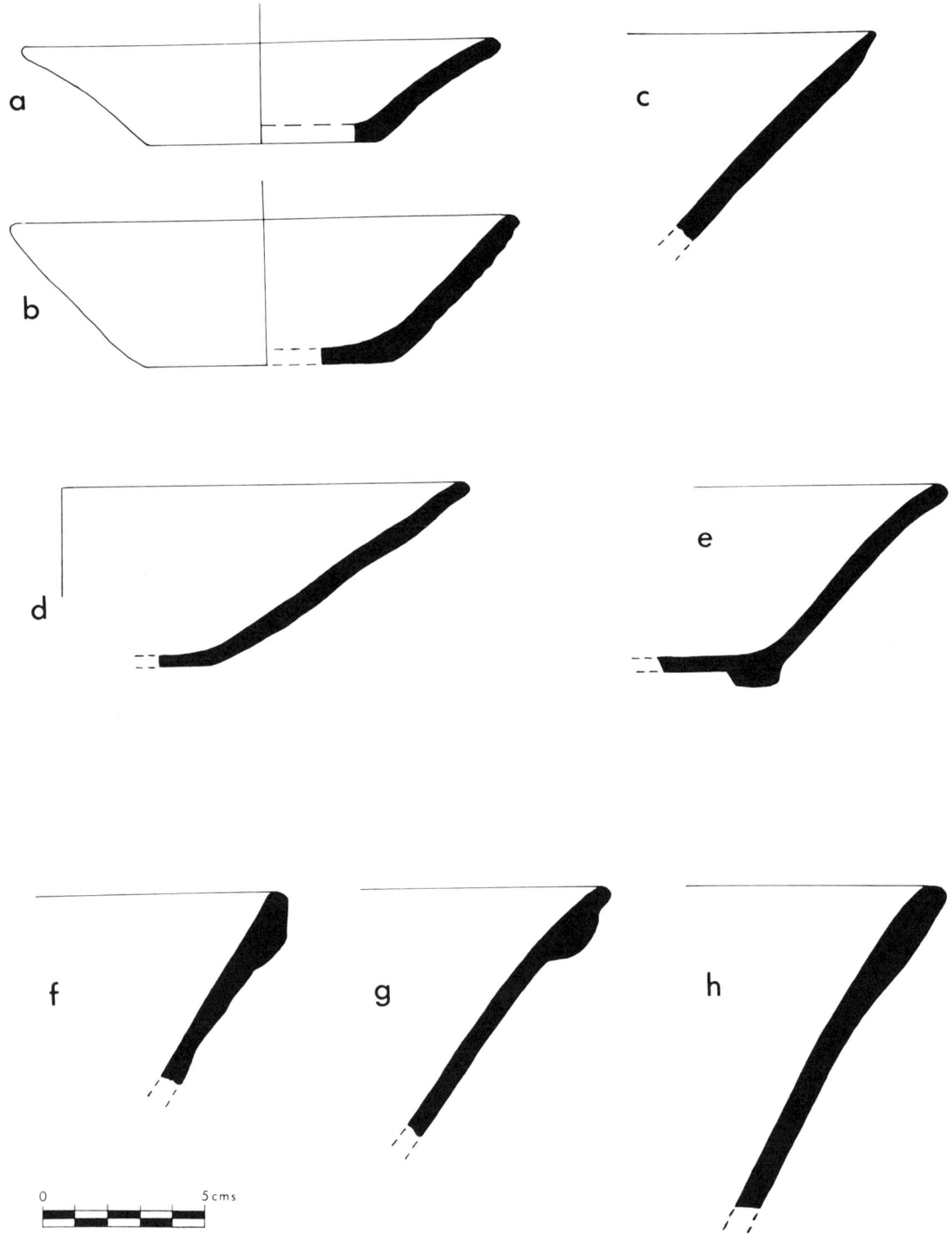

Figure 20. Trujano Gray outleaned-wall bowl rims.

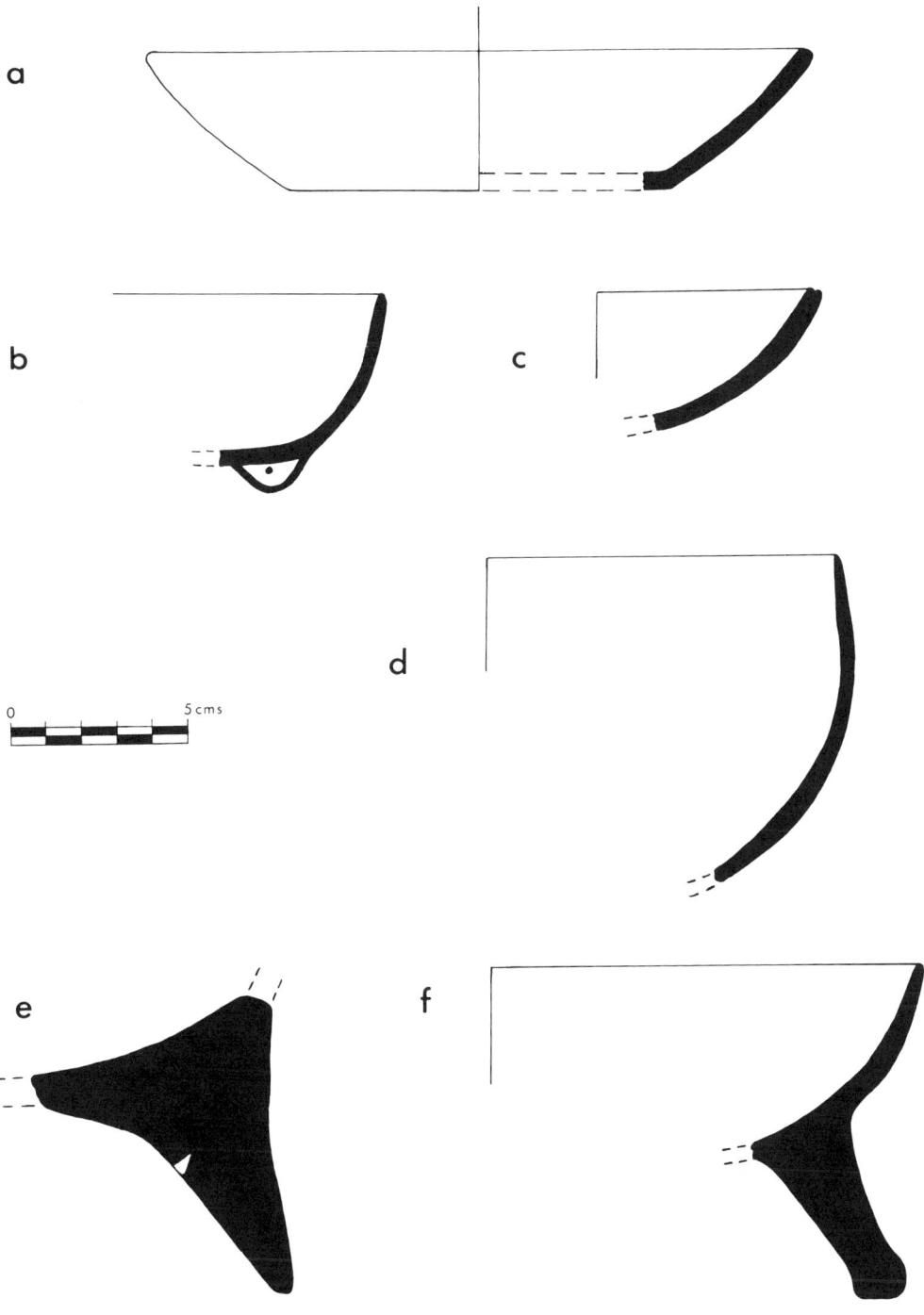

Figure 21. Trujano Gray convex-wall bowl rims (*a-d*); solid feet (*e,f*).

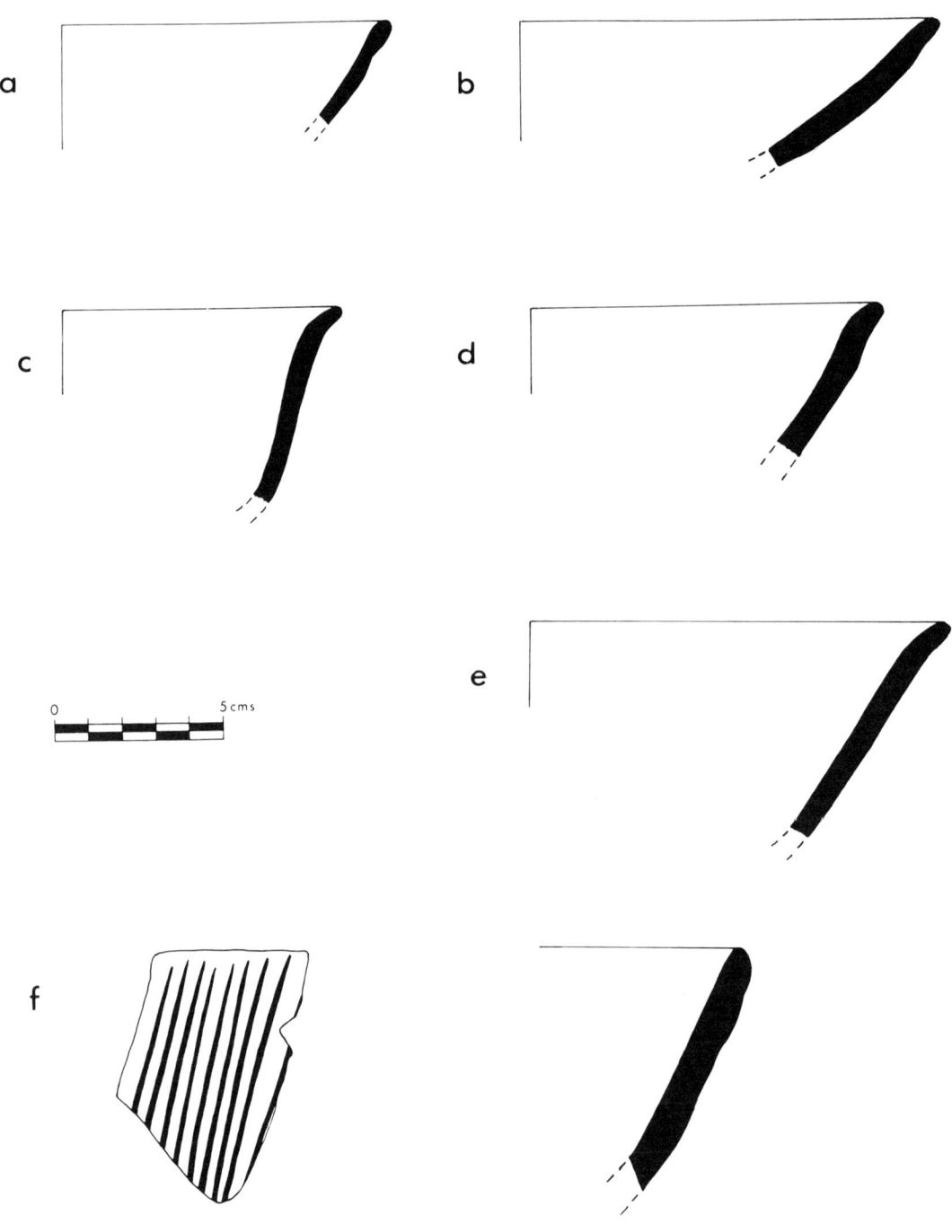

Figure 22. Trujano Gray convex-wall bowl with groove below rim (*a*); S-shaped rims (*b-e*); molcajete rim (*f*).

information with which to date site occupations as well as to carry out distributional analyses of particular artifacts between contemporaneous sites. Clearly, some way of determining contemporaneity among the surface collections is a prerequisite to these kinds of analyses. Determining contemporaneity among surface collections, however, is complicated when successive occupations on a site are represented together, resulting in mixed proveniences. Temporally diagnostic ceramics can be singled out from a mixed provenience for analysis, but other non-diagnostic artifacts cannot be assigned easily to any particular phase. How meaningful, for example, would a distributional analysis of obsidian artifacts among Perdido phase sites be, if it were not carried out using single component surface collections (i.e. surface collections yielding *only* Perdido phase material)?

Therefore, the first step in dating the surface collections involved the selection of chronologically specific ceramic variables marking the Perdido, Lomas, Trujano, and Iglesia Vieja ceramic phases. For selecting the Perdido, Lomas, and Trujano phase ceramic markers I relied upon the primary excavated proveniences recovered from the site of La Coyotera; the Iglesia Vieja phase ceramic variables were chosen after examining Hopkins' (1973) report on Postclassic ceramics from the Cañada, as well as the published descriptions of Postclassic ceramics from the neighboring Oaxaca, Tehuacán, and Nochixtlán valleys (Caso, Bernal, and Acosta 1967; MacNeish, Peterson, and Flannery 1970; Spores 1972). The selection process was conservative in nature, for it was imperative to choose those ceramics or ceramic attributes that were restricted to a single phase. Thus the number of temporally significant ceramic variables chosen was not the same for all four phases; there were 67 ceramic variables diagnostic of the Perdido phase, 32 ceramic variables diagnostic of the Lomas phase, 11 ceramic variables diagnostic of the Trujano phase, and 7 ceramic variables diagnostic of the Iglesia Vieja phase. The decreasing number of ceramic variables assignable to the successive phases is due to a number of reasons; among them is the overall decline in the variety of vessel forms, rim forms, and decorative techniques in the ceramics of successive periods, and the sharp decrease in the number of Trujano and Iglesia Vieja phase proveniences available for this purpose. A detailed description of these diagnostic ceramic variables will be presented in Redmond (n.d.).

With these chronologically specific ceramic variables, four histograms were generated in order to examine the separate distributions of Perdido phase diagnostic ceramic variables, Lomas phase diagnostic ceramic variables, Trujano phase diagnostic ceramic variables, and those of the Iglesia Vieja phase in all the 295 surface collections. This was accomplished by summing the frequencies of ceramic variables diagnostic of a particular phase in each collection, and dividing by the total frequency of diagnostic ceramics collected. Obviously, the resulting histograms were different for each of the four phases.

The four histograms were then used to construct ordinal ranks that would grade either the absence, or the light density, moderate density, and heavy density of those diagnostic ceramics of a particular phase in each collection. The cut-off points for the separate density ranks of ceramics of a particular phase were based on the breaks observed in the histogram generated for the diagnostic ceramic variables of that phase. Figure 23 depicts the histogram of the Lomas phase diagnostic ceramic variables, and shows where the cut-off points for light, moderate, and heavy densities of these Lomas phase ceramics were inserted. Light densities of Lomas phase ceramics consisted of Lomas diagnostics/total diagnostics ratios ranging between .020 and .078; moderate densities of Lomas phase ceramics included Lomas diagnostics/total diagnostics ratios between .079 and .359; and, heavy densities of Lomas phase ceramics corresponded to those collections whose Lomas diagnostics/total diagnostics ratios were greater than .360. The cut-off points for varying density ranks of diagnostic ceramics pertaining to each of the four possible phases represented in the surface collections were decided upon in this manner for all four phases.

After deciding upon the criteria for assigning ordinal density ranks to the ceramics of the four phases that might be represented in the surface collection squares, the final step in the dating procedure involved assigning a Perdido phase, Lomas phase, Trujano phase, and Iglesia Vieja phase score to each collection square, according to the density of diagnostic ceramics from each phase represented in each collection. A score of 1 meant "absent," 2 meant "light," 3 meant "moderate," and 4 meant "heavy." Each of the 295 surface collections was assessed individually and received a set of four scores based on the relative amounts of chronologically specific ceramics dating to the four phases.

This simple procedure for assigning chronological

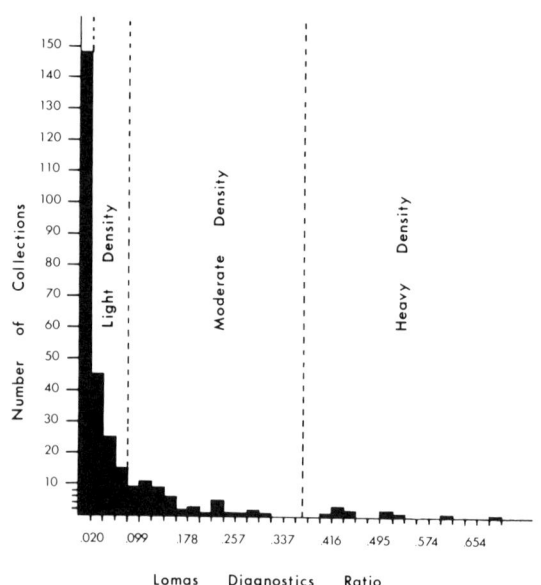

Figure 23. Histogram of Lomas phase diagnostic ceramic densities in the surface collections.

scores to the surface collections formed the basis of all my distributional analysis of particular ceramics or of other artifacts between and within Cañada sites. The assigned ranks or scores—measuring the density of ceramics of each of the four phases—always were used to select those collection squares (i.e. the cases) suitable for a certain analysis. The dating procedure provided great flexibility for grouping collection squares into relative degrees of temporally pure or mixed proveniences. For certain analyses only temporally pure proveniences would be singled out, while for others different combinations of proveniences could be selected using the date assignment scores as stratification devices. Great care was taken to select temporally pure (single component) proveniences for the distributional studies of obsidian, because obsidian artifacts are not usually considered to constitute good temporal markers in and of themselves. For example, the distributional analysis of the relative amounts of obsidian among Perdido phase sites (see Chapter 3, Table 8) used only those surface collections having Perdido phase scores of 2-4 (i.e. "light" through "heavy") combined with a Lomas phase score of 1 (i.e. "absent"), a Trujano phase score of 1 (i.e. "absent"), and an Iglesia Vieja phase score of 1 (i.e. "absent"). But, in the distributional analyses of artifacts that are themselves good chronological indicators, mixed proveniences could be included. For example, the analysis of the relative occurrence of two decorative motifs incised on Perdido Gray bowls among Perdido phase sites (see Chapter 3, Table 5) included *all* surface collections containing Perdido phase ceramics. In this case, I selected all those collection squares having Perdido phase scores of 2-4 (i.e. "light" through "heavy") together with Lomas phase scores of 1-4 (i.e. "absent" through "heavy"), Trujano phase scores of 1-4 (i.e. "absent" through "heavy"), and Iglesia Vieja phase scores of 1-4 (i.e. "absent" through "heavy").

The list of date assignment scores for all the surface collections was also relied upon to determine the outlines of separate occupations at multiple component sites. The area of a site sampled by a particular surface collection was considered occupied during a particular phase if that collection square received a score of 2-4 (i.e. "light" through "heavy") for that phase.

Neutron-Activation Analysis of Ceramics from the Oaxaca Valley and the Cuicatlán Cañada

An important part of my study of the Cuicatlán Cañada and its purported subjugation by the polity centered at Monte Albán in the Valley of Oaxaca during the Late Formative period involved examining the nature of the relationships linking these adjacent regions during the time periods before and after the proposed Zapotec conquest. One of the ways I intended to do this was by comparing the distribution of imported Oaxaca ceramics in the Cuicatlán Cañada during the Perdido phase to that obtained in the succeeding Lomas phase. As we have seen in a previous section that deals with the expectations derived from a model of the Cañada's subjugation by Monte Albán, the Cañada's transformation from an autonomous region into a tributary province of the Zapotec state might be reflected in the archaeological record by a change in the distribution of Oaxaca ceramics within the Cañada. An assumption underlying this line of reasoning was that I could differentiate visually between true Monte Albán pottery imported from the Valley of Oaxaca and any locally-produced imitations of Monte Albán wares in the Cañada (Earle and Ericson 1977:4). Therefore, the approach I eventually undertook for examining the distribution of Oaxaca ceramics in the Cuicatlán Cañada included the chemical characterization of a sample of Monte Albán ceramics from the Valley of Oaxaca and of a corresponding sample of ceramics from the Cañada by neutron-activation analysis.

Dr. Garman Harbottle of the Department of Chemistry at Brookhaven National Laboratory kindly agreed to carry out the neutron-activation analysis of ceramics from the Oaxaca Valley and the Cuicatlán Cañada. Appendix I presents a detailed description of the ceramics I selected for the procedure and reports the results of Harbottle's analysis. Interpretations based upon the neutron-activation analysis are to be found in the following chapters that deal with the Cañada during the Perdido and Lomas phases. Consequently, I will offer only a very general description of the procedure here.

Because no such analysis had ever been performed on Middle and Late Formative ceramics from the two regions, my criteria for selecting ceramics for the neutron activation analysis were twofold: (1) the general need to examine a completely representative sample of Middle and Late Formative ceramics from the two regions; and (2) the more problem-oriented need to distinguish between imported Oaxaca ceramics and any locally-produced imitations of Monte Albán wares in the Cañada during the two time periods in question. I selected 40 sherds recovered from the Cuicatlán Cañada Project that represented the region's local ceramic wares (Perdido Gray ware, Lomas Gray ware, Lomas Plain ware), and that also included some examples of what I considered to be imported Oaxaca ceramics Monte Albán Crema ware, Monte Albán Ic-II Crema ware) for the Perdido and Lomas phases. From the Valley of Oaxaca I chose a similarly representative sample of 40 sherds that included examples of the three major Monte Albán ceramic wares defined by Caso, Bernal, and Acosta (1967) for the two corresponding Oaxaca phases: Rosario/Monte Albán Ia Gray ware, Monte Albán I Crema ware, Monte Albán I Café ware, Monte Albán Ic-II Gray ware, Monte Albán Ic-II Crema ware, and Monte Albán Ic-II Café ware. Two examples of Monte Albán IIIb Gray ware were added to the sample of Oaxaca ceramics. The sherds from Monte Albán and other sites in the Oaxaca Valley were sought with the help of Dr. Marcus Winter of the INAH Centro Regional de Oaxaca. Appendix I lists the 82 sherds selected for neutron-activation analysis and provides the exact provenience and a brief description of each sherd.

The first part of the neutron-activation analysis involves preparing the sherd samples for bombardment. This includes drilling each sherd in order to remove a small 100-200 mg sample, which is then divided and packaged into capsules for separate runs. Along with the sherd samples, 6 U.S. Geological Survey Rock Standards are prepared for bombardment, their role being to provide quantitative calibration for all the elements traced in each run. These samples are then activated in the Brookhaven High Flux Beam Reactor (Abascal-M., Harbottle, and Sayre 1974:86-88).

The following stage of the analysis consists of determining the analytical values of the elements being measured. This is known as spectrum analysis, an automated procedure that combines the calibration standard data obtained from the spectra of the standard rocks with gamma-ray intensities of the unknown samples to produce the analytical values of the 23 elements measured in the sampled sherds (Hammond, Harbottle, and Gazard 1976:155). The following 23 elements were measured in this analysis: Na, K, Rb, Cs, Ba, Sc, La, Ce, Eu, Lu, Hf, Th, Ta, Cr, Mn, Fe, Co, Sb, Ca, Zn, Sm, Yb, and Sr.

With these raw data on the value of the 23 elements measured for each sherd, Harbottle and his associates at Brookhaven employed computer-based multivariate procedures to group the sampled sherds according to their chemical similarities (Harbottle 1976; Sayre 1976; Bieber Jr. et al. 1976). For the present analysis Harbottle turned to two numerical taxonomic procedures. First, a cluster analysis was performed using the program AGCLUS (Olivier 1973), which calculated a distance matrix with the log-transformed data on the 23 elements measured for the 82 sherd samples, arranged these samples in groups according to the similarities in their chemical composition, and presented these groupings in the form of a dendrogram. A simple mean Euclidean distance measure was chosen together with an average-linkage clustering procedure (Sneath and Sokal 1973). The resulting dendrogram is presented in Appendix I (Fig. 75).

The dendrogram features four groups of sherds based on the similarities in their chemical composition: Perdido and Lomas Gray wares; Lomas Plain ware; Monte Albán Ia and Ic-II Cremas; and Rosario/Monte Albán Ia and Ic-II Gray wares. An independent discriminant analysis was also performed on the raw data, using the discriminant analysis subroutine of SPSS. (For a discussion of discriminant analysis, I refer the interested reader to Davis [1973:442-453].) The discriminant analysis produced a similar set of four sherd groups, thereby supporting the results of the cluster analysis.

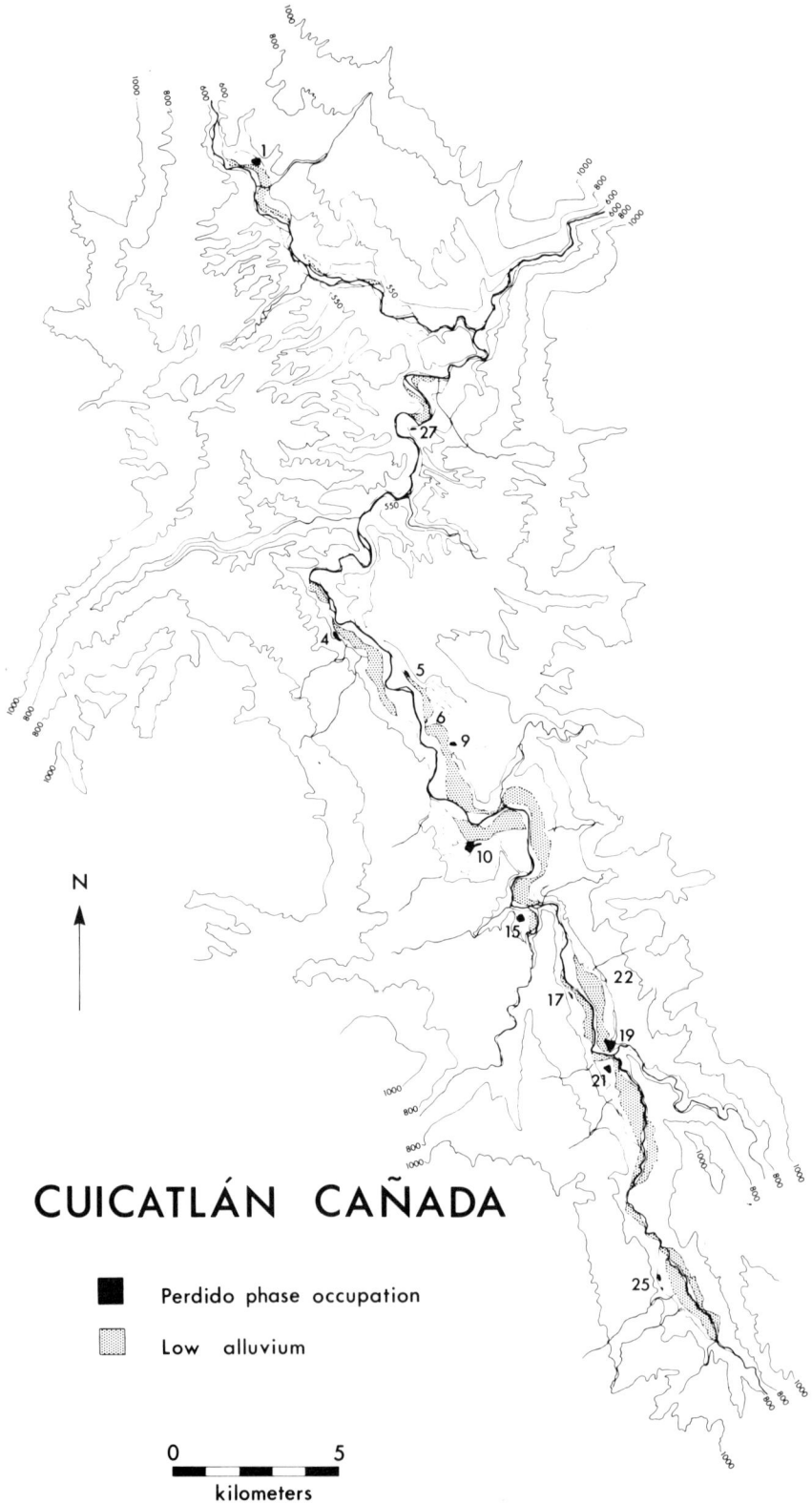

Figure 24. Perdido phase regional settlement pattern map.

Chapter 3

The Cuicatlán Cañada During the Perdido Phase

Perdido Phase Settlements and Regional Organization

It is only by the end of the Middle Formative period that we can begin to discuss the Cuicatlán Cañada's regional settlement pattern. During the course of the Cañada Survey we did surface collect some earlier Formative ceramics at Cs10, Cs19, and Cs5. Adriana Alaniz, then of the INAH Centro Regional de Oaxaca, also reported the presence of an earlier Formative occupation at the site of Rancho Dolores Ortiz (Cs22) (*Boletín* 1975). But the surface indicators of Early Formative occupations in the Cañada are simply too few and far between to enable us to determine their areal extent. At the present time we lack the information necessary to determine the sizes of these early sites and to adequately describe the corresponding regional settlement pattern.

During the Middle Formative Perdido phase, however, the Cuicatlán Cañada witnessed the growth of small farming communities on all four of its alluvial fans. The Cañada Survey located 11 Perdido phase sites along the canyon floor between the junction of the Salado and Grande rivers in the northern Cañada, and the southern closure of the canyon floor at Dominguillo. Previous to our survey, the INAH Centro Regional de Oaxaca investigations at Rancho Dolores Ortiz (Cs22) recovered three Perdido phase burials there (M. Winter, personal communication 1978). Since surface survey at Cs22 failed to produce any surface indications of a Perdido phase occupation, the evidence for a Middle Formative occupation there is confined to the excavations. Table 4 lists the 12 Perdido phase settlements and their sizes according to their geographic location on one of the Cañada's four alluvial fans. North of the Cuicatlán Cañada proper, near present-day Tecomavaca in the southern Tehuacán Valley, was the contemporaneous Late Santa María phase (MacNeish, Peterson, and Flannery 1970:102-134) component of the site of Llano de los Mogotes (Cs1), a site first reported by the Tehuacán Valley Archaeological-Botanical Project as Tr19 (MacNeish et al. 1972:411). The following discussion of the Cuicatlán Cañada during the Middle Formative period includes the 12 Perdido phase occupations in the Cañada proper as well as the site of Cs1 to the north at Tecomavaca (Fig. 24).

Eight of the Perdido phase settlements in the Cañada range in size between 1 and 5 ha. Two other settlements are presently estimated to be smaller than 1 ha (Cs6-P, Cs22). The sites of Hacienda Tecomaxtlahua (Cs19-P) and El Mirador (Cs10-P) are substantially larger; the former covers 7.76 ha and the latter assumes an area of at least 9.02 ha. North of the Cañada proper, the contemporaneous Late Santa María phase occupation at Tecomavaca (Cs1-P) extends over approximately 5.87 ha.

All these Middle Formative communities have one characteristic in common, that is, their general location on high alluvial terraces or lower piedmont slopes overlooking stretches of low alluvium along both sides of the Río Grande and its principal tributary, the Río de las Vueltas. In those areas of the canyon floor where the piedmont drops down suddenly onto the low alluvium without any intermediary zone of higher alluvium, Perdido phase sites are found on the lower piedmont slopes directly above the available low alluvium. The significant feature that appears to be shared by these communities is their proximity to the low alluvium.

Because chances for successful rainfall farming are slim in this arid region, the low alluvium is cultivated today using simple techniques of floodwater farming (Kirkby 1973:36-41). Farmers construct temporary dams from brush and river cobbles in order to divert water from the major river flows onto the flanking low alluvium (Pl. 8). Those irrigated stretches of low alluvium are extremely productive and they constitute the region's prized *tierra de primera*. A hectare of maize planted on this *tierra de primera* will yield up to 2000 kg of

Table 4. The Sizes of Perdido Phase Settlements

Alluvial Fan	Site Number	Site Name	Site Size (ha)
Quiotepec	Cs27-P	El Campanario	1.42
Cuicatlán	Cs4-P	Los Obos	2.40
	Cs5-P	Horno de Cal	1.29
	Cs6-P	Cuba Libre	.25
	Cs9-P	La Bomba	2.56
	Cs10-P	El Mirador	9.02
	Cs15-P	La Nopalera	4.77
		Total Settlement Area	20.29
El Chilar	Cs17-P	Sitio a la Entrada de Tomellín	1.32
	Cs22	Rancho Dolores Ortiz	.10
	Cs19-P	Hacienda Tecomaxtlahua	7.76
	Cs21-P	Cerro Cortés	3.89
		Total Settlement Area	13.07
Dominguillo	Cs25-P	La Coyotera (Llano Perdido)	2.64

shelled maize, and, due to the canyon's frost-free climate, at least two harvests are reaped each year (see Chapter 2).

There is good reason to believe that the Middle Formative period inhabitants of the Cañada were farming the low alluvium by means of these simple floodwater-farming techniques. We have already noted the proximity of the Perdido phase settlements to the expanses of low alluvium on all four of the region's alluvial fans. These settlements are found on high alluvial terraces that today are farmed using more sophisticated techniques of canal irrigation. Elaborate feeder canals are required to draw water from the numerous smaller tributaries of the Río Grande and to channel it onto the higher alluvium. Our survey failed to locate the remains of any irrigation canals or other hydraulic facilities in association with these Perdido phase settlements on the high alluvium.

If, on the basis of the above considerations, we assume that the inhabitants of the Perdido phase settlements were relying upon the low alluvium for their subsistence, we would expect to see a generally positive relationship between the distribution of low alluvium in the Cañada and the distribution of Perdido phase settlements. The Quiotepec and Dominguillo alluvial fans, located at the extreme ends of the canyon, contain relatively small amounts of low alluvium, and they in turn supported the smallest total Perdido phase settlement. The central alluvial fans of El Chilar and Cuicatlán have substantially larger expanses of low alluvium; correspondingly, the bulk of the Perdido phase settlement flourished on these two alluvial fans (Table 5). Figure 25 presents a scatter plot of the hectares of low alluvium and the sizes of the total Perdido phase settlement on each alluvial fan. The plot reveals an unmistakable positive association between the two variables. It might appear, then, that settlement on each of the Cañada's alluvial fans during the Perdido phase corresponds to the varying amounts of associated low alluvium.

The relationship between the Perdido phase settlement and the available low alluvium on each of the region's alluvial fans can be assessed further by comparing the estimated population residing on each alluvial fan to the agricultural potential of the associated low alluvium. Following the procedure outlined in Chapter 2, we can generate carrying capacity figures for the low alluvium on the Quiotepec, Cuicatlán, El Chilar, and Dominguillo alluvial fans (Table 5). When we compare the resulting carrying-capacity figures for each of the alluvial fans to the estimated population ranges of the associated Perdido phase settlement, we find that the total estimated Perdido phase population on each of the Cañada's four alluvial fans falls well below the estimated carrying capacity of the productive low alluvium. A similar relationship exists between the carrying capacity of the associated alluvium and the estimated population of the contemporaneous com-

Table 5. Estimated Carrying Capacity of the Cañada's Low Alluvium and Perdido Phase Settlement

Alluvial Fan	Hectares	Annual Maize Yields	Estimated Carrying Capacity	Total Perdido Phase Settlement	Estimated Perdido Phase Population @ 10-25 Persons per Hectare
Quiotepec	32.85	37,515 kg	188 persons	1.42 ha	14-35 persons
Cuicatlán	523.60	597,951 kg	2990 persons	20.29 ha	203-507 persons
El Chilar	297.43	339,665 kg	1698 persons	13.07 ha	131-327 persons
Dominguillo	142.65	162,906 kg	814 persons	2.64 ha	26-66 persons

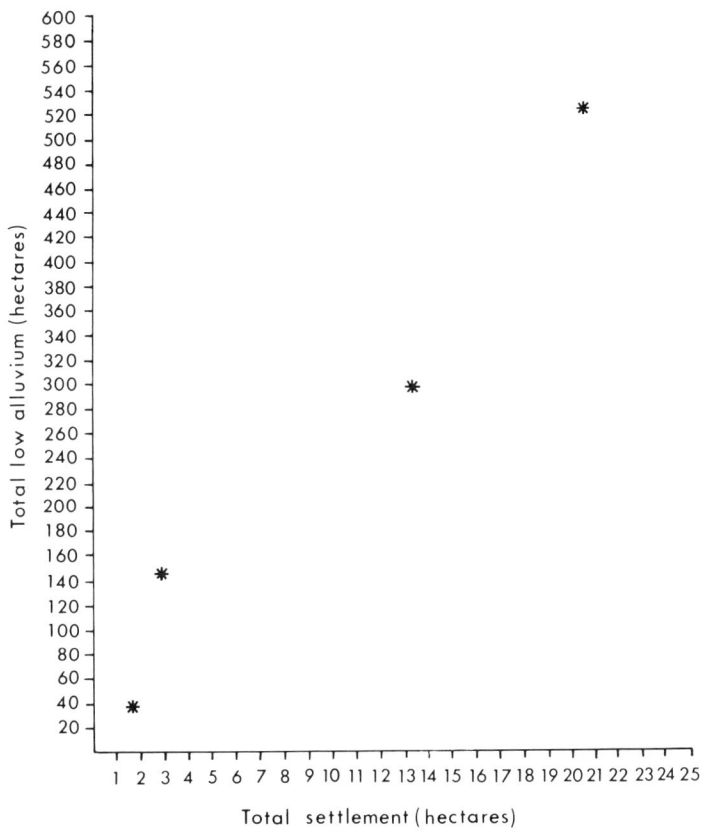

Figure 25. Scatter plot of low alluvium and Perdido phase settlement on the Cañada's four alluvial fans.

munity near Tecomavaca, just north of the Cuicatlán Cañada. In sum, while the sizes of the Middle Formative communities reflect the varying amounts of associated low alluvium, settlements on all of the Cañada's alluvial fans at this time could have been handily supported by farming the fertile stretches of low alluvium.

On the central Cuicatlán and El Chilar alluvial fans lie the region's two largest Middle Formative communities (Cs10-P, Cs19-P). A histogram of the sizes of all the Middle Formative settlements reveals a gap between those settlements smaller than 5 ha and these two larger settlements (Fig. 26). There is evidence, then, of a fairly clear two-level hierarchy of settlement sizes in the Cuicatlán Cañada at this time.

Moreover, the settlement size hierarchy is consistent with the distribution of mounded architecture among Perdido phase settlements. The two larger settlements are also the only two Perdido phase settlements in the Cañada that feature visible mounded architecture. In the center of the site of El Mirador (Cs10-P), we mapped three pyramidal mounds that were probably assembled around an open plaza (Fig. 27, Pl. 10). Two of these mounds rise 2 m above the present ground surface, the largest one of which measures approximately 50 m by 38 m at its base. We found a similar configuration of mounded architecture at the site of Hacienda Tecomaxtlahua (Cs19-P), where three pyramidal mounds rise 4 m above an open plaza located at the site's northwest end. The largest mound here has approximate basal dimensions of 35 m by 27 m (Fig. 28, Pl. 11). Thus the two largest Perdido phase communities, which emerged on the major alluvial fans of the region, exhibited a similar array of public architecture on their surfaces.

Spencer's excavation of the Perdido phase settle-

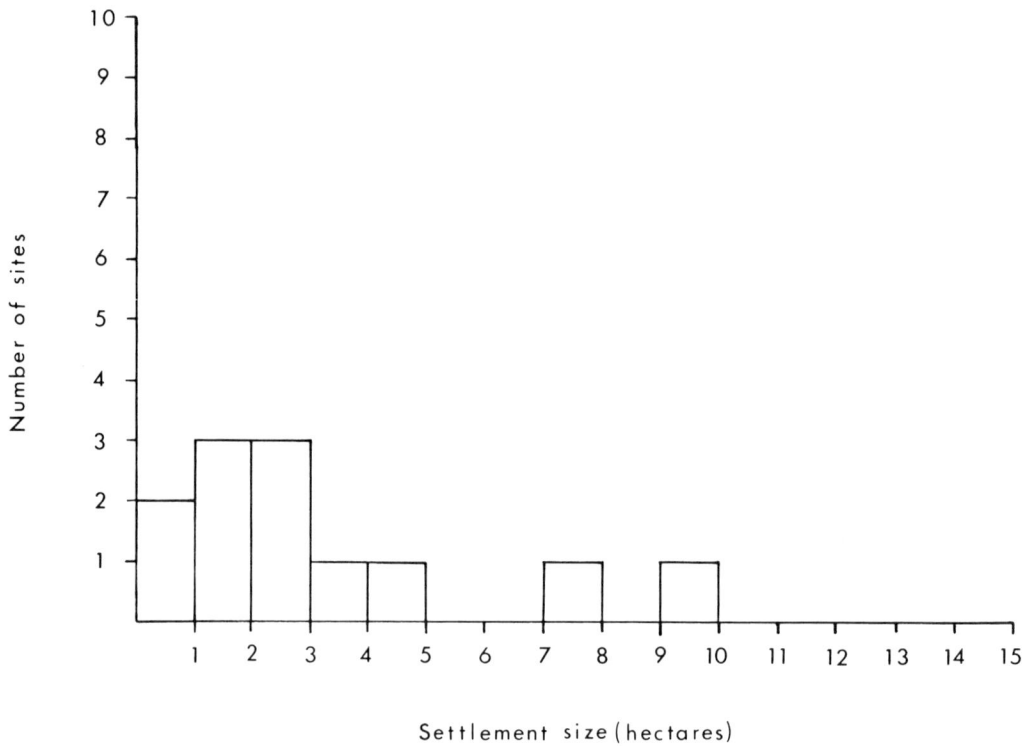

Figure 26. Histogram of Perdido phase settlement sizes.

ment at La Coyotera (Cs25-P) on the southernmost Dominguillo alluvial fan, exposed over 1600 m² of this small (2.25 ha) Middle Formative period community (see Fig. 48). The community appears to have been organized into several elaborate residential compounds, each one measuring approximately 30 to 40 m on a side. As part of Spencer's excavations at Cs25-P, we excavated one of these large compounds in its entirety and discovered that it consisted of 18 structures arranged around three courtyards (Pl. 12, Fig. 29; see also Spencer 1982:82-124). In contrast to the plazas and pyramidal mounds evident on the surface at the sites of El Mirador (Cs10-P) and Hacienda Tecomaxtlahua (Cs19-P), the public architecture uncovered at Cs25-P consisted of low platforms that were embedded within the residential compounds. The compound that we exposed completely contained the remains of six low platforms arranged around interior courtyards. These platforms varied from .30 m to 1 m in height, and their basal dimensions ranged between 5-8 m long and 4.1-5.3 m wide. Among the artifacts associated with these platforms were figurines, obsidian blades, bark beaters, red pigment, and a deer antler. Spencer's "contextual analysis" of these ritual-related artifacts leads him to propose that the low platforms and associated courtyards at La Coyotera were the loci of ritual activities; Spencer distinguishes between those ritual activities that were organized on the level of the courtyard group, and those ceremonies that encompassed the entire community (Spencer 1982:136-143; Flannery 1976d:334-336).

The public architecture uncovered at the small site of La Coyotera (Cs25-P) is significantly different in scale and configuration from the mounded architecture visible at the two large Perdido phase sites (Cs10-P, Cs19-P). The low platforms at Cs25-P are small in comparison to the pyramidal structures that rise for several meters above the present-day ground surface at Cs10-P and Cs19-P. Moreover, the low platforms at Cs25-P are contained within residential compounds, while the pyramidal structures at the two large sites are assembled around large central plazas. This evidence leads me to suggest that two orders of public architecture—in terms of volume and configuration—are associated with the two distinct levels of the Perdido phase settlement

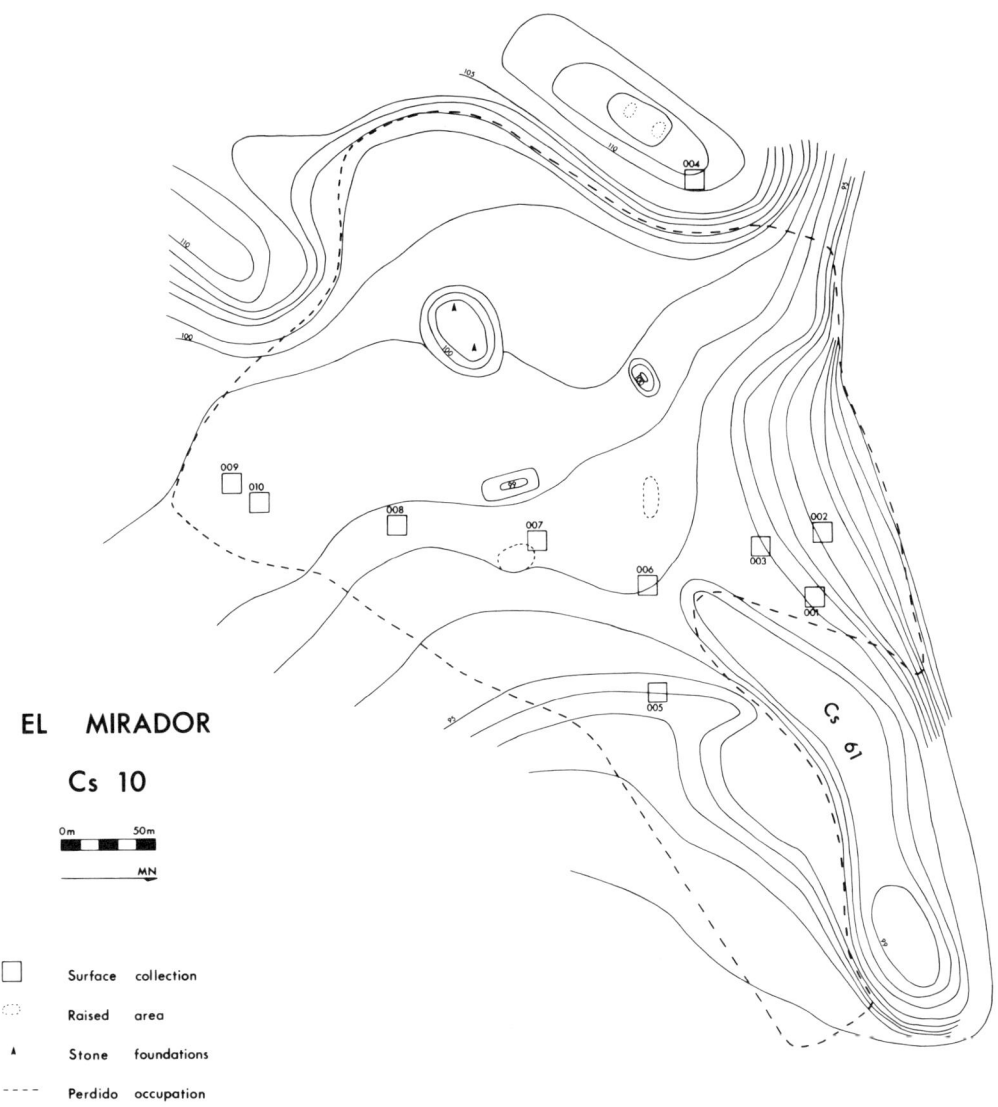

Figure 27. El Mirador site map (Cs10).

hierarchy.

On the basis of the Perdido phase settlement-size hierarchy and the corresponding order of public architecture at Perdido phase communities alone, I propose that during the Perdido phase the Cuicatlán Cañada was occupied by ranked or chiefly societies (Fried 1967; Service 1962). The regional organization of the Cañada consisted of two high chiefly centers below which ranked their subordinate secondary settlements (cf. Peebles and Kus 1977; Johnson 1973; Taylor 1975:59-78). The two high chiefly centers were the large sites of El Mirador (Cs10-P) and Hacienda Tecomaxtlahua (Cs19-P), located on the region's central and largest alluvial fans. Below these centers ranked the nine smaller communities where local chiefs probably resided. Figure 30 presents a diagram of the Cuicatlán Cañada's regional organization during the Perdido phase. My assignment of dependent settlements to one of the two high chiefly centers is based upon their proximity to that particular center. For the time being, Cs27-P will not be assigned to any chiefly center, given its isolated location at the northern extremity of the Cañada, and its intermediate position between Cs10 and Cs1.

Since our surface collections at the two large

Plate 10. Aerial view of the Cuicatlán alluvial fan, facing west. The site of El Mirador (Cs10) is located in the center of the photograph, on a high alluvial terrace overlooking the low alluvium that adjoins the Río Grande, in the right foreground. Trees dot two of the site's three pyramidal mounds.

centers included some pre-Perdido phase ceramics, I would suggest that these two centers probably represent the pioneer settlements in the region, from which in time the other Perdido phase settlements budded off. The evolution of regional settlement patterns in the Cañada might have involved the processes of colonization and hierarchization that have been outlined for other linear river valleys in Mesoamerica during the Formative period (Flannery 1976b:162-173, 1976c:173-180). In the Valley of Oaxaca, for example:

> . . . primary regional centers of the Early and Middle Formative often turn out to be among the oldest communities in the area. Such sites grow, erect ceremonial-civic structures, and increase their administrative functions while giving rise to "daughter communities" that may never develop similar functions. It may be that, as societies with ranking evolved, senior lineages of higher rank tended to remain at the parent community while cadet lineages of lower rank founded the newer sites. [Flannery 1976b:168-169]

Bonds of alliance would have linked the dependent settlements to the higher-ranking lineage at the chiefly center. These bonds would probably have been maintained by means of a number of mechanisms characteristic of chiefly societies; these include the periodic mobilization of goods and labor to the chiefly center, the exchange of goods and information between the high chief at the chiefly center and the local chiefs at dependent settlements, and certain rituals of chiefly sanctification (Earle 1978:18-19; Rappaport 1971:37-39).

The next chiefly center north of the Cuicatlán Cañada was probably Cs1-P, located just north of the present-day town of Santa María Tecomavaca. During the late Middle Formative period this settlement extended over 5.87 ha and included a 3-m-high pyramidal mound measuring 25x17 m at its base. Facing it across a flat open space was a 1-m-high platform, 16 m long and 4 m wide (see Fig. 50). The closest high chiefly center to the south of the Cuicatlán Cañada in the neighboring Etla branch of the Oaxaca Valley was likely that situated at San José Mogote, with an intermediary lower-ranking community located at Barrio del Rosario Huitzo (see Fig. 1). This administrative hierarchy is suggested by the discrepancy in size between the two contemporaneous and nearby Etla settlements (Varner

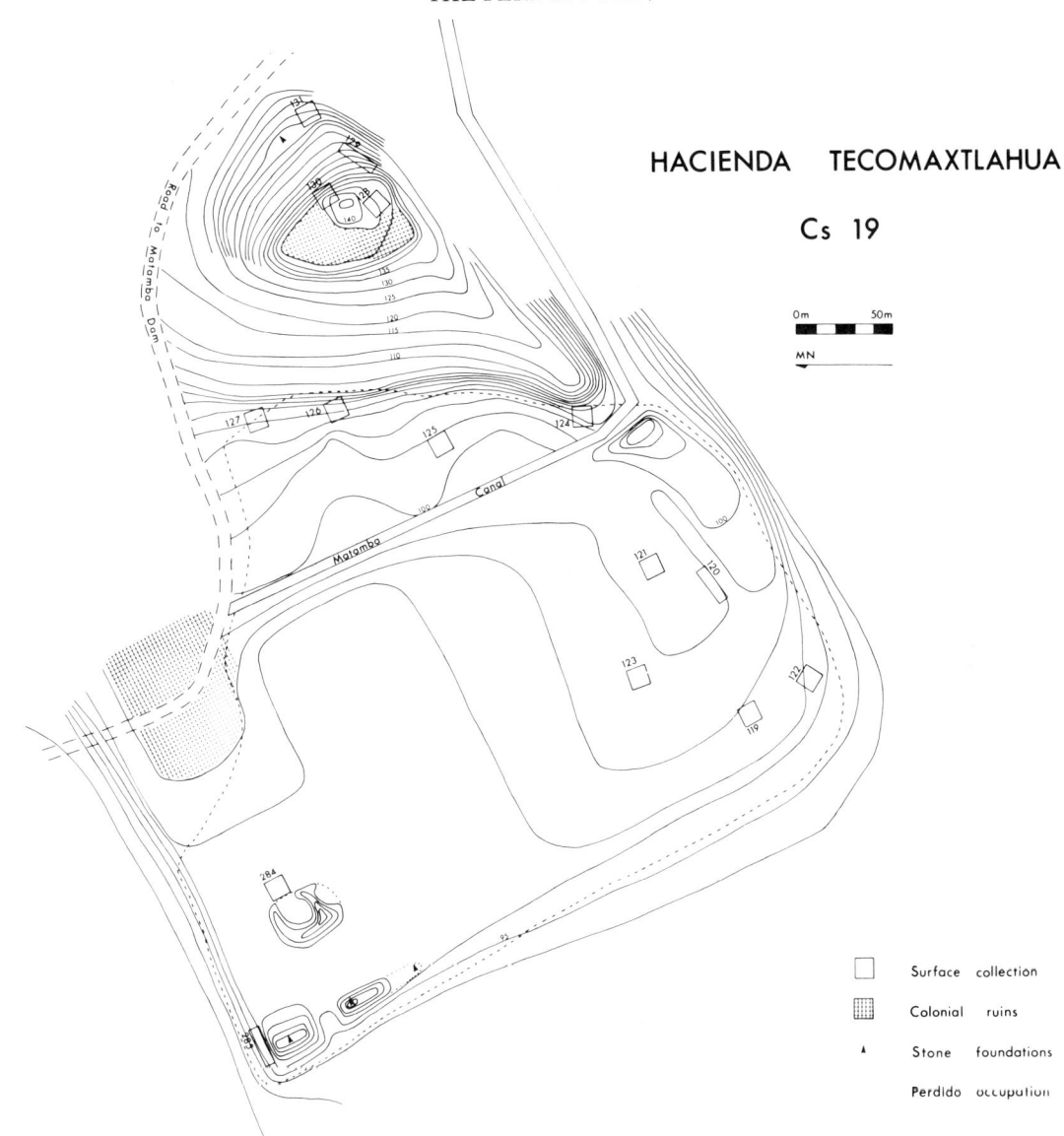

Figure 28. Hacienda Tecomaxtlahua site map (Cs19).

1974:165), and by the differences in the volume and complexity of the Middle Formative public buildings at the two sites (Flannery, Marcus, and Kowalewski 1981:75-83; Flannery and Marcus 1976a:213-215).

Within the Cuicatlán Cañada, the two chiefly centers and their associated settlements appear to have been freely interacting with one another. We find a local ceramic tradition the length of the canyon during the Perdido phase that includes certain painted, incised plain-ware vessels and a body of incised gray ceramics that are distinct from Middle Formative ceramics in adjacent regions (see Chapter 2). Two decorative motifs commonly incised on Perdido Gray outleaned-wall bowls are represented in Figure 31; Motif 5 consists of two widely-spaced horizontal lines between which other designs have been incised, while Motif 6 is made up of two narrowly-spaced horizontal lines with the addition of other designs below them. If we examine the regional distribution of these two decorative motifs, in terms of the average ratio of bowls with these motifs to total ceramic diagnostics recovered in the surface collections at 12 late Middle Formative sites in the

Plate 11. Oblique aerial view of the northern half of the site of Hacienda Tecomaxtlahua (Cs19), facing northeast. The site's three tree-lined mounds appear in the left foreground of the photograph. The Colonial period ruins for which the site is named extend across both sides of the dirt road in the background.

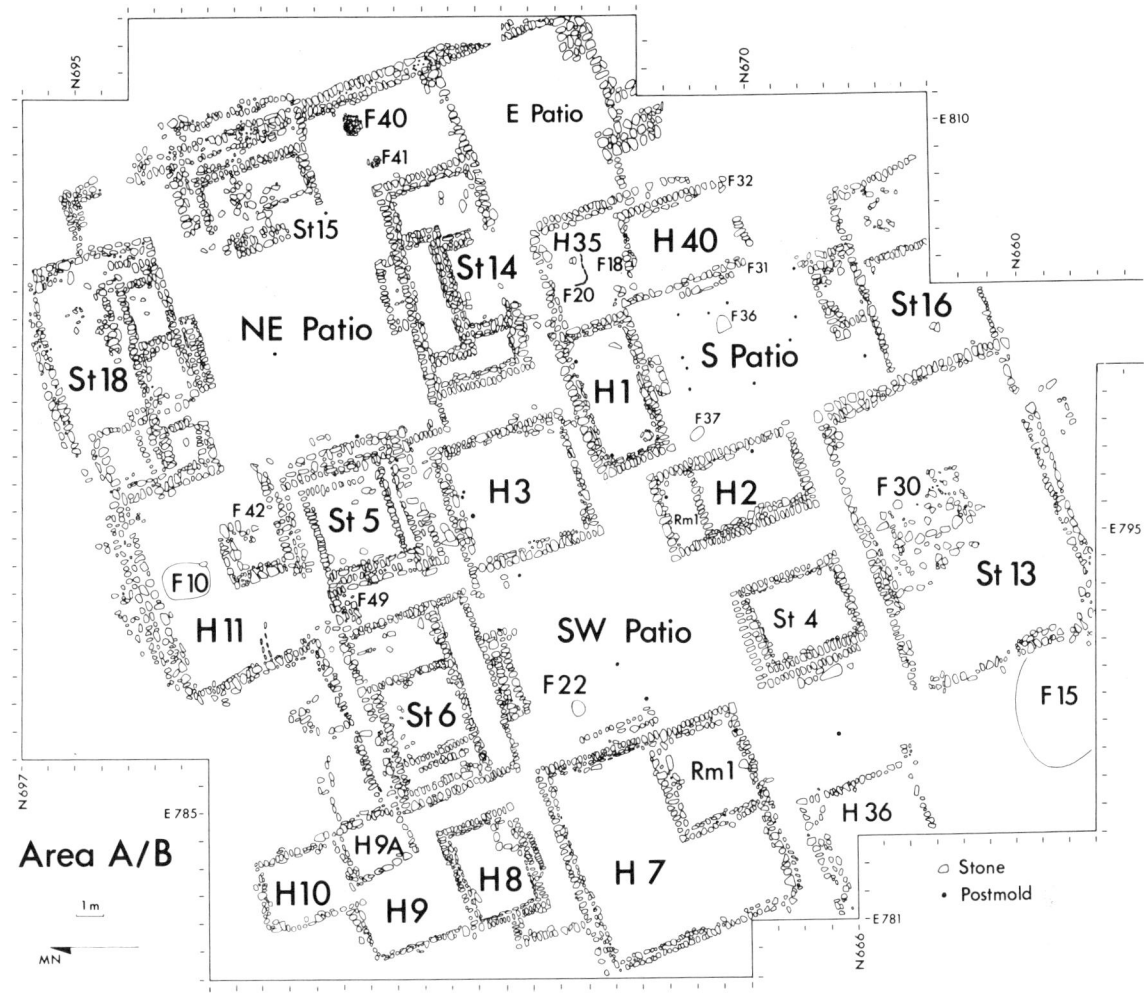

Figure 29. Plan of the Perdido phase residential compound (Area A/B) at La Coyotera (from Spencer 1982:90).

survey area, we find that they are fairly evenly distributed throughout the Cañada (Table 6). The drop-off in the relative frequency of these motifs on bowls at Cs1-P probably relates to that community's position outside the Cañada proper. To date these two decorative motifs have not been found on any late Middle Formative gray bowls in either the Tehuacán Valley or the Oaxaca Valley.

The view that these small, autonomous ranked societies were freely interacting with one another is further supported by the results of Dr. Garman Harbottle's trace-element analysis of a sample of Perdido Gray bowls (Appendix I). The ten out-leaned-wall bowl sherds that were analyzed by Harbottle came from eight Perdido phase sites in the Cuicatlán Cañada and from Cs1-P to the north; not only were they examples of the same vessel form, but they also shared the same incised decorative motif (i.e., Motif 5 illustrated in Fig. 31). Indeed, Harbottle found these representatives of the region's ceramic tradition to be unrelated to a comparable and contemporaneous sample from the Valley of Oaxaca, and instead, to constitute an unusually uniform group. With these data we cannot point to the number of actual manufacturing locales in the region during the Perdido phase, however we do know that this particular vessel was made and distributed the entire length of the canyon.

Plate 12. Aerial view of the Perdido phase residential compound (Area A/B) at La Coyotera, facing southeast (from Spencer 1982:94).

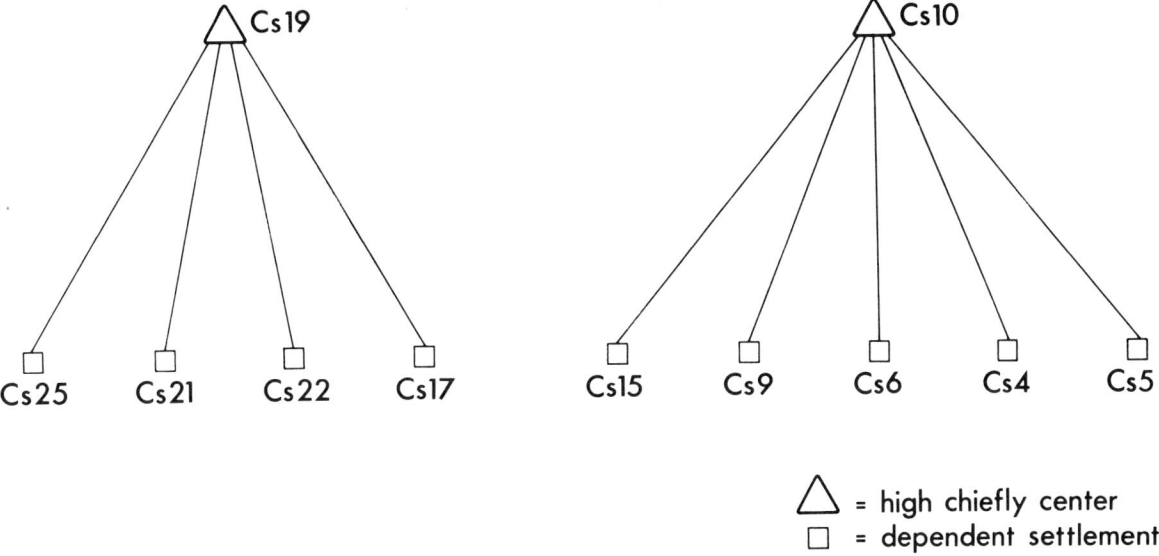

Figure 30. Diagram of the regional organization of the Cuicatlán Cañada during the Perdido phase.

In sum, the ranked societies that emerged on the Cañada's alluvial fans during the Perdido phase appear to have maintained a certain degree of regional cohesion—as evidenced by the relative homogeneity of the canyon's ceramic tradition. A network of alliance and exchange probably bound these ranked societies into a cohesive—though apparently noncentralized—regional system.

Perdido Phase Settlements and Their Highland Neighbors

Chiefly societies are distinguished from simpler egalitarian societies by the central hereditary position of the chief. By virtue of his birth, the chief stands at the apex of his region's administrative hierarchy and is regularly supplied with goods and labor from surrounding dependent communities. The chief also has control over the production of sumptuary items that are associated with his exalted position in life. Recent reappraisals of chiefdoms have shown how the traditional and central redistributive hierarchy for amassing goods and services is manipulated by a chief in order to maximize his political power (Earle 1978:180-185; Peebles and Kus 1977:424-427). A chief uses the goods that are mobilized through the redistributive hierarchy to support his chiefly retinue, to guarantee the allegiance of petty chiefs by awarding them gifts, and to build new alliances that will enlarge his political support.

While consolidating his power and position at home through the redistributive hierarchy, the chief also participates in interregional exchange networks with neighboring chiefs. These long-distance relationships between neighboring chiefs include the periodic exchange of wives and prestige goods. According to Helms (1979:75), the prestige goods used in these chiefly exchanges are scarce, non-utilitarian items that are received from distant regions and that require special craftsmanship to produce. The interregional exchange networks succeed in establishing and maintaining alliances between the chiefs of separate regions. Furthermore, they also serve to enhance and legitimize a chief's position at home. In sum,

> ... a chiefdom can be pictured as a sphere where lines of redistribution radiate from the central paramount, according to social rank order, to integrate dependent villages. Two or more such spheres may be linked in an exchange network as a result of exchanges between their respective elites. [Pires-Ferreira and Flannery 1976:291-292]

The participation by members of high-ranking lineages in interregional exchange networks is characteristic of the Formative period in Mesoamerica (Flannery 1968; Pires-Ferreira and Flannery 1976).

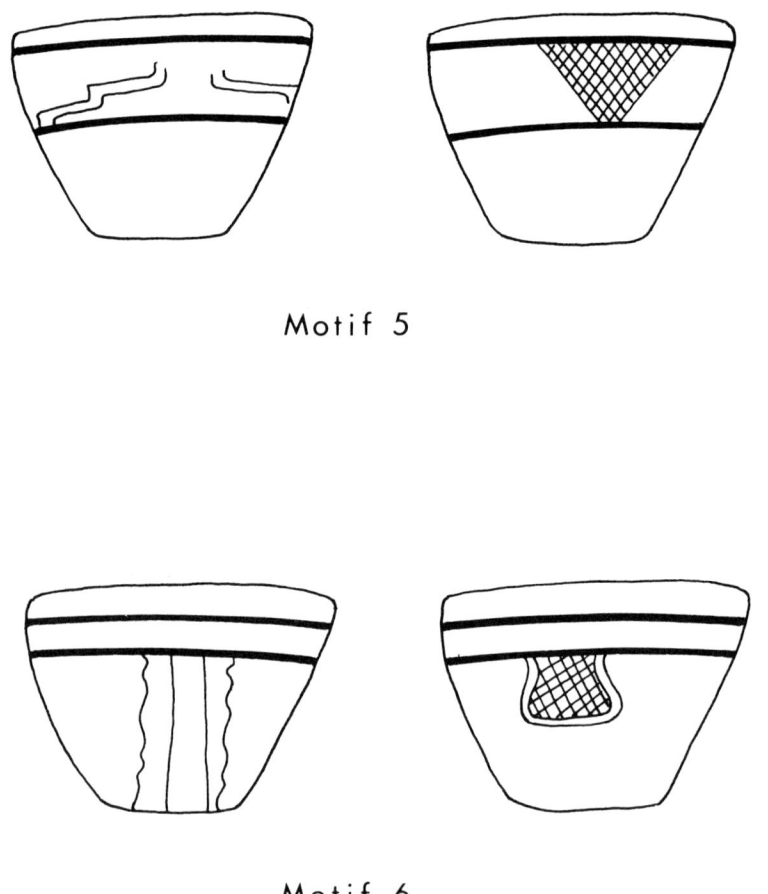

Figure 31. Two decorative motifs commonly incised on Perdido Gray bowls. Motif 5 consists of two widely-spaced horizontal lines with additional designs between them. Motif 6 consists of two narrowly-spaced horizontal lines with additional designs below them.

The nodal points of these long-distance exchange networks were the chiefly centers where the highest ranking lineages resided. Much of this exchange involved the regular flow of prestige goods between the chiefly centers of neighboring regions.

If the Cuicatlán Cañada supported two seats of high chiefly power during the Perdido phase, we would expect to find evidence of their participation in such interregional exchange networks. The interregional exchange relationships maintained by the two central chiefs at Cs10-P and Cs19-P might be manifested archaeologically by the differential distribution of exotic imported items at Perdido phase settlements. Under a system of chiefly exchange the imported items would probably have entered the Cañada by way of the chiefly centers, instead of moving through the canyon on a simple village-to-village basis. Consequently, we would expect the chiefly centers, as nodes in the interregional exchange networks, to exhibit greater frequencies of foreign prestige goods than their surrounding dependent settlements. Yet another reason to expect a differential distribution of foreign prestige goods at Perdido phase settlements is because they often serve as symbols of high status in chiefly societies (Helms 1979:75).

Accordingly, we would expect to find greater frequencies of these foreign items associated with the chiefly superstratum at the two large centers than at lower-order settlements in the region. The distribution of prestige goods among Perdido phase sites ought to assume a shape that departs from the general pattern of exponential fall-off that would be expected under conditions of simple down-the-line exchange (Renfrew 1977:85-86). Specifically, if we plot the relative quantity of imported goods at Per-

Table 6. Distribution of Perdido Gray Incised Outleaned-Wall Bowl Motifs 5 and 6 at 12 Late Middle Formative Settlements

Site	Surface Collections†	Average Ratio: Incised OWB Motif 5 / Total Ceramic Diagnostics	Average Ratio: Incised OWB Motif 6 / Total Ceramic Diagnostics
Cs1-P	9	.008	.003
Cs27-P	4	.02	.02
Cs4-P	11	.03	.01
Cs5-P	1	0	0
Cs6-P	1	0	0
Cs9-P	5	.01	.01
Cs10-P	10	.03	.02
Cs15-P	17	.03	.01
Cs17-P	6	.07	.01
Cs19-P	8	.02	.02
Cs21-P	6	.007	.02
Cs25-P	7	.03	.02

†All squares having Perdido phase material were included in this analysis (see Chapter 2).

dido phase settlements against the distance between those settlements and the sources of the goods, we should obtain a generally downward sloping curve, but with peaks that correspond to the relative concentration of foreign prestige goods at the chiefly centers.

Three kinds of foreign items were recovered in enough quantity in our surface collections at the Perdido phase sites to allow the drawing of frequency distributions: late Middle Formative ceramics from the Oaxaca Valley, late Middle Formative ceramics from the Tehuacán Valley, and obsidian artifacts from one or more obsidian sources in Central Mexico. The obsidian sources nearest to the Cañada—the Pico de Orizaba source and the Guadalupe Victoria source—are over 150 km away (Pires-Ferreira 1975:13; Zeitlin 1979:73). Marine shell was also imported to the Cuicatlán Cañada during the Perdido phase. Our best evidence comes from Spencer's excavations of the Perdido phase settlement at La Coyotera, where nearly all the shell was found to be marine (Spencer 1982: 170-172). Here I will simply discuss its occurrence at certain Perdido phase settlements, since the quantities of shell recovered in our surface collections at Perdido phase sites were too small to allow the drawing of a frequency distribution.

I selected easily identifiable Rosario and Period Early I ceramics from the Valley of Oaxaca and calculated the relative frequency of these foreign ceramics in those unmixed surface collections at the Perdido phase settlements. This was achieved by summing the readily identifiable Oaxaca ceramics collected in those surface collections, and dividing by the total number of diagnostic ceramics recovered. Table 7 lists both the total number and the

Table 7. Distribution of Late Middle Formative Ceramics Imported from Oaxaca at 12 Perdido Phase Settlements

Site	Surface Collections†	Total Ceramic Diagnostics	Oaxaca Ceramics*	Ratio	Distance from Monte Albán (km)	
					Straight Line	Ground Travel
Cs1-P	2	64	1	.016	109.41	117.29
Cs27-P	0	0	0	0	100.51	106.70
Cs4-P	6	343	6	.017	94.29	97.77
Cs5-P	0	0	0	0	91.70	95.14
Cs6-P	1	15	0	0	90.26	93.64
Cs9-P	2	155	1	.006	89.26	92.52
Cs10-P	6	389	11	.028	86.21	89.45
Cs15-P	13	252	2	.008	83.80	86.95
Cs17-P	5	229	1	.004	81.02	83.03
Cs19-P	2	298	7	.023	79.17	81.17
Cs21-P	4	116	1	.009	78.74	80.73
Cs25-P	5	427	4	.009	72.49	73.99

†Only those surface collections yielding pure Perdido phase ceramics were included in this analysis (see Chapter 2).
*Oaxaca Ceramics = Sum of C.2s, C.4s, C.5s, and other late Middle Formative ceramics (Caso, Bernal, and Acosta 1967).

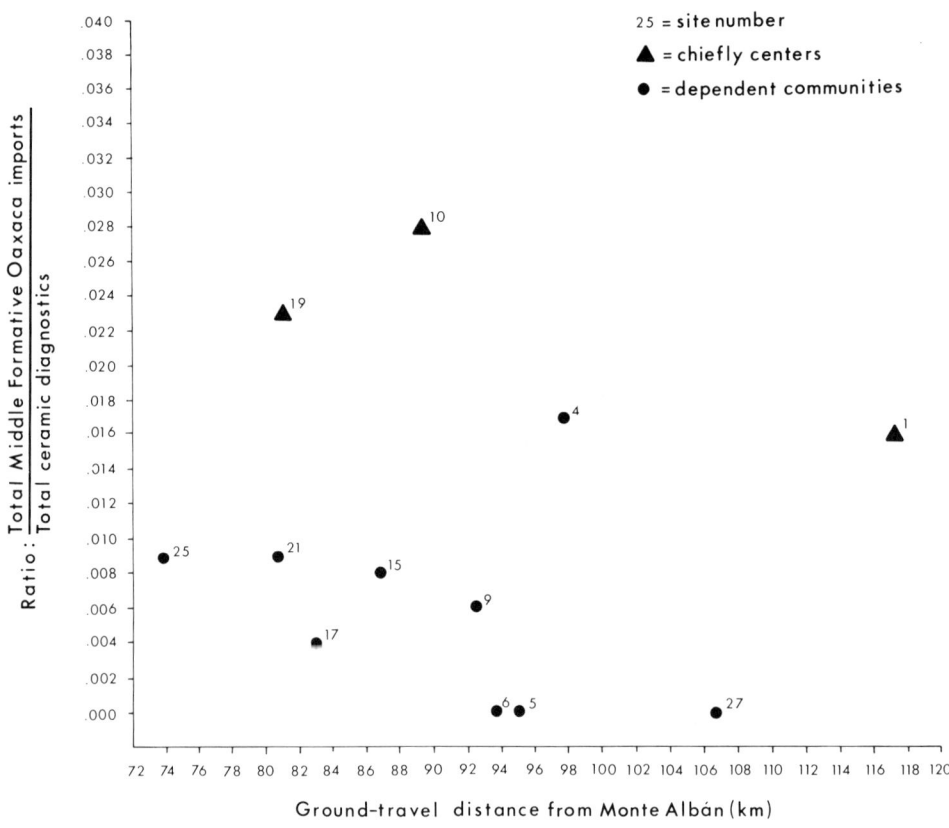

Figure 32. Scatter plot of the ratio of total Oaxaca imports/total diagnostics and distance from Monte Albán.

relative frequency of these Oaxaca ceramics at the 12 Perdido phase settlements in the survey area. The latter figures were then used to plot the relative abundance of Oaxaca ceramics at the 12 Perdido phase settlements against the distance of these settlements from Monte Albán in the Oaxaca Valley. The distance of these settlements from Monte Albán was measured in two ways: the straight-line distance in kilometers and the ground-travel distance in kilometers, which takes the nature of the intervening terrain into account and follows natural travel routes (Table 7). Figure 32 presents the scatter plot of the ratios of Oaxaca ceramics at the 12 sites against their ground-travel distance from Monte Albán. The plot reveals that in general, as distance from Monte Albán increases, the relative frequency of Oaxaca ceramics drops. But there are two exceptions to the generally subsiding slope that form peaks in the distribution; these two sites (Cs10-P, Cs19-P) exhibit noticeably higher frequencies of Oaxaca ceramics compared with nearby Cañada settlements.

Not surprisingly, the two settlements having higher frequencies of Oaxaca ceramics correspond to the two chiefly centers that were previously defined on the basis of their size and public architecture. The observed distribution of Oaxaca ceramics in the Cañada during the Perdido phase agrees closely with the distributional pattern expected under conditions of interregional prestige-good exchange, with the two peaks in the distribution, the chiefly centers, representing nodal points in the long-distance exchange of prestige goods. The distribution of Oaxaca ceramics among the Perdido phase settlements provides good evidence, therefore, for the existence of interregional exchange networks between elites in the Valley of Oaxaca and the two highest-ranking lineages in the Cuicatlán Cañada.

Figure 32 also shows the position of Cs1-P, the

next proposed chiefly center north of the Cañada, in this prestige-good exchange system. Cs1-P produced a lower relative frequency of Oaxaca ceramics than the two chiefly centers in the Cañada. This is to be expected, given its greater distance from the Valley of Oaxaca. Nevertheless, the relative frequency of Oaxaca ceramics at Cs1-P is notably higher than that at most settlements in the Cañada, and therefore, Cs1-P still represents a departure from the generally downward sloping distribution. The gradual fall-off in the slope of abundance of Oaxaca ceramics between the two chiefly centers in the Cañada and Cs1-P to the north is precisely the kind of gradual slope that Renfrew expects in his prestige-chain trading model, which accounts for the exchange of prestige goods over long distances (Renfrew 1972:467-468). Consequently, I would maintain that Cs1-P was the next chiefly center to the north that participated in the long-distance exchange network with elites in the Cuicatlán Cañada and the Valley of Oaxaca.

Below the two peaks in the distribution of Oaxaca ceramics among the Cañada settlements, Cs4-P yielded a higher frequency of Oaxaca ceramics than the remaining lower-order settlements. One possibility for this may be that it constitutes a simple accident of recovery due to the number of barrancas that dissect the site. (Detailed site descriptions will be presented in Redmond n.d.) A more intriguing possibility might be that it represents the articulation of the interregional prestige-good exchange system with the local redistributive hierarchy, whereby a portion of the foreign goods that a high chief receives through the interregional exchange networks is forwarded to local chiefs residing at dependent villages. By passing on some fraction of these highly prized goods to dependent local chiefs in the form of rewards or gifts, a high chief succeeds in maintaining the local redistributive hierarchy that supports him. In Hawaii, one of the ways a high chief guaranteed the political loyalty of local chiefs and their continuing economic support through the redistributive hierarchy was by periodically rewarding them with sumptuary items (Earle 1978: 181-182). A similar strategy was pursued by the high chiefs of sixteenth-century Panamanian chiefdoms:

> ... the best opportunities for chiefs and other high-status challengers to obtain material rewards for their supporters and to evidence personal resourcefulness and ability lay not in controlling subsistence and utilitarian resources, ... but in establishing access to "scarce" nonutilitarian resources, including gold, pearls, and textiles. The means to acquire these scarce items centered, I suggest, on chiefly participation in various regional and "long-distance" exchange systems linking Panamanian chiefs both with each other and with elites in distant regions beyond the isthmus. [Helms 1979:34]

In summary, Figure 33 diagrams the exchange of Oaxaca ceramics in the Cuicatlán Cañada and beyond to the north during the Middle Formative period. The distribution of these ceramics closely approximates the expected distribution of exotic goods exchanged between the elites of neighboring regions. The chiefly centers received Oaxaca ceramics through the interregional exchange networks that linked them with elites in the Oaxaca Valley. A fraction of these imported ceramics were then offered to local chiefs residing at dependent villages as

Table 8. Distribution of Late Middle Formative Ceramics Imported from Tehuacán at 12 Perdido Phase Settlements

Site	Surface Collections†	Total Ceramic Diagnostics	Tehuacán Ceramics*	Ratio	Distance from Quachilco (km)	
					Straight Line	Ground Travel
Cs1-P	9	443	1	.002	50.70	52.19
Cs27-P	4	269	0	0	59.60	62.78
Cs4-P	11	517	1	.002	65.82	71.71
Cs5-P	1	162	12	.07	68.41	74.34
Cs6-P	1	15	0	0	69.85	75.84
Cs9-P	5	414	0	0	70.85	76.96
Cs10-P	10	564	0	0	73.90	80.03
Cs15-P	17	341	0	0	76.31	82.53
Cs17-P	6	229	0	0	79.09	86.45
Cs19-P	8	639	0	0	80.94	88.31
Cs21-P	6	164	0	0	81.37	88.75
Cs25-P	7	517	0	0	87.62	95.49

†All surface collections having Perdido phase ceramics were included in this analysis (see Chapter 2).
*Tehuacán Ceramics = Tehuacán late Middle Formative ceramics (see MacNeish, Peterson, and Flannery 1970).

partial repayment for their continuing loyalty and support, and some were also forwarded to the chiefly elites in the Tehuacán Valley.

The distribution of late Middle Formative ceramics from the Tehuacán Valley (MacNeish, Peterson, and Flannery 1970:102-110) at Perdido phase settlements is listed in Table 8. The starting point for the distance figures of the Perdido phase settlements in Table 8 was the site of Quachilco (Ts218) in the central Tehuacán Valley. Past and present researchers in the Tehuacán Valley consider Quachilco to have been the largest settlement in that region during the Middle Formative period; as a regional center, Quachilco probably served an important role in the interregional exchange networks between high-ranking lineages (MacNeish et al. 1972:397-402; Drennan 1978:17, 78).

In general, we found smaller quantities of Tehuacán ceramics in the survey area than Oaxaca ceramics. Table 8 also reveals that Tehuacán ceramics were found only in the northern end of the survey area, at sites closest to the Tehuacán Valley. In fact, within the survey area there is only a slight overlap between the distributions of ceramics from the Tehuacán Valley and those from the Oaxaca Valley; as distance from Monte Albán increases and the relative frequency of Oaxaca ceramics at Perdido phase settlement falls off (Fig. 32), Tehuacán ceramics begin to occur, and in small quantities. And unlike the regional distribution of Oaxaca ceramics, ceramics from the Tehuacán Valley are not associated with the region's chiefly centers.

The distribution of Tehuacán ceramics in the Cuicatlán Cañada does not conform to the pattern that would be expected if these ceramics were among the items of interregional chiefly exchange. It is possible that Tehuacán ceramics did not function as prestige goods, and that perhaps other goods from the Tehuacán Valley moved through the long-distance exchange networks. The sixteenth-century *Relación* of Teotitlán del Camino, for example, mentioned the local production of lime plaster. The nearby community of Nextepec, a dependency of Teotitlán, was a major center of salt production (Paso y Troncoso 1905:223, 228-229). Salt was also produced by the town of Coxcatlán in the sixteenth century, and was used, in part, to pay tribute to the Spanish Crown (Sisson 1973:8-9). The Tehuacán Valley remains a center of "onyx" production today, due to its abundant travertine deposits. In Formative times, some of these natural resources of the Tehuacán Valley might have served the region's elite as items for prestige-good exchange with the elites of neighboring regions. In fact, Spencer's excavations at the Perdido phase site of La Coyotera in the Cañada exposed the remains of a cache of foreign prestige goods (Spencer 1982:241-242); among the cache's numerous marine shell ornaments and obsidian artifacts lay a miniature travertine bowl that might well have originated from the Tehuacán Valley.

Thus, while there is evidence of long-distance exchange between the Cuicatlán Cañada and the Tehuacán Valley, the present ceramic evidence suggests that the degree of interaction between the Cuicatlán Cañada and the Valley of Oaxaca was much greater. Perhaps certain sociopolitical developments in the Valley of Oaxaca at this time—featuring the establishment and growth of Monte Albán—involved greater ties with the chiefly elites of the Cuicatlán Cañada than did the corresponding developments in the Tehuacán Valley.

Obsidian comprises the third foreign item to be considered in this discussion of the Cuicatlán Cañada's participation in long-distance exchange networks with neighboring regions. Unfortunately, the analysis of obsidian artifacts from surface collections is complicated by the lack of an independent way to separate the obsidian chronologically. In order to minimize the possibility for confusion that can result from this problem, only unmixed Perdido phase surface collections were selected for the distributional analysis of obsidian artifacts. The two criteria used to select those unmixed Perdido phase surface collections were: (1) their abundant Perdido phase ceramic markers; and (2) their lack of ceramics diagnostic of any other phase (see Chapter 2).

Table 9 presents both the total number and the relative frequency of obsidian artifacts in the unmixed surface collections at the 12 Perdido phase settlements in the survey area (Table 9). The ratios of imported obsidian among Perdido phase settlements are generally higher than those for foreign ceramics. The question is: did obsidian reach the Cuicatlán Cañada settlements by means of a prestige-good exchange system between the elites of neighboring regions in this part of Mesoamerica, or through some other kind of exchange network?

Pires-Ferreira's study of the variation in obsidian sources used by individual households at two Formative settlements in the Valley of Oaxaca led her to suggest that imported obsidian was being pooled by

Table 9. Distribution of Obsidian
at 12 Perdido Phase Settlements

Site	Surface Collections†	Total Ceramic Diagnostics	Total Obsidian	Ratio
Cs1-P	2	64	30	.469
Cs27-P	0	0	0	0
Cs4-P	6	343	30	.087
Cs5-P	0	0	0	0
Cs6-P	1	15*	3	*
Cs9-P	2	155	9	.058
Cs10-P	6	389	42	.108
Cs15-P	13	252	17	.067
Cs17-P	5	229	20	.087
Cs19-P	2	298	27	.091
Cs21-P	4	116	6	.052
Cs25-P	5	427	41	.096

†Only surface collections yielding pure Perdido phase ceramics were included in this analysis (see Chapter 2).
*The sample is too small for meaningful analysis.

the highest-ranking lineage of a village prior to being distributed to individual households. Moreover, Pires-Ferreira discovered that the elite's control of obsidian was occurring at all levels of the regional settlement hierarchy during the Middle Formative period (Pires-Ferreira 1975:35; Winter and Pires-Ferreira 1976:310-311). Her study provides evidence from the Valley of Oaxaca for the articulation between the long-distance exchange system—whereby obsidian was imported to the valley—and the local redistributive hierarchy. Imported obsidian was received, pooled, and redistributed by the high-ranking lineages at the chiefly centers; it was then received, controlled, and further redistributed by lower-ranking lineages at dependent settlements.

On the basis of these data from the Valley of Oaxaca, we have reason to believe that obsidian moved through the interregional exchange networks that were maintained by the chiefly elites of diverse regions. Pires-Ferreira (1975:35) attributes the practice of pooling the imported obsidian to the increasing demand by the elite for obsidian blades. Obsidian blades are considered to have been one of the instruments used in ritual bloodletting in Mesoamerica (Flannery 1976d:341; Joralemon 1974:59-62). During the latter part of the Middle Formative they were probably utilized in rituals of chiefly sanctification (Drennan 1976b:348, 357-358) that involved members of the highest-ranking lineages who occupied positions of sanctified authority.

The distribution of obsidian among late Middle Formative settlements in the Cuicatlán Cañada (Table 9) supports the claim that obsidian moved through the long-distance exchange networks linking high-ranking lineages. The region's two chiefly centers (Cs10-P, Cs19-P), which would have been nodal points in this exchange system, exhibit higher obsidian ratios than all but one of the smaller communities in the region. That exception is Cs25-P, whose obsidian ratio falls between the values for the two chiefly centers; a single collection square (Cs25/298), located in a highly-eroded area of the site, was the principal contributor to the site's unexpectedly high obsidian ratio (see Spencer 1982:88-89, Fig. 3.5). The only other higher obsidian ratio was obtained at Cs1-P, the next chiefly center north of the Cañada and closer to the obsidian sources of the Puebla Basin.

With the exception of Cs25-P, the distribution of obsidian among the Perdido phase settlements in the Cañada conforms to the distribution expected under conditions of interregional prestige-good exchange. The region's two chiefly centers that would have participated in these long-distance exchange networks have the greatest relative frequencies of obsidian. Below these fall the values for obsidian at the smaller communities in the region. These dependent communities probably received their obsidian through the chiefly redistributive hierarchy, in the manner described by Pires-Ferreira (Winter and Pires-Ferreira 1976:310-311).

Moreover, the distribution of obsidian within the Cuicatlán Cañada is similar to that of late Middle Formative ceramics from the Oaxaca Valley (Table 10). The peak of both distributions occurs at the site of El Mirador (Cs10-P), the largest Perdido phase settlement in the Cañada and one of the region's two chiefly centers. The second such center at Hacienda Tecomaxtlahua (Cs19-P) exhibits the second highest ratio of Oaxaca ceramics and third highest obsidian ratio. The prominent position of the next chiefly center north of the Cañada at Cs1-P in both distributions also conforms to the distributional pattern expected under conditions of interregional chiefly exchange. As a chiefly center, Cs1-P probably acted as a node in the interregional exchange networks that bound elites in the Oaxaca Valley and the Cuicatlán Cañada with elites to the north who controlled the major obsidian sources in the central Mexican highlands.

The occurrence of shell in our Perdido phase surface collections also conforms with the distributions of obsidian and Oaxaca ceramics. It is safe to

Table 10. Distribution of Obsidian and Late Middle Formative Ceramics Imported from Oaxaca at 9 Perdido Phase Settlements

Site	Ratio: Total Obsidian / Total Ceramic Diagnostics	Ratio: Total Oaxaca Ceramics / Total Ceramic Diagnostics
Cs1-P	.469	.016
Cs4-P	.087	.017
Cs9-P	.058	.006
Cs10-P	.108	.028
Cs15-P	.067	.008
Cs17-P	.087	.004
Cs19-P	.091	.023
Cs21-P	.052	.009
Cs25-P	.096	.009

assume that the shell in the Perdido phase collection is marine, since 98% of the shell recovered from the excavations of the Perdido phase community at La Coyotera (Cs25-P) was identified as marine shell (Spencer 1982:170-172). Marine shell would obviously have been imported to the Cuicatlán Cañada from coastal regions. Only two fragments of shell were recovered on the surfaces of Perdido phase settlements: one fragment was collected at Cs10-P, and the other fragment came from Cs19-P. The two Perdido phase sites in question correspond to the region's two chiefly centers, where we expected to find evidence of their involvement in interregional exchange networks.

The evidence at hand suggests that obsidian, Valley of Oaxaca ceramics, and marine shell functioned as prestige items in an elite interregional exchange network during the Middle Formative period. What might the Cañada elites have produced and exchanged in order to receive these foreign items? Midden deposits excavated at the Perdido phase community at La Coyotera (Cs25-P) contained the carbonized remains of various tropical fruits and nuts in addition to remains of the usual Mesoamerican staples. The tropical fruits and nuts represented include the black zapote and the coyol palm (Smith 1979:238-240), which cannot be grown at the higher elevations of the valleys bordering the Cuicatlán Cañada. The coyol palm has a wide variety of traditional uses: its fronds can be used for roof thatching and basket weaving; its sap can be fermented into an alcoholic beverage; and the nut inside its fruit can be ground and boiled to extract a fine oil for cooking or for burning in lamps (Smith 1979:239-24). The latter two uses of the coyol palm might have been of particular interest to the chiefly elites of the highland valleys of Oaxaca and Tehuacán. First of all, the wine produced from the coyol palm might have been desired for intoxication.

Intoxicants are known to be an important ingredient of most rituals performed by native peoples of the New World (Helms 1979:115), and it has been suggested that the chiefly elites of the Middle Formative period in Mesoamerica were steeped in rituals of sanctification, which served to legitimize their political authority (Drennan 1976b:348, 355-358). Moreover, we know that only members of the Valley Zapotec elite were entitled to imbibe fermented fruit drinks later during the Postclassic period (Burgoa 1674b:125). The coyol palm might also have been a major source of oil in Mesoamerica, an area where other plant species bearing a high content of readily extractable oil are rare (Smith 1979:240).

There is a long history of interest in these *tierra caliente* products of the Cuicatlán Cañada by inhabitants of the surrounding highland valleys. The early Colonial-period *Relación* of Cuicatlán noted that the region specialized in the production of tropical fruits, fruits which were traded and bought by highlanders—particularly those from the Oaxaca Valley (Gallego 1580:187-188; Hopkins 1974:78-79). The botanical remains from the site of La Coyotera indicate that such tropical fruits were cultivated in the Cañada during the late Middle Formative period. At that time these native products probably functioned as items of exchange in the interregional exchange relationships that the Cañada elites maintained with elites of other regions.

It appears that during the Perdido phase the Cuicatlán Cañada supported a line of farming communities, whose inhabitants cultivated the stretches of productive low alluvium. The region was administered by two chiefly centers, which were defined on the basis of their position in the regional settlement-size hierarchy and their corresponding public sectors. Below these centers ranked a series of smaller dependent communities.

THE PERDIDO PHASE

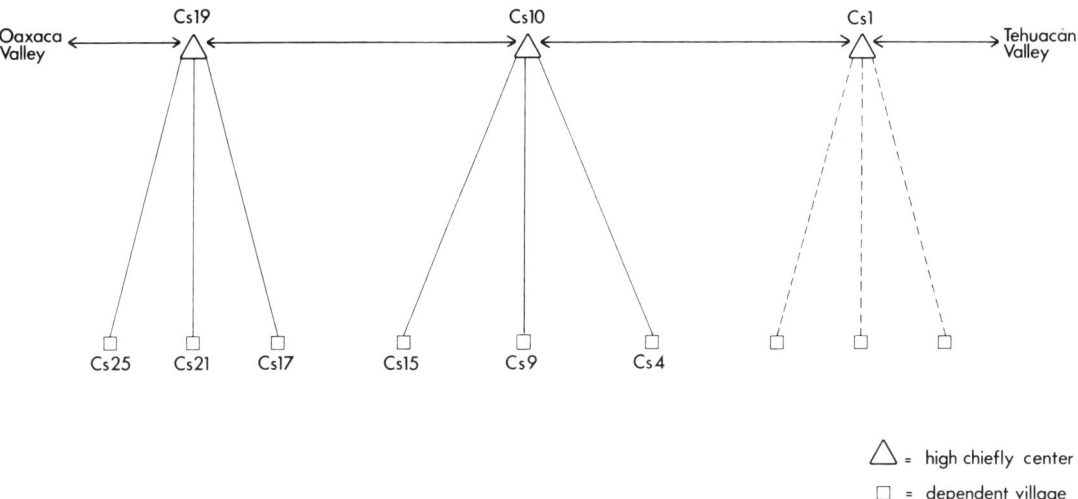

Figure 33. Diagram of the exchange of Oaxaca ceramics in the Cuicatlán Cañada and beyond during the late Middle Formative period.

The distributions of imported prestige goods among Perdido phase settlements support this view of the Cañada's regional organization, and further suggest that the two chiefly centers formed nodal points in an interregional exchange network that linked elites from across a large part of Mesoamerica at this time.

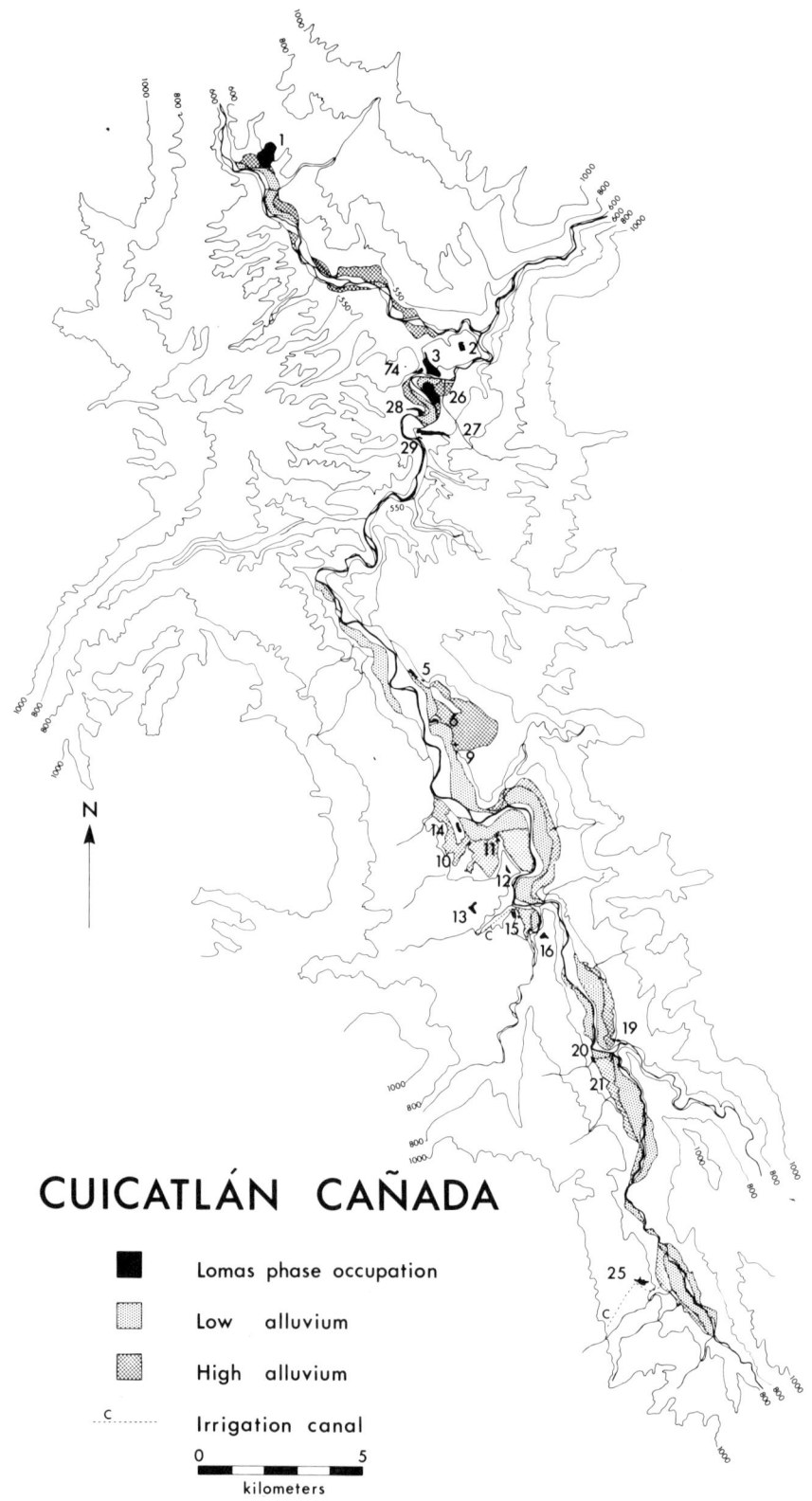

Figure 34. Lomas phase regional settlement pattern map.

Chapter 4

The Cuicatlán Cañada During the Lomas Phase

Transition

The Lomas phase is the time period when, according to the conquest slabs on Building J in the Main Plaza of Monte Albán, the Valley Zapotec embarked upon a policy of imperial expansion into neighboring regions, one of these regions being the Cuicatlán Cañada (Marcus 1976:130-131, 1980:56). The effects that such an imperial policy might have had upon the Cañada are included in the conquest model presented in Chapter 2.

The transition from the Perdido phase to the Lomas phase entailed major developments in the regional settlement pattern of the Cuicatlán Cañada (Fig. 34). The most widespread changes involved: (1) the virtual abandonment of the Perdido phase communities, which we have seen were located on high alluvial terraces or low piedmont slopes flanking the fertile low alluvium; and (2) the establishment of settlements on piedmont spurs and ridges rising above both the low and high alluvium of the canyon floor. Although the number of settlements in the Cuicatlán Cañada increases to 21 during the Lomas phase, a histogram of the settlement sizes (Fig. 35) reveals that most of these settlements remain under 5 ha in size. Table 11 lists the 21 Lomas phase settlements, their corresponding sizes, and their geographic position on one of the Cañada's four alluvial fans.

Another striking development in the regional distribution of settlement occurred on the Quiotepec alluvial fan at the Cañada's northern boundary. Extending west of the junction of the Río Grande with the Río Salado is a mountain ridge that nearly seals off the northern Cañada from the Tehuacán Valley. Entry to the Cañada from the north is restricted to a narrow pass cutting through this mountain ridge. A major ford on the Río Grande that is still in use today lies immediately south of the mountain pass.

In contrast to the single 1.42-ha community in the Quiotepec area during the previous Perdido phase (Cs27-P), seven settlements were established here during the Lomas phase. These communities were the largest settlements in the Cañada at this time (Table 11). Cs3-L covers both sides of the critical mountain pass, and a defensive wall fortifies a large plaza with a ballcourt, surrounding platforms, and numerous residential structures. Presiding above this settlement is an elaborate hilltop fortress featuring two monumental mound groups, a ballcourt, and associated elite residences, all contained within stone fortifications (Cs2-L). On another ridgetop above the pass stands an isolated plaza supporting a 10-12-m-high mound (Cs74-L). Directly south of the mountain pass and the river ford on the Quiotepec alluvium is a large plaza delimited by elongated mounds, 6 m high, through which any traveler using the ford would have had to pass (Cs26-L). Additional settlements extend along the piedmont ridges overlooking the large plaza on the south bank of the Río Grande (Cs27-L, Cs28, Cs29). The total Lomas phase occupation on the Quiotepec alluvial fan is 44.34 ha, forming an unprecedented expansion of settlement here, and making Quiotepec by far the most densely settled of the Cañada's four alluvial fans at this time (Table 12). As I will demonstrate later on in this chapter, this sudden concentration of settlement at Quiotepec could not have been supported locally, for the estimated population far exceeds the carrying capacity of the available farmland on the Quiotepec alluvial fan.

South of Quiotepec in the central and southern Cañada, a different settlement distribution emerged during the Lomas phase. The 14 hilltop settlements here are uniformly smaller than 4 ha in size (Fig. 36). Furthermore, if we examine the total settlement on each of the alluvial fans we find that there is little or no population growth in the central and southern Cañada. Although the Lomas phase occupation at the southern Dominguillo end of the canyon marks a slight increase over that seen there during the previous period, there is no comparable growth in settlement on the two central alluvial fans (Table 12).

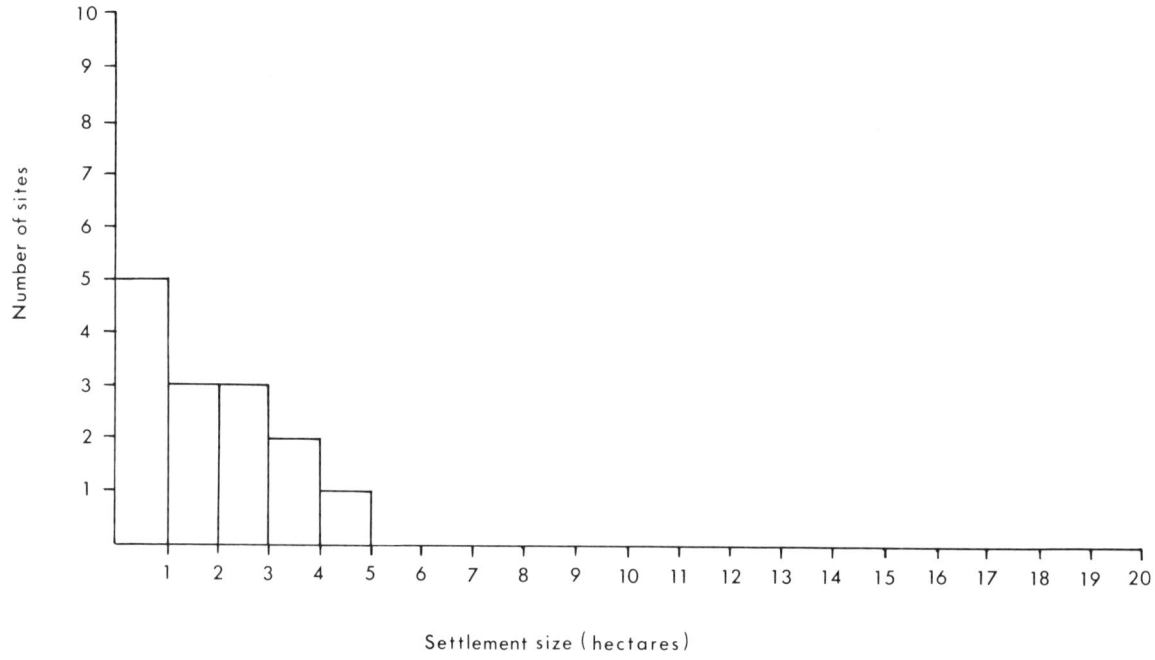

Figure 35. Histogram of Lomas phase settlement sizes in the Cuicatlán Cañada.

These developments in the region's settlement pattern during the Lomas phase were accompanied by changes in the regional distribution of imported items. The distribution of imported Oaxaca ceramics among settlements in the Cañada during the previous Perdido phase, which we have seen formed a generally subsiding curve as distance from Monte Albán increased (see Chapter 3, Fig. 32), was reversed during the Lomas phase. Table 13 lists the relative frequencies of imported Late Monte Albán I and II ceramics at the 17 Lomas phase settlements that were intensively mapped and surface collected, together with the distance of each site from Monte Albán. If we compare this table to a similar one drawn up for the distribution of Oaxaca ceramics at the previous Perdido phase settlements (Chapter 3, Table 7), we can detect several overall changes. First of all, the transition from the Perdido to the Lomas phase marked an overall decrease in the amount of imported ceramics from the Valley of Oaxaca to the Cuicatlán Cañada. Moreover, the regional distribution of these imported Monte Albán ceramics became highly discontinuous during the Lomas phase; Monte Albán ceramics are found in smaller quantities and at fewer settlements in the Cañada at this time. Finally, it is clear that distance from Monte Albán ceased to be a major factor affecting the distribution of Oaxaca ceramics during the Lomas phase, since the greatest abundance of these imported ceramics in the region at this time occurs at sites on the Quiotepec alluvial fan, the most distant from the Valley of Oaxaca (Table 14, Fig. 37). Thus, the observed distribution of Monte Albán ceramics in the Cuicatlán Cañada during the Lomas phase—featuring an unprecedented concentration of these items at the region's northern boundary—probably represents an entirely new form of exchange linking the two regions.

Another item imported to the Cuicatlán Cañada is obsidian, and during the Lomas phase we observe a reversal in the distribution of obsidian similar to that seen in the distribution of Oaxaca ceramics. Table 15 lists the relative frequencies of obsidian, chert, and quartz at the 13 settlements where surface collections recovered relatively unmixed Lomas phase ceramics. The table reveals that Lomas phase settlements in the central and southern Cañada have lower frequencies of obsidian relative to chert and quartz, whereas the opposite is true at the four settlements in the northern Quiotepec end of the canyon where higher obsidian ratios are consistently obtained.

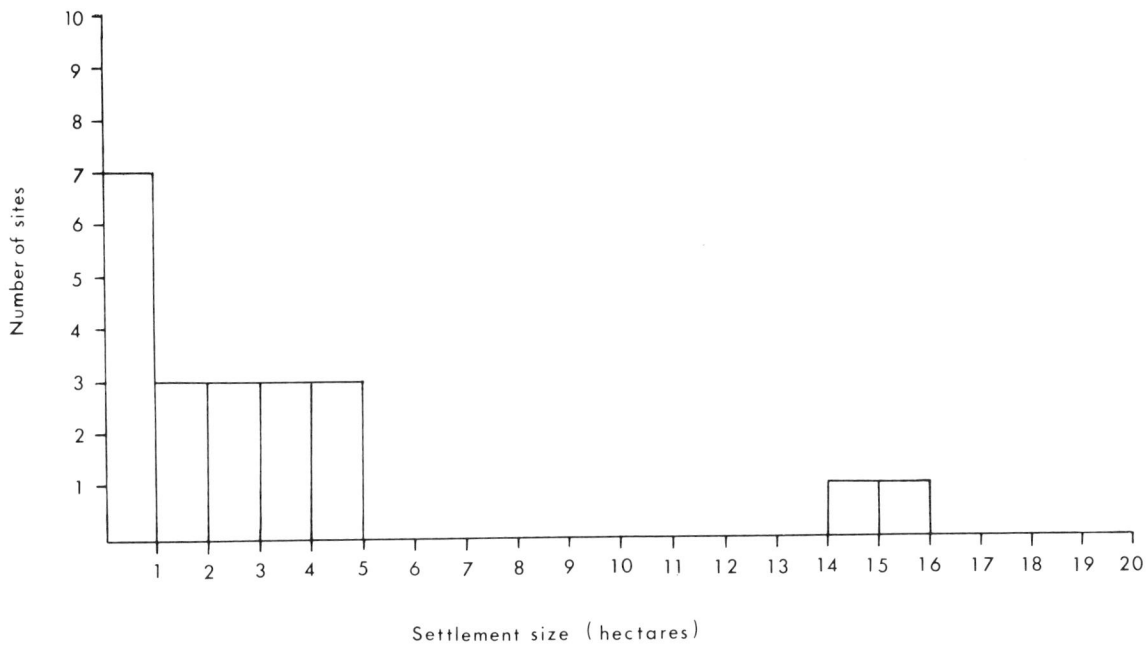

Figure 36. Histogram of Lomas phase settlement sizes in the central and southern Cañada.

Table 11. The Sizes of Lomas Phase Settlements

Alluvial Fan	Site Number	Site Name	Site Size (ha)
Quiotepec	Cs2-L	Cerro de Quiotepec	4.55
	Cs3-L	Paso de Quiotepec	14.67
	Cs74-L	Quiotepec Lookout Post	0.13
	CS26-L	Campo del Panteón	15.80
	Cs28	La Hacienda	3.85
	Cs27-L	El Campanario	4.79
	Cs29	La Estación	0.55
		Total Settlement Area	44.34
Cuicatlán	Cs5-L	Horno de Cal	2.79
	Cs6-L	Cuba Libre	1.87
	Cs9-L	La Bomba	0.96
	Cs14-L	Loma Larga	2.82
	Cs10-L	El Mirador	0.49
	Cs11-L	Loma del Llano Chiquito	0.76
	Cs12-L	Cerro Mixteco	1.65
	Cs13-L	Loma Grande	4.04
	Cs15/66-L	La Nopalera/Cerrito del Río Apoala	2.77
		Total Settlement Area	18.15
El Chilar	Cs16-L	Sitio Entre Dos Ríos	3.78
	Cs19-L	Hacienda Tecomaxtlahua	0.62
	Cs20-L	Las Monjas	1.33
	Cs21-L	Cerro Cortés	0.38
		Total Settlement Area	6.11
Dominguillo	Cs25-L	Loma de la Coyotera	3.04

If we plot the obsidian ratios for the 13 settlements against their distance from Monte Albán (Fig. 38) two clusters of points are produced representing, on the one hand, the sites in the central and southern Cañada, and, on the other, the sites in the Quiotepec area with their substantially higher obsidian ratios. Although obsidian appears to be more widely distributed in the Cañada than Monte Albán ceramics during the Lomas phase, the distribution of obsidian shares two characteristics with the distribution of Monte Albán ceramics: in contrast to the situation observed during the Perdido phase, the obsidian ratios increase with distance from Monte Albán; moreover, the sites at the northern Quiotepec boundary of the region exhibit an unprecedented concentration of obsidian. Obsidian was no doubt being imported to the Cañada from the obsidian sources in the Central Mexican highlands to the north. But I do not think that the higher obsidian ratios obtained at the region's northern boundary necessarily comprise the source end of a sloping distribution that gradually falls off as distance southward from the obsidian sources increases. As was the case for Oaxaca ceramics, the settlements in the Quiotepec area appear to have received substantially higher quantities of imported obsidian, suggesting that they were supplied preferentially.

In the process of surveying north of the Cuicatlán Cañada to include the general area of Santa María Tecomavaca in the southern Tehuacán Valley, we discovered that Quiotepec marks the northern limit of the distribution of Lomas phase and Monte Albán ceramics. At Tecomavaca, where previously the Late Santa María phase community (Cs1-P) shared ceramic decorative motifs with the contemporaneous and neighboring Perdido phase settlements in the Cuicatlán Cañada (see Chapter 3), the settlement contemporaneous with the Lomas phase settlement at Quiotepec (Cs1-L) is covered with the Palo Blanco phase pottery of Tehuacán (MacNeish, Peterson, and Flannery 1970:145-176). Thus the transition from the Perdido phase to the Lomas phase witnessed the sudden appearance of a ceramic boundary at Quiotepec, which separated the settlements in the Cañada from their neighbors to the north in the Tehuacán Valley.

These developments in the regional settlement pattern of the Cuicatlán Cañada and the regional

Table 12. Comparison of Perdido and Lomas Phase Settlement on the Cañada's Alluvial Fans

Alluvial Fan	Total Area of Perdido Phase Settlement (ha)	Total Area of Lomas Phase Settlement (ha)
Quiotepec	1.42	44.34
Cuicatlán	20.29	18.15
El Chilar	13.07	6.11
Dominguillo	2.64	3.04

distribution of imported items during the transition from the Perdido phase to the Lomas phase agree with many of the expectations derived from a model of the Cañada's subjugation by the Valley Zapotec centered at Monte Albán during the Late Formative period (ca. 300 B.C.-A.D. 200). There were abrupt discontinuities in the region's settlement pattern and large fortified settlements were established suddenly at the northern boundary of the Cañada, in strategic positions along both sides and at the southern terminus of the mountain pass leading in and out of the region (see Frontispiece). The regional distributions of imported items point to a disruption of the reciprocal exchange relations that the Cañada had previously maintained with the

Table 13. Distribution of Late Formative Ceramics Imported from Oaxaca at 17 Lomas Phase Settlements

Alluvial Fan	Site	Surface Collections†	Total Ceramic Diagnostics	Oaxaca Ceramics*	Ratio	Distance from Monte Albán (km) Straight Line	Distance from Monte Albán (km) Ground Travel
Quiotepec	Cs2-L	10	812	8	.010	103.18	110.10
Quiotepec	Cs3-L	24	1690	12	.007	102.21	108.86
Quiotepec	Cs26-L	2	90	0	0	101.51	107.89
Quiotepec	Cs27-L	11	840	7	.008	100.51	106.70
Cuicatlán	Cs5-L	6	1225	1	.0008	91.70	95.14
Cuicatlán	Cs6-L	9	547	4	.007	90.26	93.64
Cuicatlán	Cs9-L	2	274	0	0	89.26	92.52
Cuicatlán	Cs10-L	1	17	0	0	86.21	89.45
Cuicatlán	Cs11-L	3	123	0	0	86.06	89.14
Cuicatlán	Cs12-L	3	133	0	0	85.08	88.16
Cuicatlán	Cs13-L	10	595	1	.0017	85.24	88.43
Cuicatlán	Cs15/66-L	1	27	0	0	83.80	86.95
El Chilar	Cs16-L	6	568	0	0	82.94	85.37
El Chilar	Cs19-L	6	743	0	0	79.17	81.17
El Chilar	Cs20-L	3	135	2?	.015	79.00	81.00
El Chilar	Cs21-L	3	57	0	0	78.74	80.73
Dominguillo	Cs25-L	25	2263	1	.0004	72.49	73.99

†All surface collections yielding Lomas phase ceramics were included in this analysis (Chapter 2).
*Oaxaca Ceramics = Sum of C.6s, C.7s, C.11s, C.13s, C.20s, and specular red cremas (see Caso, Bernal, and Acosta 1967).

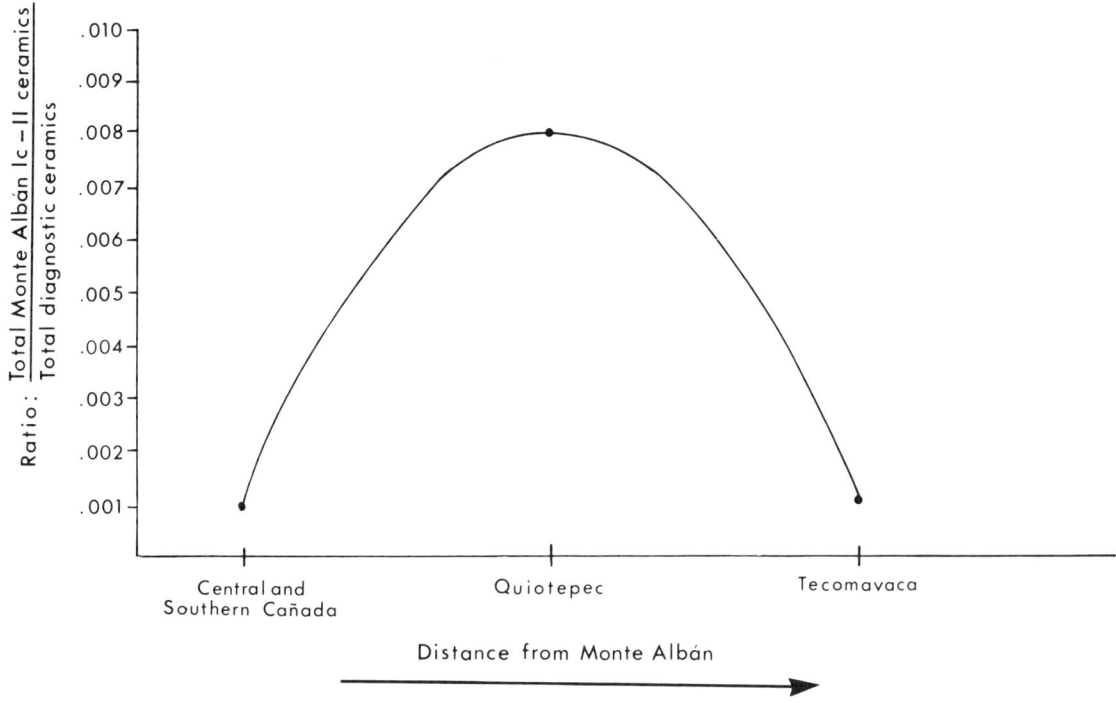

Figure 37. Distribution of Monte Albán Ic-II phase ceramics within and beyond the Cuicatlán Cañada.

Table 14. Distribution of Monte Albán Ic-II Ceramics Within and Beyond the Cuicatlán Cañada

Area	Sum of Monte Albán Ic-II Ceramics†	Total Ceramic Diagnostics	Ratio
Tecomavaca	4	3345	.001
Quiotepec	27	3432	.008
Central and Southern Cañada	9	6707	.001

†Sum of Monte Albán Ic-II ceramics = Sum of C.6s, C.7s, C.11s, C.13s, C.20s, and specular red cremas (see Caso, Bernal, and Acosta 1967).

neighboring Valleys of Oaxaca and Tehuacán. Instead, Monte Albán ceramics and obsidian were concentrated now at settlements on the northern Quiotepec border of the Cañada, suggesting that these communities were being preferentially supplied. The disruption of previous interregional exchange relations was further accompanied by the appearance of a ceramic boundary differentiating the settlements in the Quiotepec area and in the remainder of the Cañada from those beyond the region in the southern Tehuacán Valley. I suggest that the transition from the Perdido phase to the Lomas phase signaled the Zapotec subjugation of the Cuicatlán Cañada and the transformation of this previously autonomous region into a frontier region of the expanding Monte Albán state.

The Structure of a Frontier Region

Faced with the task of analyzing the spatial organization of Zapotec imperial control in the Cañada, I find it useful to adopt an analytical framework similar to the one proposed by Owen Lattimore in his study of imperial China and its expanding frontiers (Lattimore 1962). Lattimore contrasts China's southern expansion and its incorporation of groups practicing intensive agriculture there with the radically different Great Wall frontier created on the northern steppe where pastoral nomads existed. He notes the significance of regional variability in economic potential for the implementation of various control policies and for the formation of different kinds of frontiers. Frontiers can be compared according to

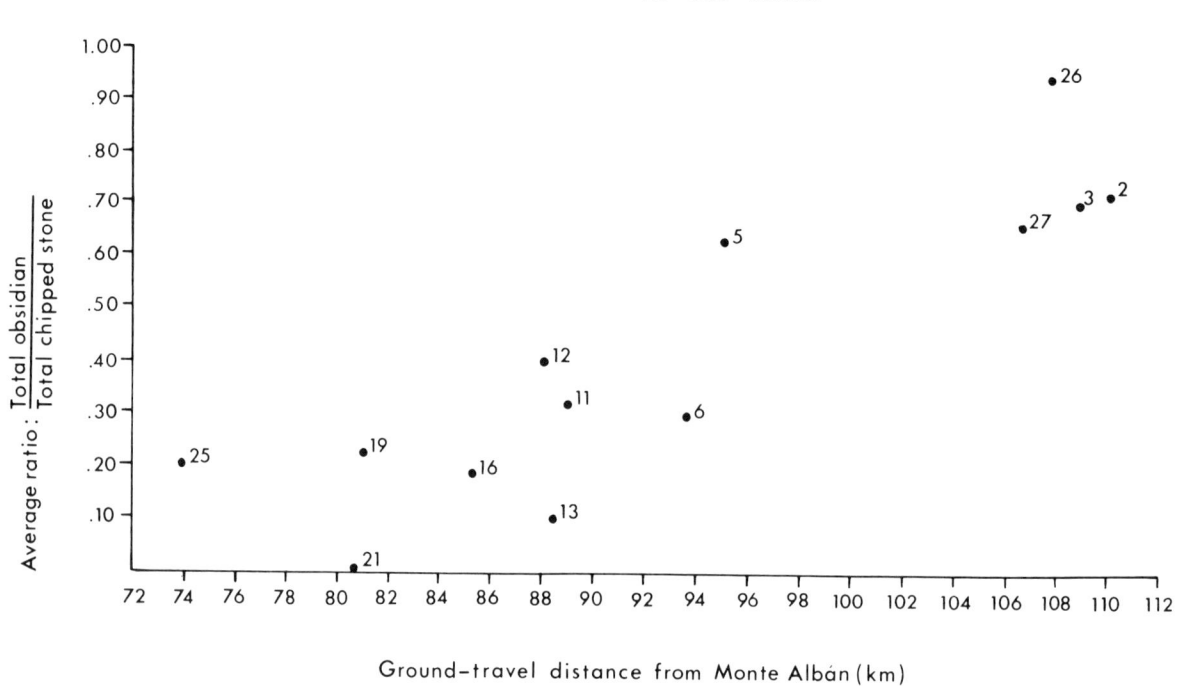

Figure 38. Scatter plot of obsidian at 13 Lomas phase settlements and distance from Monte Albán.

... their differences of latitude, terrain, climate, vegetation, and animal life. From the point of view of sociology and the evolution of institutions they can be described in terms of the alternative processes through which a society either continues a trend of development on which it is already launched, intensifying and sophisticating its characteristics but not changing them in kind, or diverges to a trend that will result in creating a different kind of society. [Lattimore 1962:477]

These differences stemming from a subjugated region's environment, economic potential and existing sociopolitical organization, form the specific preconditions of conquest and have a significant bearing upon the nature of imperial control there.

The terms of Lattimore's model are the geographic ranges of three different kinds of control: (1) unification by military action; (2) centralization under civil administration; and (3) economic integration by means of incorporation into the state market system (Lattimore 1962:480). In this model the range of military action is greater than that of civil administration, which is in turn greater than the range of incorporation into the state market system; the geographic ranges of military, civil, and economic control can be conceived as forming concentric rings of control policy (Fig. 39).

Table 15. Distribution of Chipped Stone*
at 13 Lomas Phase Settlements

Alluvial Fan	Site Number	Surface Collections†	Average Ratios		
			Obsidian	Chert	Quartz
Quiotepec	Cs2-L	5	.72	.26	.01
	Cs3-L	19	.70	.28	.02
	Cs26-L	2	.94	.05	0
	Cs27-L	7	.66	.34	0
Cuicatlán	Cs5-L	3	.63	.37	0
	Cs6-L	4	.30	.49	.17
	Cs11-L	2	.32	.60	.07
	Cs12-L	1	.40	.60	0
	Cs13-L	8	.11	.66	.22
El Chilar	Cs16-L	4	.19	.43	.38
	Cs19-L	3	.23	.48	.29
	Cs21-L	1	0	0	1.00
Dominguillo	Cs25-L	6	.21	.69	.10

†Those surface collections yielding Lomas phase ceramics, including those having a light amount of Trujano phase ceramics, were selected for this analysis (see Chapter 2).
*Chipped Stone ratios = Total Obsidian/Total Chipped Stone, Total Chert/Total Chipped Stone, and Total Quartz/Total Chipped Stone.

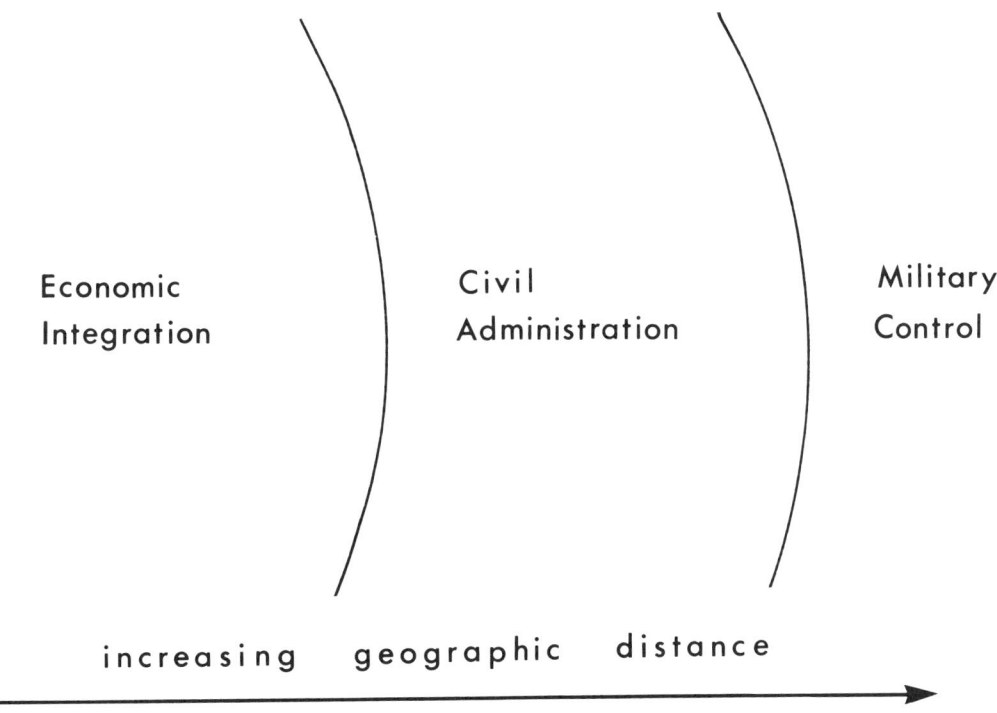

Figure 39. Lattimore's model for the structure of a frontier region.

In this dynamic view of frontier expansion, the military range of imperial control reaches over regions that could, after conquest, be added to the state. Beyond this range military action consists of occasional raids for plunder in outlying territories that cannot be successfully annexed. Within the zone of civil administration, the solidarity of the state is maintained by establishing uniform and duplicate administrative units in each of the conquered regions. In the case of China's northern frontier,

> at which an attempt was made to exclude the barbarians, was also the limit beyond which uniform blocks of cultivated territory with a uniform complement of cities and administrative services could not be added to the state; the limit within which a standardized tribute largely in kind and not costing too much in transport could be gathered by the state and beyond which trade was essentially centrifugal, draining the state of more than it brought in. [Lattimore 1962:487]

Thus, a frontier established on the outer limit of a subjugated region should feature a distinctive military presence. Moreover, the frontier should emerge at the limit within which a standardized tribute can be exacted and beyond which the effort required to subjugate and control outlying territories would far outweigh the expected return in tribute collection.

Lattimore's model for the structure of a state's expanding frontiers can be readily applied to the study of other cases of imperial expansion. Adams (1974) draws upon Lattimore's work in his study of certain ecological and historical processes in ancient Mesopotamia and claims:

> His work invites attention to the ecological processes that have set the boundaries for other great long-lived civilizations, and to the relationship of these boundaries to internal processes of growth and dissolution. [Adams 1974:1]

Returning to the case at hand, the Cuicatlán Cañada's transformation into a frontier region of the Monte Albán state between the Perdido and Lomas phases, we realize that: (1) we cannot fully understand the frontier region without placing it in the context of the larger expanding polity, i.e., the Monte Albán state; and (2) in this frontier region we are probably dealing with the outer ranges of

Plate 13. General view of the Quiotepec alluvial fan, facing north. The Río Grande flows northward and bends eastward toward its junction with the Río Salado at the right edge of the photograph. Immediately north of the Río Grande rises the mountain ridge that constitutes the northern boundary of the Cuicatlán Cañada.

Figure 40. Quiotepec glyph in the Codex Fernando Leal (redrawn from Hunt 1972:181).

Zapotec military control and civil administration. The inner range of economic integration, defined by Lattimore (1962:480) as the zone within which the state market system serves to transport bulk goods (especially food) regularly, would likely be confined to the Oaxaca Valley.

In keeping with Lattimore's framework, I will begin my discussion of the Cañada's transformation into a frontier region of the Monte Albán state by examining the ranges of Zapotec military control and civil administration in the Cuicatlán Cañada during the Lomas phase. I will describe the outer range of Zapotec military control on the region's northern Quiotepec boundary and the inner-lying zone under civil administration in the central and southern Cañada. I will then turn to the question of how the Monte Albán state might have interacted with polities beyond its frontier.

The Quiotepec Frontier

Above the junction of the Río Salado and the Río Grande rises a mountain ridge that forms the northern boundary of the Cuicatlán Cañada. Only a narrow pass through the mountain ridge permits entry into the region from the north. The place glyph for Quiotepec—"hill of the *quiote* (agave shoots)"—in the Codex Fernando Leal (Fig. 40) depicts this mountain ridge, which is notable for its impressive ridgetop towering above the river junction. The mountain ridge encloses the Cañada's northernmost alluvial fan, named for the present-day community of Santiago Quiotepec that occupies it (Pl. 13). Compared to the other three alluvial fans of the central and southern Cañada, the Quiotepec alluvial fan is small and remote.

We have seen how during the Lomas phase the Quiotepec area witnessed an enormous settlement expansion that included the construction of fortifications above the crucial pass through the mountain ridge. Moreover, during the Lomas phase the physical boundary of the Cañada here at Quiotepec also delimited some sort of "cultural" boundary, since the Quiotepec settlements marked the northern extent of both Cañada and Monte Albán ceramics. In light of these developments I have proposed that during the Lomas phase the Quiotepec alluvial fan became the northern frontier of the expanding Monte Albán state. We must now examine the settlement components at the frontier and begin to glean the range of activities, personnel, and organization associated with this northern outpost of the Monte Albán state.

The Frontispiece is a bird's-eye reconstruction of the Quiotepec frontier with its seven settlement components. The site of Paso de Quiotepec (Cs3-L) covers both the east and west sides of the natural pass leading through the Quiotepec mountain ridge, and extends over an area of 14.67 ha (Pl. 14,

Plate 14. View of the Quiotepec alluvium and of the natural pass through the Quiotepec mountain ridge, facing north. The site of Paso de Quiotepec (Cs3) straddles the pass. The isolated lookout post (Cs74) sits atop the ridge rising immediately west above the pass.

Fig. 41). Two defensive walls (3-5 m wide and 1.5-3.0 m tall), built of masonry and connected by ramps, protect the more gradual eastern slope above the pass; a single opening between the defensive walls serves to restrict access to this area of the site, especially to its sunken central plaza.

Bordering the south side of the plaza is an I-shaped ballcourt, 75 m long and oriented N 47° E. On the west side rises a 6-m-high platform mound that supports a series of structures arranged on three sides of an open courtyard; this pattern is repeated once again in smaller dimensions atop the 3-m-high mound bordering the west side of this elevated courtyard. South of the plaza and ballcourt lie the remains of 4 to 5 low mound groups consisting of small housemounds arranged around central courtyards. A 4-m-high mound rises at the east end of this broad terrace.

The remainder of Cs3-L consists of numerous housemounds; they are scattered for almost 400 m along the edge of the river bluff east of the pass, as well as along a series of terraces ascending the steep ridgetop flanking the pass on the east. Only a single broad terrace—located at the northern and highest point of this steep ridgetop—might have held a non-residential function, as it is substantially larger than the other terraces, and it offers an excellent view of the Río Salado and the southern Tehuacán Valley.

Above the pass to the west rises another ridge, which is also terraced and dotted with numerous housemounds. In all, we located and mapped 210-225 housemounds at Cs3-L, located on both sides of the mountain pass. If we use the estimate of 5 persons per house (Kirkby 1973:127; Spencer 1979), our population estimate for this site is between 1050 and 1125 persons. A separate population estimate based solely on hectares of settlement is also listed in Table 16.

Paso de Quiotepec's strategic location overlooking both sides of the crucial mountain pass as well as its defensive walls suggest that one of its functions was to control this single entry point into the Cañada from the north. The broad terrace on the northern and highest point of the settlement overlooking the pass might also have served as a lookout post. The settlement contains both a civic-ceremonial sector centered upon the ballcourt and an extensive residential sector spanning both sides of the pass. This differentiation of Cs3-L into public and residential sectors on the basis of architectural remains is supported by the distribution of ground stone tools (manos, metates), which are usually associated with domestic activities (Table 17). Only one ground stone artifact was recorded in the civic-ceremonial sector of Cs3-L, in surface collection square Cs3/191, which is associated with a probable elite residence atop the mound platform immediately west of the plaza, whereas a total of seven ground stone artifacts were noted in the surface collections associated with the housemounds and residential terraces forming the site's residential sector.

High above the mountain pass and the western portion of Cs3-L lies an isolated plaza (30x15 m) with a single 10-12-m-high mound at its western edge (Cs74-L) (Pl. 14). Unfortunately, pottery at Cs74-L was extremely sparse and non-diagnostic. A trail connects the Lomas phase settlement down on the lower slope of the ridge west of the pass (Cs3-L) with this isolated plaza, and for this reason, I would venture to guess that the two settlements were contemporaneous. Like the broad terrace of Cs3-L located at the northern end of the steep ridgetop rising across the pass to the east, this plaza with its pyramidal mound provides an excellent view to the north beyond the frontier extending towards the southern Tehuacán Valley; I believe that Cs74-L probably functioned as a lookout post or watchtower guarding the Quiotepec frontier.

On the highest point of the mountain ridge rising immediately west of the river junction lies the hilltop fort known as Cerro de Quiotepec (Cs2) (Pl. 15). Constantine Rickards visited the Quiotepec area in the mid-1920s, and his report includes a brief description and some photographs of Cs2 and of the Postclassic site (Cs71) located on a lower western arm of the ridge (Rickards 1926). Rickards' visit to Cerro de Quiotepec was followed by that of Martín Bazán, who conducted an archaeological reconnaissance of the mountain ridge and contributed the first map of the site (Bazán 1928; Fig. 42, this volume). But most of the information we had about Cerro de Quiotepec prior to our survey came from Eduardo Pareyón, who directed one short season of tomb salvage and preliminary excavations at both the Classic and Postclassic period sites here in 1957 (Pareyón 1960).

Our map of the fortified settlement on the highest point of the Quiotepec mountain ridge is presented in Figure 43. Two large plazas occupy the highest artificially-raised terrace here, supported by well-preserved masonry retaining walls along their eastern faces and enclosed by mound platforms of stag-

94 A FUEGO Y SANGRE

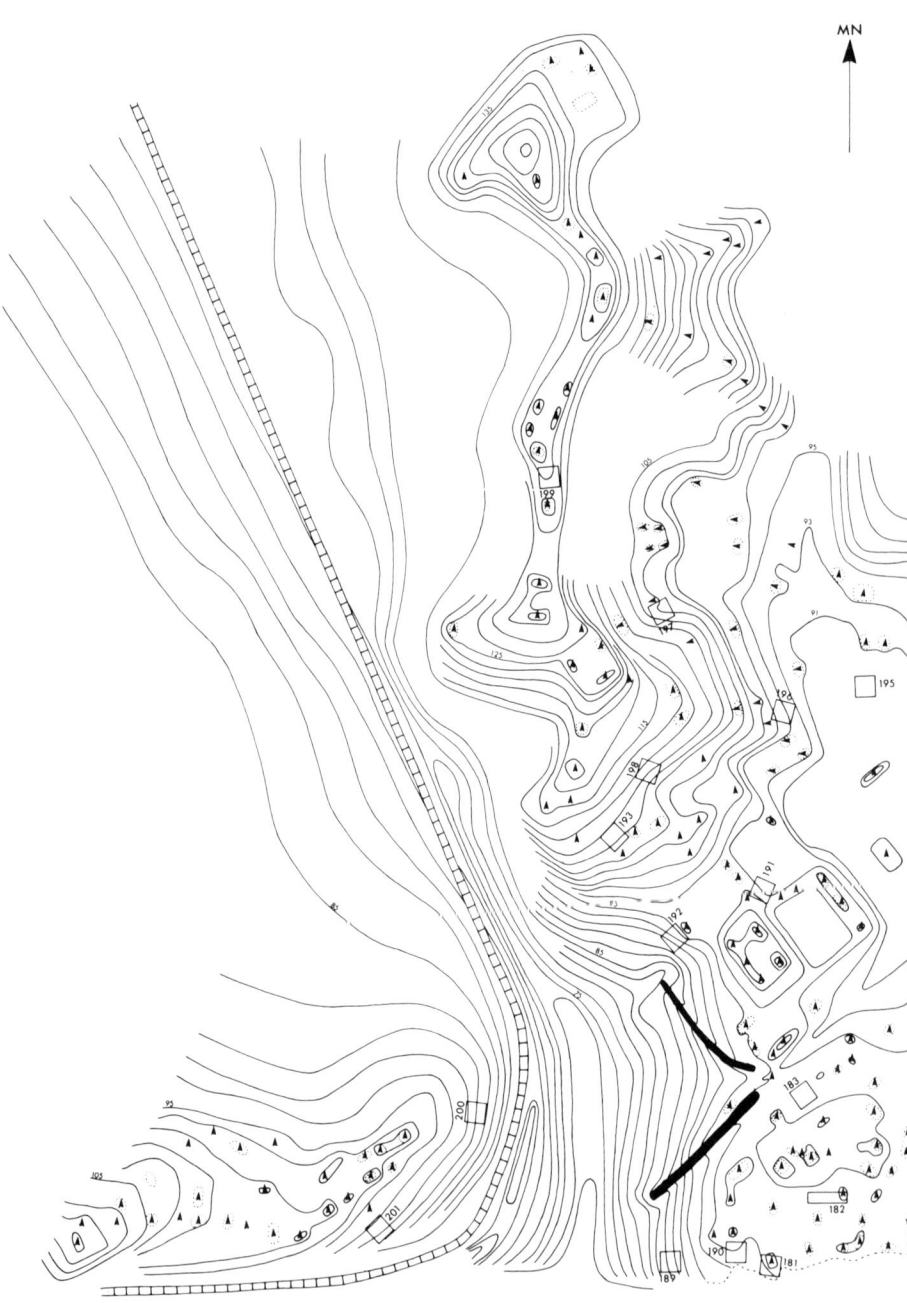

Figure 41. Paso de Quiotepec site map (Cs3).

PASO DE QUIOTEPEC
Cs 3

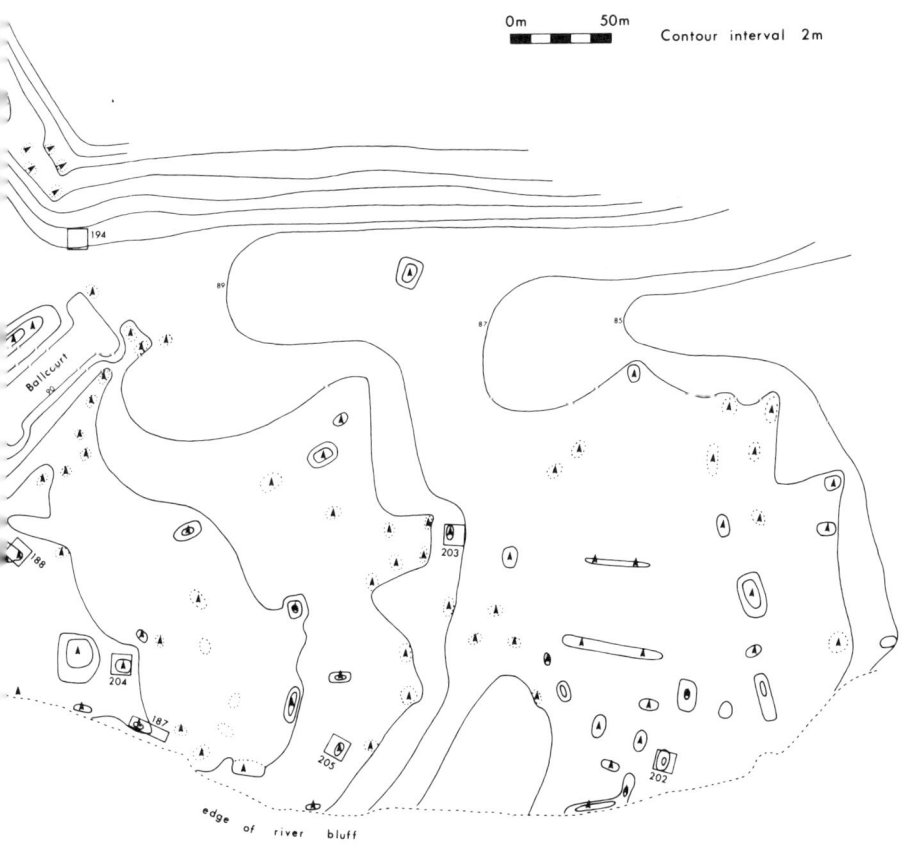

Table 16. Estimators of Population at Lomas Phase Settlements in the Quiotepec Area

Site	Size (ha)	Population Estimate @ 10-25 Persons per Hectare	Number of Housemounds	Population Estimate @ 5 Persons per House
Cs2-L	4.55	45-114	30	150
Cs3-L	14.67	147-367	210-225	1050-1125
Cs74-L	0.13	1-3	0	0
Cs26-L	15.80	158-395	0	0
Cs28	3.85	38-96	40-45	200-225
Cs27-L	4.79	48-120	90	450
Cs29	0.55	5-14	18-20	90-100
Totals	44.34	443-1108	338-410	1940-2050

gering dimensions (see Pls. 16-17). The northern plaza is dominated on its north side by a mound platform measuring 60x55 m at its base and rising 8 m above the plaza floor. On its surface once stood an elaborate residence or palace consisting of several raised masonry structures arranged around an interior patio. Another massive mound platform separates the two plazas; it is 64 m long, 21 m wide, and rises 7 m above the northern plaza floor (Fig. 43). It, too, supported a multi-chambered structure. Three narrow ramps or staircases allow entry to the two adjoining plazas from the east. Along the sheer western slope of the ridge below these two plazas extend fortifications built of cut stone slabs and mortar (Pl. 18).

East of the two plazas on the next terrace below extends a 65-m-long, I-shaped ballcourt, which is oriented N 10°E. In the middle and at the ends of the ballcourt floor we located eight stone monuments and one river boulder, which might have functioned as ballcourt markers. They appear not to have been carved, only covered with stucco and possibly painted (Pl. 19). A 5-m-high platform north of the ballcourt supports a series of structures arranged around a sunken interior patio.

These two artificially-raised terraces, with their large plazas, massive mound platforms, multi-chambered structures and ballcourt, constitute the public sector of Cs2 during the Lomas phase (Pl. 16). On the terrace below the 12-m-high retaining wall east of the ballcourt are numerous housemounds, one of which features a looted tomb that was salvaged by Pareyón (1960:98, 101-102), and which I will describe later in this chapter. An arm of the ridge that projects in a northeasterly direction below the northern plaza, where four residential terraces descend the arm in a stepped fashion, was also occupied during the Lomas phase. Farther down the arm we mapped five small, scattered residential terraces, which also might have been occupied at this time. The southeastern arm of Cerro de Quiotepec, however, appears not to have been occupied during the Lomas phase. Thus, the Lomas phase occupation at Cs2 extends over approximately 4.55 ha, an area within which we counted a total of 30 housemounds; the resulting population estimate for Cs2-L is therefore 150 persons (Table 16). All the ground stone implements found at Cerro de Quiotepec were associated with these housemounds in the residential sector (Table 17).

Cerro de Quiotepec apparently consisted of an isolated, walled precinct containing two large plazas, impressive mound platforms, a ballcourt, and approximately 30 residences. Entry to this hilltop fortress was limited to a single narrow gateway piercing the stone fortifications at the southwestern corner of the ridge; a small pillar-shaped masonry structure that stands beside the gateway probably functioned as a guardhouse (Pl. 20).

Cerro de Quiotepec shares a number of features with Guiengola, a Zapotec fortress dating to the Postclassic period. Guiengola is situated on the top of a mountain ridge overlooking the Tehuantepec River, which forms the major communication route to the Isthmus of Tehuantepec from the Valley of Oaxaca (Peterson and MacDougall 1974). Fray Francisco de Burgoa described this fortress in his account of the Zapotec campaign against the Mex-

Table 17. Distribution of Ground Stone Tools*
at Lomas Phase Settlements in the Quiotepec Area

Site	Site Sector	
	Civic-Ceremonial	Residential
Cs2-L	0	3
Cs3-L	1	7
Cs26-L	0	0
Cs27-L	0	2

*Counts of ground stone artifacts from surface collection squares.

Plate 15. Distant view of Cerro de Quiotepec (Cs2), from where the natural pass meets the Río Grande, facing northeast.

ican armies in Tehuantepec. It was from this hilltop fortress that the Zapotec armies silently descended upon the unsuspecting Mexican troops who were marching through the mountain pass below (Burgoa 1674a:394, 1674b:340). Like Guiengola, Cerro de Quiotepec is strategically situated on a mountaintop overlooking a major communication route.

The site of Guiengola is contained within a series of defensive walls, 1.5 m thick and 3 m high, and sometimes aligned parallel to one another; only two openings in the fortifications permit entry to the site. Similar to Cerro de Quiotepec, Guiengola has two plazas surrounded by massive mound platforms, one 7 m high and another 9 m high, which support multi-chambered structures. The civic-ceremonial sector of Guiengola also features an I-shaped ballcourt, in which Peterson reports finding a smoothed spheroid stone (Peterson and Mac-Dougall 1974:10-23). These structures are constructed from stacked limestone blocks and clay mortar faced with stucco.

A final point of resemblance between the two hilltop fortresses is the relatively small resident population represented at both sites. According to Peterson, the residential sector at Guiengola consisted of only 41 rooms arranged around 11 patios; he also notes a corresponding paucity of domestic refuse here. If we assign 5 persons to each room—which admittedly results in a higher estimate than that for a structure—the resulting population estimate of 205 persons for the "Elite Residential Area" of Guiengola is not much higher than the resident population estimated for Cerro de Quiotepec (see Table 16). Nevertheless, the population of both these fortified sites could easily have swelled during times of war. As Peterson suggests for Guiengola, Cerro de Quiotepec could have served as a temporary place of refuge for a large number of people (Peterson and MacDougall 1974:51).

The site of Campo del Panteón (Cs26-L) is situated on a high alluvial terrace flanking the Río Grande, directly south of the natural pass cutting through the Quiotepec mountain ridge, and across a perennial ford on the river (Pl. 21). A large plaza measuring approximately 200 m on a side is delimited on its eastern and southern ends by two elon-

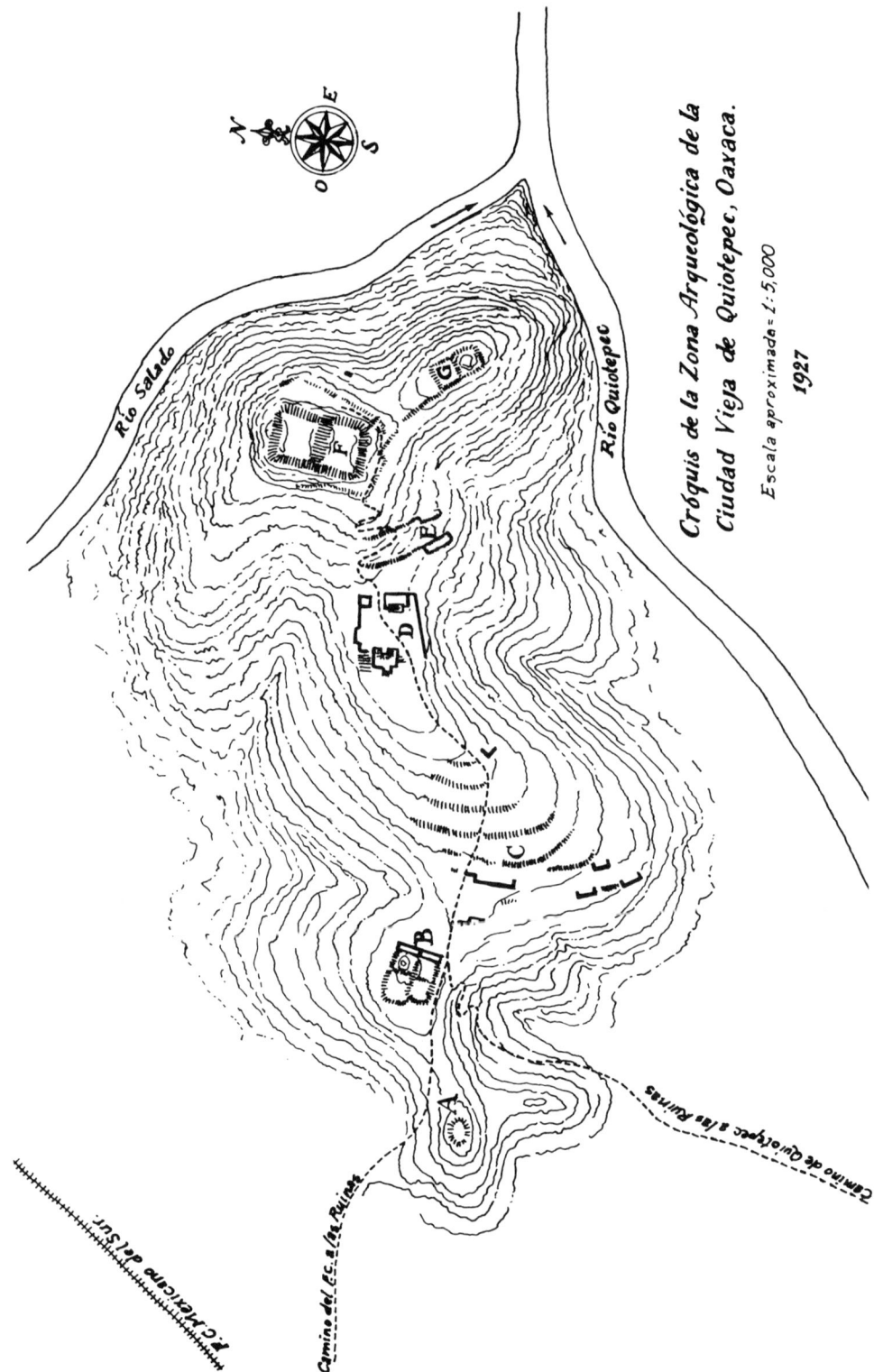

Figure 42. Martín Bazán's map of La Ciudad Vieja de Quiotepec (redrawn from Bazán 1928:120). The hilltop fort of Cerro de Quiotepec (Cs2) corresponds to groups F and G on his map.

Plate 16. View of the public sector of Cerro de Quiotepec (Cs2), facing northwest, with its massive mound platforms and well-preserved masonry retaining walls.

gated mounds, 6 m high (Fig. 44, Pl. 22). Another elongated mound forms the western border of the plaza. In the center of this vast plaza are two mounds: one measures 88x20 m at its base and is 4 m high, while the other mound measures 40x25 m and rises 7 m above the plaza floor. All these mound platforms have the masonry foundations of structures along their surfaces.

Any traveler entering the Quiotepec area from the north would have journeyed through the mountain pass, forded the Río Grande, and entered this plaza. Two ramps or staircases located at the southeast corner of the plaza would have led the traveler out of the plaza and on south. The position of this grand plaza with its large-scale buildings opposite the single entry point to the Quiotepec frontier suggests that it might have functioned to regulate the flow of traffic into and out of the Cuicatlán Cañada during Monte Albán's hegemony.

The configuration of public buildings at Cs26-L extends over approximately 9.39 ha of the available high alluvium on the Quiotepec alluvial fan. Lomas phase occupation here extends south of the plaza over an area where unfortunately there are no architectural remains visible on the modern cultivated surface; therefore, the maximum area of the high alluvial terrace occupied by Cs26-L is 15.8 ha. In the absence of residential architecture here, only a rough population estimate can be generated for Cs26-L using its site size (see Table 16). Moreover, since the public building sector of Cs26-L extends over 9 ha and is devoid of any ground stone artifacts (Table 17), this estimate is probably a maximum one. It is possible that much of the manpower staffing this frontier facility actually resided at other settlements in the Quiotepec area.

The site of El Campanario (Cs27-L) spans the entire length of a piedmont ridge overlooking the Quiotepec alluvial fan from an upstream position south of the settlements at the mountain pass (see Frontispiece, Fig. 34). In contrast to those settlements, which we have seen either contain civic-ceremonial sectors with associated residential areas (Cs2-L, Cs3-L), or else consist solely of a civic-

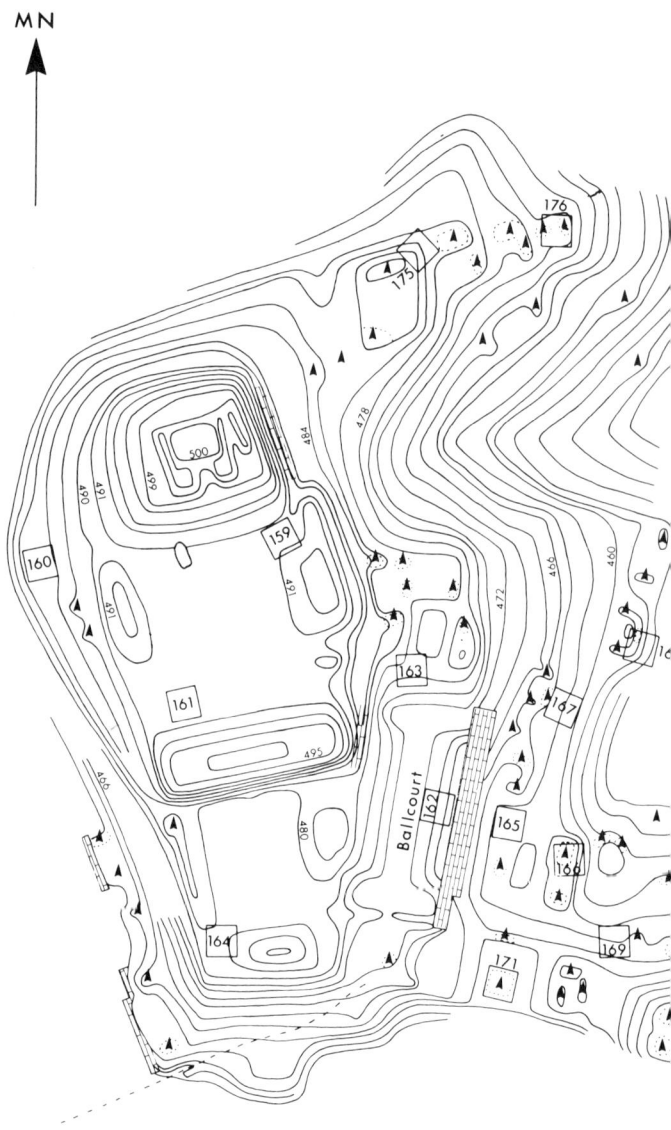

Figure 43. Cerro de Quiotepec site map (Cs2).

THE LOMAS PHASE

Plate 17. Cut stone slab and mortar retaining wall, 10 m high, at Cerro de Quiotepec (Cs2).

ceremonial sector (Cs26-L, Cs74-L), the site of El Campanario is comprised principally of residences that occupy the string of terraces descending the ridge, covering a total area of 4.79 ha (Fig. 45). There are only three terraces that might have supported structures other than residences, and they are not concentrated in any one part of the site. The terrace occupying the summit of the ridge has two long and narrow mounds (33x2 m; 43x2 m) flanking its eastern side and two accompanying structures perpendicular to them. At a saddle in the ridge below lies a broad terrace with a 2-m-high mound rising along its eastern end. Another isolated mound is situated at the southernmost foot of the ridge, bordering the east side of a small terrace.

Otherwise, Cs27-L appears to have consisted of 45-48 residential terraces. A total of 90 housemounds are evident on the terraced slope of Cs27-L, some of which are arranged around interior courtyards. The distribution of ground stone tools recorded at the site is consistent with this interpretation, since all the ground stone was associated

Plate 18. View of stone fortifications along sheer western slope of Cerro de Quiotepec (Cs2), facing northeast.

with housemounds (Table 17). At 5 persons per house, the resulting population estimate for Cs27-L is 450 persons (Table 16).

On another piedmont ridge across the Río Grande to the west extends a 3.85 ha settlement whose configuration is similar to that seen at the site of El Campanario. The site of La Hacienda (Cs28) has only two candidates for public buildings: a 2-m-high mound located on the ridgetop and another 2-m-high mound situated on the lower broad piedmont slope traversed by the railroad.

Fifteen terraces descend the east slope of the ridge down to the broad terrace cut by the railroad. Approximately 25 housemounds dot the lower piedmont slope and extend east and south across the railroad tracks (see Fig. 34, Frontispiece). In all we counted 40-45 housemounds at Cs28; the resulting population estimate for this settlement is between 200-225 persons (Table 16).

The site designated La Estación (Cs29) is the final Lomas phase settlement component of the Quiotepec frontier. Located on a piedmont spur directly south across a barranca from the ridge occupied by Cs27 (see Fig. 34), the site of Cs29 covers .55 ha. Along with Cs27-L and Cs28, this site constitutes another settlement located upstream from the critical mountain pass, and appears to have consisted mainly of residences. Only a single low and narrow mound measuring 50 m long, 6 m wide, and 1 m high on the highest point of the spur might have served in a non-residential capacity. Along the remainder of the piedmont spur we noted 18-20 housemounds. The population estimate for Cs29 therefore ranges between 90-100 persons (Table 16). The interpretation of Cs29 as a residential component of the Quiotepec frontier is supported by the occurrence of ground stone artifacts here, which were noted on the site report form filled out for Cs29.

These seven settlement components established at the Quiotepec frontier during the Lomas phase comprise both public and residential sectors. The four sites (Cs2-L, Cs3-L, Cs74-L, Cs26-L) that feature plazas, pyramidal mound groups, ballcourts, and stone fortifications all occupy strategic positions vis-à-vis the pass through the Quiotepec mountain

Plate 19. *Above and below*, stone monuments in the ballcourt at Cerro de Quiotepec (Cs2). Traces of stucco are evident on the upturned surface of the stone monument in the lower photograph.

Plate 20. Single entryway to Cerro de Quiotepec (Cs2), facing northeast. The pillar-shaped masonry structure was probably a guardhouse.

ridge. Farther upstream, and south of the pass lie three additional residential components (Cs27-L, Cs28, Cs29). The total area occupied by these Lomas phase settlements is 44.34 ha, which constitutes by far the largest concentration of settlement found on any of the Cañada's alluvial fans during this time period (Tables 11, 16). If we add the population estimates generated on the basis of the number of housemounds found at each of the settlement components in the Quiotepec area (Table 16), the estimated population in the Lomas phase ranges between 1940 and 2050 persons.

Immediately, a question comes to mind: How did this smallest of the region's alluvial fans support a population of this size? The Quiotepec alluvial fan includes 32.85 ha of low alluvium and 59.55 ha of high alluvium (see Table 3, Chapter 2). The figure for the high alluvium drops to 45.15 ha during the Lomas phase when the site area of Campo del Panteón (Cs26-L), located precisely on the high alluvium, is subtracted from that figure. If we follow the procedure outlined in Chapter 2 for estimating the carrying capacity of the Quiotepec alluvial fan in the Lomas phase, and add the estimates of the potential yearly maize yields rendered on the low and high alluvium respectively, the resulting carrying-capacity estimate for the Quiotepec alluvial fan during the Lomas phase is only 393 persons (Table 18). Because the corresponding population estimate generated for the Quiotepec frontier at this time is 1940-2050 persons (Table 16), there were over four times as many people residing at the Quiotepec frontier during the Lomas phase than could have been supported by farming the available alluvium.

A similar discrepancy between the size of the population residing at a frontier and the amount of available farmland apparently existed in the frontier region of another expanding state in Mesoamerica. The Central Quiché people began to expand outside the Quiché Basin of highland Guatemala beginning early in the A.D. 1400s (Fox 1978). An adjacent region that became incorporated into the Central Quiché state was the Río Negro Basin, a natural corridor bound on the north by the Sierra de Cuchumatanes, and home of the Sacapulas-Quiché. One of the settlements that Fox labels a regional

Plate 21. Aerial view of the natural pass through the Quiotepec mountain ridge, the ford on the Río Grande, and the site of Campo del Panteón (Cs26) on the Quiotepec alluvium, facing north. Trees line the site's large mounds. The site is named after the modern cemetery in the right foreground of the photograph.

capital of the Central Quiché state is situated at the eastern end of the Río Negro Basin, the most distant point from the pass leading to the Quiché Basin where the state capital of Utatlán was located. This site of Chutinamit-Sacapulas is strategically located on a steep ridge overlooking the narrow basin, and is contained within a series of defensive walls and a moat (Fox 1978:77-81).

In outlining the territorial organization of the imperial Central Quiché state, Fox generalizes about the locations of the regional capitals established in the tributary regions, and claims that most of these regional centers controlled fairly large tracts of good farmland, capable of supporting large numbers of non-food producers. The only exception, Fox notes, is the regional capital of the Río Negro Basin, Chutinamit-Sacapulas, which is not situated near a broad-based sustaining area (Fox 1978:301). I would propose that the site of Chutinamit, together with the neighboring fortified settlements of Chutixtiox and Xolpacol, became for a time the northern frontier of the Central Quiché

Table 18. Estimated Carrying Capacity of the Cañada's Alluvium during the Lomas Phase

Alluvial Fan	Low Alluvium		High Alluvium		Estimated Carrying Capacity
	Hectares	Annual Maize Yields (kg)	Hectares	Annual Maize Yields (kg)	
Quiotepec	32.85	45,859	45.15	32,689	393 persons
Cuicatlán	523.60	730,946	514.77	372,693	5518 persons
El Chilar	297.43	415,212	118.20	85,577	2504 persons
Dominguillo	142.65	199,139	59.20	42,861	1210 persons

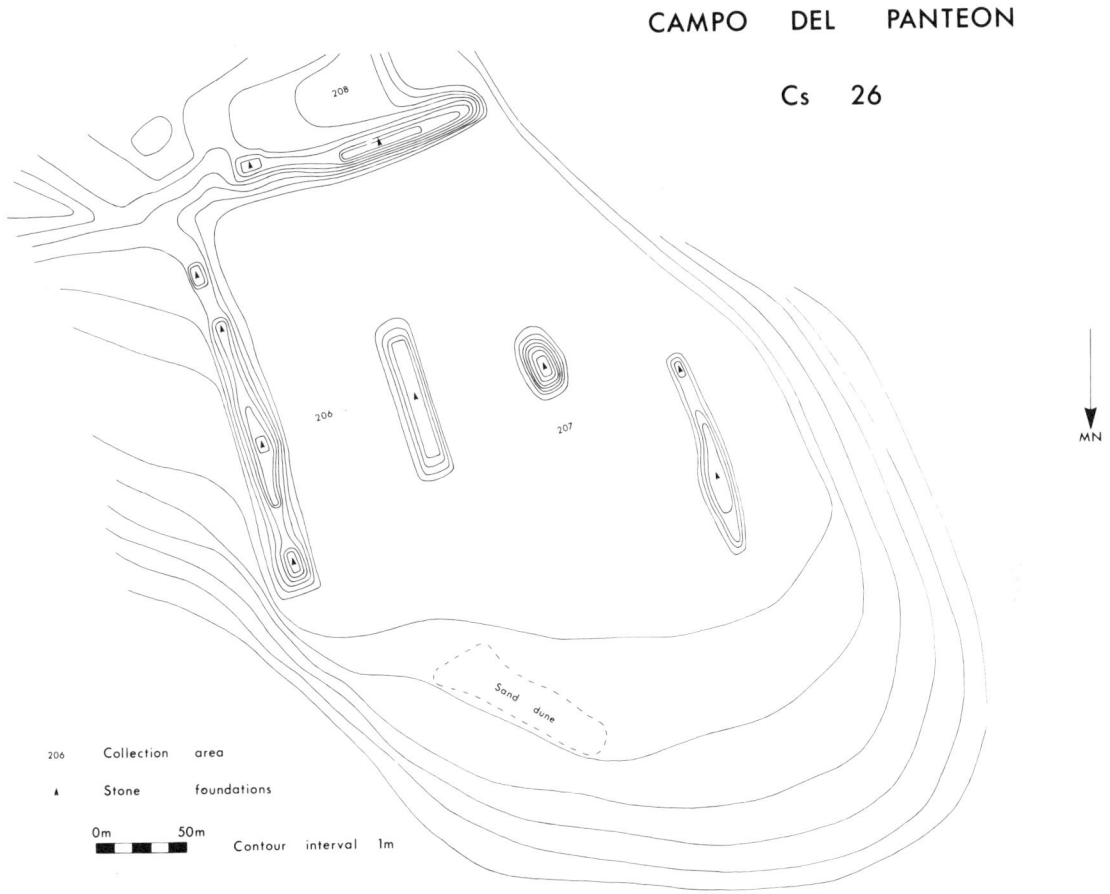

Figure 44. Campo del Panteón site map (Cs26).

state under firm military control; I suggest they were probably established and supported by the expanding state.

Settlements in frontier regions such as those at the eastern end of the Río Negro Basin controlled by the Central Quiché state, and those at the Quiotepec frontier of the Monte Albán state, must be viewed in a larger than local context in order to be understood properly, since non-local processes clearly contributed to their development and support. To quote from yet another study of intrusive imperial overlay in a subjugated region:

> The hand of the state is clearly evident in the character of the centers, as well as in their founding and rapid growth. [Morris 1972:393]

Military Control and Administration at the Quiotepec Frontier

The Quiotepec frontier of the Monte Albán state does appear to have been under Zapotec military control. We must now turn to the various functions of this military control represented at the Quiotepec frontier and consider their administrative implications. At least two major military functions are represented at the Quiotepec frontier: (1) to define and guard the frontier in order to provide a "protective umbrella" (Rowlands 1972:457) for the social and economic developments taking place behind it in the zone under civil administration; and (2) to regulate the flow of traffic in and out of the state's borders.

Plate 22. Two views of the large plaza at Campo del Panteón (Cs26), facing south. *Above*, elongated mound, 6 m high, bordering east side of the plaza. *Below*, the entire length of plaza, with trees lining the mounds along its eastern and southern borders, and a 4-m-high elongated mound to the right.

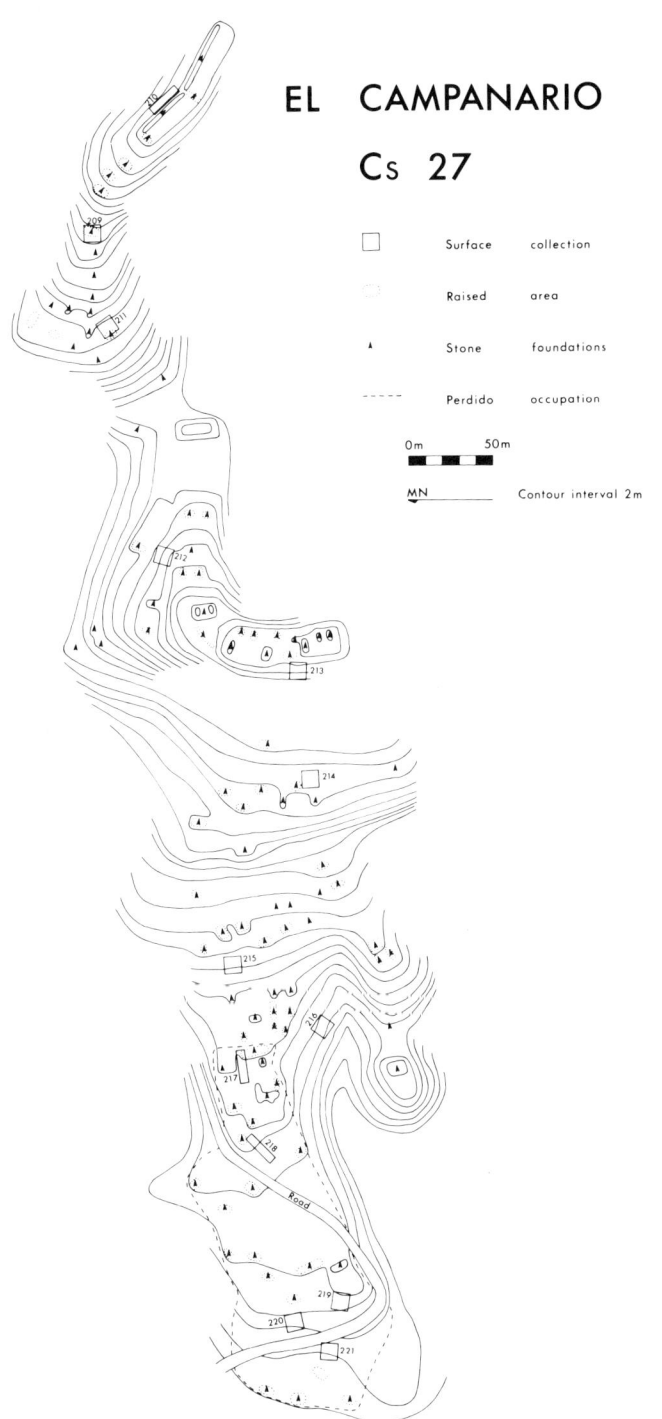

Figure 45. El Campanario site map (Cs27).

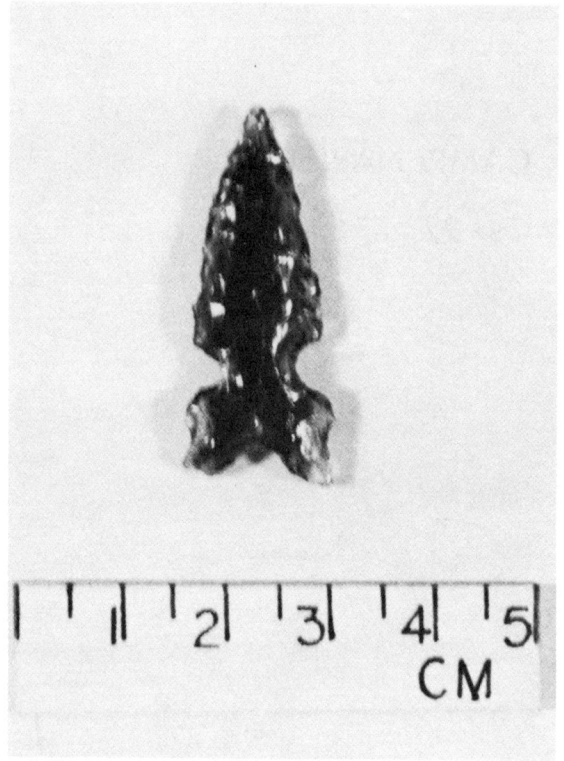 

Plate 23. Stone projectile points found at settlements on the Quiotepec frontier. *Left*, obsidian projectile point (Cs3/068). *Right*, chert projectile point (Cs2/169).

Table 19. Distribution of Projectile Points in the Survey Area during the Lomas Phase

Alluvial Fan	Site	Material	
		Obsidian	Chert
Tecomavaca	Cs1-L	1	0
Quiotepec	Cs2-L	0	2
	Cs3-L	1	0
	Cs27-L	1	1
Cuicatlán	none		
El Chilar	Cs16-L	0	1
Dominguillo	none		

Consistent with what we know about Zapotec militaristic practices in frontier regions of the Zapotec state during the Postclassic period, settlements were erected in strategic positions guarding the mountain pass that leads into the Cuicatlán Cañada from the north. Three settlements are situated in strategic positions above the pass: Cs3-L, Cs74-L, and Cs2-L; moreover, two of these are enclosed by defensive walls. The hilltop fort of Cerro de Quiotepec (Cs2-L), which had a relatively small resident population, could have served as a temporary place of refuge if the frontier were ever to come under severe attack. Another defensive strategy involving long-distance sighting—perhaps even the monitoring of long-distance communication signals—is evident in the establishment of possible lookout posts on ridgetops here (Cs74-L, Cs3-L). Thus, guarding the single entry point to the region from behind fortifications, as well as long-range sighting from lookout posts, were among the likely functions of these settlements established by the Zapotec at the northern boundary of the Cuicatlán Cañada. If the number of housemounds found at these settlements reflects the manpower engaged in

Table 20. Distribution of Stone Labrets at Settlements in the Quiotepec Area

Site and Collection Square	Material	
	Travertine	Greenstone
Cs2/170	1	0
Cs2/173	1	0
Cs3/187	0	1

frontier defense, the size of the resident military arm at Quiotepec would have been approximately 1200-1275 persons (see Table 16).

The settlement on the Campo del Panteón (Cs26-L) probably served a different function from those overlooking the pass. Located on the Quiotepec alluvium directly opposite the southern terminus of the pass, Campo del Panteón occupies a strategic but indefensible position. Its 42,000 m² plaza bounded by monumental buildings would have received all the traffic entering the frontier region from the north through the mountain pass—as well as all the traffic exiting the Cuicatlán Cañada. I would suggest that this frontier facility functioned to regulate the flow of traffic across the Zapotec state's northern boundary in conjunction with the fortified settlements above the pass. The maximum number of people stationed here is estimated to have been between 158-395 persons (see Table 16). Similar military functions are attributed to the wall and fortifications established by Hadrian across the Solway-Tyne Isthmus along the northern frontier of Roman Britain in the second century A.D. The wall delimited the territory occupied by the Romans and controlled the movement of people into and out of the frontier region (Frere 1974:149-158).

What artifactual evidence do we have of the actual military personnel stationed at the Quiotepec frontier? The surface evidence is slim yet consistent with the model of Zapotec subjugation outlined in Chapter 2. One artifact type that can be associated with military activities is the stone projectile point, which formed the head of an arrow. Gorenstein's excavations at the Postclassic fortified hilltop site of Tepexi el Viejo in Puebla produced 33 stone projectile points, leading her to suggest that bows and arrows were used to repel attackers (Gorenstein 1973:55). Furthermore, we know that bows and arrows were among the weapons used in warfare by the sixteenth-century Zapotec (see Chapter 2). If we examine the distribution of projectile points in the Cuicatlán Cañada during the Lomas phase (Table 19), we discover that 5 out of 6 projectile points recovered in the Cuicatlán Cañada at this time come from settlements at Quiotepec (Pl. 23). Beyond the Quiotepec frontier we collected one projectile point at the contemporaneous site of Llano de los Mogotes (Cs1-L).

In addition to the weapons used by the military personnel at Quiotepec, we would expect to find evidence of the dress and sumptuary paraphernalia worn by the military orders. Our ethnohistorical sources tell us that Zapotec warriors who excelled in battle received awards and became entitled to many of the same privileges and sumptuary rules of dress enjoyed by the Zapotec elite. Furthermore, we know that *chosen* military captains and garrison troops—who presumably wore the badges of past military achievements—manned the forts established in those regions conquered by the Zapotec state (see Chapter 2).

One type of ornament known to have been awarded to brave warriors in Mesoamerican society was the lip-plug (labret) or the nose-plug. We know, for example, that one of the important moments in the history of the Mixtec hero named 8 Deer was the occasion when he delivered a prisoner of war and in return received a nose-plug, which signified that he had become a great lord or *tecuhtli* (Smith 1973:16). Gorenstein reports finding an obsidian lip-plug at Tepexi el Viejo, a site where the occurrence of other military artifacts and defensive features is unquestionable (Gorenstein 1973:6,59).

The only ornaments of this kind recovered anywhere in the Cuicatlán Cañada came from the two fortified settlements at Quiotepec (Table 20, Pl. 24): one greenstone labret was collected at Paso de Quiotepec (Cs3-L); two travertine labrets were found at Cerro de Quiotepec (Cs2-L), though admittedly in collection squares with many Trujano phase ceramics. Although not conclusive in and of itself, the distribution of these ornaments in the Cuicatlán Cañada during the period of Zapotec subjugation is consistent with the other evidence we have of military activities in the Quiotepec area at this time.

Aside from their military duties, the soldiers guarding the Quiotepec frontier might well have played the Mesoamerican ballgame. The only Lomas phase settlements in the Cuicatlán Cañada that have standard I-shaped ballcourts are Cerro de Quiotepec (Cs2-L) and Paso de Quiotepec (Cs3-L). At Cs3-L the 70-m-long ballcourt borders the main plaza, and the 65-m-long ballcourt at Cs2-L occupies the terrace directly below the two central plazas (see Figs. 41, 43).

In a study of the Mesoamerican ballgame, Borhegyi alludes to the connections between the ballgame and warfare (Borhegyi 1980). Borhegyi claims that formal I-shaped ballcourts were in use all over Mesoamerica by the proto-Classic period. Using illustrations of the ballgame rendered in Postclassic codices, Borhegyi finds a close associa-

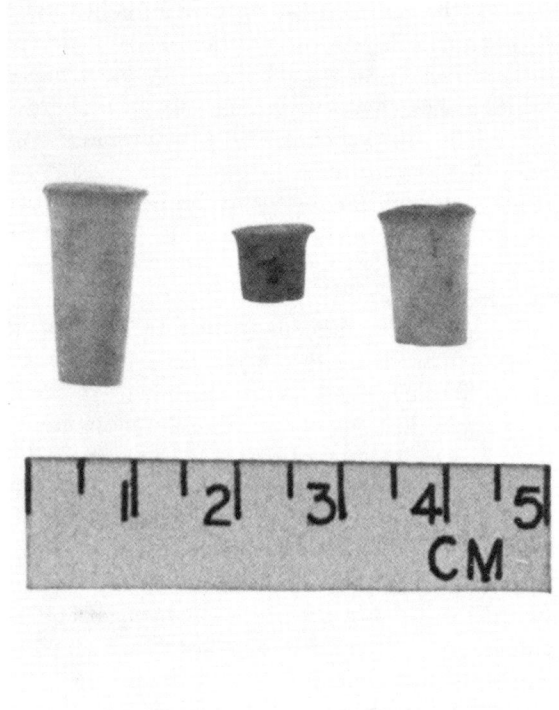

Plate 24. Stone labrets found at settlements on the Quiotepec frontier. *Left*, alabaster labret (Cs2/173). *Center*, greenstone labret fragment (Cs3/187). *Right*, alabaster labret fragment (Cs2/170).

tion between the military orders and the ballgame: "Opposing teams or single warriors dressed in full martial regalia are frequently shown in the courts playing a game (Codex Vindobonensis, p. 29)" (Borhegyi 1980:20).

We do not have to go far afield to find a society in which the ballgame was directly associated with the military organization. Gearing's study of the four recurrent structural poses assumed annually by the male population of an eighteenth-century Cherokee village (Gearing 1958, 1962) details the composition of the Cherokee organization for war. Winter was the season for warfare, when men—who at other times of the year acted simply as household heads, or as separate clan members—became organized for war under elected war officials who functioned separately from the village council. During other seasons of the year, the structural pose for war was resumed for the purpose of playing ballgames:

> Periodically, during the summer when warfare was rare, the young men joined together for ballplays with other villages. They assumed then a set of relations with one another, and with the village at large, which was analogous to the structure of the village for war. [Gearing 1962:27]

Thus the ballgame—referred to by the Cherokee as "the companion of battle"—was a summer substitute for warfare and was played by warriors. Not only did the ballplayers have war priests conjuring for their victory, but after the ballgames, they had to pass through purifying rites analogous to the rites they performed on their return from war (Gearing 1962:60-61).

Acknowledging this association between the ballgame and the military organization, I would argue that the ballcourts at the two fortified settlements guarding the Quiotepec frontier are yet another indication of the military presence there. If the ballgame was commonly played by young warriors, the fact that ballcourts are found *only* at settlements on the Quiotepec alluvial fan during the Lomas phase would be consistent with the concentration of Zapotec military strength at the northern boundary of the subjugated region.

If the Quiotepec frontier formed the outer range of Zapotec military control, we must examine the evidence of other activities and personnel here that formed an integral part in maintaining the frontier. A major activity occurring in the Quiotepec area during the Lomas phase involved the building of elaborate fortifications and monumental buildings. Nowhere else in the Cuicatlán Cañada at this time do we find such large-scale buildings and fortifications. It is likely that one of the functions of the nonmilitary personnel associated with the Quiotepec frontier was to provide the necessary manpower for building projects on a scale "that only a state could build" (Sanders 1974:109). Providing labor for state building projects, of course, is a common form of tribute exacted in regions subjugated by expanding states (Morris 1972:398-400); Sanders and Price 1968:166).

We have artifactual evidence of specialized craft activities in the Quiotepec area during the Lomas phase. Two craft-related artifacts that are found only

Table 21. **Distribution of Craft-Related Artifacts at Settlements in the Quiotepec Area**

Site	Spindle Whorls	Notched Stones	Adzes, Celts
Cs2-L	2	0	1
Cs3-L	0	0	1
Cs26-L	0	0	0
Cs27-L	1	2	3

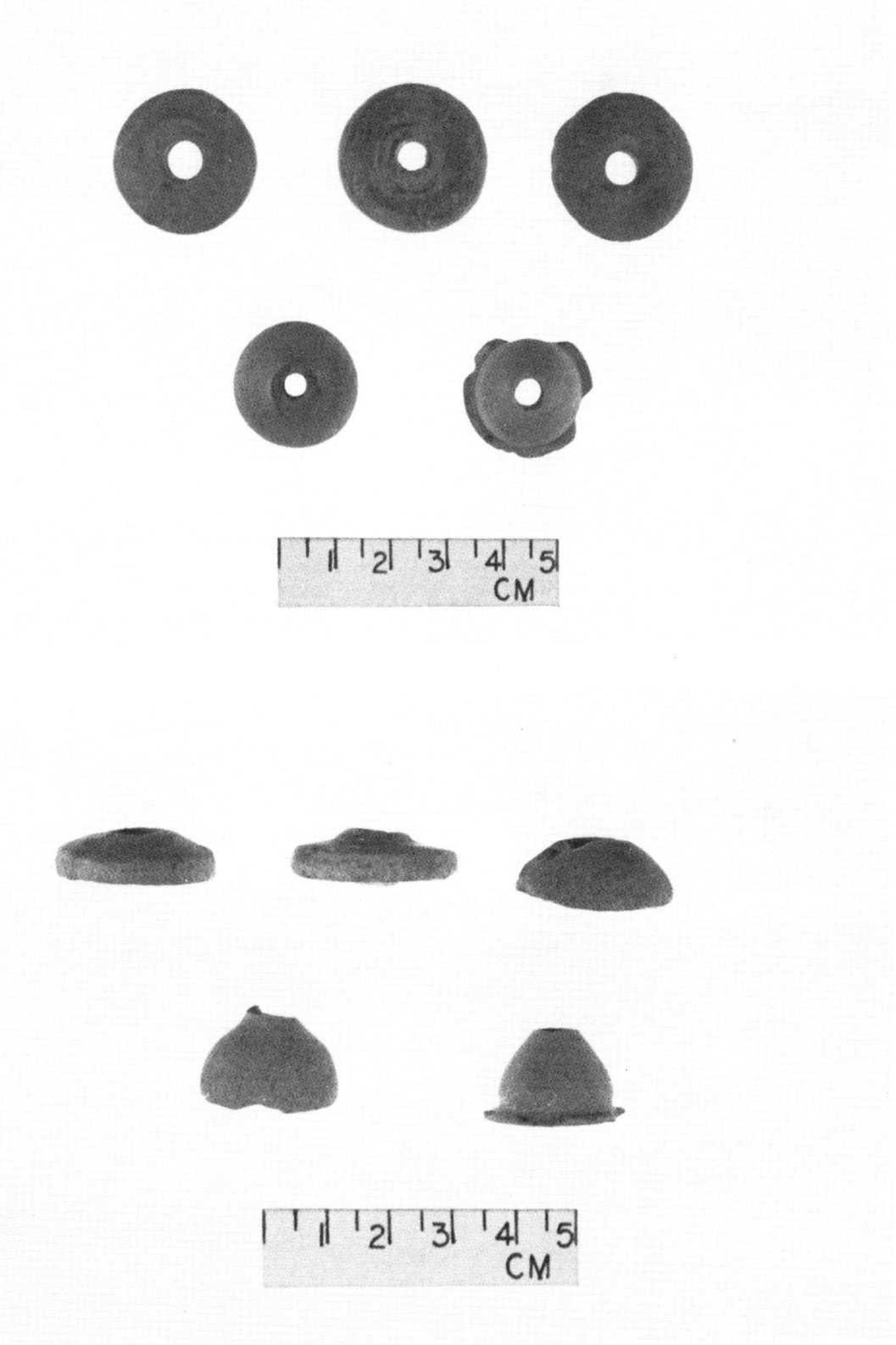

Plate 25. Clay spindle whorls found at settlements on the Quiotepec alluvial fan. Top row: left (Cs2/172), center (Cs27/210), right Cs2/177). Bottom row: left (Cs71/178), right (Cs71/178). *Above*, plan view. *Below*, profile view.

Table 22. Dimensions of Clay Spindle Whorls Recovered from the Cuicatlán Cañada Survey

Provenience	Overall Diameter (mm)	Hole Diameter (mm)	Weight (g)	Proportion of Whole Whorl	Estimated Total Weight (g)
Cs6/017	24	4.0	4.0	.80	5.0
Cs3/069	13	3.5	2.0	.80	2.5
Cs2/172	25	7.0	4.1	1.00	4.1
Cs2/177	25	5.0	5.8	1.00	5.8
Cs71/178	23	4.0	4.8	.90	5.3
Cs71/178	21	4.0	5.5	1.00	5.5
Cs27/210	26	5.0	5.4	1.00	5.4
Cs14/280	26	4.0	5.7	1.00	5.7
Cs8/290	28	5.0	2.2	.45	4.9

at settlements in the Quiotepec area during the Lomas phase are spindle whorls and notched stones (Table 21). In a study of the spindle whorls recovered from the Teotihuacán Valley, Mary Parsons (1972) was able to differentiate between those spindle whorls used for spinning maguey fiber and those used for spinning cotton fiber. The larger whorls were used for spinning maguey fiber and range in overall diameter between 35-73 mm, with hole diameters between 5.5 and 14.5 mm; the smaller whorls used for spinning cotton fiber range between 15-31 mm in diameter, with hole diameters between 1.5-6.5 mm. Using Parsons' criteria, the spindle whorls found at two settlements in the Quiotepec area (see Pl. 25) were probably used for spinning cotton (Parsons 1972:61-62). For that matter, *all* of the spindle whorls recovered during our survey of the Cuicatlán Cañada exhibit the smaller dimensions of whorls used to spin cotton fiber (see Table 22).

Two notched stones were collected at the Lomas phase settlement of El Campanario (Cs27-L) (Pl. 26). Although the function of these stones is not certain, Morris reports finding a similar artifact at the Inca administrative center of Huánuco Pampa. In a compound of residence-workshops Morris excavated over 200 spindle whorls and more than 100 other artifacts that he considered to be related to the production of textiles; among the artifacts were rectangular notched stones, which Morris suggests were used for spacing threads in looms (Morris 1974:53-55).

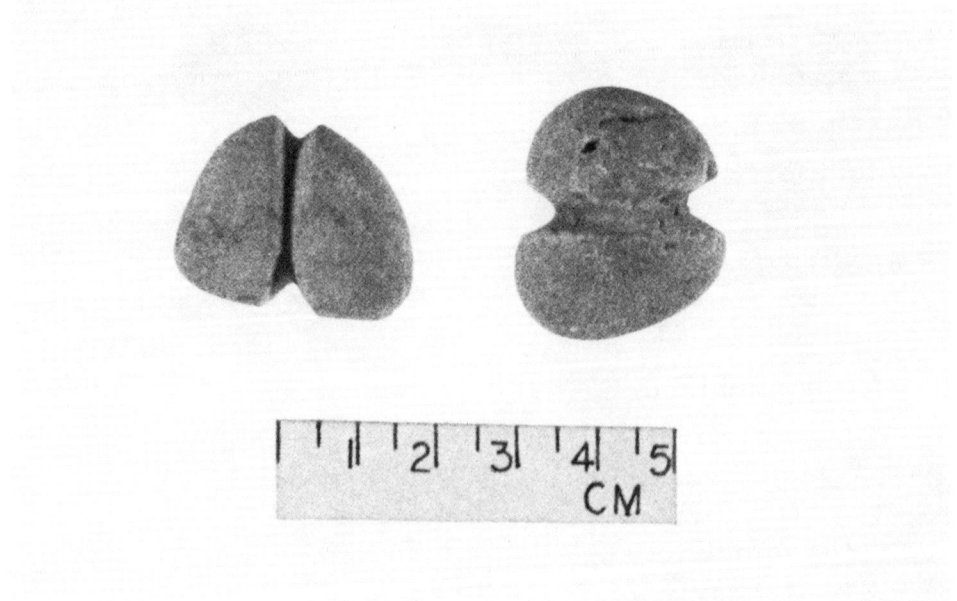

Plate 26. Notched stones collected at El Campanario (Cs27). *Left*, (Cs27/212). *Right*, (Cs27/217).

Plate 27. Polished stone artifacts collected at settlements on the Quiotepec alluvial fan. *Above*, adzes—left, green-black fragment (Cs2/170); right—black-with-white streaks fragment (Cs27/213). *Below*, green-black celt (Cs27/218).

The spindle whorls and the notched stones found at Quiotepec, particularly at the site of El Campanario (Cs27-L), probably reflect the local production of cotton textiles. We know from the ethnohistorical sources that only the Zapotec elite were entitled to wear cotton mantles, and that Zapotec warriors wore padded cotton armor (Chapter 2). The cotton textiles produced in the Quiotepec area were probably supplied to the military forces stationed there. Yet, one thing is certain: The Zapotec did not introduce this craft activity to the Cuicatlán Cañada. Prior to the Zapotec takeover, residents at the Perdido phase community of La Coyotera (Cs25-P) in the southern Cañada were spinning and possibly weaving cotton fiber (Spencer 1982:111, 127, 144-145). The apparent restriction of this activity to the Quiotepec area during the succeeding Lomas phase represents a change in the

Table 23. Distribution of Obsidian Artifacts at Settlements in the Quiotepec Area

Site	Total Obsidian† Artifacts	Blades		Flakes		Débitage	
		Frequency	Percentage	Frequency	Percentage	Frequency	Percentage
Cs2-L	81	53	65.4%	10	12.3%	18	22.2%
Cs3-L	147	25	17%	71	48.3%	50	34%
Cs26-L	13	9	69%	3	23.1%	1	7.7%
Cs27-L	24	7	29.2%	9	37.5%	7	29.2%

†Obsidian artifacts from those surface collections yielding Lomas phase ceramics, including those having a light amount of Trujano phase ceramics (see Chapter 2).

nature of local craft production concurrent with the Cañada's transformation into a frontier and tributary region of the Monte Albán state.

Polished stone adzes and celts, which may have been hafted onto wooden handles, constitute other artifacts found only in the Quiotepec area during the Lomas phase (Table 21, Pl. 27). Although their function is unclear, their distribution in the Cuicatlán Cañada during the time period of Zapotec domination suggests that they might have been used in an activity that was also restricted to the Quiotepec frontier. One possibility is that they might have been used to make those weapons and shields that we know the Zapotec constructed from perishable materials such as wood and cane.

We have seen how the Lomas phase settlements in the Quiotepec area received markedly higher quantities of imported obsidian (Table 15). Clearly, another craft activity occurring at the Quiotepec frontier was obsidian working. If we examine the distribution of obsidian blades, flakes and débitage at the Quiotepec settlements we find that the greatest percentage of blades occur at Cs2-L and Cs26-L, which contain impressive public building sectors (Table 23). Obsidian flakes and débitage, on the other hand, are found in greater amounts at Cs3-L and Cs27-L, the two settlements having large residential sectors. It would seem that obsidian was imported to the Quiotepec area as a raw material, and worked locally to produce blades and other artifacts.

We know from the ethnohistorical sources that obsidian blades—and possibly also obsidian flakes—were used by the Zapotec to make the broadswords they wielded in warfare (Chapter 2). A possible archaeological example comes from the site of Huitzo in the Valley of Oaxaca, a border settlement at the northern end of the valley's Etla arm whose name means "military watchtower" (see Fig. 1). Nine obsidian blades said to form part of a broadsword (*macana*) were among the funerary accompaniments of a prominent individual buried in a Period V tomb here (Moser 1969:45). Another possible use for obsidian blades, which constitute the largest percentage of the obsidian artifacts collected in the Quiotepec area (Table 23), might have been for rituals performed by the military forces stationed there. Obsidian blades are known to have been one of the instruments used in bloodletting rituals in Mesoamerica (Joralemon 1974:59-62; Flannery 1976d:341), and they might well have been used for this purpose by the Zapotec warriors posted at Quiotepec. We are familiar with some of the ideological aspects of Zapotec militarism during the Postclassic period (see Chapter 2), which might have included ritual bloodletting. In this light, it is significant that the greatest percentages of blades occur at Cs2-L and CS26-L, the two settlements having large plazas and monumental public buildings where ceremonies of this kind would probably have taken place.

The supply of obsidian to the Quiotepec area and the production of obsidian tools there was probably crucial, therefore, to the maintenance of military control at the Quiotepec frontier. Just how the Zapotec state secured the obsidian it needed to supply its frontier regions is a subject that I will return to later.

On all the Lomas phase settlements in the Quiotepec area we noted the occurrence of a local ceramic (Lomas Plain) imitation of Period Late I and II cremas from the Valley of Oaxaca. A representative sample of these ceramics was sent to Dr. Garman Harbottle at Brookhaven National Laboratory, where they were subjected to neutron activation along with other Lomas Plain ceramics and with actual Monte Albán Ic-II cremas from the Valley of Oaxaca. The results of Harbottle's analysis support the view that these were locally manufactured imitations of Monte Albán Ic-II cremas; the resulting dendrogram groups these ceramics together with other local Lomas Plain samples, and separates them from the group of Period Late I-II cremas from the Oaxaca Valley, which have a much lower iron content (see Appendix I). If we examine the distribution of these local imitations of Monte Albán ceramics within the Cuicatlán Cañada at large (Table 24), we discover that the settlements on the Quiotepec alluvial fan have the greatest abundance of these ceramics, especially the sites designated Cs27-L and Cs3-L.

The distribution of these Lomas Plain imitations of Monte Albán pottery in the Cuicatlán Cañada is analogous to another imperial situation in the New World, the Inca empire. Morris (1972, 1974) has investigated the Inca administrative centers along the Inca road, and he notes profound differences between these imperial centers and neighboring local settlements in regions incorporated into the Inca empire. One of these differences is expressed in the regional distribution of ceramics; Morris finds that the pottery at the imperial centers along the

Table 24. Distribution of Lomas Plain Imitations of Monte Albán Ic-II Cremas at 17 Lomas Phase Settlements

Alluvial Fan	Site	Surface Collections†	Total Ceramic Diagnostics	Lomas Plain Imitations*	Ratio
Quiotepec	Cs2-L	10	812	10	.012
	Cs3-L	24	1690	234	.138
	Cs26-L	2	90	3	.033
	Cs27-L	11	840	144	.171
Cuicatlán	Cs5-L	6	1225	13	.011
	Cs6-L	9	547	21	.038
	Cs9-L	2	274	3	.011
	Cs10-L	1	17	0	0
	Cs11-L	3	123	2	.016
	Cs12-L	3	133	2	.015
	Cs13-L	10	595	0	0
	Cs15/66-L	1	27	1	.037
El Chilar	Cs16-L	6	568	0	0
	Cs19-L	6	743	5	.007
	Cs20-L	3	135	0	0
	Cs21-L	3	57	0	0
Dominguillo	Cs25-L	25	2263	1	.0004

†All surface collections yielding Lomas phase ceramics were included in this analysis (see Chapter 2).
*Total Lomas Plain Imitations = Sum of Lomas Plain C.7 finish, Lomas Plain C.11 finish, and Lomas Plain with specular red.

Inca road consisted of local imitations of the major Cuzco-style vessel forms, while villages in the subjugated regions adhered to their pre-Inca ceramic traditions (Morris 1972:394-395).

Morris looks to the institutional basis underlying the expanding Inca empire and, with the use of documentary evidence, suggests an explanation for the differences in ceramic assemblages between the Inca administrative centers and the local subject villages. Because tribute within the Inca empire was collected in the form of a labor tax (the *mit'a*), Inca centers were established in the subjugated regions, to which household heads periodically went to render their *mit'a* in services that included cultivating state fields, performing military duties, and working on state building projects. In return for their labors, the state provided them with housing, food, and whatever else they needed during their period of service to the state at these Inca centers. For this reason, it is only at the Inca centers in the subjugated territories that these Inca-style ceramics were provided (Morris 1972:398-399). Likewise, the Lomas Plain imitations of Monte Albán ceramics discovered at all the settlements in the Quiotepec area were probably manufactured there in deliberate imitation of Monte Albán ceramics, with the intention of supplying ceramics to the population residing at the frontier. The production of these ceramics constitutes another specialized craft activity associated with the Quiotepec frontier.

In addition to the military personnel stationed at the Quiotepec frontier, there was apparently a variety of specialized craft producers attached to the frontier settlement. Among them were producers of cotton textiles, military equipment, and ceramics. Although I cannot estimate the total number of non-food producers residing at the Quiotepec frontier on the basis of the distribution of craft-related artifacts, I can attempt to estimate the number of food producers that would have been required to farm the

Table 25. Estimated Labor Requirements for Farming the Cañada's Alluvium during the Lomas Phase

Alluvial Fan	Farmers Needed @ 2 ha per Farmer		Estimated Population @ 5 Persons per House	Potential Farmers @ 2 Persons from Each House
	Low Alluvium	High Alluvium		
Quiotepec	16	23	1940-2050	776-820
Cuicatlán	262	257	1090-1430	436-572
El Chilar	149	59	324-345	130-138
Dominguillo	71	30	275-300	110-120

Plate 28. Entrance to Monte Albán-style tomb at Cerro de Quiotepec (Cs2), facing east.

available alluvium at Quiotepec, using the figure of 2 for the number of hectares that can be farmed by an individual using the traditional *coa* or digging stick (Kirkby 1973: Table 10). By dividing the hectares of available low and high alluvium on each of the Cañada's alluvial fans during the Lomas Phase (Table 18) by this figure I can estimate the amount of labor that would have been needed to farm each alluvial fan. Table 25 lists the estimated labor needed to farm the available alluvium on each alluvial fan during the Lomas phase together with the potential number of available farmers, which is based on the estimated number of houses. It turns out that 39 farmers would have been able to cultivate the available farmland on the Quiotepec alluvial fan, roughly 2% of the total estimated population residing there during the Lomas phase. Obviously, the bulk of the population represented at the Quiotepec frontier must have been non-food producers.

It is clear that the supply of food to the Quiotepec area was critical to the maintenance of the frontier region and that it must have been administered by the Zapotec state. As we shall see shortly, the food imported to the Quiotepec frontier probably constituted part of the tribute exacted from the Cuicatlán Cañada by the Monte Albán state. Although food was necessarily imported to the Quiotepec frontier, the distribution of ground stone manos and metates in the residential sectors of the Quiotepec settlements (Table 17) suggests that individual residential units here prepared their own food.

A final factor to be considered in the administration of the Quiotepec frontier is the remuneration of the military personnel stationed here. We know from ethnohistorical sources on the Zapotec that great warriors, military captains, and frontier administrators were honored with awards and privileges, including elaborate burial at their deaths (Chapter 2). In his study of the relationships between military organization and social structure, Andrzejewski (1954) demonstrated that conquest fosters the emergence of a privileged group of warriors. According to Andrzejewski, a government can maintain greater control over its troops if: (1) the troops depend on the central government for their supplies and equipment; and (2) the troops depend on the central government for their income (Andrzejewski 1954:29, 81-87). If the Monte Albán state administered the remuneration of its military personnel at the Quiotepec frontier, we would expect to find evidence of direct recompense in kind or privilege from Monte Albán to the settlements at Quiotepec.

One possible line of evidence is the distribution of Monte Albán ceramics imported to the Cuicatlán Cañada from the Valley of Oaxaca during the Lomas phase. One of the expectations of the proposed Zapotec subjugation of the Cañada was a decrease in the relative frequency of Oaxaca ceramics imported to the tributary region. After the Zapotec take-over, the importation of goods from the Valley of Oaxaca would be directed as provisions or rewards to the Zapotec military and civil servants stationed in the region and not to the local tributary Cañada population; accordingly, I would expect the highest frequencies of Oaxaca ceramics to be associated with the loci of Zapotec military and civil administration in the Cañada (Chapter 2). On the basis of my visual identification of Late Formative Monte Albán pottery types, my expectations concerning their distribution in the Cuicatlán Cañada during the Lomas phase were apparently borne out by the archaeological record (Table 13). The quantities of Monte Albán Ic-II crema ceramics entering the region are small, and appear mainly at settlements on the Quiotepec frontier.

Nevertheless, four examples of what I classified as Monte Albán Ic-II cremas were the subject of a chemical trace-element analysis at Brookhaven National Laboratory, along with Middle Formative Oaxaca cremas and other Middle and Late Formative ceramics from the Cañada and the Valley of Oaxaca (see Appendix I). The trace-element analysis and subsequent cluster analysis revealed that while one of these imported Period Late I and II cremas fell firmly within the group of Monte Albán I and II cremas (i.e., Monte Albán I crema ware from Monte Albán, Monte Albán I crema ware imported by the Cañada, Monte Albán Ic-II crema ware from Monte Albán), the remaining three specimens appeared to be closely related to the Cañada's local plain ware tradition (i.e. Lomas Plain ware, Lomas Plain ware imitations of Monte Albán Ic-II cremas). According to the trace-element analysis, the three examples from settlements at Quiotepec were *not* imported crema ceramics from the Valley of Oaxaca. Instead, they were extremely good locally-produced copies of Monte Albán ceramics, such that someone familiar with Monte Albán pottery might not be able to tell them apart. We have seen that the Lomas phase settlements on the Quiotepec alluvial fan had the greatest abundance of these local imitations of Monte Albán ceramics (Table 24), and I have suggested that these ceramics were probably manufactured in the Quiotepec area in order to supply ceramics to the population residing at the frontier.

So, while my visual classification of Monte Albán cremas found at Lomas phase settlements in the Cañada reveals a concentration of these imported ceramics at setlements on the region's northern boundary, the results of the trace-element analysis suggest that few, if any, Monte Albán ceramics were being imported to the Quiotepec area. This discrepancy between the visual and chemical identifications of Late Formative Oaxaca ceramics in the Cañada is significant in the case of Late Formative Monte Albán ceramics, because the two methods for identifying imported Oaxaca pottery during the earlier Middle Formative period were in close agreement. Indeed, the three examples of what I classified as Monte Albán I cremas imported to Perdido phase settlements in the Cañada were closely related to the sample of Monte Albán I cremas from Monte Albán (see Appendix I). I conclude that with the transformation of the Cuicatlán Cañada into a tributary region of the Monte Albán state, few if any ceramics from the Valley of Oaxaca were being sent to this outlying canyon, not even to the Zapotec military personnel stationed there. I would suggest that considerations of travel and of bulk led the Monte Albán state to establish a local ceramic ware in the Cañada that deliberately imitated Monte Albán ceramics.

What evidence is there, then, of the ways the Monte Albán state remunerated the military personnel who controlled its frontier regions? Consistent with the known Zapotec practice of rewarding great warriors, military captains, and frontier administrators with elaborate burial upon their deaths is the discovery of Monte Albán-style tombs at the Quiotepec frontier, at Cerro de Quiotepec (Cs2-L). One of our designated surface collection areas at Cs2 (square Cs2/168) overlapped the exposed entrance and remains of a looted tomb (Pl. 28), which was salvaged and described by Eduardo Pareyón (1960). The main chamber of Tomb 5, as it was referred to, contained three niches and the central wall was decorated with modeled stucco; the panels located on either side of the entrance to the chamber had traces of murals, including the depiction of a human face from which an elaborate speech scroll emerges (see Rickards 1926: Fig. 5). According to Pareyón (1960:101-102), the modeled stucco and murals decorating Tomb 5 are rendered in straightforward Monte Albán style. Apparently, an important individual residing at Quiotepec was interred in this Zapotec-style tomb. Of the three surface collections at Cs2-L containing what I considered to be imported Monte Albán ceramics, one was the aforementioned surface collection square Cs2/168, which overlapped with the backdirt of this looted tomb; another surface collection area that yielded a possible Monte Albán ceramic import also overlapped with the backdirt of another looted tomb (square Cs2/175). Thus, the individuals buried in tombs at Cerro de Quiotepec were probably accompanied by ceramic vessels, which, if not imported from the Valley of Oaxaca, were fashioned locally in clear Monte Albán style.

The foregoing discussion has outlined the nature of Zapotec military control at the Quiotepec frontier, and the variety of other activities necessary to its maintenance. Clearly, the organizational implications of establishing and maintaining this frontier outpost for the state were considerable. An entire military and administrative hierarchy was required to guard the frontier and to regulate the movement of people across the state's boundary. Military equipment, provisions, and manpower had to be garnered. Although food and labor were likely supplied from the subject region, the Zapotec state probably maintained direct control over the production of armament, the supply of imported items, and the remuneration of its forces.

Civil Administration of the Central and Southern Cañada

South of Quiotepec, in the central and southern Cañada, the transition from the Perdido phase to the Lomas phase involved significant changes in the settlement pattern. The Perdido phase communities on the high alluvium were all abandoned and 14 new settlements were established on the piedmont ridges overlooking the canyon floor (Fig. 34, Table 11). In contrast to the large fortified settlements found in the Quiotepec area, the settlements in the central and southern Cañada are all smaller than 4 ha in size and lack fortifications. I would suggest that these settlements were situated within the "protective umbrella" of the Zapotec military forces stationed at the Quiotepec frontier and thus fall within a zone of civil administration similar to that proposed by Lattimore in his model of the structure of a frontier region.

If the three alluvial fans of the central and southern Cañada correspond to a zone under civil administration, then what policies did the Zapotec state pursue here? Lattimore defines the range of civil administration as the territory subjugated by an expanding state within which a standardized tribute can be exacted (Lattimore 1962:487). Two policies are implicit in his definition: (1) control over the subject population; and (2) the exaction of tribute. We know that such policies were enforced in regions conquered by the Zapotec state during the Postclassic period. Consequently, the effects of these related policies upon the Cuicatlán Cañada are among the expectations of the conquest model presented in Chapter 2.

With the abandonment of the Perdido phase communities during the transition from the Perdido phase to the Lomas phase, we witness the dissolution of the region's indigenous administrative hierarchy, which during the Perdido phase featured two chiefly centers located on the central alluvial fans of the region (Chapter 3). Instead, a different picture emerges when we examine the sizes of the 14 Lomas phase settlements in the central and southern Cañada and the configurations of public architecture found on them. A histogram of the sizes of these settlements reveals a simple unimodal distribution lacking any breaks (Fig. 36, Table 11). Moreover, 12 of these settlements feature essentially the same array and volume of public architecture on their central plazas. A typical hilltop settlement in the central and southern Cañada during the Lomas phase will contain a single small plaza with one or two small mounds, each some 2 m or less in height (see Figs. 46, 47, 48, and Pls. 30, 33).

On the basis of settlement size and public architecture alone, there seems to have been a less clearly defined regional administrative hierarchy in the central and southern Cañada during the Lomas phase than previously. It is difficult to rank settle-

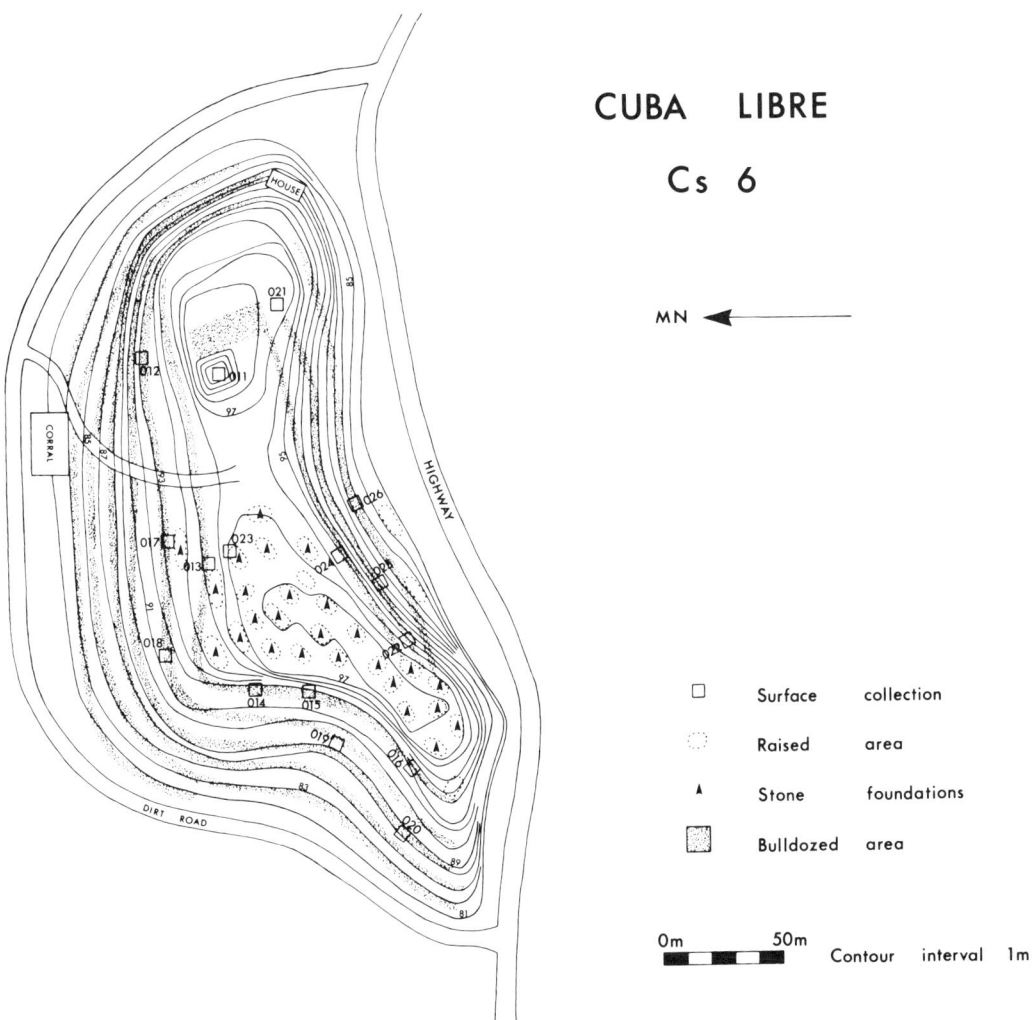

Figure 46. Cuba Libre site map (Cs6).

ments here according to their size and the public architecture they exhibit. I suggest that under direct intervention by the conquering Zapotec, the two-level regional administrative hierarchy that obtained in the Cañada during the Perdido phase was eliminated. While the "hand of the state" (Morris 1972:393) is clearly evident at the Quiotepec frontier, no single regional center emerges in the central and southern Cañada during the succeeding Lomas phase. This apparent reduction in the region's administrative hierarchy probably reflects a Zapotec policy of curtailing native political institutions in the subjugated regions. Instead, the Zapotec apparently wanted to establish equivalent administrative units in the central and southern Cañada as a way of controlling the subject population (cf. Lattimore 1962; Hodder 1972).

With the disappearance of the Perdido phase regional centers (Cs10-P, Cs19-P) on the two central alluvial fans of the Cuicatlán Cañada, we might expect to find a consequent disruption of the interregional exchange relationships maintained by the native ruling elite that resided at those centers. Upon the Cañada's transformation into a tributary province of Monte Albán, the reciprocal exchange ties between the elites of the Cañada and the Valley of Oaxaca might well have been replaced by the flow of tribute from the Cañada to the Oaxaca Valley. Under this new tributary relationship to Monte Albán, the Cañada might no longer have been entitled to receive trade items from the Valley of Oaxaca in return for the items that it sent as tribute. One archaeological manifestation of the switch from the prior reciprocal exchange relationship between the two

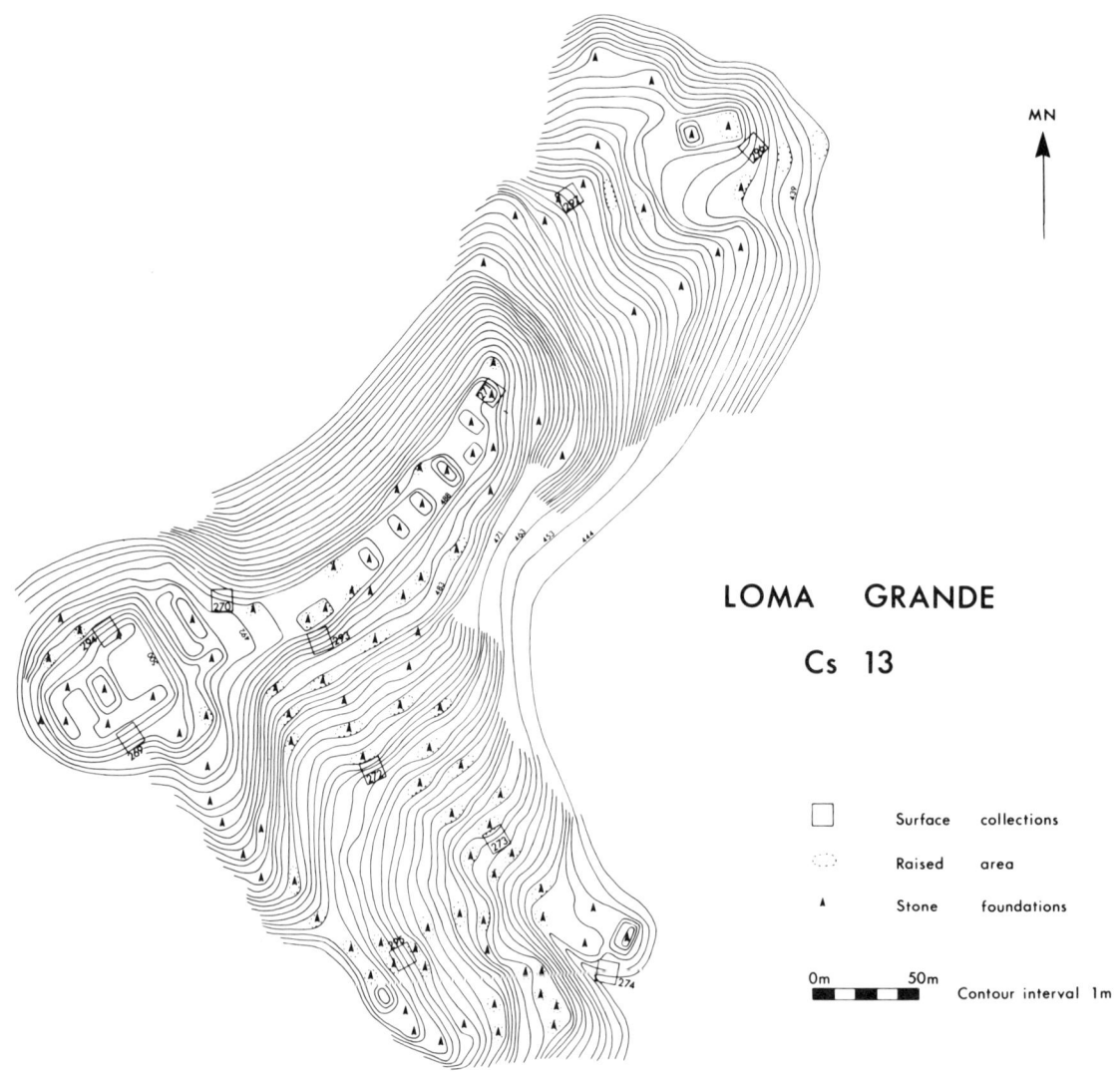

Figure 47. Loma Grande site map (Cs13).

regions to one characterized by the flow of tribute from the Cañada to the Oaxaca Valley might be a decrease in the relative frequency of imported Oaxaca ceramics in the Cuicatlán Cañada.

The transition from the Perdido phase to the Lomas phase does, in fact, include significant changes in the distribution of imported Oaxaca ceramics in the central and southern Cañada (see Tables 13, 14; Fig. 37). As we saw earlier, smaller amounts of Monte Albán ceramics are found at Lomas phase settlements than at previous Perdido phase settlements. Furthermore, the regional distribution of Oaxaca ceramics becomes highly discontinuous; fewer settlements have smaller quantities of these items. Unlike the distribution of Oaxaca ceramics during the Perdido phase, which was characterized by a general fall-off in their abundance as distance from Monte Albán increased, the greatest abundance of Monte Albán—or Monte Albán-style—ceramics in the Cañada during the Lomas phase occurs at sites on the Quiotepec frontier, the most distant from the Valley of Oaxaca.

Obsidian, another item previously imported to the regional centers in the central and southern Cañada during the Perdido phase, also reached settlements at the Quiotepec frontier in much greater abundance than those settlements lying in the zone under civil administration (Table 15). I have suggested that obsidian was preferentially supplied to the military forces stationed at the Quiotepec frontier. The distribution of obsidian in the Cuicatlán Cañada during the Lomas phase agrees with a model of state-administered exchange, whereby the Quiotepec frontier is supplied directly with these imported items.

With the transformation of the Cuicatlán Cañada into a frontier tributary region of the Monte Albán state, we witness the elimination of the previous regional centers—the seats of native political institutions—and the concomitant disruption of the reciprocal exchange relationships that were maintained by the elites residing at these centers with the elites of other regions, including the Valley of Oaxaca. Under direct civil administration by the Monte Albán state, the central and southern Cañada assumed a new status as a tributary province and was no longer in a position to exchange freely with other regions.

Given this apparent reorganization of the Cañada's regional administrative hierarchy—with its consequent implications for the breakdown in the previous reciprocal exchange relationships maintained between the Cañada and the Valley of Oaxaca—how can we determine whether the Zapotec were actually exacting a standardized tribute from the central and southern Cañada? According to the conquest model, we would expect to find evidence of changes in the Cañada's local economy in order to meet large-scale tribute demands.

We do, in fact, find a significant change in the typical location of settlements in the central and southern Cañada during the transition from the Perdido to the Lomas phase. The Perdido phase communities on the high alluvium were abandoned and new settlements were established on adjacent piedmont ridges (Pls. 29, 31). At the same time, the transition from the Perdido phase to the Lomas phase was characterized by little or no settlement growth in the central and southern Cañada (Table 12). If we add the sizes of all the settlements found on the Cuicatlán, El Chilar, and Dominguillo alluvial fans during the Lomas phase (Table 11), we find that the total settlement here is far lower than that seen on the Quiotepec alluvial fan. Two estimators of the population of these settlements are listed in Table 26: one estimate is based on site size; the second is calculated on the basis of the number of residential units (i.e. residential terraces, housemounds) that are visible on the surfaces of these sites.

Two of the hilltop settlements in the central and southern Cañada (Cs25-L, Cs15/66-L) had the remains of irrigation canals associated with them (see Fig. 34). We traced the trajectory of these canals and discovered that they channeled water from tributary streams onto high alluvial terraces, which had previously been the loci of settlement (Cs25-P, Cs15-P). One of these irrigation facilities is associated with the site of Loma de la Coyotera (Fig. 48), where Spencer conducted excavations designed to investigate the nature of local economy and sociopolitical organization at this community (see Spencer 1982:215-242). As happened elsewhere in the central and southern Cañada, the establishment of this hilltop settlement followed the abandonment of the Perdido phase community (Cs25-P) located on the high alluvium below. In terms of settlement size alone, the new settlement established on Loma de la Coyotera is less than half a hectare larger than the earlier community on the high alluvium (see Table 12).

By means of excavation and intensive surface collections, Spencer was able to assign a Lomas phase date to the construction and earliest use of the irrigation facility at Loma de la Coyotera (Spencer 1982:224-225). A long and well-built canal brought water down from a tributary stream behind the community to the expanse of high alluvium below. Eleven aqueducts lifted the canal across intervening arroyos before it emptied onto the high alluvium at precisely the location of the Perdido phase settlement (see Fig. 48, and Pl. 32). Concurrent with the abrupt settlement shift off the high alluvium, therefore, we have evidence that irrigation facilities were being built in order to channel water onto expanses of high alluvium. As we saw in a previous chapter (Chapter 2), cultivation of the Cañada's high alluvium today is totally dependent upon techniques of canal irrigation. It would appear that, with the addition of the high alluvium to the land under cultivation by means of canal irrigation, the Lomas phase witnessed a major expansion in the scale of agricultural production.

In order to examine the relationship between this expanded productive regime and the associated

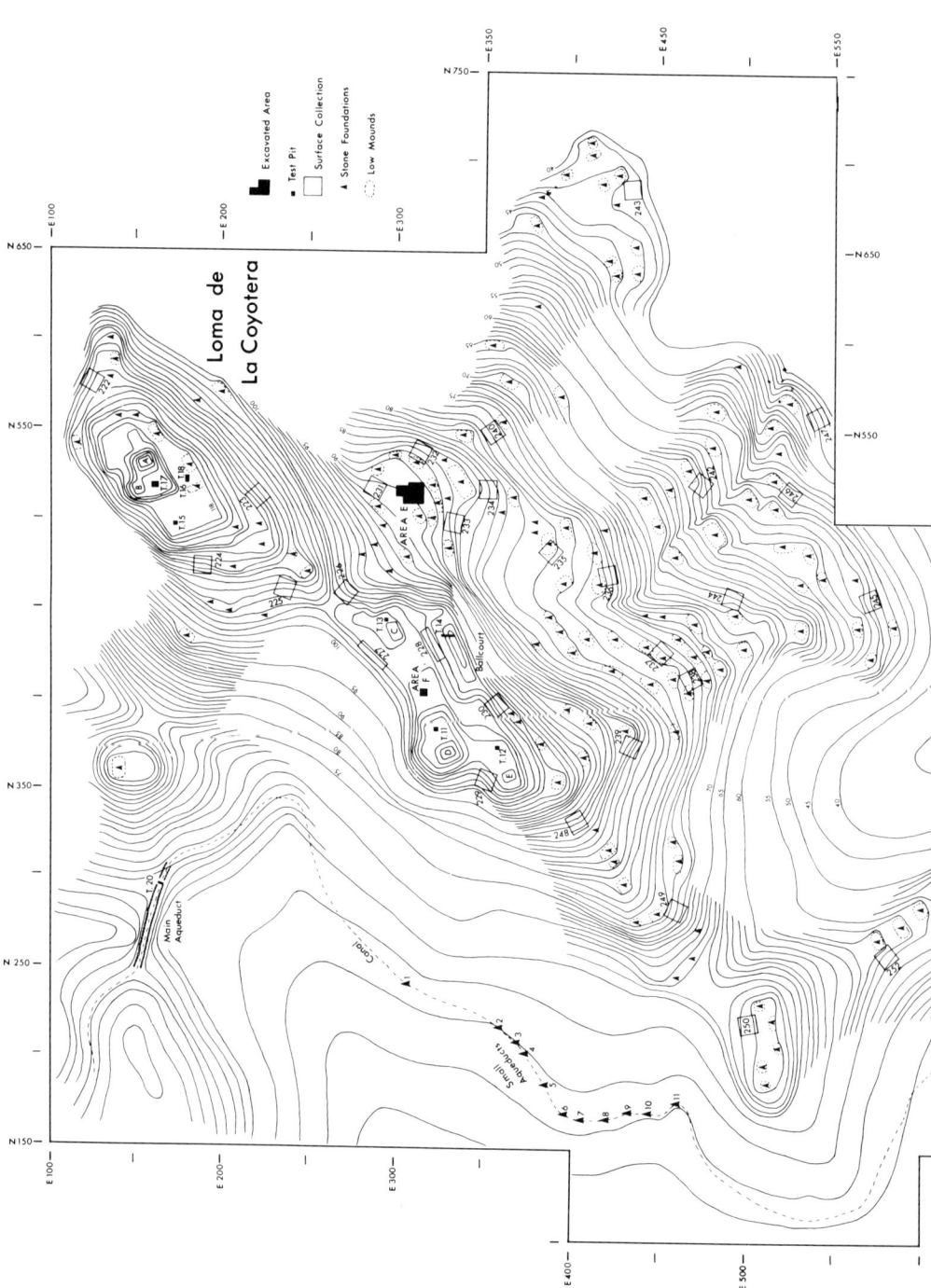

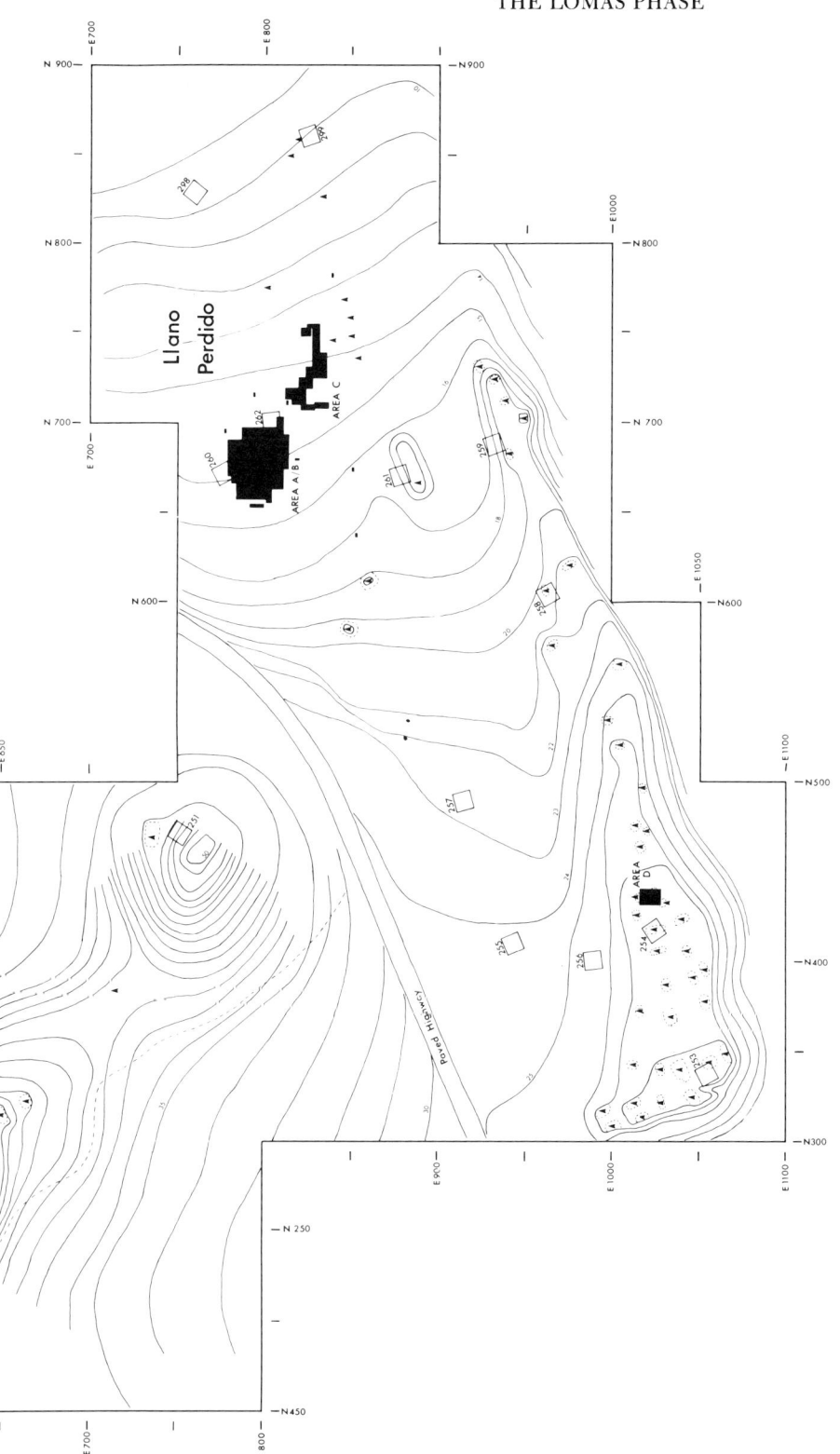

Figure 48. La Coyotera site map (Cs25) (from Spencer 1982:86–87).

Plate 29. View of hilltop site of Cuba Libre (Cs6), from across the Río Grande, facing east.

Lomas phase settlement in the central and southern Cañada, I calculated the carrying capacity of the Cuicatlán, El Chilar, and Dominguillo alluvial fans, following the procedure outlined in Chapter 2. To do this, the potential annual maize yields harvested on the low and high alluvium were added for each of these alluvial fans and then divided by the estimated average annual maize consumption of an individual (see Table 18). In contrast to the relationship noted between the estimated carrying capacity and the observed Lomas phase population on the Quiotepec alluvial fan, where population far and away exceeds the carrying capacity, the reverse is true for the Cuicatlán, El Chilar, and Dominguillo alluvial fans: the estimated carrying capacity of these alluvial fans significantly exceeds the observed Lomas phase population. Therefore, the noticeable expansion in the scale of agricultural production in the Cuicatlán Cañada during the Lomas phase did *not* appear to correspond to any observable growth in the local population there.

We can determine the basic labor requirements for this expansion in the region's agricultural production by using Kirkby's (1973: Table 10) figure for the number of hectares that an individual can farm with the traditional digging stick (see Table 25). If we calculate the labor needed to farm the available low and high alluvium on the Cuicatlán, El Chilar, and Dominguillo alluvial fans and compare these figures with the estimated number of farmers residing on the alluvial fans, we find a close relationship between the estimated labor requirements and the available work force in this expanded agricultural regime. Only in the case of the El Chilar alluvium did the available work force of 130-138 farmers fall short of the 208 farmers needed to farm both the low and high alluvium; of course, additional farmers could have been supplied from settlements on the two adjacent alluvial fans, where the available work force exceeded the estimated number of farmers required to farm those alluvial fans.

Certain clues needed to elucidate the factors responsible for the apparent expansion in the scale of the region's agricultural production come from the site of Loma de la Coyotera (Cs25-L). Midden deposits excavated on a residential terrace here (see Spencer 1982:227-230) produced a tremendous density of carbonized plant remains suggesting that

Plate 30. Eastern face of mound at Cuba Libre (Cs6), facing west.

in the Lomas phase the cultivation of a few special tropical plants was emphasized to a much greater extent than previously. Four plant species were especially well represented in these deposits: (1) the coyol palm (*Acrocomia mexicana*); (2) another palm, presently unidentified as to species (*Palmae*); (3) the black zapote (*Diospyros digyna*); and (4) the ciruela (*Spondias mombin*) (Smith 1979:244). Thus much of the high alluvium that was brought under cultivation here through canal irrigation at this time was probably used for intensifying the cultivation of these tropical plants. The increased production of the coyol palm and the black zapote in the Lomas phase represents a major reorganization of the local economy from that we reconstructed for the previous Perdido phase community, where these tropical plants merely supplemented the usual Mesoamerican staples (Spencer 1982:145-147).

These developments in the settlement pattern and local economy of the central and southern Cañada during the Lomas phase agree with many of the expectations of the conquest model and are consistent with Lattimore's definition of an expanding state's range of civil administration. The implementation of Zapotec policies here involved dramatic changes for the Cañada's population. First of all, the local population was forcibly moved off the high alluvium and re-settled in communities established atop piedmont ridges. Given the unprecedented population concentration on the Quiotepec alluvial fan, it is possible that some fraction of the subject population was re-settled on the Quiotepec alluvial fan in order to supply the manpower that we have seen was needed to maintain the Quiotepec frontier. At the same time, the Zapotec implemented a major reorganization of the local economy by bringing large expanses of high alluvium under irrigation agriculture and by stepping up the production of certain tropical products. In view of the fact that there was little or no population growth in the central and southern Cañada at this time, it would appear that these developments relate instead to newly-dictated tribute demands imposed upon the Cañada's inhabitants by the Monte Albán state.

These tribute demands were probably of various kinds. First, the additional maize or other staples cultivated under this expanded regime were probably sent as provisions to the large population resid-

Plate 31. View of site of Loma Grande (Cs13) on piedmont ridge rising above high alluvium, facing south.

ing at the Quiotepec frontier. The supply of food to Zapotec garrisons was a common form of tribute demanded of subject populations in regions conquered by the sixteenth-century Zapotec state (Chapter 2). The special *tierra caliente* products, on the other hand, were probably sent as tribute to the Valley of Oaxaca.

One possibility is that the Zapotec enforced a policy of local economic specialization in the Cañada during the Lomas phase, as a way of meeting their diverse tribute demands. Communities on the various alluvial fans in the region may have been encouraged by their Zapotec overlords to specialize in the production of particular tribute items. While this is only one possibility and definitely subject to future archaeological test, certain data gathered by the 1977-78 Cuicatlán Cañada Project enable me to raise it here. We have seen how the community at La Coyotera stepped up the cultivation of certain tropical fruits and nuts during the Lomas phase. At the same time, Spencer has found evidence of a marked decline in other productive activities at this community. The notable drop in the occurrence of craft-related artifacts such as perforated sherd disks and notched stones (see Spencer 1982:230-231) might reflect a reduction of textile-making activities at this community during the Lomas phase. The production of cotton textiles is an activity that, on the basis of our surface collections, appears to have been restricted to communities in the Quiotepec area during the Lomas phase (see Table 21).

Perhaps then, the Zapotec "encouraged" communities in various parts of the subjugated region to specialize in different productive tasks; tropical fruit and nut cultivation in the southernmost Dominguillo area, textile making—in addition to other specialized military activities—on the Quiotepec alluvial fan, and so forth. The inhabitants of the region's largest and central Cuicatlán alluvial fan might have been charged with providing the much-needed supply of food to the Quiotepec frontier. Such a policy of enforced economic specialization would not only have provided the Zapotec with their desired tribute items, but might also have undermined the relative self-sufficiency of the Cañada's communities in preconquest times, thereby constituting another strategy designed to enhance their control over the local population.

There is some evidence of direct political intervention by the Zapotec at a number of communities in the Cañada. If we re-examine the distribution of Oaxaca ceramics at settlements in the central and southern Cañada (see Table 13) we find that four or five of them (Cs25-L, Cs20-L?, Cs13-L, Cs6-L, Cs5-L) had small amounts of Oaxaca ceramics. The possibility that the ceramics from these sites that I classified as Monte Albán Ic-II cremas are, in fact, imported cremas from the Valley of Oaxaca is corroborated by the trace-element analysis of an example from Cs25-L, which did prove to be closely related to the group of Monte Albán Ic-II cremas from Monte Albán (see Appendix I). Furthermore, those few Lomas Gray ceramics in the Cuicatlán Cañada that Harbottle identified as actual imports from the Oaxaca Valley—of the G.12 type (Caso, Bernal, and Acosta 1967:25-27)—were found at sites Cs25-L and Cs13-L (Appendix I). In keeping with an expectation of the conquest model, which stated that the regional distribution of imported items within the Cuicatlán Cañada during the Lomas phase would reflect the Zapotec administration of this tributary province, this spotty distribution of Oaxaca ceramics in the central and southern Cañada probably represents the resident Zapotec administrators or tribute collectors in the service of the Monte Albán state.

The best evidence for the intrusion of the state into the affairs of local communities in the central and southern Cañada comes once again from excavations at the site of Loma de la Coyotera (Cs25-L). Similar to other hilltop communities established in the Lomas phase, the civic-ceremonial sector at Loma de la Coyotera contains a central plaza with two pyramidal mounds raised on a platform (see Fig. 48, Pl. 33). A test excavation placed directly in front of the larger of these two mounds encountered a concentration of 61 human skulls, roughly aligned in rows. Spencer interprets this deposit as the remains of a toppled over skull rack, what the Aztec termed a *tzompantli* (Spencer 1982:236-239) (see Fig. 49). The discovery of this skull rack at Loma de la Coyotera agrees perfectly with the terror tactics known to have been practiced by the Postclassic Zapotec in conquered regions, which included massive executions and the construction of skull racks with the butchered remains (Chapter 2). These skull racks were among the symbols of Zapotec conquest; they were designed to terrorize the subject population and help keep them submissive and responsive to the interests of the imperial state.

It is appropriate that together with the skull rack Spencer found another symbol of Zapotec imperial power, the paw of a hollow jaguar statue or urn (Pl. 34), similar to the one discovered at the contemporaneous site of Suchilquitongo in the Valley of Oaxaca (Caso and Bernal 1952:62-63) (see Fig. 60). As we

Table 26. Estimators of Population at Lomas Phase Settlements in the Central and Southern Cañada

Alluvial Fan	Site	Site Size (ha)	Estimated Population @ 10-25 Persons per Hectare	Number of Residential Terraces	Number of Housemounds	Estimated Population @ 5 Persons per House
	Cs5-L	2.79	28-70	15	15-30	75-150
	Cs6-L	1.87	19-47	4	22-24	110-120
	Cs9-L	.96	10-24	0	2-3?	10-15
	Cs14-L	2.82	28-70	20-22	20-40	100-200
Cuicatlán	Cs10-L	.49	5-12	0	2	10
	Cs11-L	.76	8-19	7	13-14	65-70
	Cs12-L	1.65	16-41	18-20	35-40	175-200
	Cs13-L	4.04	36-91	66-68	90-95	450-475
	Cs15/66-L	2.77	28-69	19-28	19-38?	95-190
Total		18.15	177-443		218-286	1090-1430
	Cs16-L	3.78	34-85	30	45	225
	Cs19-L	.62	6-15	0	5-6?	25-30
El Chilar	Cs20-L	1.33	13-33	0	7-10?	35-50
	Cs21-L	.38	4-10	0	8	40
Total		6.11	57-143		65-69	325-345
Dominguillo	Cs25-L	3.04	30-76	35-38	55-60	275-300

Plate 32. Main aqueduct of irrigation facility associated with Loma de la Coyotera (Cs25), facing southwest.

shall see in Chapter 6, many Oaxaca scholars have reason to believe that the ancient name for Monte Albán might have been "Hill of the Jaguar" (Caso et al. 1967:84; Marcus 1976:131, 1980:58; Blanton 1978:5-6). The presence of this symbol of the Monte Albán state alongside the skull rack in the central plaza of Loma de la Coyotera (Cs25-L) probably reflects the enforcement of Zapotec imperial policies at this community during the Lomas phase. The discovery of another such jaguar paw fragment in the plaza area of the Lomas phase site of Cuba Libre (Cs6-L) (Pl. 34) is also possible evidence of the Zapotec state's intrusion into the affairs of local communities in the central and southern Cañada at this time.

The implementation of Zapotec policies in tributary regions like the Cuicatlán Cañada had important administrative implications for the Monte Albán state. At local communities within one of these tributary regions, we find evidence of the intrusion of state-level administrators, charged with maintaining control over the subject population and implementing those policies related to the exaction of a standardized tribute here. Some tribute demands were probably met by supplying provisions and labor to the Zapotec garrisons stationed in the region, while other tribute demands involved the wholesale shipment of certain items to the Valley of Oaxaca. The functions of the zones of Zapotec military control and civil administration were interdependent: the frontier guarded the central and southern Cañada and this inner-lying zone under civil administration in turn supplied food and manpower to the frontier. Yet, to the central state that directed these policies, the Cuicatlán Cañada was only one of many tributary regions to be administered in this way. Recall that some 40 subjugated places were recorded on stone slabs at Monte Albán, attesting to the extent of the Zapotec tributary empire in Late Formative times.

A Port of Trade Beyond the Frontier

Monte Albán's imperial expansion into surrounding regions like the Cuicatlán Cañada undoubtedly disrupted those long-distance exchange relationships that had linked the Oaxaca Valley with

Plate 33. Mound A at Loma de la Coyotera (Cs25), facing northwest. The corner of test excavation 17 is visible in the foreground.

other regions. We have seen how the exchange ties maintained between the elites of the Valley of Oaxaca, the Cuicatlán Cañada, and the Tehuacán Valley during the Perdido phase ceased in the succeeding Lomas phase when the Zapotec state subjugated the Cuicatlán Cañada and established a military outpost at the northern boundary of this region. The Zapotec apparently did not carry their conquest activities beyond the Quiotepec alluvial fan of the Cuicatlán Cañada. In contrast to the settlements in the Quiotepec area, the next settlement to the north at Tecomavaca (Cs1-L) is covered with ceramics belonging to the contemporaneous Early Palo Blanco phase of the Tehuacán Valley sequence (MacNeish, Peterson, and Flannery 1970:145-161). In the Tehuacán Valley at this time we find the development of a number of autonomous polities, not incorporated into the Monte Albán state (Drennan 1979; Spencer 1979).

With Monte Albán's expansion into the Cuicatlán Cañada and its control over this major artery of communication, how did the Monte Albán state trade with those regions with which it had previously interacted by way of the Cañada? It is likely that the Monte Albán state would still have desired exchanges with regions beyond its frontiers in order to receive those items that were not available within the territory it controlled. Obsidian was one trade item of special interest to the Zapotec, one which was not available within the confines of Zapotec-controlled territory. Blanton, for example, has found that obsidian was intended for use by the Zapotec elite residing at Monte Albán (Blanton 1978:93-95). I maintain that the Zapotec also used obsidian to fashion broadswords and arrows used in warfare. Thus, the procurement of obsidian for the military outposts established in frontier regions—as well as for the Oaxaca Valley elite—would be in the vital interests of the Monte Albán state. Moreover, one way for the Monte Albán state to ensure command over its troops stationed in these frontier outposts would be for it to control the supply of raw materials like obsidian that were used in the production of military equipment (Andrzejewski 1954:87).

The eighteenth-century West African state of Dahomey, which traded the captives gained in war

Figure 49. An artist's reconstruction of the skull rack at Loma de la Coyotera.

for guns and powder from European traders at the coastal port of Whydah, came to face a similar problem (Arnold 1957a:154-176). The Dahomey state depended upon its trade with Europeans at Whydah in order to secure its firearms, yet it did not want to come into close contact with the European powers with which it traded. For this reason, Dahomey favored leaving the port of Whydah in the hands of the Whydasians, so long as Dahomey's access to the port was secure. When Dahomey was suddenly denied access to the crucial port of Whydah, its security was threatened:

> This war between Dahomey and Whydah had not only disorganized the ordinary channels of trade and closed off the trade routes, but there was as well a "great Destruction of the Inhabitants of the neighbouring Countries, who used to carry on a regular Trade with the far Inland People." Obviously, trade could not operate under such disturbed conditions. On the other hand, peace might be equally disruptive of trade so far as it cut off the supply of slaves. [Arnold 1957a:163]

In the context of the Dahomey state's expansionistic strategies, how did it solve the problem of maintaining those trade relations with the foreign powers that provided the military equipment necessary to its security and survival? Dahomey took over Whydah and established a port of trade there, an institution which was politically neutral and open to all nations. All foreign exchange was conducted at the port of trade, under close supervision by native officials. Foreign traders were generally barred from entering Dahomey territory; they needed royal permission for their occasional state visits to the capital. The Dahomey state traded war captives and palm oil in return for the firearms it needed in warfare, as well as for a variety of luxury items such as cloth, cowrie shells, and coral, which were circulated only among the Dahomey elite (Arnold 1957a:164-174). In the case of Dahomey, the port of trade developed as an institution for resolving the disruptive effects that war has upon previous long-distance trade relations.

The port-of-trade model of interregional exchange is not foreign to Mesoamericanists, due largely to Anne Chapman's (1957) pioneering study

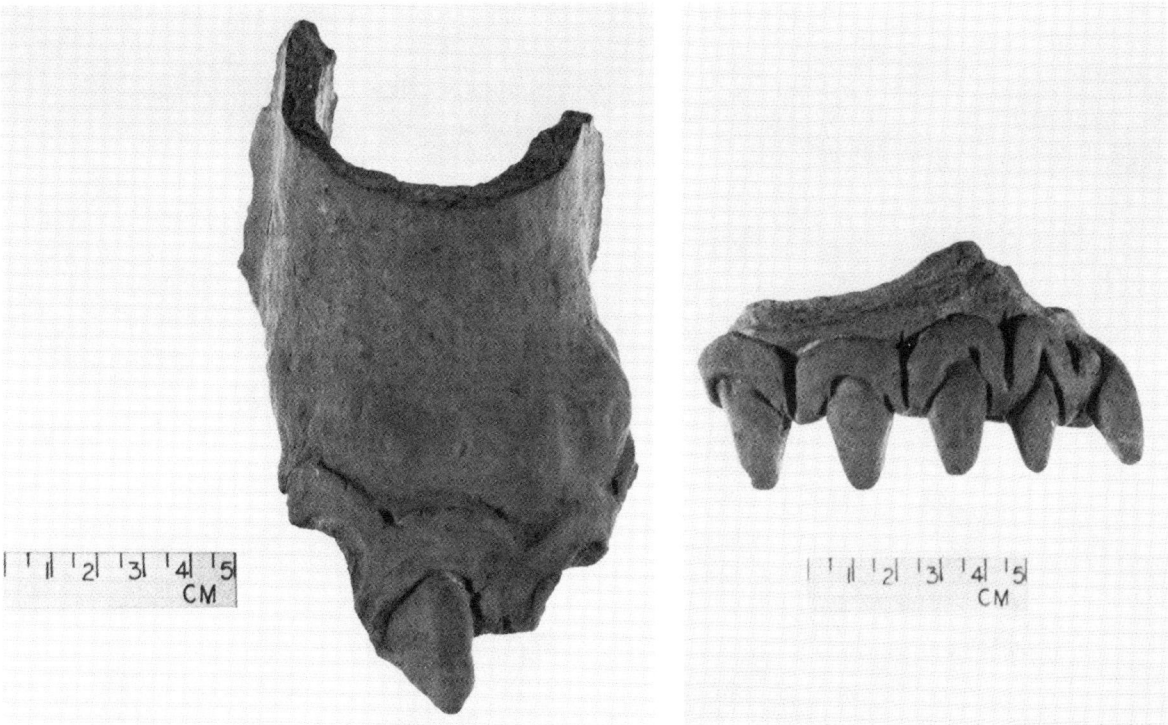

Plate 34. Ceramic jaguar-paw urn fragments recovered from plaza areas of two Lomas phase sites in the Cuicatlán Cañada. *Left*, Loma de la Coyotera (Cs25/874). *Right*, Cuba Libre (Cs6/021).

of the ports of trade maintained by the Aztec and Maya during the Postclassic period. More recently, a number of archaeologists have applied the port-of-trade model to potential pre-Columbian examples of ports of trade in Mesoamerica (Rathje and Sabloff 1973; Sabloff et al. 1974; Sabloff and Freidel 1975; Sabloff and Rathje 1975; Brown 1977; Henderson et al. 1979).

Ports of trade are a vehicle for exchange between rulers of separate polities. They are frequently established on the borders of environmentally distinct regions, and/or in politically neutral buffer zones outside the boundaries of powerful states. Such a marginal location reduces the distances traveled by the traders from the separate regions, and provides a neutral meeting place for the representatives of neighboring polities (Chapman 1957:116).

A specialized group of traders often carries out this trade at the ports of trade under the close administration of local port officials. Trade is treaty-based; all competition is excluded and prices are fixed. The ports of trade provide the trading facilities, which include warehouses for storing the trade goods and temporary residences for the foreign traders. The native residents at the ports of trade render ancillary services to the foreign traders through the local market but generally do not have access to the items being exchanged there (Chapman 1957:116; Leeds 1961:27; Arnold 1957b:182).

The trade conducted at ports of trade is considered an affair of state between the rulers of the politically independent states in part because the objects being traded are special items, which are not exchanged in the general marketplace and which consequently do not reach the population at large. These items are circulated to state officials and members of the ruling class. The port of trade is therefore "a way of moving goods necessary for military needs, elite consumption, public works or public payments" (Leeds 1961:28).

In view of the foregoing discussion on the characteristics and functions of ports of trade, we must return to the problem of how the Monte Albán state traded with polities beyond its expanded frontiers. As we have seen, the Quiotepec alluvial fan of the Cuicatlán Cañada marked the northern extent of Zapotec expansion during the Late Formative period. The Tehuacán Valley to the north remained

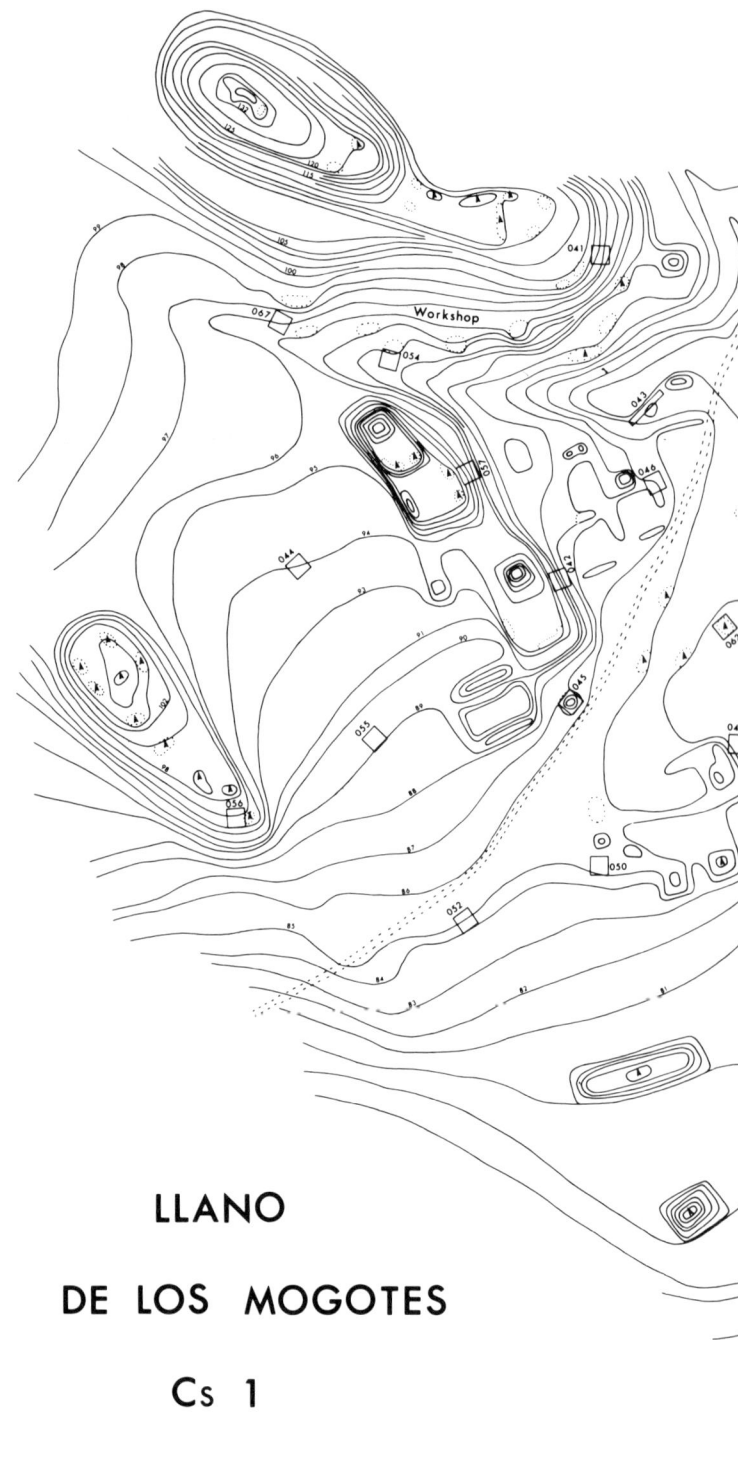

Figure 50. Llano de los Mogotes site map (Cs1).

THE LOMAS PHASE

Plate 35. View of site of Llano de los Mogotes (Cs1) on high alluvium and low piedmont from opposite side of Río Salado, facing east.

free from Zapotec control and witnessed instead the development of autonomous polities at this time. If certain raw materials such as obsidian were desired by the Zapotec and derived from obsidian sources controlled by polities in the Central Mexican highlands, we might expect to find the establishment of neutral ports of trade beyond Monte Albán's northern frontier in the Late Formative period, in order for Monte Albán to maintain its prior exchange relations with the polities who controlled the obsidian sources. The emergence of ports of trade here would be intimately tied to Monte Albán's expansion. This trade would constitute a vehicle for resolving the disruptive effects that Monte Albán's expansion had upon previous interregional trade relations. It would also be necessary for the very maintenance of Monte Albán's frontier regions—considering how the military forces stationed in regions like the Cuicatlán Cañada needed to be outfitted and remunerated with certain items supplied by these interregional exchange relationships.

Let us examine the site of Llano de los Mogotes (Cs1-L), situated near the present-day town of Santa María Tecomavaca in the southern tip of the Tehuacán Valley (Fig. 34). It lies on the border between the Cuicatlán Cañada and the southern Tehuacán Valley, along the major communication route connecting these two regions. While surveying this Late Formative settlement north of the Cañada we discovered the ceramic boundary at the Quiotepec frontier; in contrast to the Monte Albán and Lomas ceramics recovered from the settlements in the Cuicatlán Cañada, the ceramics collected on the surface here conform to the ceramics of the Palo Blanco phase in the Tehuacán Valley sequence (MacNeish, Peterson, and Flannery 1970:145-174). If, as I have suggested, this ceramic boundary coincided with the northernmost limits of Zapotec military expansion during the Late Formative period, then the settlement at Llano de los Mogotes lay just outside the territory subjugated by Monte Albán.

During the transition from the Late Santa María phase to the Early Palo Blanco phase—the same transition as that from the Perdido phase to the Lomas phase in the Cuicatlán Cañada sequence—

Plate 36. View of central civic-ceremonial area of Llano de los Mogotes (Cs1) from the top of the piedmont eminence at the site's northeastern end, facing southwest.

the site of Cs1 grew over five times in size, from 5.87 ha in the Late Santa María phase to 29.58 ha in the succeeding Early Palo Blanco phase. The site of Llano de los Mogotes became one of the largest settlements in the Tehuacán Valley at this time (cf. Nowack 1977; Drennan 1979; Spencer 1979). Unfortunately, because much of the site is under cultivation at present, and the non-mounded architectural remains are not generally evident on the plowed surface of the site, the only population estimate that I can generate for Cs1-L is based on its size. At 10-25 persons per hectare of occupation, the estimated population for Cs1-L ranges between 296 and 739 persons.

The site extends across a high alluvial terrace and adjoining low piedmont slope east of the Río Salado (Pl. 35). This location is a surprising one, since most Early Palo Blanco centers in the Tehuacán Valley occupy hilltops and piedmont ridges; access to some of these centers is further restricted by means of defensive walls (Nowack 1977; Drennan 1979; Spencer 1979). Unlike other contemporaneous settlements in the Tehuacán Valley, therefore, defense does not appear to have been a consideration in the location of Cs1-L. We have already discussed the fortified settlements on the Quiotepec alluvial fan directly to the south in the Cuicatlán Cañada.

In contrast to the general settlement shift off the high alluvium seen in the Cuicatlán Cañada, which appears to have been related to an expansion in that region's agricultural production, Cs1-L's location on a stretch of cultivable land suggests that a strategy of local agricultural intensification by bringing the

Table 27. Distribution of Ground Stone Tools and Comales† at Llano de los Mogotes

Site Sector	Total Ground Stone	Average Ratio: Comal Rims / Total Ceramic Diagnostics
Civic-ceremonial	4	.012
Residential	13	.038
Workshop	4	.003

†Only those collection squares yielding Early and Late Palo Blanco ceramics were included in this analysis.

Table 28. Density of Sherds in the Ceramic Workshop

Collection Square	Sherd Density (per m^2)	Gray		Plain		Gray/Plain Ratio
		Rims, Decorated Body Sherds	Undecorated Body Sherds	Rims, Decorated Body Sherds	Undecorated Body Sherds	
Cs1/041	20.60	297	1261	10	485	3.15
Cs1/054	14.61	206	973	13	258	4.35
Cs1/067	62.22	833	4846	60	466	10.80
Average for Workshop Squares	32.48					6.10
Average for Other Squares	5.27					1.63

high alluvium under cultivation was not being pursued here. We can measure the relationship between the available sustaining area and the associated Early Palo Blanco phase population at Cs1-L by following the procedure outlined in Chapter 2. The potential maize yields rendered on the low alluvium and that portion of the high alluvium not occupied by Cs1-L would have supported at most 943 persons. There is a small margin between this figure and the maximum range of the Early Palo Blanco phase population estimate for Cs1-L. It would appear that agricultural production here in the Early Palo Blanco phase was designed to meet only the needs of the local population.

Plate 37. Misfired sherds from the ceramic workshop at Llano de los Mogotes (Cs1/067).

True to its name, the site of Llano de los Mogotes contains a vast array of public buildings and interconnected courtyards (Fig. 50), which are distributed across a large area of the site. A massive multi-tiered mound platform supporting two pyramidal mounds and a number of associated structures forms the focus of the site's civic-ceremonial sector (Pl. 36). A ballcourt projects northward from the western end of this mound platform. South of the mound platform extend five interconnected courtyards measuring roughly 20-25 m on a side, surrounded on all four sides by low elongated mounds. There were probably more of these courtyard groups than can be seen on the heavily cultivated surface of the site today, since traces of at least three additional courtyard groups extend south and west of here. A second ballcourt and two large mounds rise in the northwestern quarter of the site. In all, the civic-ceremonial sector of Cs1-L assumes approximately 50% of the settlement's total area.

The definition of the civic-ceremonial sector of Cs1-L as the area of the site featuring public architecture is supported by the distribution of ground stone tools and comal rims across the different sectors of the site (Table 27). Ground stone implements and comales are good indicators of domestic activities, so it is not surprising to find the greatest numbers of these two artifacts outside the civic-cer-

Table 29. Craft-Related Artifacts in the Ceramic Workshop

Collection Square	Misfired Gray Sherds	Slag	Bark-Beater
Cs1/041	0	0	0
Cs1/054	1	0	0
Cs1/067	169	8	1

emonial sector in the residential sector of the site. The differences in the number of ground stone tools collected in the various sectors of the site and the average ratios of comal rims obtained in these sectors conform to the public and residential sectors defined here.

On the lower slope of the piedmont eminence rising east of the civic-ceremonial sector we discovered the surface remains of a ceramic workshop (Fig. 50). The workshop sector is characterized by the occurrence of large densities of ceramics, misfired sherds, fragments of misfired clay or slag, and other craft-related artifacts. Surface collection squares Cs1/041, Cs1/054, and Cs1/067 yielded unusually large numbers of El Riego Gray ceramics (Table 28) (MacNeish, Peterson, and Flannery 1970:146-155). Among these large quantities of ceramics were a total of 170 misfired sherds or kiln wasters, which indicate that El Riego Gray ceramics were being produced in this workshop (Pl. 37). Fragments of misfired clay or slag were found amid the workshop debris, as was a polished stone bark-beater (Table 29, Pl. 38). Many of these surface characteristics resemble those associated with the ceramic workshop discovered at another Palo Blanco phase center to the north in the Arroyo Lencho Diego area of the southern Tehuacán Valley, which also produced El Riego Gray ceramics (Redmond 1979). Misfired El Riego Gray ceramics have also been reported at other Palo Blanco phase centers in the Tehuacán Valley (Nowack 1977; Drennan 1979). It would appear that the ceramic workshop at Llano de los Mogotes, like those at other Palo Blanco phase centers, was producing El Riego Gray ceramics to meet the settlement's local needs.

On the basis of the following characteristics of Cs1-L: (1) its location on the geographic boundary between the Cuicatlán Cañada and the Tehuacán Valley; (2) its position just outside the territory subjugated by Monte Albán during the Late Formative; (3) its non-defensive location on the valley floor; (4) its size and estimated population relative to the associated catchment area; and (5) its configuration

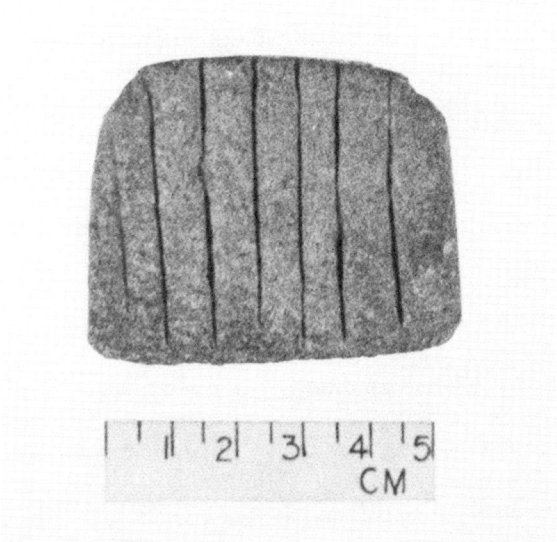

Plate 38. Polished stone bark-beater from the ceramic workshop at Llano de los Mogotes (Cs1/067).

of public buildings and interconnected courtyard groups, I would propose that Cs1-L functioned as a port of trade. Located as it was beyond the Quiotepec frontier of the Monte Albán state in an undefended position, the site of Llano de los Mogotes would have served as a neutral meeting place for Zapotec traders to exchange with traders from polities existing beyond the borders of Zapotec-controlled territory.

The rapid growth of this settlement during the transition from the Late Santa María phase to the Early Palo Blanco phase and the unusual elaboration of its civic-ceremonial sector would be consistent with its role as a specialized trading center. Unfortunately, to date we lack detailed descriptions of the internal structures of ports of trade with which to compare Llano de los Mogotes (Brown 1977:309-310). One Mesoamerican port of trade, the town of Itzamkanac on the Río Candelaria, was described by the early Spanish explorers as having a large population. The center consisted of between 900 and 1000 residences, and was organized into four quarters, each quarter having its patron deity (Scholes and Roys 1948:53-57, 110, 160). Although we are told that ports of trade such as Itzamkanac contained warehouses and associated trading facilities for use by foreign traders, we lack precise descriptions of them.

The lattice of interconnected courtyards surrounded by low platforms in the heart of the civic-ceremonial sector of Cs1-L might well have been among the facilities built to "implement exchange, storage, transport, and resupply transactions" (Sabloff and Rathje 1975:14) between the foreign traders meeting here. Among the goals of recent archaeological investigations on the island of Cozumel off the east coast of the Yucatán Peninsula, which is known to have functioned as a trading center during the Postclassic period, was the archaeological identification of the facilities associated with a port of trade. According to members of the Cozumel Archaeological Project, the site of Buena Vista functioned as a major storage area for perishable commodities being transshipped through the port of trade (Sabloff and Freidel 1975:397-400; Sabloff and Rathje 1975:77-87, Map 1). At Buena Vista, they mapped a network of "agglutinated" low rubble platforms extending over approximately 5 ha, which they suggest functioned as storage areas for exchange and resupply transactions. The series of interconnected courtyards and low platforms at Llano de los Mogotes might have served a similar function as the rubble platforms at Buena Vista.

Although certain characteristics of the site of Llano de los Mogotes match some of the known features of ports of trade, what artifactual evidence do we have from Cs1-L that would be consistent with this interpretation? Before I present the evidence, however, I should offer two cautionary notes. The first warning concerns the complete intermixing of Early and Late Palo Blanco ceramics in all the surface collections at Cs1, making it difficult to distinguish between the two occupations. The second problem is one that has already been considered by other archaeologists investigating a port of trade. In outlining the archaeological correlates of a port of trade, Rathje and Sabloff bring up an important point:

> It is often assumed that a trade center will be identified by the presence of large quantities of trade goods. This assumption ignores the constraints upon the function of trading centers, not as final destination[s] of goods, but merely as facilities which rapidly effect their transshipment. A trading system which "leaks" large quantities of goods locally would not be functioning as a useful trading center. [Sabloff and Rathje 1975:13]

The distribution of items being exchanged at a port of trade like Cs1 might not be as clear-cut as we would like it to be.

Given the difficulty of differentiating between the Early and Late Palo Blanco phase occupations at Cs1, I must assume that the function of the site remained the same during the two time periods represented. Actually, our most complete artifactual evidence on the distribution of trade items at Cs1 comes from the Late Palo Blanco phase or Classic period occupation (see Fig. 8). Two trade items controlled by the city of Teotihuacán during the Early Classic period were Thin Orange ceramics and green obsidian blades (Millon 1981:224; Séjourné 1966:148; Hirth 1981:142). Robert Drennan and Judith Nowack have examined the distribution of these two items at Palo Blanco phase centers in the Tehuacán Valley; they find the concentration of these items at certain centers in the Tehuacán Valley to be related to their proximity to major travel routes through the region (Drennan and Nowack 1977). One of the Palo Blanco phase centers having a notable abundance of Thin Orange ceramics and green obsidian is Llano de los Mogotes (Cs1).

We can examine the distribution of Thin Orange ceramics and green obsidian blades among the different sectors of Llano de los Mogotes (Table 30). If

Table 30. Distribution of Thin Orange Ceramics and Green Obsidian at Llano de los Mogotes†

Site Sector	Average Ratio: Thin Orange / Total Ceramic Diagnostics	Average Ratio: Green Obsidian / Total Chipped Stone
Civic-ceremonial	.118	.249
Residential	.066	.188
Workshop	.026	0

†Only those collection squares yielding Early and Late Palo Blanco ceramics were included in this analysis (see Chapter 2).

we compare the average ratios of these trade items in the three sectors of Cs1, we find that the civic-ceremonial sector has much higher average ratios of Thin Orange ceramics and green obsidian blades. Not only does the general concentration of these trade items at Llano de los Mogotes support the view that the site functioned as a port of trade, but the internal distribution of these items within the site suggests that the civic-ceremonial sector, which contains the interconnected courtyard groups, was probably the major locus of foreign exchange. The concentration of trade items within this public sector of the port of trade would further agree with the possibility that this exchange was administered by native officials here.

The artifactual evidence supporting the role of Llano de los Mogotes as a port of trade during the Early Palo Blanco phase is not quite as abundant. Table 31 lists the frequencies of foreign ceramics collected at the site. In addition to Thin Orange ceramics of the Classic period from Central Mexico, Period Late I and II ceramics from the Valley of Oaxaca are present, as well as a differentially fired, white-rimmed black ware, a major ceramic ware in lowland regions during the Late Formative and Protoclassic periods (Zeitlin 1979:60-61, 67, 357-365; Coe and Diehl 1980:211). Also listed are a variety of unidentifiable ceramics, which might well be trade wares from other regions of Mesoamerica. The Monte Albán Ic-II ceramics and the white-rimmed black ceramics come from three surface collections located directly east and north of the site's principal mound platform (see Fig. 50). The distribution of these Late Formative ceramics from foreign regions at the site is not conclusive in and of itself; nevertheless, it does support the view that Llano de los Mogotes functioned as a port of trade during the Early Palo Blanco phase.

If Llano de los Mogotes became a port of trade in response to Zapotec expansion into the Cuicatlán Cañada, what might the port of trade's relationship have been to the Zapotec military installations at the Quiotepec frontier? Some portion of the obsidian received by Zapotec traders at the port of trade was probably supplied directly to the Quiotepec frontier, where the greatest densities of obsidian are found during the Lomas phase (Table 15). Moreover, with one exception, the Quiotepec sites are the only settlements in the Cuicatlán Cañada during the Lomas phase that received green obsidian. I would propose, therefore, that the port of trade at Llano de los Mogotes was fostered by the Monte Albán state in the Late Formative period for the purpose of trading with independent polities beyond its borders to the north, where the major obsidian sources lay.

Given such a relationship between the Quiotepec frontier and the port of trade at Tecomavaca, it is interesting to note a "leakage" in the ceramic boundary separating the Cuicatlán Cañada from the

Table 31. Distribution of Foreign Ceramics at Llano de los Mogotes

Surface Collection	Total Ceramic Diagnostics	Oaxaca Ceramics	White-Rim Black Ware	Other Wares	Thin Orange
Cs1/041	314	0	0	1	6
Cs1/042	127	0	0	0	2
Cs1/043	80	0	0	0	12
Cs1/044	171	2	1	2	7
Cs1/045	111	0	0	0	3
Cs1/046	85	0	0	0	30
Cs1/047	241	0	0	2	34
Cs1/048	123	0	0	0	3
Cs1/049	113	0	0	0	16
Cs1/050	130	0	0	1	7
Cs1/051	112	0	0	2	15
Cs1/053	98	0	0	0	9
Cs1/054	230	0	1	0	10
Cs1/055	61	0	0	1	3
Cs1/056	155	0	0	1	15
Cs1/057	84	0	0	1	2
Cs1/058	131	0	0	0	8
Cs1/062	189	0	0	1	13
Cs1/067	910	2	0	2	13

Table 32. Distribution of El Riego Gray Decorated Ceramics at 17 Lomas Phase Settlements

Alluvial Fan	Site	Surface Collections†	Total Ceramic Diagnostics	El Riego Gray Decorated	Ratio
Quiotepec	Cs2-L	10	812	0	0
	Cs3-L	24	1690	10	.006
	Cs26-L	2	90	0	0
	Cs27-L	11	840	0	0
Cuicatlán	Cs5-L	6	1225	1	.0008
	Cs6-L	9	547	0	0
	Cs9-L	2	274	0	0
	Cs10-L	1	17	0	0
	Cs11-L	3	123	0	0
	Cs12-L	3	133	0	0
	Cs13-L	10	595	1	.0017
	Cs15/66-L	1	27	0	0
El Chilar	Cs16-L	6	568	0	0
	Cs19-L	6	743	0	0
	Cs20-L	3	135	0	0
	Cs21-L	3	57	0	0
Dominguillo	Cs25-L	25	2263	0	0

†All surface collections yielding Lomas phase ceramics were included in this analysis (see Chapter 2).

Tehuacán Valley—aside from the handful of Monte Albán Ic-II ceramics recovered at the port of trade. At the site of Paso de Quiotepec (Cs3-L) we collected a smattering of gray ceramics having the distinctive incised decoration found on El Riego Gray ceramics that we know were being produced at Llano de los Mogotes, as well as at a number of other Palo Blanco phase centers in the Tehuacán Valley (Table 32) (MacNeish, Peterson, and Flannery 1970:146-155). Only two other examples of El Riego Gray decorated pottery were recovered during our intensive survey of Lomas phase settlements in the Cuicatlán Cañada.

Not only does the occurrence of these El Riego Gray decorated ceramics at Paso de Quiotepec confirm the contemporaneity of the Quiotepec settlements and the site of Llano de los Mogotes, but it provides independent archaeological evidence of the direct relationship between the Quiotepec frontier and the port of trade. I believe that the port of trade was partnered by the Monte Albán state in order to preserve those trade relations with other political powers, especially with those polities who controlled the obsidian sources lying outside the confines of Zapotec territory. The trade items received by the Monte Albán state through ports of trade like the one at Llano de los Mogotes were probably channeled as supplies and rewards to the military forces in the service of the state and to the Zapotec elite residing at Monte Albán.

Once again, we must consider the administrative implications of this form of state-administered exchange for the Monte Albán state. We might expect to find the emergence of a permanent body of long-distance traders in the service of the state at this time, who conducted their exchange at ports of trade located beyond the borders of the territory held by the Zapotec. The establishment of distant ports of trade like the one at Llano de los Mogotes, and the development of a specialized body of Zapotec traders who journeyed there, would have placed further demands upon Monte Albán's administrative organization during the Late Formative.

Summary

Evidence has been presented that supports the hypothesized conquest of the Cuicatlán Cañada by the Valley Zapotec sometime during the Late Formative period. We have seen how the Cuicatlán Cañada was transformed from a previously autonomous region into a frontier tributary region of the Monte Albán state. The nature of Monte Albán's control over this frontier region resembles that in frontier regions of other imperial states, in which the range of military control reaches beyond the area that can, after conquest, be added to the civil territory of the state.

Zapotec military control was concentrated on the Quiotepec alluvial fan at the northern boundary of the Cuicatlán Cañada. The functions of the Quiotepec frontier were to define and guard the Monte Albán state's expanded boundary enclosing the subjugated region and to regulate the flow of traffic across the state's border. Settlements in the central and southern alluvial fans of the Cuicatlán Cañada lay within the zone under direct Zapotec administration. A standardized tribute in the form of *tierra caliente* agricultural products—among other goods and services—was exacted and enforced on the local level here by state-level administrators. The functions of the zones of Zapotec military control and civil administration were interdependent: the Quiotepec frontier guarded the central and southern Cañada, and the inner-lying zone under civil administration in turn supplied food and manpower to the frontier.

The Zapotec military expansion into hinterland regions like the Cuicatlán Cañada disrupted the interregional exchange relationships maintained by the elites of these previously autonomous regions. A new mechanism of interregional exchange arose, involving the establishment of neutral ports of trade beyond the borders of Zapotec-controlled territory. One port of trade was established at Llano de los Mogotes (Cs1-L), just north of the Quiotepec frontier at the southernmost end of the Tehuacán Valley. Zapotec traders in the service of the Monte Albán state came here to meet with foreign traders. Those special items that were previously exchanged between the elites of adjacent regions in this part of Mesoamerica—including the Cuicatlán Cañada and the Valley of Oaxaca—were now supplied directly to the Monte Albán state by means of this state-administered trade. The introduction and maintenance of this form of interregional exchange was probably in the vital interests of the militaristic state, whose security and cohesion depended upon it.

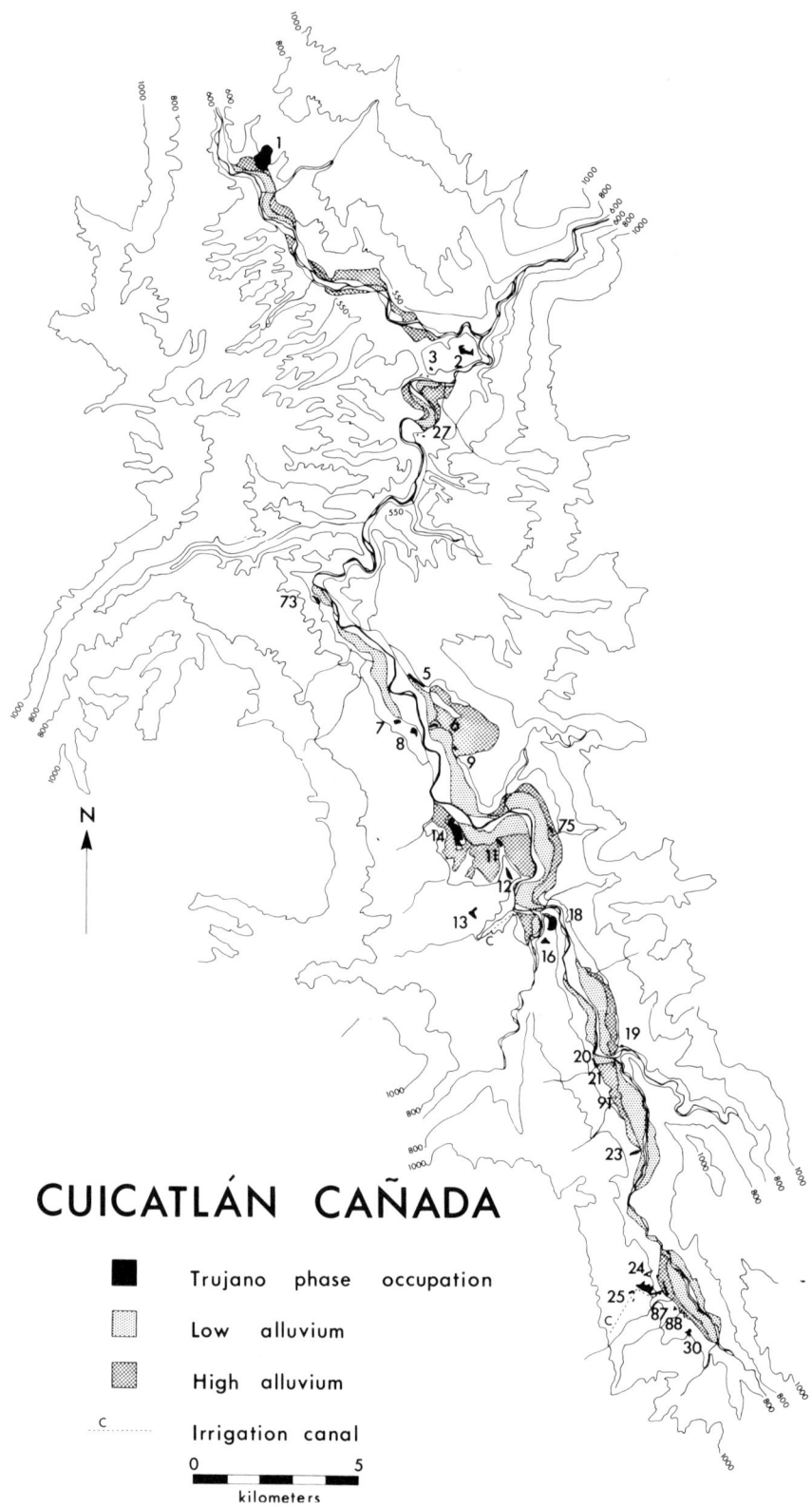

Figure 51. Trujano phase regional settlement pattern map.

Chapter 5

The Cuicatlán Cañada During the Trujano Phase

Transition

Considerable change occurred in the region's settlement pattern during the transition from the Lomas phase to the Trujano phase (Fig. 51). First of all, the settlement on the Quiotepec alluvial fan at the Cañada's northern boundary—which had expanded to such an extent during the Lomas phase—shrank dramatically. Four of the seven Lomas phase settlements in the Quiotepec area were abandoned, including the lookout post above the mountain pass at the northern point of entry to the region (Cs74-L), as well as the public facility located on the Quiotepec alluvium directly south across a ford on the Río Grande from the mouth of the pass (Cs26-L). The hilltop fortress of Cerro de Quiotepec (Cs2-L) became the only major settlement here. The other two settlements that continued to be occupied in the Trujano phase—one of which had previously spanned both sides of the critical mountain pass—were reduced to the size and status of small hamlets (Cs3-T, Cs27-T) (see Table 33).

If the Quiotepec alluvial fan formed the outer zone of a frontier region under Zapotec military administration during the previous Lomas phase (Chapter 4), the abandonment of major military facilities here in the Trujano phase suggests that the Zapotec were no longer interested in controlling the northern boundary of the Cuicatlán Cañada and in regulating the flow of traffic in and out of the region. Associated with the apparent abandonment of the major Zapotec installations at the Quiotepec frontier is a notable reversal in the relationship between the total settlement and the available farmland there (Tables 34, 36). Unlike the disparity seen during the Lomas phase between the size of the settlement on the Quiotepec alluvial fan and the estimated carrying capacity of the available farmland—which reflected the specialized and artificial character of Zapotec military control here—settlement in the Quiotepec area became commensurate with the estimated carrying capacity of the alluvial fan. In light of these developments on the Quiotepec alluvial fan, therefore, I suggest that the Quiotepec area ceased to be in the hands of Zapotec military forces during the Trujano phase.

The alluvial fans of the central and southern Cañada, on the other hand, witnessed a resurgence and growth in settlement during the Trujano phase. Of the 23 settlements occupying hilltop locations here, half represent enlarged Lomas phase settlements; the other half were newly founded at this time. Table 33 lists the 26 Trujano phase sites found on the region's four alluvial fans together with their sizes. If we compare the total settlement on each of the region's alluvial fans during the Lomas phase to that during the Trujano phase (Table 34), we find that while settlement dropped sharply on the northern Quiotepec alluvial fan, there was up to a threefold or fourfold increase in settlement associated with the Cuicatlán, El Chilar, and Dominguillo alluvial fans. The concentration of settlement shifted away from the Quiotepec area to the central and southern Cañada, where there are signs of definite population growth.

North of the Cañada proper near present-day Santa María Tecomavaca lies the largest Classic period site in the survey area. The Late Palo Blanco phase occupation at Llano de los Mogotes (Cs1-T) maintains the 29.58 ha that the site had assumed over the preceding Lomas phase. Because Cs1-T lies outside the Cuicatlán Cañada, however, I will not include it in my discussion of Classic period developments in this region.

If we construct a histogram of Trujano phase settlement sizes in the Cuicatlán Cañada (Fig. 52), we find a clear departure from the unimodal distribution of settlement sizes that characterized the central and southern Cañada during the previous Lomas phase (see Fig. 36)—which probably represented the curtailment of native political institutions under the administrative policies introduced by the conquering Zapotec. For the Trujano phase there is a definite hierarchy of settlement sizes in

Table 33. The Sizes of Trujano Phase Settlements in the Cuicatlán Cañada

Alluvial Fan	Site Number	Site Name	Site Size (ha)
Quiotepec	Cs2-T	Cerro de Quiotepec	7.80
	Cs3-T	Paso de Quiotepec	1.44
	Cs27-T	El Campanario	.46
		Total Settlement Area	9.70
Cuicatlán	Cs73-T	none	2.33
	Cs5-T	Horno de Cal	7.44
	Cs6-T	Cuba Libre	1.87
	Cs7-T	none	2.50
	Cs8-T	El Tablero	3.00
	Cs9-T	La Bomba	1.37
	Cs11-T	Loma del Llano Chiquito	1.37
	Cs12-T	Cerro Mixteco	3.16
	Cs13-T	Loma Grande	3.17–4.04
	Cs14-T	Loma Larga	11.95
	Cs75-T	La Gasolinera	1.50
		Total Settlement Area	40.09
El Chilar	Cs16-T	Sitio Entre Dos Ríos	3.78
	Cs18-T	Puente del Río Grande	9.70
	Cs19-T	Hacienda Tecomaxtlahua	.43
	Cs20-T	Las Monjas	2.29
	Cs21-T	Cerro Cortés	.38
	Cs23-T	none	2.55
	Cs91-T	El Panteón	.20
		Total Settlement Area	19.33
Dominguillo	Cs24-T	Las Bugambilias	1.95
	Cs25-T	Loma de la Coyotera	9.73
	Cs30	Loma del Panteón	2.60
	Cs87-T	La Peñita	.70
	Cs88-T	Loma del Barrio del Ticolute (Tecolote)	.60
		Total Settlement Area	15.58

the region; while the majority of settlements range up to 4 ha in size, four settlements are substantially larger (Cs2-T, Cs25-T, Cs18-T, Cs14-T). Thus, there is an unequivocal two-level hierarchy and probably a three-level hierarchy of settlement sizes in the Cañada at this time.

Each of the four largest Trujano phase settlements in the Cañada is associated with one of the region's four alluvial fans. Moreover, the ranking of the sizes of these four settlements agrees with the ranking of the sizes of the associated alluvial fans

Table 34. Comparison of Lomas and Trujano Phase Settlement on the Cañada's Alluvial Fans

Alluvial Fan	Total Lomas Phase Settlement (ha)	Total Trujano Phase Settlement (ha)
Quiotepec	44.34	9.70
Cuicatlán	18.15	40.09
El Chilar	6.11	19.33
Dominguillo	3.04	15.58

(Table 37). The largest settlement in the Cuicatlán Cañada during the Trujano phase (Cs14-T), for example, occurs on the region's major alluvial fan. The association of a large settlement with each alluvial fan in the region contrasts with the previous concentration of large settlements on the smallest alluvial fan at Quiotepec during the Lomas phase. Trujano phase settlement on each alluvial fan consists of a large nucleated center (8–12 ha) with associated smaller settlements (see Table 33).

Furthermore, if we examine the public sectors of Trujano phase settlements here we find that they vary in terms of the sizes of their plazas, the volumes of their mound platforms, and the presence of ballcourts (Table 38). Three of the four large settlements (Cs2-T, Cs25-T, Cs14-T) on the Quiotepec, Dominguillo, and Cuicatlán alluvial fans respectively, have single or double plazas surrounded by sizable mounds, and they all include a ballcourt (see Figs. 43, 48, 53). Although the largest settlement associated with the El Chilar alluvial fan, Cs18-T,

Table 35. Estimators of Population at Trujano Phase Settlements in the Cuicatlán Cañada

Alluvial Fan	Site	Site Size (ha)	Population Estimate @ 10-25 Persons per Hectare	Number of Residential Terraces	Number of Housemounds	Population Estimate @ 5 Persons per House
Quiotepec	Cs2-T	7.80	78-195	50-60	110-115	550-575
	Cs3-T	1.44	14-36	0	5-10	25-50
	Cs27-T	.46	5-11	3	8-16	40-80
Total		9.70	97-242		123-141	615-705
Cuicatlán	Cs73-T	2.33	23-58	0	23-28	115-140
	Cs5-T	7.44	74-186	43-45	44-88?	220-440
	Cs6-T	1.87	19-47	4-?	26-28	130-140
	Cs7-T	2.50	25-62	0	30	150
	Cs8-T	3.00	30-75	25	50-75	250-375
	Cs9-T	1.37	14-34	0	5-10?	25-50
	Cs11-T	1.37	14-34	15-17	29-34	145-170
	Cs12-T	3.16	32-79	46-48	69-76	345-380
	Cs13-T	3.17-4.04	36-90	48-50	80-85	400-425
	Cs14-T	11.95	119-299	80-84	117	585
	Cs75-T	1.50	15-37	0	5-10?	25-50
Total		40.09	401-1002		478-581	2390-2905
El Chilar	Cs16-T	3.78	38-94	35-37	55	275
	Cs18-T	9.70	97-242	0	40-60	200-300
	Cs19-T	.43	4-11	0	4-5?	20-25
	Cs20-T	2.29	23-57	0	12-24?	60-120
	Cs21-T	.38	4-9	0	8-10	40-50
	Cs23-T	2.55	25-64	25-30	27-55?	135-275
	Cs91-T	.20	2-5	0	2-4?	10-20
Total		19.33	193-483		148-213	740-1065
Dominguillo	Cs24-T	1.95	19-49	21	36-40	180-200
	Cs25-T	9.73	97-243	95-97	169-179	845-895
	Cs30	2.60	26-65	40	40-80?	200-400
	Cs87-T	.70	7-17	10-12	18-24	90-120
	Cs88-T	.60	6-15	5-6	6-12	30-60
Total		15.58	156-389		269-335	1345-1675

lacks any public architecture, it lies at the foot of the hill occupied by Cs16-T, which does feature a central plaza delimited by public buildings (Fig. 54). For this reason, it is possible that Cs18-T was a residential sector or *barrio* of Cs16-T. Settlements in the smaller size mode tend to have plazas that occupy narrow terraces, a lower volume of mounded architecture, and the majority of them lack ballcourts (see Fig. 55). The Trujano phase settlement-size hierarchy is evidently reflected in the complex-

Table 36. Estimated Carrying Capacity of the Cañada's Alluvium and Trujano Phase Settlement

Alluvial Fan	Low Alluvium		High Alluvium		Estimated Carrying Capacity	Total Trujano Phase Settlement (ha)	Trujano Phase Population @ 10-25 Persons per Hectare	Trujano Phase Population @ 5 Persons per House
	Hectares	Annual Maize Yields (kg)	Hectares	Annual Maize Yields (kg)				
Quiotepec	32.85	58,407	59.55	54,905	567 persons	9.70	97-242 persons	615-705 persons
Cuicatlán	523.60	930,961	514.77	474,618	7028 persons	40.09	401-1002 persons	2390-2905 persons
El Chilar	297.43	528,830	118.20	108,980	3189 persons	19.33	193-483 persons	740-1065 persons
Dominguillo	142.65	253,632	59.20	54,582	1541 persons	15.58	156-389 persons	1345-1675 persons

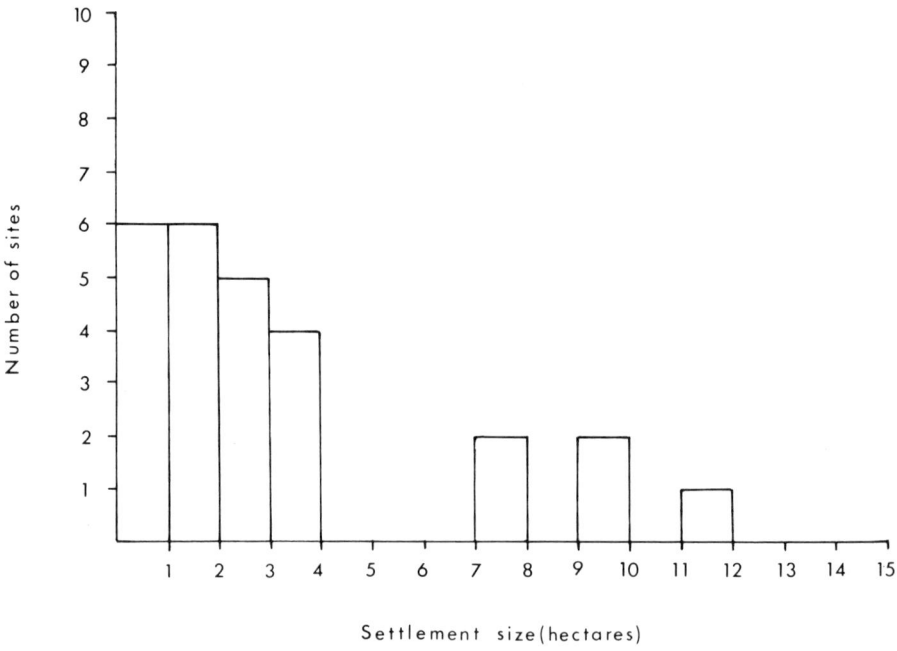

Figure 52. Histogram of Trujano phase settlement sizes.

ity and abundance of public architecture associated with Trujano phase settlements of different size ranges.

On the basis of the hierarchy of settlement sizes during the Trujano phase and the array and volume of public architecture associated with these settlements, I propose that the Cuicatlán Cañada was no longer directly administered by the Zapotec state during the Trujano phase. In response to the power vacuum left by the Zapotec administrators, native political institutions apparently arose on the separate alluvial fans to govern the region. What we observe during the transition from the Lomas phase to the Trujano phase is the dissolution of the administrative hierarchy imposed upon the region by the Zapotec in the Lomas phase and, as I shall elaborate upon later, a return in some ways to the general form of regional political organization that existed in the Cañada during the time period prior to the Zapotec subjugation, when autonomous ranked societies flourished on the region's alluvial fans (Chapter 3).

At Loma de la Coyotera (Cs25-T), the largest of the five Trujano phase communities occupying the Dominguillo alluvial fan, we have recovered evidence that documents the developments taking place at an individual community during the transition from the Lomas phase to the Trujano phase. At this time, the settlement expanded from 3.04 ha to 9.73 ha in size. Whereas 35-38 residential terraces had been occupied during the Lomas phase, the Trujano phase occupation at Loma de la Coyotera extended over 95-97 residential terraces, and its estimated population grew to between 845-895 persons (Table 35). On the basis of his excavations here, Spencer has determined that in the Trujano phase the main public building sector of the community shifted away from the small plaza where during the Lomas phase a skull rack had been raised in front of the principal mound. On the ridgetop 200 m to the southeast a new plaza area was established, which included the building of a 3-m-high mound platform to support a 2-m-high mound on its south end, and a 45-m-long ballcourt along its eastern edge (see Fig. 48) (Spencer and Redmond 1979:211-212). Such a major shift in the location of the public sector of this community—with the constructon of a new plaza area and the introduction of a ballcourt—probably reflects a change in the political order ruling here.

Excavation in the major aqueduct of the irrigation canal associated with Loma de la Coyotera suggests

Table 37. Ranking of Largest Trujano Phase Settlements and the Cañada's Four Alluvial Fans

Ranking of Largest Settlements		Ranking of Alluvial Fans	
Site	Site Size (ha)	Alluvial Fan	Size (ha)
Cs2-T	7.80	Quiotepec	92.40
Cs25-T	9.73	Dominguillo	201.85
Cs18-T	9.70	El Chilar	415.63
Cs14-T	11.95	Cuicatlán	1038.37

that this facility continued to be used throughout the Trujano phase. We have seen how this irrigation canal was constructed along the base of Loma de la Coyotera during the Lomas phase in order to channel water from a tributary stream behind the community onto the expanse of high alluvium below (Chapter 4). But, in contrast to the Lomas phase midden deposits excavated at Loma de la Coyotera, which yielded enormous quantities of carbonized tropical fruit and nut remains, the deposits associated with the Trujano phase occupation contained much lower densities of these *tierra caliente* products. The drop in the frequencies of these fruit and nut remains suggests that during the Trujano phase the irrigated high alluvium below Loma de la Coyotera appears to have been used principally to support the community's growing population. We saw in Chapter 4 how the high alluvium was first cleared and irrigated during the Lomas phase in order to intensify the production of tropical fruits and palm nuts demanded as tribute by the conquering Zapotec.

These changes in the settlement size, in the location and composition of the public sector, and in the local economy of an individual community like Loma de la Coyotera between the Lomas and Trujano phases are not consistent with a model of subjugation and tribute exaction. Instead, they constitute evidence on the community level to support the claim I made on the basis of changes in the regional organization: that the Cuicatlán Cañada was no longer directly dominated and administered by the Monte Albán state during the Trujano phase.

Classic Period Developments in Highland Mesoamerica

In order to understand the developments taking place on the alluvial fans in the Cuicatlán Cañada during the Trujano phase, we must survey the major developments occurring in highland Mesoamerica at this time. By the Early Classic period (ca. A.D. 200-300) a powerful political entity centered at Teotihuacán had emerged in the Basin of Mexico (Millon 1973:56-59; Parsons 1976b:85-89; Sanders, Parsons, and Santley 1979:105-129). The city of Teotihuacán had assumed its maximum size (20 km^2) and its characteristic urban layout, and two monumental pyramids had been erected at the north end and east side of the city's great north-south avenue. Large numbers of people from outside the Teotihuacán Valley in the Basin of Mexico were drawn to the urban center.

Teotihuacán's impact went beyond the bound-

Table 38. Public Sectors of Trujano Phase Settlements in the Cuicatlán Cañada

Alluvial Fan	Site	Site Size (ha)	Presence of a Plaza	Presence of Mounded Architecture	Presence of a Ballcourt
Quiotepec	Cs2-T	7.80	X	X	X
	Cs3-T	1.44			
	Cs27-T	.46			
Cuicatlán	Cs73-T	2.33			
	Cs5-T	7.44	X	X	
	Cs6-T	1.87	X	X	
	Cs7-T	2.50			
	Cs8-T	3.00	X	X	
	Cs9-T	1.37			
	Cs11-T	1.37	X?	X	
	Cs12-T	3.16	X	X	
	Cs13-T	3.17-4.04	X	X	X
	Cs14-T	11.95	X	X	X
	Cs75-T	1.50			
El Chilar	Cs16-T	3.78	X	X	
	Cs18-T	9.70			
	Cs19-T	.43	X		
	Cs20-T	2.29		X?	
	Cs21-T	.38		X?	
	Cs23-T	2.55	X	X	X
	Cs91-T	.20			
Dominguillo	Cs24-T	1.95			
	Cs25-T	8.03	X	X	X
	Cs30	2.60	X	X	X
	Cs87-T	.70			
	Cs88-T	.80			

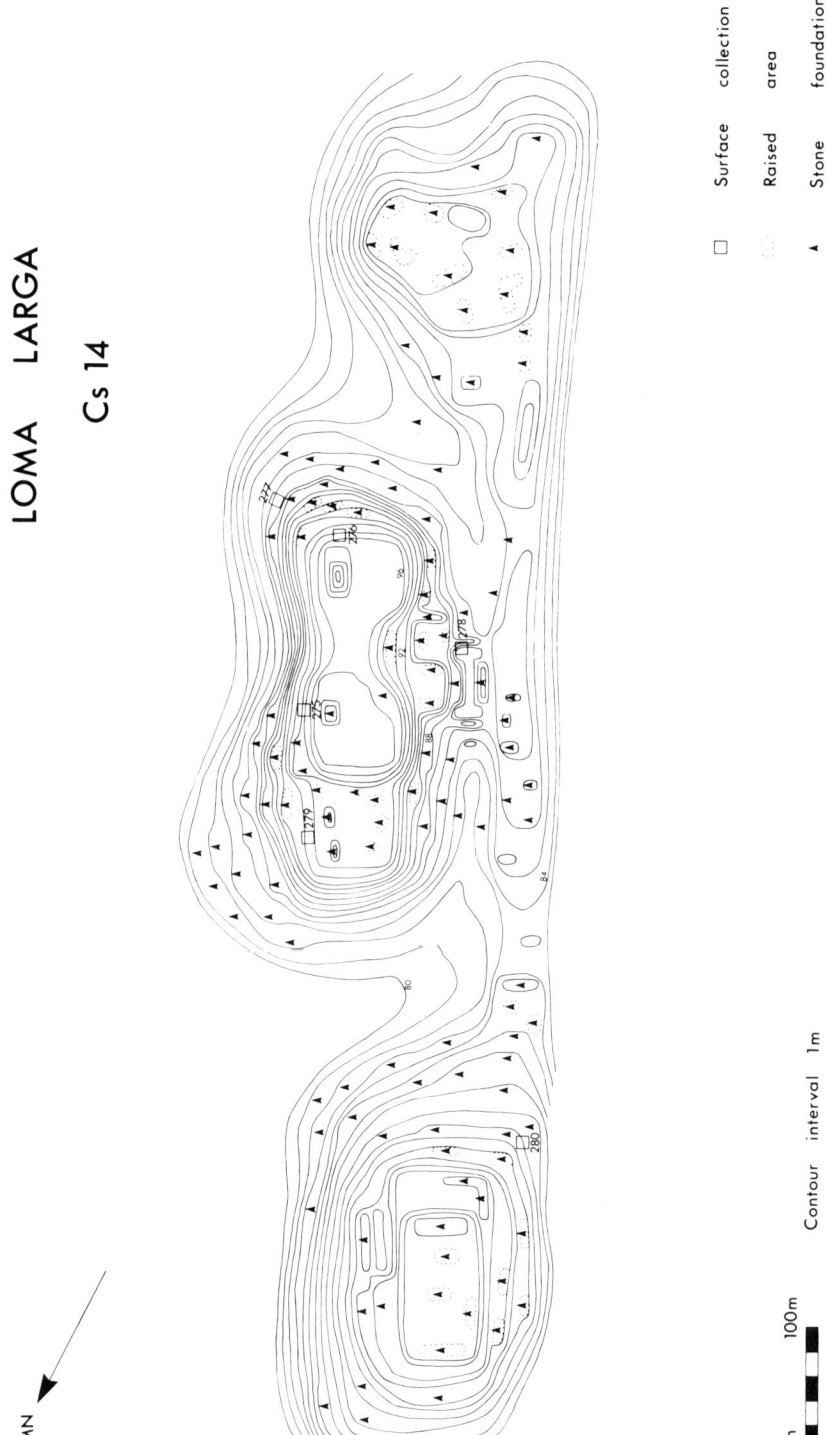

Figure 53. Loma Larga site map (Cs14).

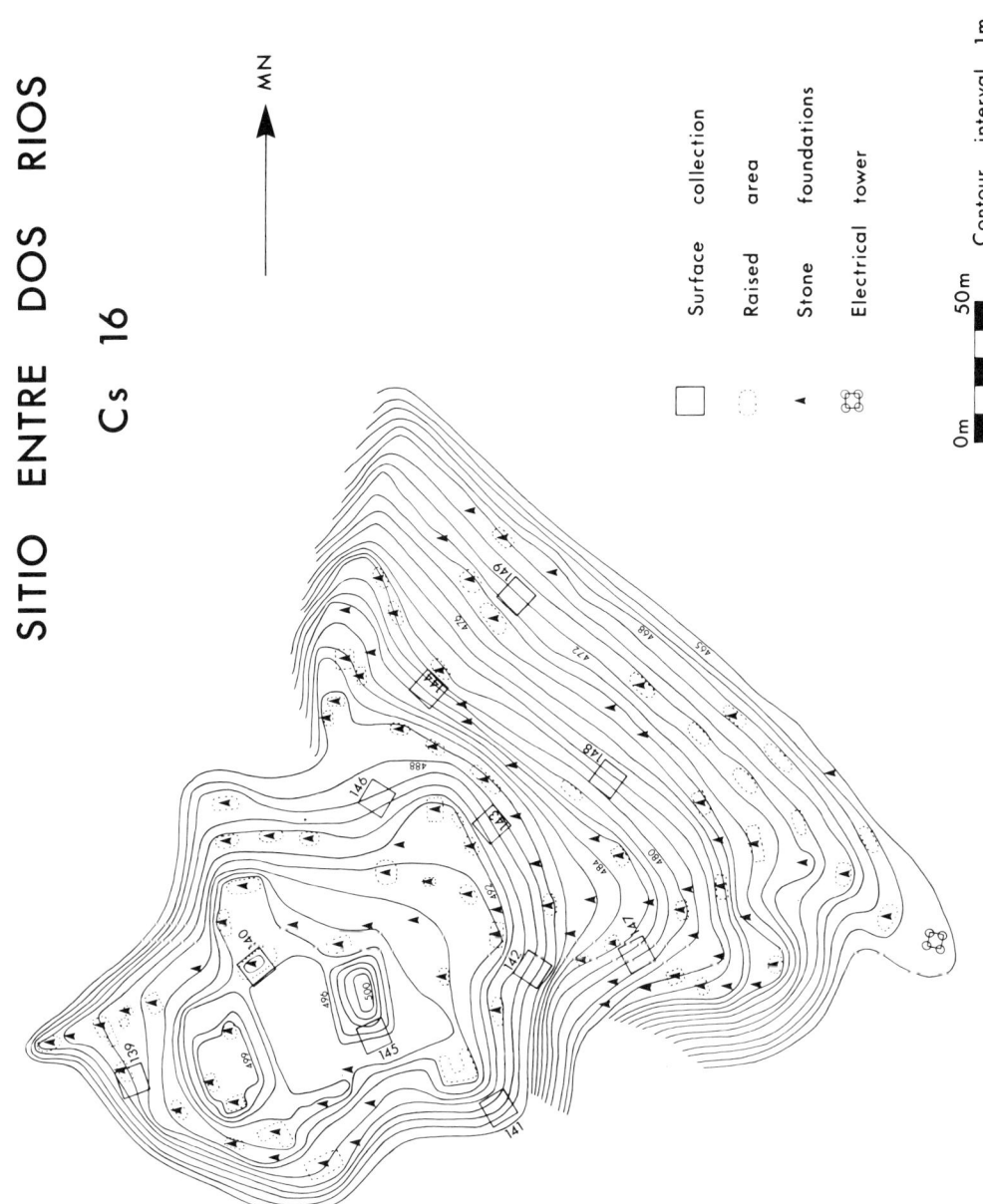

Figure 54. Sitio Entre Dos Ríos map (Cs16).

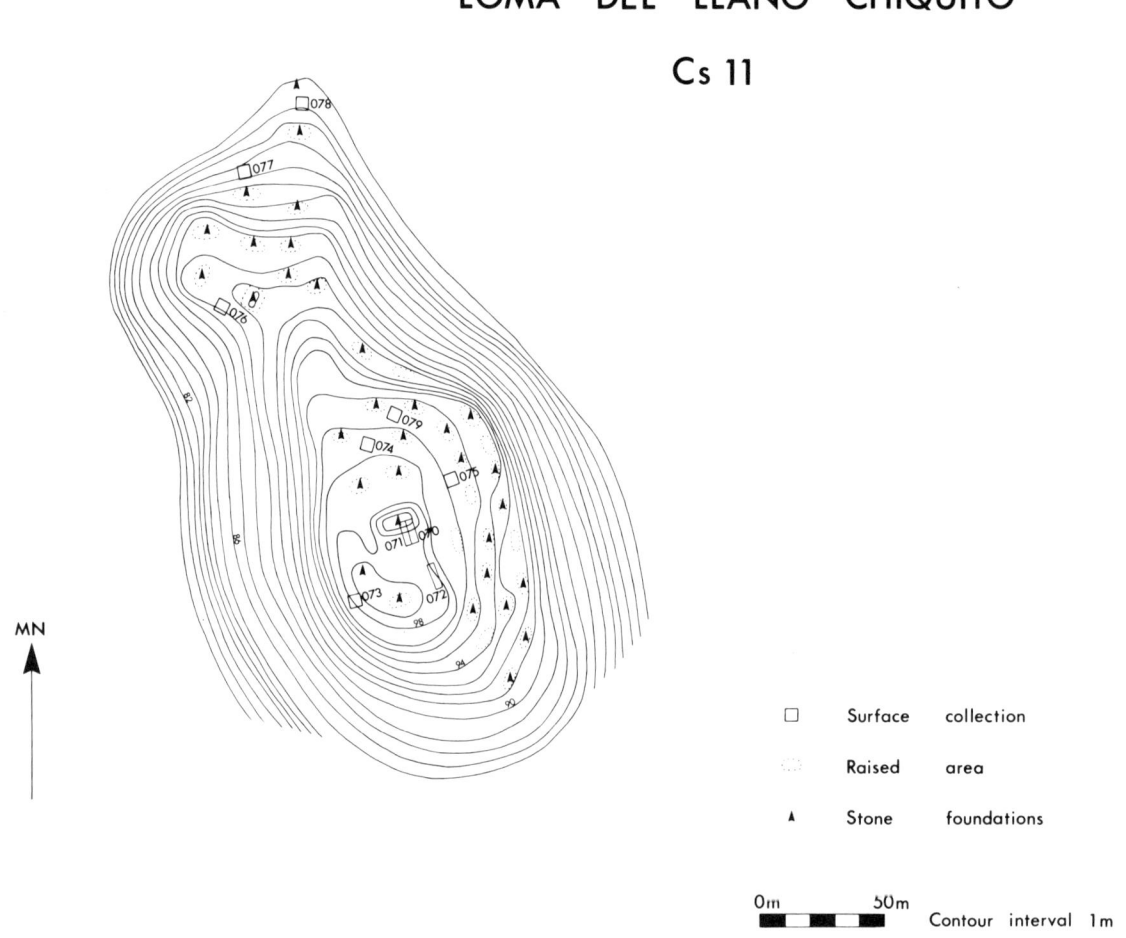

Figure 55. Loma del Llano Chiquito site map (Cs11).

aries of the Basin of Mexico, for we have evidence that Teotihuacán's political and economic influence were beginning to be felt over much of Mesoamerica during the Early Classic period; it is clear that many regions became incorporated into its empire. The Valley of Mexico and regions immediately surrounding it formed Teotihuacán's sustaining area. One of the hinterland regions controlled by Teotihuacán was the Río Amatzinac Valley in eastern Morelos, where changes in regional settlement pattern at the start of the Classic period appear to have been in response to Teotihuacán's demand for local agricultural produce (Hirth 1978:325-328, 1981: 145-148). Direct archaeological evidence of Teotihuacán's intervention at distant sites like Kaminaljuyú in the Valley of Guatemala (Kidder, Jennings, and Shook 1946; Sanders and Michels 1977) suggests that Teotihuacán maintained administrative outposts at critical points along major communication routes in order to control the flow of foreign trade goods.

Although the Central Mexican state centered at Teotihuacán might have desired to control the Valley of Oaxaca, evidence supporting a conquest has not surfaced. Blanton (1978:57) proposes that the Valley of Oaxaca with its capital at Monte Albán never became incorporated into Teotihuacán's empire, since Teotihuacán's influence on Monte Albán's ar-

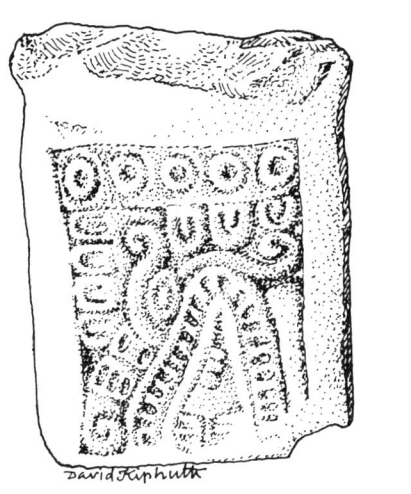 

Figure 56. This solid ceramic slab-foot support with its bas-relief depiction of the Central Mexican fire-serpent, Quetzalcoatl, was recovered in the ballcourt of Cerro de Quiotepec (Cs2), in collection square Cs2/162, which yielded predominantly Trujano phase ceramics. It measures 6.8 by 5.3 cm and is .8 cm thick.

chitecture and ceramics during the Early Classic (Periods IIIa-IIIb) is limited. But Blanton believes that Teotihuacán's unprecedented growth and expansion at the start of the Classic period would have presented a considerable military threat to the Zapotec state, and he suggests that "this probably more than any other factor explains Monte Albán's growth beginning in Period IIIa (ca. A.D. 200-400), and continuing into Period IIIb (ca. A.D. 400-600)" (Blanton 1978:57). In response to Teotihuacán's rise to prominence then, the regional capital of the Valley Zapotec at Monte Albán grew to reach its maximum population of between 15,000 to 30,000 persons, and the civic and elite residential area centered on the Main Plaza—bordered on two sides by the massive North and South Platforms—assumed its final form (Blanton 1978:57-63, 108).

I believe we can characterize the relations between Monte Albán and Teotihuacán as a peaceful, though wary, détente. During the Early Classic period a Zapotec enclave was established on the western outskirts of Teotihuacán where representatives from the Valley of Oaxaca resided, perhaps in some ambassadorial capacity, with a full complement of ceremonial and domestic ceramic wares from their homeland (Millon 1973:41-42). At the same time, stone monuments located at the corners of the South Platform at Monte Albán record ceremonial visits by Teotihuacán personages to Monte Albán, and a travertine slab from Monte Albán known as the Lápida de Bazán registers a possible agreement between representatives of the two cities (Marcus 1980: 57-59). Marcus suggests that

> . . . it was probably through diplomatic encounters such as this one that Monte Albán and its far larger neighbor Teotihuacán maintained a healthy social distance, regulated their tributary boundaries and preserved their special relationship. [Marcus 1980:59]

Table 39. Population Estimates for the *Cacicazgo* Centers in the Cuicatlán Cañada

Center	1548 *Suma de Visitas*	Hopkins' Population Estimate
Quiotepec	40 households	300 persons
Cuicatlán	140 households	1063 persons
Dominguillo	22 households	63 persons

The changes in regional settlement pattern in the Cuicatlán Cañada at the start of the Classic period must therefore be viewed in light of the major developments taking place in highland Mesoamerica at this time, particularly in the face of Teotihuacán's rise to prominence and the potential military threat it posed for Monte Albán. Changes in the regional organization of the Cuicatlán Cañada and in the organization of individual communities between the Lomas and Trujano phases probably reflect the repercussions that Teotihuacán's tremendous expansion had upon the Zapotec state centered at Monte Albán and upon the imperial strategies that Monte Albán had pursued in neighboring regions like the Cuicatlán Cañada during the Lomas phase. Remember that in the Cañada at this time we witness the abandonment of the major Zapotec military installations at the northern Quiotepec frontier (see Fig. 56). South of Quiotepec on the alluvial fans of the central and southern Cañada, we observe the dissolution of the administrative hierarchy imposed by the Zapotec for the purposes of exacting a standardized tribute from the local population there, and the resurgence of local political institutions.

Changes are also evident in the regional organization of the Valley of Oaxaca during the Early Classic period. Blanton and his collaborators (Blanton 1978; Blanton et al. 1979, 1981:88-92, 1982: 85-95) find a substantial increase in the population of Monte Albán as well as in the central and southern portions of the valley floor. Several large administrative centers were established at this time in the southern arm (Valle Grande) of the Oaxaca Valley. They view the sudden agricultural development of the high alluvium and piedmont zones in the Valle Grande in terms of the immense potential for generating agricultural surpluses. Among the factors they consider important for understanding these changes in the regional organization of the Valley of Oaxaca during the Early Classic period is the external threat posed by Teotihuacán (Blanton 1978:57; Blanton et al. 1979:382, 1981:91, 1982: 97-98). At the same time that Monte Albán was withdrawing its direct control over tributary regions like the Cuicatlán Cañada, the Valley of Oaxaca was undergoing major changes that included the establishment of secondary and tertiary administrative centers in its southern arm, and the intensification of agricultural production.

So, although Teotihuacán's expansion over much of Mesoamerica during the Early Classic period does not appear to have included the subjugation of the Oaxaca Valley, the Zapotec state centered at Monte Albán underwent changes in its administrative organization at this time, probably in response to the rise of Teotihuacán. These changes included: (1) the withdrawal of direct control over tributary regions such as the Cuicatlán Cañada; (2) the growth of the regional capital at Monte Albán; (3) the establishment of secondary and tertiary administrative centers in the southern arm of the valley; and (4) the intensification of agricultural production within this southern branch of the valley.

Ethnohistory and Postclassic Period Developments in the Cuicatlán Cañada

If Zapotec domination of the Cuicatlán Cañada ceased at the start of the Classic period, what kind of regional political organization emerged in this newly-autonomous region during the Trujano phase? We can begin to address this question by turning to the early Spanish accounts about the Cuicatec speakers who inhabited the Cuicatlán Cañada at the time of the Spanish Conquest. The major authority on the subject is Eva Hunt, and the following discussion relies principally upon her ethnohistorically-based study of the Cuicatec polities in the region during the Postclassic and early Colonial periods (Hunt 1972).

The regional organization of the Cuicatlán Cañada during the immediately pre-Conquest and early Colonial periods comprised a series of small, autonomous polities. Hunt refers to them as *cacicazgos* and defines them as territorially-bounded, autonomous political units that were ruled by *caciques* who resided at the major centers (Hunt 1972:171). The three Cuicatec *cacicazgos* in the Cañada were centered on the Atlatlauca, Dominguillo (formerly Alpizagua), and Cuicatlán alluvial fans. On the Quiotepec alluvial fan lay a minor *cacicazgo* of Mazatec speakers. Thus, the Cuicatlán Cañada as I have defined it (Chapter 2) contained three *cacicazgos*, each located on the Quiotepec, Cuicatlán, and Dominguillo alluvial fans respectively. Settlement on the El Chilar alluvial fan formed part of the Dominguillo *cacicazgo* (Hopkins 1974:164).

Each *cacicazgo* had a major center (*cabecera*) where the governing elite resided. These centers contained impressive public sectors and large resident populations (Hunt 1972:237). Peripheral villages and hamlets belonging to the *cacicazgo* were scattered on spurs and ridges rising above the irrigated alluvium, within walking distances of 12 hours or less from the major center. Hunt suggests that these satellite communities represented offshoots of the major centers, which were the oldest and largest communities (Hunt 1972:232).

The *cacicazgos* delimited their territories with natural landmarks such as barrancas or by erecting markers such as painted boulders along the boundaries of their territories. Each of these political units controlled all the land and all the water sources that lay within its territory. The boundaries of each *cacicazgo* usually coincided with the limits of the potentially cultivable land on the alluvial fan that it occupied (Hunt 1972:234). According to Joseph Hopkins, who has compiled the available information on the population history of the Cuicatec region, the estimated population of the largest Cuicatec *cacicazgo* (probably Atlatlauca) was under 5000 persons. The sizes of the other *cacicazgos*—including the three *cacicazgos* in the Cuicatlán Cañada—were all under 3000 persons (Hopkins 1974:98). Table 39 lists the population estimates that Hopkins generated for the centers of Quiotepec, Cuicatlán, and Dominguillo, using the earliest available figures found in the *Suma de Visitas* of 1548 (Hopkins 1974:134-166).

Our picture of the regional organization of the Cuicatlán Cañada during the Postclassic and early Colonial periods consists of three autonomous *cacicazgos*

> . . . in which small hamlets were located on spurs, ridges, and flats near and above irrigated agricultural fields, in a territory partially surrounding a larger "urbanized" settlement, or nucleus, major in population size, antiquity, and political might. [Hunt 1972:202]

At the head of each *cacicazgo* was the *cacique*, who in return for his administrative duties was supported by tribute rendered in kind or in service by his subjects.

Relations between the *cacicazgos* were peaceful. Peace was maintained by means of a regional exchange network, as well as by the formation of marriage alliances between the ruling elites. Binding the *cacicazgos* of the central and southern Cañada further was their language, and their mythology of common descent, which was transmitted by their oral traditions and codices. Like the patron-saint fiestas celebrated in the Cañada towns today, the pre-Hispanic *cacicazgos* participated in an annual round of ceremonies dedicated to the patron deities of each *cacicazgo* (Hunt 1972:205-207).

While solutions to any territorial conflicts between the *cacicazgos* of the Cañada were reached by peaceful means, conflicts with non-Cuicatec polities in surrounding regions frequently erupted in warfare. War was usually precipitated by neighboring polities who wished to encroach upon the water sources and the fertile alluvial fans of the Cañada. The *cacicazgos* in the Cuicatlán Cañada frequently had to defend their territories from foreign incursions (Hunt 1972:209-211). At the same time, the Cañada *cacicazgos* traded the lowland fruits they cultivated for the products of their highland Cuicatec counterparts. They also maintained long-distance exchange relationships with polities in the neighboring valleys of Tehuacán and Oaxaca, as well as with lowland regions of the Gulf Coast.

Be that as it may, the Cañada became incorporated into the Aztec empire shortly before the Spanish Conquest, during the reign of Moctezuma II (A.D. 1502-1520) (Hunt 1972:209-210; Hopkins 1974:104-115). Communities in the Cañada became part of the Aztec tributary province centered at Coixtlahuaca in the Mixteca Alta, where the Aztec established a garrison for the purposes of enforcing their *Pax Azteca*. Tribute collectors (*calpixqui*) in the service of the Aztec state periodically traveled from Coixtlahuaca to the *cacicazgo* centers in the Cañada to collect the specified tribute items, which included feathers, gold, precious stones, and cotton mantles. Occasionally, some communities in the Cañada sent tribute in the form of manpower, food, and other provisions to the Aztec garrison at Coixtlahuaca (Hopkins 1974:110-111). Aside from imposing tribute demands upon the Cañada *cacicazgos*, however, the Aztec did not meddle in their internal affairs.

Although a discussion of the imperial policies of the Late Postclassic Aztec lies beyond the scope of this study, a useful comparison can be drawn between the Zapotec and Aztec conquests of the Cuicatlán Cañada. The Aztec exacted their tribute demands from the Cañada by simply tapping the region's administrative hierarchy. The native rulers continued to administer their respective *cacicazgos* and to draw tribute from their loyal subjects, only they were obliged to render tribute periodically to Moctezuma's tribute collectors. The Aztec were able to exploit the existing tributary obligations that characterized the Cañada's *cacicazgos*, without having to administer them directly. Accordingly, "for the purposes of internal politics, the Cuicatec states . . . remained relatively independent until Spanish entry" (Hunt 1972:210).

In the earlier proposed period of Zapotec domination, however, the Cañada's populations experienced the dramatic effects of *direct* Zapotec control. Where small, autonomous chiefly societies had previously flourished, the Zapotec introduced their own regional administrative hierarchy for the purposes of enforcing their imperial policies. Forts and garrisons were raised, communities were forcibly resettled, and unprecedented tribute demands were imposed upon the Cañada's inhabitants by their new Zapotec overlords, which resulted in a major reorganization of the region's political economy (see Chapter 4).

That the Aztec did not carry out a comparable administrative overhaul in Late Postclassic times attests to differences in the nature of Zapotec and Aztec imperial control here. In my opinion, these differences stem in large part from the existing sociopolitical organization and economic potential in the Cañada prior to the two periods of subjugation. These preconditions of conquest, as I have referred to them (see Chapter 2), will have a great bearing upon the nature of imperial control (Lattimore 1962:477). The Zapotec of the Formative period subjugated a series of small chiefly communities in the Cañada, whose inhabitants farmed nearby stretches of low alluvium by means of simple floodwater-farming techniques. In order to raise their desired tribute demands, the Zapotec apparently found it necessary to take on the direct administration of the Cañada and introduce a policy of agricultural expansion there. By the time of the sixteenth-century Aztec penetration here, however, the Cañada was occupied by a series of significantly larger Cuicatec *cacicazgos*, whose boundaries coincided with the practicable limits of irrigation agriculture, and whose rulers received standardized tribute payments from their subjects. By the Late Postclassic period, the preconditions of conquest in the Cuicatlán Cañada were suited to the indirect form of imperial control that the Aztec evidently exercised there.

The *cacicazgos* that occupied the alluvial fans of the Cuicatlán Cañada never achieved any greater level of political centralization before their subjugation by the Aztec, and shortly thereafter, by the Spaniards. In the first place, the region's topography did little to favor tendencies toward higher-level political centralization. As we have seen, all settlements in the Cañada were confined—and still are today—to the alluvial fans of the canyon floor where tributary streams join the Río Grande. The boundaries of each *cacicazgo* on one of these alluvial fans were easily demarcated and usually represented the viable limits of agricultural expansion (Hunt 1972:233-234). Although the extension of marriage alliances between the elites of these *cacicazgos* could have served to unify these polities into a large power, Hunt sees the process whereby daughter communities budded off from the major centers as a force that counteracted any attempts at regional political unification. The forces of regional political growth were opposed by local processes of territorial fission, and "a precarious balance of allegiances and enmities maintained the Cuicatec state dynasty in a state of flux, without achieving greater political centralization" (Hunt 1972:228, 173, 223).

Let us compare Hunt's ethnohistorically-based reconstruction of the Cañada's regional organization during the Postclassic and early Colonial periods with the corresponding settlement pattern obtained in the region for the contemporaneous Iglesia Vieja ceramic phase (ca. A.D. 1000-1520) (Fig. 57). My discussion of the Iglesia Vieja phase settlement pattern will be brief, since the study of this time period lay beyond the immediate goals of our Cuicatlán Cañada Project. For one thing, we did not carry out excavations at any Iglesia Vieja phase site, and therefore we lack the primary ceramic samples needed to improve upon Hopkins' ceramic report (Hopkins 1973), which deals principally with Postclassic period ceramics. At the moment we are not in any position to subdivide the long Iglesia Vieja phase into early and late components. Moreover, we did not return to map and conduct systematic surface collections at the Iglesia Vieja phase sites. We have only very general information on the internal configuration of these settlements and we lack complementary artifactual data. Future research on the Postclassic period will undoubtedly serve to refine and perhaps alter the general remarks presented here.

Settlement expanded on the alluvial fans of the central and southern Cañada during the Iglesia Vieja phase (Table 40). If we compare the total Iglesia Vieja phase settlement obtained on each of the Cañada's four alluvial fans to that seen during

THE TRUJANO PHASE

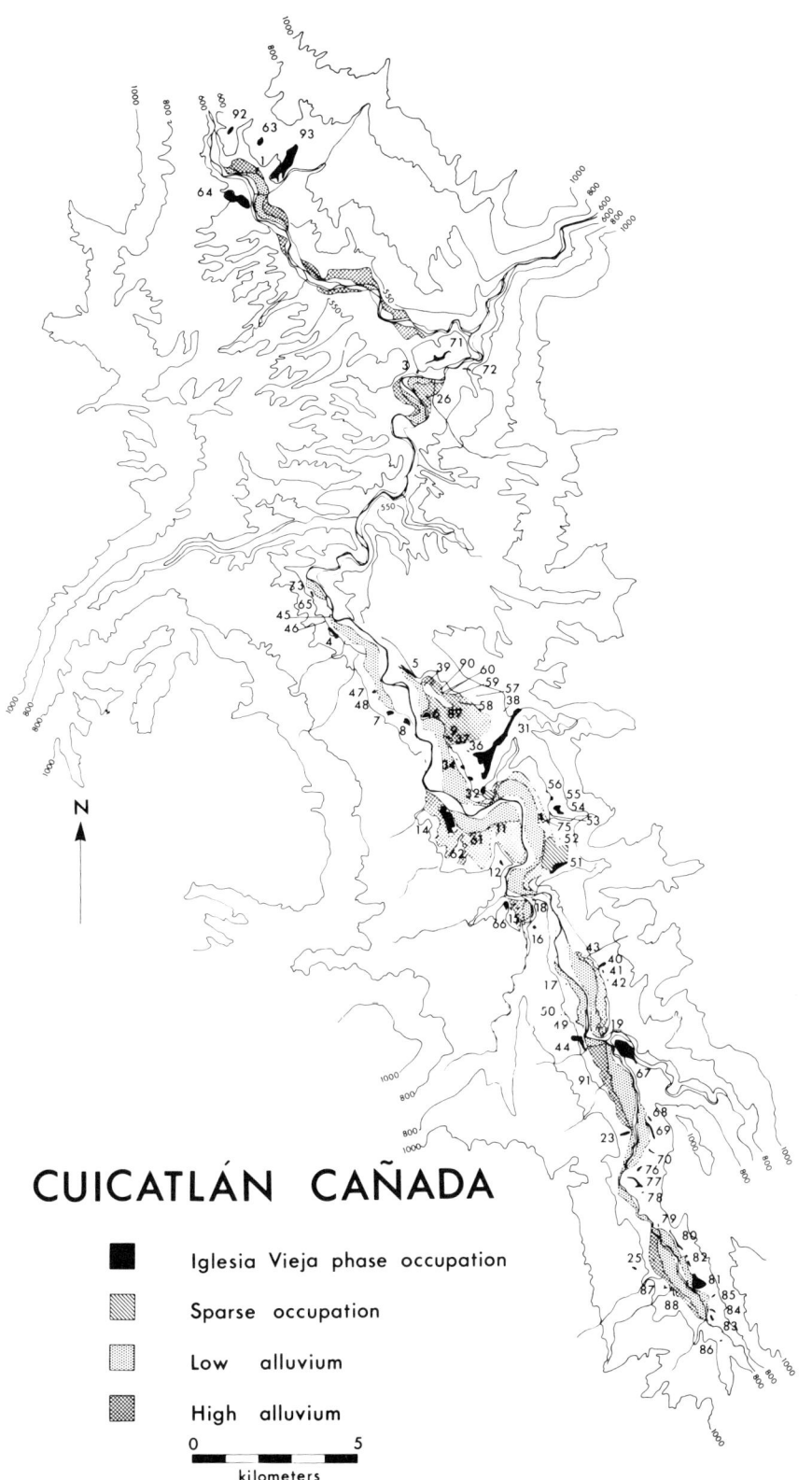

Figure 57. Iglesia Vieja phase regional settlement pattern map.

Table 40. The Sizes of Iglesia Vieja Phase Settlements in the Cuicatlán Cañada

Alluvial Fan	Site Number	Site Name	Site Size (ha)
Quiotepec	Cs71	Quiotepec Viejo	6.60
	Cs72	Loma del Guaje	.87
	Cs3-IV	Paso de Quiotepec	.18
	Cs74-IV?	none	.13
	Cs26-IV	Campo del Panteón	.83
		Total Settlement Area	8.61
Cuicatlán	Cs73-IV	none	.16
	Cs65	none	.10
	Cs45	none	.15
	Cs46	none	.20
	Cs4-IV	Los Obos	1.95
	Cs47	none	1.10
	Cs48	none	.15
	Cs7-IV	none	2.50
	Cs8-IV	El Tablero	3.00
	Cs6-IV	Horno de Cal	3.70
	Cs39	Loma Larga de la Sabana	.10
	Cs90	none	.07
	Cs60	Lomita de la Laguna II	.18
	Cs59	Lomita de la Laguna I	.20
	Cs57	La Canoa	.10
	Cs58	none	.05
	Cs38	none	.10
	Cs89	none	.15
	Cs6-IV	Cuba Libre	1.72
	Cs9-IV	La Bomba	1.20
	Cs37	none	.30
	Cs35	none	.30
	Cs36	El Carrizal	.35
	Cs31	Iglesia Vieja	47.80
	Cs34	El Zapotillo	1.40
	Cs33	La Mesquitera	1.88
	Cs32	Valencia	2.85-10.75
	Cs14-IV	Loma Larga	15.20
	Cs61	none	.60
	Cs10-IV	El Mirador	1.02
	Cs11-IV	Loma del Llano Chiquito	.20
	Cs62	none	.25
	Cs12-IV	Cerro Mixteco	1.90
	Cs66-IV	Cerrito del Río Apoala	1.50
	Cs15-IV	La Nopalera	1.15
	Cs56	La Cardonera	.15
	Cs55	La Cardonera	.90
	Cs54	La Cardonera	5.10
	Cs53	none	.55
	Cs75-IV	La Gasolinera	1.50
	Cs52	none	.20
	Cs51	Iglesia Vieja	6.85-56.50
		Total Settlement Area	166.38
El Chilar	Cs18-IV	Puente del Río Grande	.17
	Cs16-IV	Sitio Entre Dos Ríos	1.20
	Cs43	none	.15
	Cs40	none	2.25
	Cs41	none	.50
	Cs42	none	.15
	Cs17-IV	none	.10
	Cs50	none	.20
	Cs49	none	.20
	Cs44	none	8.40
	Cs20-IV	Las Monjas	1.08
	Cs19-IV	Hacienda Tecomaxtlahua	.50
	Cs67	El Picacho	22.70

Table 40, Continued

Alluvial Fan	Site Number	Site Name	Site Size (ha)
	Cs91-IV?	El Panteón	.20
	Cs23-IV?	none	2.55
	Cs68	none	1.00
	Cs69	none	3.40
	Cs70	none	1.10
	Cs76	none	1.40
		Total Settlement Area	47.25
Dominguillo	Cs77	none	4.30
	Cs78	none	.30
	Cs79	El Plan del Obo	.20
	Cs80	none	3.00
	Cs82	Llano de la Plaza	1.65
	Cs81	Iglesia Vieja	11.50
	Cs85	none	.70
	Cs84	none	.80
	Cs83	Cueva de los Tejones	1.20
	Cs86	El Picachito	.30
	Cs25-IV	Loma de la Coyotera	.53
	Cs87-IV	La Peñita	.70
	Cs88-IV	Loma del Barrio del Ticolute (Tecolote)	.60
		Total Settlement Area	25.78

the previous Trujano phase (Table 41), we discover up to a threefold increase in settlement associated with the Cuicatlán, El Chilar, and Dominguillo alluvial fans. Settlement on the Quiotepec alluvial fan, by contrast, continued to decline as it had previously during the Lomas to Trujano phase transition.

A histogram of the sizes of Iglesia Vieja phase settlements in the Cuicatlán Cañada reveals several developments in the regional settlement pattern (Fig. 58). If we compare it to the distribution of Trujano phase settlement sizes (Fig. 52) we find the following changes in the distribution of Postclassic period site sizes: (1) a proliferation of isolated households and hamlets, less than 1.50 ha in size; and (2) the emergence of major nucleated centers of population. Whereas the largest center in the region during the previous Trujano phase measured approximately 12 ha in size, during the Iglesia Vieja phase we see large centers of up to four times that size.

Settlement on each alluvial fan consists of a single large nucleated center, surrounded by an array of smaller settlements. This hierarchy of settlement sizes on each alluvial fan is generally matched by the distribution of public architecture among sites occupying each alluvial fan; the largest settlement of each alluvial fan features an impressive civic-ceremonial sector with a central plaza and substantial mounded architecture. The major centers in the region, defined in terms of their size, volume, and configuration of their public buildings are Cs31, Cs81, and Cs71 (Redmond n.d.). Cs31 is situated on top of the boot-shaped ridge directly north of the modern town of San Juan Bautista Cuicatlán on the region's central alluvial fan. Cs81 covers a foothill across the Río de las Vueltas from the present-day community of Santiago Dominguillo on the southernmost alluvial fan of the Cañada, and Cs71 extends along the top of a narrow ridge that delimits the northern end of the Quiotepec alluvial fan. Table 42 lists the sizes and population estimates I have assigned to these three nucleated centers. North of the Cañada, the Venta Salada phase site of Cs93—designated Tr299 by MacNeish and his collaborators (MacNeish et al. 1972:433)—covers the top of a prominent piedmont ridge that rises directly north of the modern town of Santa María Tecomavaca, over an area of about 30.40 ha. Cs93 formed the next major center north of the Cuicatlán Cañada during the time period immediately preceding the Spanish Conquest.

On the region's central and largest alluvial fans we find the following secondary centers, defined on the basis of their size and the configuration of public architecture found on them: Cs51, Cs67, and Cs14-IV (see Table 40). North of the Cañada and west

Table 41. Comparison of Trujano and Iglesia Vieja Phase
Settlement on the Cañada's Alluvial Fans

Alluvial Fan	Total Trujano Phase Settlement (ha)	Total Iglesia Vieja Phase Settlement (ha)
Quiotepec	9.70	8.61
Cuicatlán	40.09	166.38
El Chilar	19.33	47.25
Dominguillo	15.58	25.78

across the Río Salado from the modern town of Santa María Tecomavaca we surveyed the site of Cs64, a center which extends along the top of a steep river bluff and ascends an adjoining mountain ridge to cover a total area of about 20.50 ha (Redmond n.d.). I believe that two of these secondary centers (Cs14-IV, Cs64) date specifically to the Early Postclassic period, and that at this time they formed the major nucleated centers of their respective alluvial fans. In the Late Postclassic period, they were replaced by new centers—Cs93 and Cs31—which were established on the opposite side of the river.

Surrounding the major centers of each alluvial fan is a variety of associated communities, which are scattered on top of eminences and foothills that rise

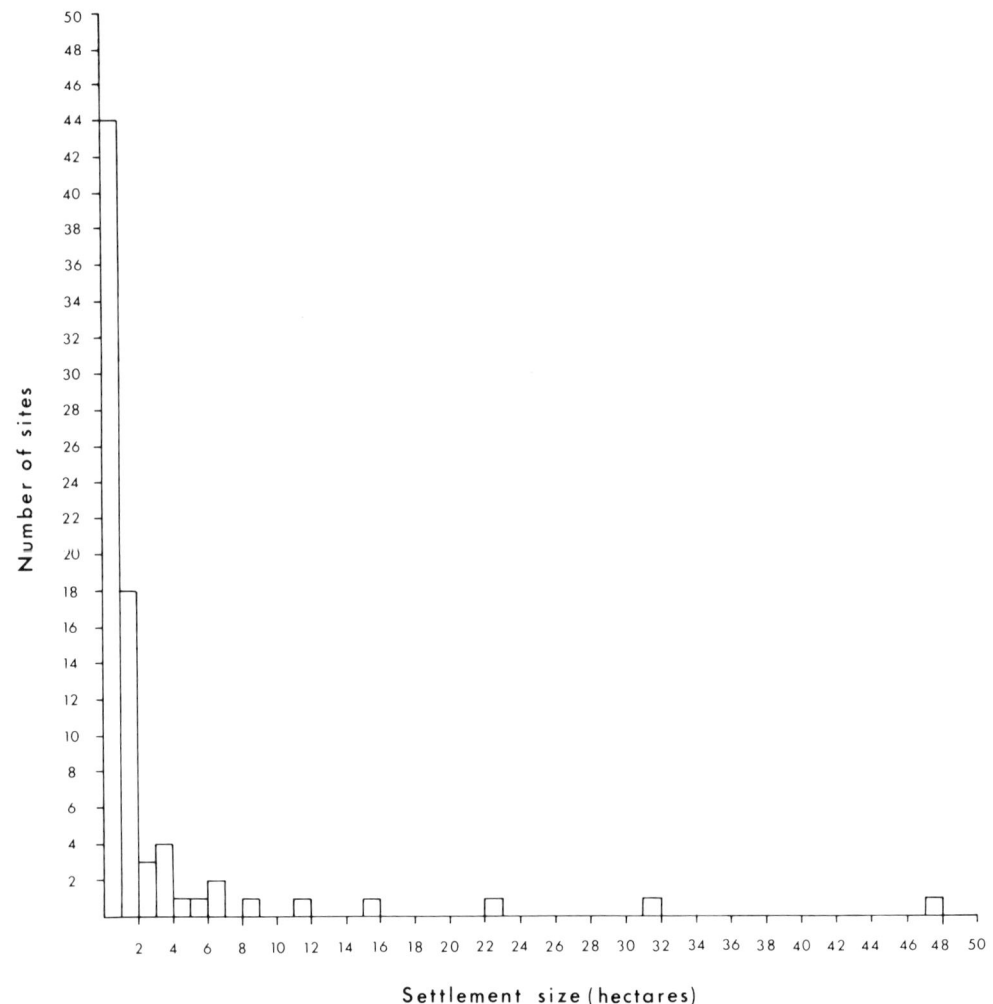

Figure 58. Histogram of Iglesia Vieja phase settlement sizes.

from the canyon floor. By far the greatest number of these satellite communities are hamlets and isolated housemounds, less than 1.50 ha in size (see Table 40).

How close is the fit, then, between Hunt's ethnohistorically-derived model of the autonomous *cacicazgos* that occupied the Cañada's alluvial fans at the time of the Spanish Conquest, and the corresponding regional organization that is based upon the actual Iglesia Vieja phase settlement pattern obtained there? I consider the fit to be surprisingly close, in spite of the very long chronological period and the general nature of the results of the regional settlement pattern survey.

On each alluvial fan we find a major hilltop center that features a sizable public sector, flanked by numerous residential terraces. These centers correspond to the *cacicazgo* centers referred to in the sixteenth-century Spanish accounts. The largest of these centers is the site named Iglesia Vieja (Cs31), on the Cuicatlán alluvial fan. The earliest population estimate of 1063 persons that Hopkins calculated for the town of Cuicatlán on the basis of the *Suma de Visitas* (Table 39) falls within the estimated population range of 1050-1150 persons that I have generated on the basis of the number of housemounds and residential terraces at Cs31 (Table 42). The ethnohistorical sources tell us that the *cacicazgo* on the Cuicatlán alluvial fan was the largest and most powerful of the polities in the region before the arrival of the Spaniards. South of the Cuicatlán Cañada lay another major Cuicatec *cacicazgo* at Atlatlauca, and to the north lay a Mazatec *cacicazgo* at Tecomavaca (Hunt 1972:173-184).

The Iglesia Vieja phase hilltop center on the Dominguillo alluvial fan (Cs81) corresponds to the Dominguillo (Alpizagua) *cacicazgo* center. If, as Hopkins proposes, the Dominguillo *cacicazgo* included the adjacent alluvial fan that today is marked by the town of San José El Chilar (Hopkins 1974:164), this would explain the absence of a major nucleated center on the El Chilar alluvial fan. The largest Iglesia Vieja phase settlement on the El Chilar alluvial fan is Cs67, which has only a single 3-m-high mound. Since the El Chilar alluvial fan was lightly populated during the Trujano phase (Fig. 51, Table 33), the Iglesia Vieja phase occupation here probably represents the colonizing process described by Hunt (1972:173, 232), whereby daughter communities budded off from the major settlements on the Dominguillo alluvial fan.

The third *cacicazgo* known to have existed in the Cuicatlán Cañada was centered on the Quiotepec alluvial fan. There we find the hilltop center of Quiotepec Viejo (Cs71). Hunt's discussion of the Quiotepec *cacicazgo* further strengthens the fit between the ethnohistorical identification of this *cacicazgo* and our investigation of the Iglesia Vieja phase settlement here. Hunt describes it as a minor *cacicazgo* which:

> ... has an interesting history of decay from a politically powerful center to a minor town subject to the headtown of a neighboring cacicazgo. During the Classic Period it was a large fortified settlement. Its inhabitants fought against the Chichimec-Nonoalca in their migrations southward. After losing a war against Papalo (ca. 1172) the inhabitants moved north across the river and became dependent on the Mazatec allies of Tecomavaca. At the time of the Spanish Conquest they were a small cacicazgo settlement whose lords intermarried with Cuicatec cacique children of Papalo, Cuicatlán, and Tonaltepec.[Hunt 1972:181-182]

The process of decline described above is readily supported by the changes in settlement pattern seen on the Quiotepec alluvial fan during the transition from the Trujano phase to the Iglesia Vieja phase. At this time, the mountaintop fortress of Cerro de Quiotepec (Cs2-T) was abandoned, and a settlement (Cs71) was established on a lower arm of the same mountain ridge. Cs71 comprises groups A-E on Martín Bazán's map of the Quiotepec mountain ridge (see Fig. 42). The population estimate of 225-240 persons that I have assigned to Cs71, which is based upon the number of residential terraces at that Iglesia Vieja phase site (Table 42), agrees with the earliest available estimate of 300 persons for the town of Quiotepec that is derived by Hopkins from the *Suma de Visitas* (Table 39).

Furthermore, the establishment of ties with the nearby *cacicazgo* at Tecomavaca during the twelfth century A.D. is manifested archaeologically by the architectural and ceramic similarities that Cs71 shares with Cs64 to the north (Redmond n.d.). I have proposed that Cs64 was the major center in the Tecomavaca area during the Early Postclassic pe-

Table 42. Estimators of Population for Three Iglesia Vieja Phase Centers in the Cuicatlán Cañada

Center	Site Size (ha)	No. of Residential Terraces	No. of House-mounds	Population Estimate
Cuicatlán (Cs31)	47.80		210-230	1050-1150
Dominguillo (Cs81)	11.50	55-70		275-350
Quiotepec (Cs71)	6.60	45-48		225-240

riod, the time period when, according to Hunt, the Cuicatec *cacicazgo* at Quiotepec became subject to the Mazatec *cacicazgo* at Tecomavaca. Thus the architectural and ceramic styles shared by these two neighboring centers probably reflect the Quiotepec *cacicazgo*'s new status as subject to the Mazatec *cacicazgo* centered at Tecomavaca Viejo (Cs64).

Along with the *cacicazgo* centers, we find a variety of associated Iglesia Vieja phase settlements on each of the region's alluvial fans. In addition to clarifying the status of the communities on the El Chilar alluvial fan—which as we have seen formed part of the Dominguillo *cacicazgo*—the ethnohistorical sources resolve the otherwise questionable status of the hilltop center of Cs51, which is located on the piedmont ridge rising directly above the modern community of San Pedro Chicozapote at the southern end of the Cuicatlán alluvial fan. Cs51 contains a plaza surrounded on all four sides by pyramidal mounds, in the center of which stands an *adoratorio*. Flanked by 25 to 30 residential terraces, the core of Cs51 comprises 6.85 ha. North of the piedmont ridge, however, a light but continuous distribution of Iglesia Vieja phase pottery extends over approximately 49.70 ha (see Fig. 57). In my analysis of the Cañada's regional organization during the Iglesia Vieja phase, which is based on the settlement size hierarchy and the distribution of public architecture, Cs51 would rank as a major center, alongside Cs31, on the Cuicatlán alluvial fan. According to Hunt, however, the earliest documented settlement at San Pedro Chicozapote was one of the four *barrios* of the *cacicazgo* center of Cuicatlán (Cs31) referred to in the *Suma de Visitas* (Hunt 1972:176-177). Cs51 was therefore not a satellite community in the usual sense, but rather an integral part of the Cuicatlán *cacicazgo* center of Cs31.

In sum, the regional settlement pattern during the Iglesia Vieja phase is consistent with Hunt's model of autonomous *cacicazgos* in the Cuicatlán Cañada during the Postclassic period. The nucleated hilltop centers of Cs31, Cs81, and Cs71 correspond to the *cacicazgo* centers of the Cuicatlán, Dominguillo, and Quiotepec polities, respectively. The absence of such a center on the El Chilar alluvial fan confirms the associated communities' documented status as subject to the Dominguillo *cacicazgo*. Moreover, Hunt's description of the satellite settlements belonging to these *cacicazgos*—"on spurs, ridges, and flats near and above irrigated agricultural fields"(Hunt 1972:202)—agrees with the results of the regional settlement pattern survey; the Iglesia Vieja phase sees a proliferation of hamlets and isolated households perched on eminences and hilltops overlooking the canyon floor.

We can investigate Hunt's claim that each *cacicazgo* was

> . . . a small political aggregate, extended to the viable ecological limits of expansion. . . . Although marginal lands were exploited for gathering wild products, collecting firewood, establishing nopaleras [nopal cactus groves], and so forth, the limits of the potentially controllable irrigated territory . . . , established the political frontiers of each primitive state. [Hunt 1972:233-234]

We can do so by examining the relationship between the total Iglesia Vieja phase settlement on each alluvial fan that—with the exception of settlement on the El Chilar alluvial fan—would have comprised separate *cacicazgos*, and the estimated carrying capacity of the associated farmland found on each alluvial fan. The procedures for estimating the carrying capacity of the available farmland on each alluvial fan as well as for generating the actual Iglesia Vieja phase population estimates are outlined in Chapter 2. For the Iglesia Vieja phase sites, however, we lack information on the number of housemounds with which to calculate the usual population estimates. Therefore, in addition to

Table 43. Estimated Carrying Capacity of the Cañada's Alluvium and Iglesia Vieja Phase Settlement

Alluvial Fan	Low Alluvium		High Alluvium		Estimated Carrying Capacity	Total Iglesia Vieja Phase Settlement (ha)	Iglesia Vieja Phase Population @ 10-25 Persons/ha	Iglesia Vieja Phase Population @ 25-50 Persons/ha
	Hectares	Annual Maize Yields (kg)	Hectares	Annual Maize Yields (kg)				
Quiotepec	32.85	100,217	59.55	94,089	971 persons	8.61	86-215 persons	215-430 persons
Cuicatlán	523.60	1,595,933	514.77	813,337	12,046 persons	166.38	1664-4159 persons	4159-8319 persons
El Chilar	297.43	906,567	118.20	186,756	5,467 persons	47.05	470-1176 persons	1176-2352 persons
Dominguillo	142.65	434,797	59.20	93,536	2,642 persons	25.78	258-644 persons	644-1289 persons

using the population density figure of 10-25 persons per hectare of settlement, I have added a second population estimate for the Iglesia Vieja phase sites, one which is based on the higher density figure of 25-50 persons per hectare of settlement. This higher density figure characterizes modern "compact high-density villages" in highland Mexico (Sanders 1965:50; Parsons 1971:23; Sanders, Parsons, and Santley 1979:39). I believe that this higher density figure reflects more accurately the density of surface remains seen at most Iglesia Vieja phase sites in the region than the density figure that I have usually listed. Table 43 lists the estimated carrying capacity of the region's four alluvial fans during the Iglesia Vieja phase together with these two population estimates.

When we compare the estimated carrying capacity of each alluvial fan with the actual population estimates for that alluvial fan, we find that while the region's population did increase during the Iglesia Vieja phase, the population residing on each alluvial fan remained below the productive potential of the associated farmland. The sizes of each of the region's three autonomous *cacicazgos* centered on the Cuicatlán, Dominguillo, and Quiotepec alluvial fans appear to have remained within 30-50% of the estimated carrying capacity of the available farmland within their territories. Of course, the figure would be higher if a large percentage of the available farmland were under the cultivation of non-staple, tropical products. But the results of the catchment analysis suggest that the autonomous *cacicazgos* occupying the Cañada's alluvial fans during the Postclassic period still had plenty of room in which to expand and develop.

The Emergence of Autonomous *Cacicazgos* in the Cuicatlán Cañada

Armed with the knowledge of the Cuicatlán Cañada's regional organization during the Postclassic period, we must return to discuss the Classic period developments in the region. We have seen that this was the time period when—in the face of Teotihuacán's imperial expansion—the Zapotec state withdrew its direct control over tributary regions like the Cuicatlán Cañada. In the wake left by the retreating Zapotec, what political institutions arose to govern this newly-autonomous region?

I believe that the autonomous *cacicazgos* that are known to have existed in the Cañada during the Postclassic and early Colonial periods first emerged during the Trujano phase. After the withdrawal of the Zapotec military forces and administrators from the Cañada, three settlements that had been established during the Lomas phase became large nucleated centers. We have seen how each of these Trujano phase centers presided over one of the region's alluvial fans: Cs2-T on the Quiotepec alluvial fan, Cs14-T on the Cuicatlán alluvial fan, and Cs25-T on the Dominguillo alluvial fan (Fig. 51). The biggest center, Cs14-T, occurred on the region's major alluvial fan; the ranking of the sizes of the other two Trujano phase centers agrees with the ranking of the sizes of their associated alluvial fans (Table 37). In addition to their larger size, these three centers also featured impressive public sectors that contained central plazas, pyramidal mounds, and ballcourts. Surrounding these hilltop centers on each alluvial fan were smaller settlements dispersed on spurs and eminences above the canyon floor. By far the greatest number of satellite settlements occurred on the Cuicatlán alluvial fan (Table 33).

Thus, the three autonomous *cacicazgos* known to have been centered on the Quiotepec, Cuicatlán, and Dominguillo alluvial fans during the Iglesia Vieja phase appear to have emerged in the Trujano phase, when the region became free from direct Zapotec domination. These alluvial fans became the territories of autonomous political units of roughly comparable size, though the *cacicazgo* located on the central Cuicatlán alluvial fan was certainly the largest polity and probably the most powerful. Similar to the Iglesia Vieja phase settlement pattern (Fig. 57), settlement on each of the Cañada's alluvial fans during the Trujano phase consisted of a nucleated hilltop center, surrounded by smaller dependent settlements (Fig. 51).

The status of the region's fourth alluvial fan, which today is occupied by the town of San José el Chilar, remains to be explained. During the Trujano phase a large settlement grew at its northern end (Cs18-T), but unlike the other large Trujano phase centers in the region, Cs18-T was newly-founded at this time and it lacked a public sector. I have already mentioned the possibility that Cs18-T might have formed a residential sector, or *barrio*, of adjacent Cs16-T, which did contain a central plaza delimited by mound platforms. We know that during the Postclassic period the El Chilar alluvial fan formed part of the *cacicazgo* centered on the Dominguillo alluvial fan, which explained the absence of a major Iglesia Vieja phase nucleated center on the El Chilar alluvial fan. Similarly, settlement on the El Chilar alluvial fan during the Trujano phase lacks a large nucleated center. These parallels in settlement on the El Chilar alluvial fan during the Trujano and Iglesia Vieja phases suggest that this alluvial fan and its associated settlements might have formed part of the *cacicazgo* centered on the Dominguillo alluvial fan during both the Classic and Postclassic periods.

If, as I am proposing, three independent polities arose on the Cañada's alluvial fans in the Trujano phase, there are a number of expectations derived from Eva Hunt's (1972) model of autonomous *cacicazgos* that we should investigate. First of all, Hunt characterizes the *cacicazgos* as small political aggregates, territorially-bounded, and politically autonomous. Accordingly, if the Quiotepec, Cuicatlán, and El Chilar-Dominguillo alluvial fans formed the sustaining areas of independent polities, we might expect their political autonomy to be reflected in a self-sufficient local economy. We would consequently expect the sizes of these polities to be in line with the productive potential of their respective territories.

We can assess this expectation by measuring the relationship between the total Trujano phase settlement obtained on each alluvial fan and the estimated carrying capacity of the associated farmland. Following the procedure outlined in Chapter 2, we can estimate the number of persons that could have been supported on each of the Cuicatlán Cañada's alluvial fans during the Trujano phase (Table 36). For the Trujano phase we have two independent estimates of the actual population residing on the region's alluvial fans: the first estimate is based simply on the sizes of the settlements found on each alluvial fan; the second estimate is based on the number of housemounds at settlements on each alluvial fan (Table 35).

If we compare the latter population estimate of each alluvial fan during the Trujano phase to the estimated carrying capacity of the associated alluvium, we find that settlement on all the alluvial fans falls within the productive potential of the available farmland. This suggests that the settlements constituting the separate polities on the Cañada's alluvial fans could have supported themselves locally by farming the alluvium within their territories. But the estimated population residing on some of the alluvial fans during the Trujano phase formed higher percentages of the potential population than could have been locally supported. While settlement on the Cuicatlán alluvial fan remained within 38% of its potential population, settlement on the Dominguillo alluvial fan formed 98% of its potential population, and the population estimated to have resided on the Quiotepec alluvial fan might have assumed an even higher percentage of its potential population. The higher percentage of actual population to the potential population of the Dominguillo alluvial fan drops if—as the ethnohistorical sources propose—we consider the Trujano phase settlement on the El Chilar alluvial fan as part of the Dominguillo *cacicazgo*. Together, settlement on the El Chilar-Dominguillo alluvial fans remained within 51% of their combined carrying capacities. This more favorable man-land relationship helps to explain the aforementioned lack of a major Trujano phase center on the El Chilar alluvial fan, which may have been controlled by the *cacicazgo* centered on the Dominguillo alluvial fan.

Following from Hunt's model of autonomous *cacicazgos*, we do find that the nascent *cacicazgos* occupying the Cañada's alluvial fans during the Trujano phase were generally self-sufficient in terms of their subsistence. The varying relationship of their settlement sizes to the productive potential of their territories probably affected their ability to generate agricultural surpluses. The low margin for surplus production on the Quiotepec alluvial fan and the Dominguillo alluvial fan during the Trujano phase is probably reflected in later developments there. We have seen how the Quiotepec *cacicazgo* declined and eventually allied itself with the Tecomavaca *cacicazgo* during the Postclassic period. This process of decline may have been partially precipitated by stresses emanating from the close man-land relationship on the Quiotepec alluvial fan during the Trujano phase. The relatively high percentage of actual population to the potential Trujano phase population of the Dominguillo alluvial fan, on the other hand, probably resulted in the process of colonization of the adjacent El Chilar alluvial fan during the transition between the Trujano and Iglesia Vieja phases. As population was reaching the potential carrying capacity of the Dominguillo alluvial fan, daughter communities budded off and settled on the El Chilar alluvial fan, which formed part of the Dominguillo *cacicazgo*'s territory.

THE TRUJANO PHASE

Table 44. Distribution of Chipped Stone* at 10 Trujano Phase Settlements

Alluvial Fan	Site	Surface Collections†	Average Ratio, Obsidian	Average Ratio, Chert	Average Ratio, Quartz
Quiotepec	Cs2-T	8	.76 (.07 green)	.17	.07
Cuicatlán	Cs11-T	5	.32	.41	.27
	Cs12-T	1	.67	.33	0
	Cs14-T	3	.89 (.54 green)	.11	0
El Chilar	Cs16-T	2	.35	.27	.37
	Cs18-T	1	.50	.50	0
	Cs19-T	1	.33	0	.67
	Cs20-T	1	0	0	0
	Cs21-T	2	.64 (.35 green)	.24	.12
Dominguillo	Cs25-T	10	.12	.81	.07

†Only those surface collections yielding pure Trujano phase ceramics were included in this analysis (see Chapter 2).
*Chipped stone ratios = Total Obsidian/Total Chipped Stone, Total Chert/Total Chipped Stone, Total Quartz/Total Chipped Stone.

According to Hunt (1972:205-206, 212), the Cuicatec *cacicazgos* maintained regional exchange networks. At local markets the *cacicazgos* within the Cañada exchanged their *tierra caliente* products for those special products of their highland counterparts. The Cañada *cacicazgos* also participated in interregional exchange networks with neighboring regions; we know, for example, that the *cacicazgos* exchanged cotton mantles and native fruits in order to receive exotic items such as salt from the Tehuacán Valley, cotton from the Veracruz lowlands, and green beads (Hunt 1972:212). Information on the precise mechanism of this interregional exchange is scanty; however, Hunt alludes to the role of traveling traders or middlemen—"provided" by the Cuicatlán *cacicazgo*—in the trade of salt with the polity centered at Coxcatlán in the Tehuacán Valley. The long-distance trade in exotic items appears to have been handled by the ruling elite of the *cacicazgos*, and particularly by the ruling elite of the dominant Cuicatlán *cacicazgo*.

If the Trujano phase was the time period when autonomous *cacicazgos* emerged in the Cuicatlán Cañada, we would expect these *cacicazgos* to have participated in similar interregional exchange networks. We saw in Chapter 4 how a port of trade was established at Tecomavaca (Cs1) during the Late Formative period, and I have assumed that it continued to operate as a port of trade during the Classic period. One line of evidence supporting Cs1's role as a port of trade was the concentration of Thin Orange pottery and green obsidian artifacts

Table 45. Distribution of Thin Orange Ceramics at 14 Trujano Phase Settlements

Alluvial Fan	Site	Surface Collections†	Total Ceramic Diagnostics	Total Thin Orange	Ratio
Quiotepec	Cs2-T	18	1574	0	0
Cuicatlán	Cs5-T	2	569	0	0
	Cs6-T	10	620	0	0
	Cs9-T	3	267	3	.011
	Cs11-T	7	334	1	.003
	Cs12-T	5	246	1	.004
	Cs13-T	6	405	0	0
	Cs14-T	6	547	16	.029
El Chilar	Cs16-T	3	327	0	0
	Cs18-T	1	110	0	0
	Cs19-T	4	688	1	.001
	Cs20-T	5	212	3	.014
	Cs21-T	2	131	0	0
Dominguillo	Cs25-T	36	3079	0	0

†All surface collections having Trujano phase ceramics were included in this analysis (see Chapter 2).

Table 46. Distribution of Ceramic Urn Fragments at 10 Trujano Phase Settlements

Alluvial Fan	Site	Surface Collections†	Total Ceramic Diagnostics	Urn Fragments	Ratio
Quiotepec	Cs2-T	8	762	9	.012
Cuicatlán	Cs11-T	5	251	1	.004
	Cs12-T	1	29	0	0
	Cs14-T	3	220	5	.023
El Chilar	Cs16-T	2	184	0	0
	Cs18-T	1	110	0	0
	Cs19-T	1	32	0	0
	Cs20-T	1	52	0	0
	Cs21-T	2	131	0	0
Dominguillo	Cs25-T	10	752	9	.012

†Only those surface collections yielding pure Trujano phase ceramics were included in this analysis (see Chapter 2).

there. The middlemen that Hunt refers to would probably have journeyed to trade centers like the one at Tecomavaca to exchange with traders from other regions. If this long-distance trade was handled by the ruling elite of the Cañada *cacicazgos*, we might expect to find higher densities of trade items at the *cacicazgo* centers, where the ruling elite are known to have resided.

The distributions of obsidian artifacts and Thin Orange ceramics at Trujano phase settlements in the Cañada are generally consistent with this expectation (Tables 44, 45). Of the three proposed Trujano phase *cacicazgo* centers (Cs2-T, Cs14-T, Cs25-T), our Trujano phase collection squares at Cs14-T and at Cs2-T have notably higher average obsidian ratios; both centers are further distinguished by the occurrence of green obsidian there. Collection squares at the third proposed *cacicazgo* center on the Dominguillo alluvial fan (Cs25-T) produced a low average obsidian ratio—and in turn a high average chert ratio. Two of the three proposed Trujano phase *cacicazgo* centers in the Cuicatlán Cañada—and particularly the center of the nascent *cacicazgo* on the region's major alluvial fan—appear to have been nodal points in the interregional exchange of obsidian.

The distribution of Thin Orange ceramics is restricted to fewer settlements in the Cañada, but like the distribution of obsidian artifacts, the greatest number of Thin Orange ceramics occurs at Cs14-T, the proposed center of the Cuicatlán *cacicazgo* during the Trujano phase (Table 45). While Thin Orange ceramics were not collected on the surfaces of the region's other two proposed *cacicazgo* centers, minor quantities of this trade item were recovered from three smaller settlements on the Cuicatlán alluvial fan, as well as from two small settlements on the El Chilar alluvial fan. But at least we have evidence from the proposed center of the region's largest *cacicazgo* of its participation in interregional exchange networks with polities to the north. The greatest densities of two Classic period trade items present at the port of trade at Tecomavaca are found at the major Trujano phase *cacicazgo* center in the heart of the Cuicatlán Cañada.

A final characteristic of the Postclassic *cacicazgo* centers in the Cuicatlán Cañada that we can examine in terms of their possible predecessors during the Classic period is their role as ceremonial centers. The three Trujano phase centers that I propose were the centers of autonomous *cacicazgos* (Cs2-T, Cs14-T, Cs25-T) all feature public sectors consisting of central plazas, pyramidal mounds, and ballcourts. Hunt suggests that the Cuicatec *cacicazgos* were bound by their mythology of common descent, and by their shared religious traditions. According to Hunt: "in the realm of ritual, ceremonialism, and organized religion, there was also a division of labor between the states of the Cuicatec. The different town temples were dedicated to different gods whose ceremonies were held at different times of the year" (Hunt 1972:206). The *cacicazgos* participated in an annual round of ceremonies dedicated to the patron deities of each *cacicazgo*.

If the three Trujano phase centers were indeed the centers of independent *cacicazgos*, we would expect their public sectors to have been the loci of ceremonies dedicated to their patron deities. Consequently, we might expect these centers to have greater densities of ritual artifacts that commemorated their deities. Ceramic effigy urns might con-

THE TRUJANO PHASE

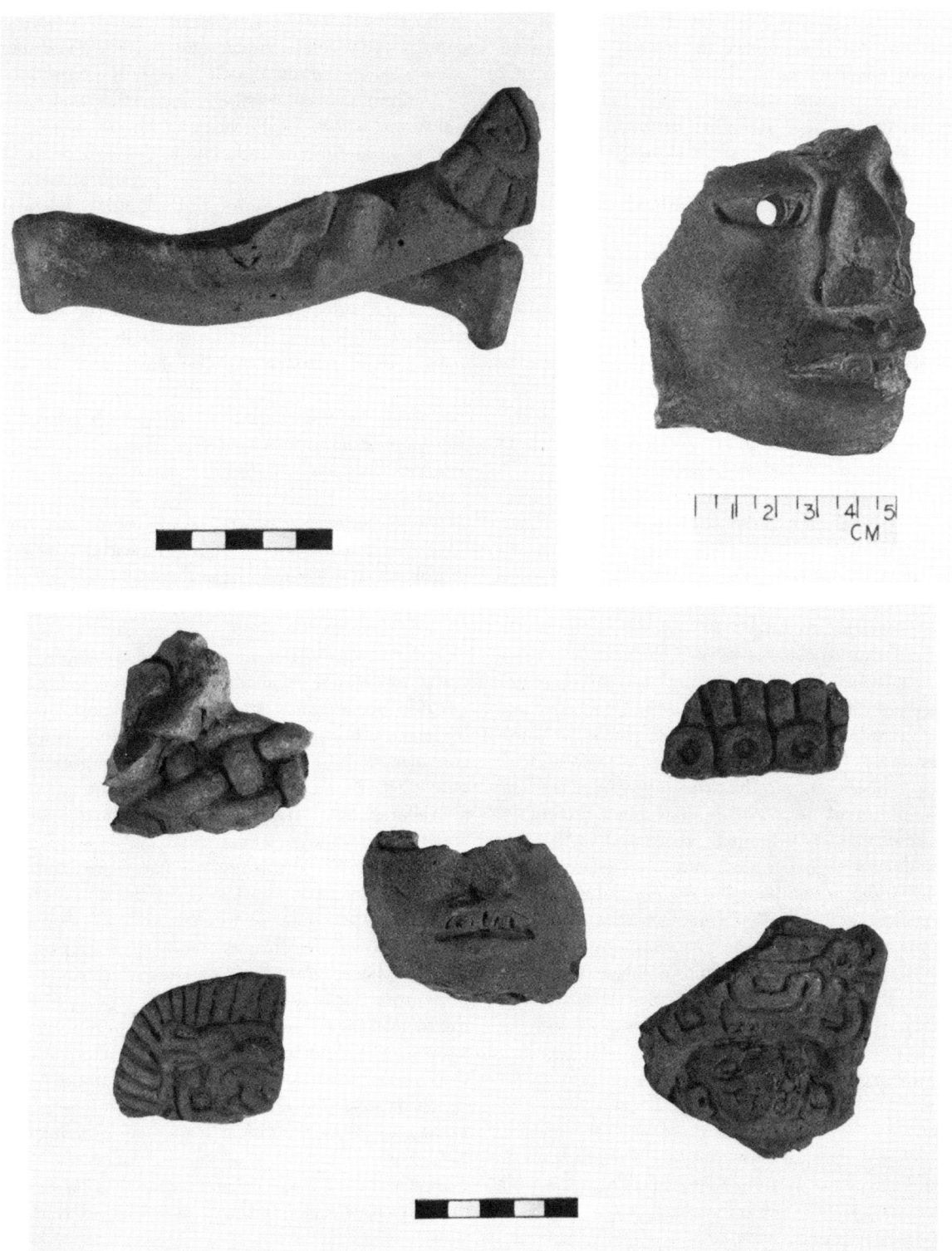

Plate 39. Ceramic urn fragments from Trujano phase centers. *Top left*, seated urn fragment from Cerro de Quiotepec (Cs2/170). *Top right*, urn fragment of face from Loma Larga (Cs14/276). *Bottom*, urn fragments from Loma de la Coyotera. Top row: headdresses, left (Cs25/227), right (Cs25/222). Center: hollow face (Cs25/245). Bottom row: headdresses, left (Cs25/228), right (Cs25/222).

stitute one such ritual artifact. Traditionally, effigy urns have been considered to be representations of ancient Mesoamerican deities (Caso and Bernal 1952:10-12). Joyce Marcus (1983b:141) has suggested alternatively that effigy urns represent royal ancestors who assumed supernatural attributes in their role as mediators between their living descendants and the divine entities with whom they resided in the afterlife. Accordingly, royal ancestors were often revered and commemorated as if they were divine themselves (Marcus 1978:175-176). Be they representations of deities or royal ancestors, both interpretations view effigy urns as images of special beings who were commemorated in temples with special ceremonies. In the case of the Postclassic Cuicatec *cacicazgos*, we know that the center of each *cacicazgo* erected temples and held ceremonies dedicated to these divine beings.

When we examine the distribution of urn fragments at 10 Trujano phase settlements in the Cañada (Table 46), we discover that three of the four settlements where our surface collections recovered urn fragments correspond to the proposed Trujano phase *cacicazgo* centers (Pl. 39). The highest urn fragment ratio occurs at Cs14-T, the large center on the Cuicatlán alluvial fan; I computed the same urn fragment ratio for the centers on the Quiotepec and Dominguillo alluvial fans (Cs2-T; Cs25-T). Moreover, most of the urn fragments are associated with the public sectors of these three hilltop centers. The distribution of effigy urns in the Cañada during the Trujano phase is principally restricted to the proposed *cacicazgo* centers, and is consistent with Hunt's discussion about the ceremonial role of the *cacicazgo* centers. Unfortunately, the urn fragments are too incomplete to attempt an analysis of their representations; it would be interesting to examine the possibility that particular deities or revered ancestors might have been associated with the separate *cacicazgo* centers.

In sum, then, the polities that emerged on the Cañada's alluvial fans during the Trujano phase have many of the characteristics of the autonomous *cacicazgos* that are known to have existed there in the Postclassic period. Like their later counterparts, the Classic period *cacicazgos* that emerged on the Quiotepec, Cuicatlán, and El Chilar-Dominguillo alluvial fans consisted of large ceremonial centers and satellite villages and hamlets. The size of each *cacicazgo* remained in line with the productive potential of its territory, suggesting that each polity was able to locally sustain its population.

Free from Zapotec domination, the ruling elite of these nascent *cacicazgos* of the Trujano phase appear to have participated in interregional exchange networks with neighboring regions. In this way, the Cañada's *cacicazgo* centers—and particularly the *cacicazgo* center on the region's major alluvial fan—were supplied with trade items from the central Mexican highlands. Furthermore, like the ceremonial role assumed by the Postclassic period *cacicazgo* centers, which revolved around yearly ceremonies commemorating their patron deities or royal ancestors, our evidence enables us to assign a similar function to their Classic period predecessors.

The regional organization evident in the Cuicatlán Cañada after the Zapotec withdrawal resembles in some respects the regional organization that first emerged there in the Middle Formative period, prior to the Zapotec conquest. We saw in Chapter 3 how autonomous ranked or chiefly societies arose on the Cañada's alluvial fans during the Perdido phase. They supported their populations by farming the low alluvium, their chiefly centers constituted the loci of regional administration and chiefly rituals, and they participated in interregional exchange networks with polities in the Tehuacán and Oaxaca valleys. These small autonomous societies represented the region's native political institutions that were curtailed by the conquering Zapotec in the Lomas phase. Similarly autonomous native political institutions re-emerged during the Trujano phase, when their Zapotec overlords withdrew from the region. Consequently, we can trace the roots of the Classic and Postclassic period autonomous *cacicazgos* in the Cuicatlán Cañada back to the chiefly societies that emerged there in the Middle Formative period. The only major interruption in the region's local political history came during the Late Formative period, when the Valley Zapotec conquered the Cuicatlán Cañada and transformed it into a frontier region of the Monte Albán state.

Chapter 6
Summary and Conclusion

Summary

This study of the impact of Zapotec militarism upon the Cuicatlán Cañada began with a consideration of the founding and development of the Monte Albán state in the Valley of Oaxaca. The evidence presented in Chapter 1 suggested that Monte Albán's ascension to statehood in the Late Formative period was concurrent with a campaign of Zapotec military conquests in regions outside the Valley of Oaxaca. Thus, the early Zapotec state apparently arose in the context of militaristic expansion, and, to better understand the factors that contributed to this significant administrative transformation, I considered it necessary to investigate the role that militarism might have played in that development.

With the aid of ethnohistorical information on Zapotec militaristic practices during the Postclassic period, I constructed a model that attempted to relate the determinants and consequences of a Zapotec conquest for the Cuicatlán Cañada. Beginning in the Middle Formative period, the time period prior to the proposed Zapotec take-over, I discussed those aspects of the Cuicatlán Cañada that might have been of sufficient interest to the Valley Zapotec that they would have mounted a military conquest of the region. A second component of the conquest model examined the impact of a Zapotec take-over upon a previously autonomous region such as the Cañada, which would have been transformed by the conquering Zapotec in the Late Formative period into a tributary province of the Monte Albán state. The final component of the conquest model considered the effects of the conquest strategy upon the emergent Zapotec state centered at Monte Albán in the Valley of Oaxaca.

The expectations of the conquest model for the Cuicatlán Cañada have been evaluated with archaeological evidence from that region. The preconditions of conquest were outlined in Chapter 3, which described the Cuicatlán Cañada's regional organization during the Perdido phase. At this time, a series of small, ranked societies inhabited the Cañada, whose chiefly elites were participating in interregional exchange networks that linked the elites of neighboring polities across much of Mesoamerica.

The succeeding Lomas phase is when, according to the conquest slabs on Building J at Monte Albán, the Valley Zapotec expanded militarily into adjacent regions. We saw in Chapter 4 how the changes in the Cuicatlán Cañada's settlement pattern during the transition from the Perdido phase to the Lomas phase agreed with many of the expectations derived from the model of Zapotec conquest of this *tierra caliente* region. Accordingly, I have suggested that the previously autonomous Cañada was transformed into a frontier tributary region of the Monte Albán state during the Lomas phase. Zapotec military control was concentrated on the northern boundary of the region, so as to guard the Monte Albán state's frontier and to direct the flow of traffic across the state's border. Thus enclosed and protected, the Cañada's heartland became a tributary province, wherein tribute in the form of tropical agricultural products, other goods, and services was probably exacted and enforced by administrators in the service of the Monte Albán state.

The Zapotec subjugation of regions surrounding the Valley of Oaxaca disrupted the reciprocal exchange relationships that had been maintained by the elites of these previously independent regions. In response to this disruption, a new mechanism of interregional exchange was instituted during the Lomas phase. This was the establishment of neutral ports of trade beyond the borders of Zapotec-controlled territory. One such port of trade emerged at Tecomavaca in the southernmost Tehuacán Valley, just outside the northern border of the Monte Albán state. Ports of trade usually serve as vehicles for the exchange of special items between rulers of separate polities. For this reason, I have suggested that this new form of interregional exchange essentially bypassed the regions subjugated by Monte Albán, and was designed to link Monte Albán's rulers with foreign polities beyond the confines of Zapotec territory.

Monte Albán's imperialistic control over regions like the Cuicatlán Cañada appears to have waned at the start of the Classic period. In the Cañada, the transition from the Lomas phase to the Trujano phase was marked by the withdrawal of Zapotec military forces from the region's northern boundary, by the dissolution of the Zapotec administrative hierarchy that was imposed upon the Cañada in the Lomas phase, and by the re-emergence of native political institutions on the region's alluvial fans (Chapter 5). The withdrawal of direct Zapotec control over tributary regions like the Cuicatlán Cañada in the Early Classic period can perhaps be best understood as a strategic response on the part of the Monte Albán state to the emergence of a powerful competitor centered at Teotihuacán in the Basin of Mexico. At the same time that the Monte Albán state was retreating from its expanded frontiers, it was intensifying its control over the immediate Valley of Oaxaca—as reflected in the growth of its capital at Monte Albán, the establishment of secondary and tertiary centers on the valley floor, and the intensification of local agricultural production.

Conclusion

I would first like to outline some of the ways in which this study might contribute to the investigation and understanding of early state development in general. To begin with, the *interregional perspective* that I adopted for the study of Zapotec militarism and the rise of the Monte Albán state has convinced me of the general need to expand the usual regional framework for dealing with the question of primary state formation. As Wright (1977:382) has noted, states seem to develop in the context of interacting chiefdoms regulated by warfare and alliance. In the case at hand, I constructed an interregional model in order to monitor the effects of Zapotec militarism upon existing interregional relationships during the period of Zapotec state formation. The effects of Zapotec military expansion were felt directly in one of the regions that was impinged upon and transformed into a tributary province. At the same time, the Zapotec conquest strategy disrupted the existing mechanisms of interregional exchange and introduced new forms of long-distance exchange. The model was also designed to measure the effects of the interregional conquest strategy upon the expanding polity itself—the emergent Monte Albán state in the Oaxaca Valley. We are dealing with a series of changing interregional relationships that are clearly important in the transition from chiefdoms to states, and yet which remain to be examined fully in other areas of the world where primary states developed.

The focus of this investigation has been the role of military expansion, or *imperialism*, in the administrative transformation between chiefdoms and states. By *imperialism*, I mean a policy of military expansion and conquest, one that extends the expanding polity's territorial control over the regions and foreign polities it subjugates. The conquered regions are brought under the hegemony of the expanding polity, very often by means of direct military control and administration. In the context of a complex chiefly society, military expansion encourages the addition of new components to the central decision-making organization and thereby helps to promote the internally-specialized decision-making apparatus that is characteristic of the state. I wish to emphasize, however, that I do not regard this form of warfare as the *only* leading factor responsible for the emergence of the state, but rather as one of many socioenvironmental factors that can contribute to the administrative developments associated with nascent states.

For example, a campaign of interregional military conquests like the one described here will favor the establishment of a permanent military organization. As regions are subjugated and incorporated, the expanding chiefly polity must develop the administrative capability to govern them directly. The administration of such an imperial network involves not only the maintenance of direct control over subject populations in outlying regions, but also the extraction and mobilization of tribute from those regions in the form of goods and services. These activities will result in the addition of specialized components to the central decision-making organization and in the concomitant emergence of higher-order control units to integrate these newly instituted components within the administrative hierarchy; accordingly, the central decision-making organization becomes internally specialized.

Particular attention should be paid to the changing nature of a military order itself in the administrative transformation between chiefdoms and states, especially under conditions of warfare and military expansion. The military organization of a chiefdom, which is frequently embedded in a crosscutting, multi-purpose warrior or dance society, is transformed into a special military arm of the state. The permanent institutionalization of the military organization out of a previously ephemeral and multi-purpose organization is entirely consistent with the changing political strategy on the part of the central decision maker in the transition from chiefdoms to states, a strategy that is designed to promote specialization within the administrative hierarchy (Wright 1977:383). The changes observed in the military sphere will be diagnostic of the entirely new organizational strategy exercised by the ruler of a state, and these changes should constitute a salient feature of the administrative transformation from chiefdoms to states.

It is also important to consider the power-seeking role of the military organization in discussions of early state development. In the process of mounting military campaigns and subjugating foreign territories, the military order can gain the necessary strength, organization, and authority that might enable it to assume a central position in the state's decision-making organization. I suggest, in fact, that a military organization's dynamic, power-seeking potential is ultimately responsible for the "militaristic states" that have been recognized in both the archaeological and historical past.

In light of these general remarks, I wish to return to the specific case of early state development and to conclude this study with a consideration of the final component of the conquest model, which examines the effects of the Zapotec conquest strategy upon the polity centered at Monte Albán. In Chapter 2 I outlined some of the possible consequences of such a conquest strategy for the development of the Monte Albán state. The effects of the imperial strategy for the Monte Albán state were expected to stem from the military organization required to subjugate neighboring regions like the Cuicatlán Cañada in the first place, and subsequently from the military and administrative apparatus responsible for managing a vast imperial network. Although I have alluded to the military and administrative implications of this imperial policy at various times during the study, it is time to consider four interrelated consequences of the conquest strategy for the development of the early Zapotec state: (1) the establishment of a permanent military organization; (2) the administration of a tributary network; (3) the appearance of new interregional exchange mechanisms; and (4) the eventual rise to political prominence of the military organization.

Establishment of a Permanent Military Organization

In order for the Valley Zapotec to have mounted a campaign of interregional military conquests in the Late Formative period, they would have needed to assemble a strong military organization. If there previously had existed no permanent body of military specialists and warriors, we would expect that such an institution would have arisen at this time. Based upon our knowledge of Zapotec militarism during the Postclassic period, we might expect Monte Albán's early military organization to have been led by military captains and differentiated into ranked warrior orders.

What evidence is there that such an institution arose in the Late Formative period? Consistent with the early Spanish chroniclers' descriptions of the armor, special insignia, and distinctive hair knots worn by Zapotec warriors is the appearance in Period II of anthropomorphic ceramic urns and standing ceramic figures at Monte Albán that display definite warrior characteristics (Caso and Bernal 1952:116, 336) (Fig. 59). In fact, Bernal has summarized the Period II anthropomorphic figures from Monte Albán in the following way:

> They are clothed by this time. Male attire gets more elaborate, and the headdresses are more complicated with chinstraps, plumes, top knots, and ribbons which fall to the neck. [Bernal 1965:801]

Aside from these probable representations of male warriors is the discovery in Period II tombs and burials at Monte Albán of certain ornaments that are known to have been commonly awarded to brave warriors in Mesoamerica. Along with the profusion of jade ear-plugs and necklaces found in tombs and burials of this time period, Caso notes the appearance of jade nose-plugs here (Caso 1965b:900). That the nose-plug was a military insignia in Mesoamerica is exemplified by an important moment in the history of the Mixtec hero named "8 Deer," when he delivered a prisoner of war and was awarded a nose-plug (Smith 1973:16).

Furthermore, since chosen warriors in Postclassic Zapotec society are known to have joined special warrior orders that were under the patronage of wild

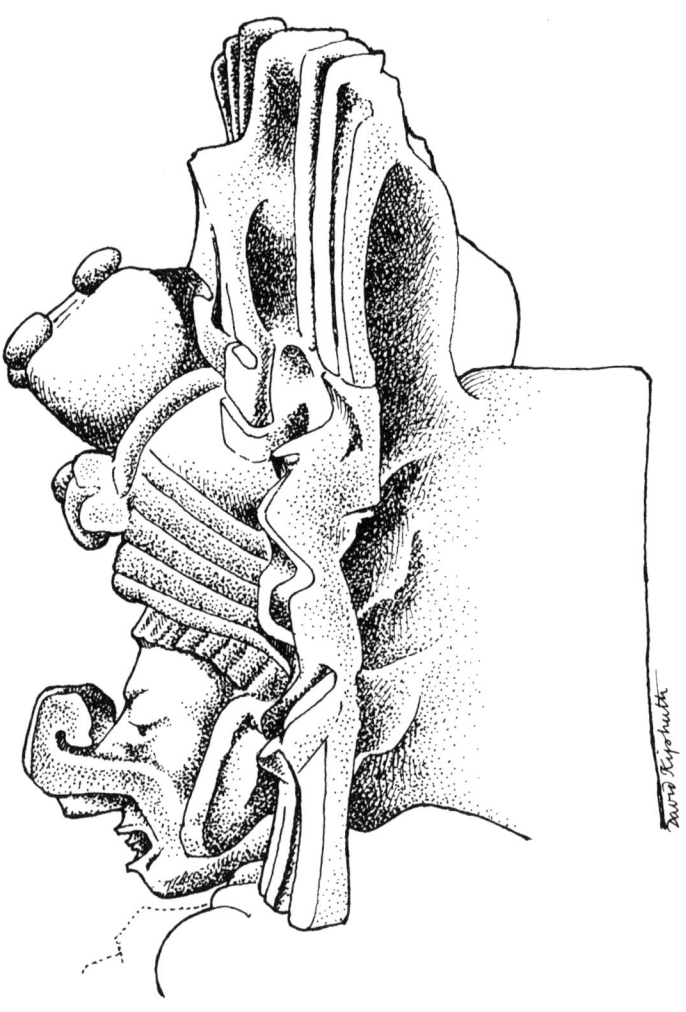

Figure 59. Profile of an anthropomorphic ceramic urn from Monte Albán that displays many of the insignia associated with warriors (redrawn from Caso and Bernal 1952:116).

animals such as the jaguar, and to have dressed in costumes appropriate to their orders (Chapter 2), evidence of the earliest Zapotec warrior orders might be traced in the archaeological record by means of their known association with jaguars and other wild animals. There is, in fact, little doubt as to the emergence of the jaguar in Zapotec iconography during Period II. In their iconographic study of Zapotec urns, Alfonso Caso and Ignacio Bernal (1952:54-64) describe the representations of a jaguar deity they name *Dios Tigre*. The earliest known portrayal of this being is a large, seated jaguar statue that was discovered in a Period II context on the Main Plaza at Monte Albán, and depictions of jaguars apparently become common at Monte Albán thereafter.

> Las representaciones de tigres concebidas como un animal, y no ya con características humanas, son bastante abundantes. La más antigua encontrada en Monte Albán, es la de un gran tigre de la época II, que apareció en el basurero de la Plataforma Oeste (Fig.82). El animal está sentado, tiene un moño al cuello y está totalmente policromado. A partir de esta época, las representaciones de tigres son muy frecuentes en Monte Albán. . . . [Caso and Bernal 1952:55]

Not only are free-standing jaguar statues found at

Plate 40. Jaguar paws decorate the inset panels that flank the staircase of Mound X at Monte Albán.

Monte Albán, but jaguar heads, and jaguar attributes—such as jaguar paws and jaguar fangs—become important elements in the Zapotec iconography of this time period. For example, jaguar heads and jaguar-paw vases are frequently found in offerings and tombs at Monte Albán (Caso and Bernal 1952:55-64). Even the architectural styles of the period adopted the jaguar motif; representations of jaguar paws decorate the sunken *tablero* of the Period II temple platform at Monte Albán that is named Mound X (Pl. 40) (Marquina 1964:330, 334, Lámina 93).

Jaguar statues and vessels decorated with jaguar characteristics have also been recovered at Period II sites on the valley floor. A magnificent seated jaguar statue, similar to the one from the Main Plaza at Monte Albán, was found in a tomb at the site of Suchilquitongo at the northern end of the Etla arm of the valley (Fig. 60) (Caso and Bernal 1952:62-63, Fig. 98). Furthermore, there is evidence that the jaguar was recognized in the outlying regions that were incorporated by the Zapotec. Recall that fragments of similar jaguar statues were recovered from the plazas of two contemporaneous sites in the Cuicatlán Cañada (see Chapter 4, Pl. 34). In Chapter 4, I suggested that these jaguar statues were displayed at communities subjugated by the Valley Zapotec as a symbol of Zapotec imperial power.

I propose that the warrior orders, which are known to have embodied Zapotec imperial power during the Postclassic period, are also manifested in Monte Albán's iconography by portrayals of men wearing jaguar costumes. Among the representations of "humanized jaguars," as Caso and Bernal (1952:54-55) refer to them, are seated figures attached to urns who are portrayed wearing jaguar headdresses and jaguar masks. In fact, Caso and Bernal report an actual clay helmet shaped in the form of a jaguar head that was probably worn by these kinds of figures (Caso and Bernal 1952:58, Fig. 86). Perhaps the best example of a "humanized jaguar" from Monte Albán is found on the Lápida de Bazán carving (Caso and Bernal 1952:54-55), where the important figure on the right is clearly portrayed wearing a jaguar costume, complete with a jaguar mask, jaguar paws, and a jaguar tail (Fig. 61). I will return to discuss the significance of this jaguar personage later.

Figure 60. Ceramic jaguar statue from Suchilquitongo (redrawn from Caso and Bernal 1952:63).

Representations of men outfitted as jaguars are also found at other Period II sites in the Oaxaca Valley. Joyce Marcus has summarized the themes of carved stone monuments from settlements on the valley floor, where "jaguars and various ritual themes are particularly conspicuous" (Marcus 1976:133). Of the 100 or more carved stones found at valley floor settlements, at least 80 of them come from the site of Dainzú in the Tlacolula arm of the valley (see Fig. 1), and date to the end of Period I or the beginning of Period II. Marcus believes that the Dainzú monuments portray:

1) Seated and standing human figures with large headdresses.
2) Seated *"humanized" jaguars or men outfitted as jaguars.*
3) Ball players. [Marcus 1976:133, emphasis added]

Carved stone monuments from a nearby site at Teotitlán del Valle, which date to Period II or Period IIIa, depict jaguars and human figures wearing elaborate animal headdresses and carrying weapons. Similar figures appear on carved stones from Tlacochahuaya (Marcus 1976:133, 135).

All these figures displaying jaguar characteristics match the descriptions we have of Zapotec warriors who belonged to the jaguar order (Chapter 2). I suggest that a military organization made up of warrior orders such as these was instituted in the Valley of Oaxaca—both at Monte Albán and at settlements on the valley floor—by the very end of Period I or the beginning of Period II, exactly the time period when the Zapotec were evidently pursuing the military conquest of regions outside the Valley of Oaxaca.

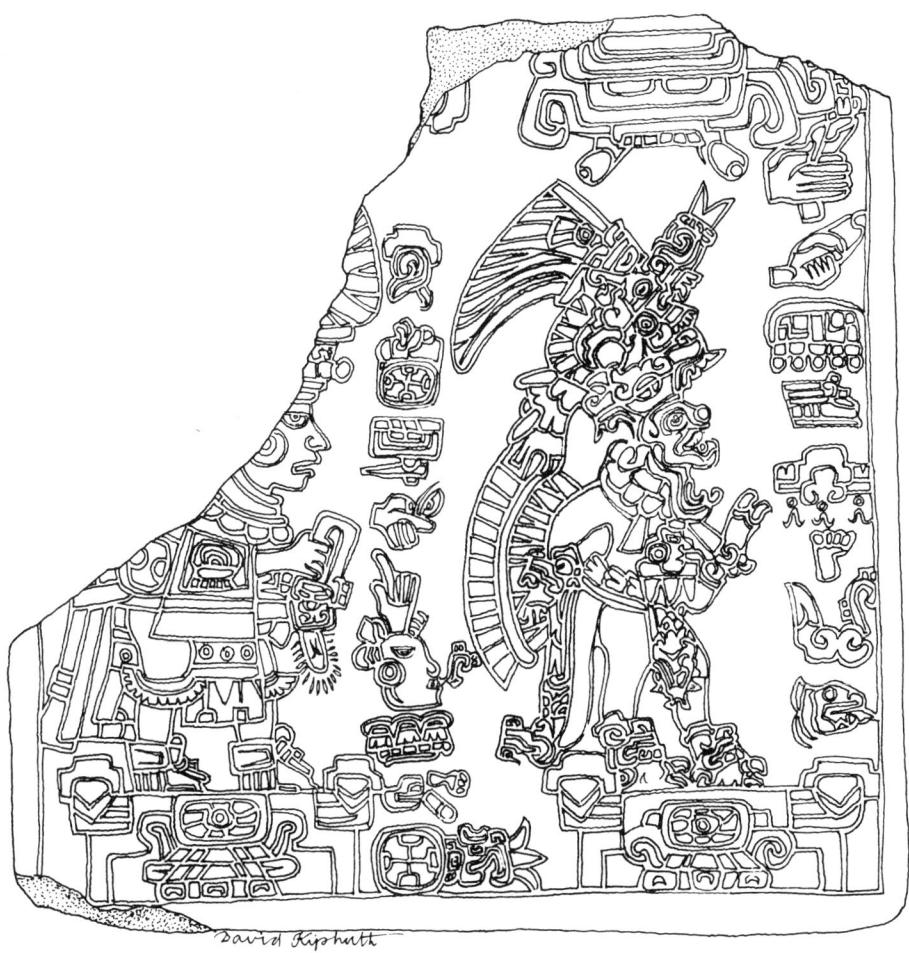

Figure 61. Lápida de Bazán (redrawn from Caso and Bernal 1952:55).

There is also some evidence in Zapotec iconography during Period II of warrior orders associated with animals other than jaguars. For example, Caso and Bernal describe a series of male deities portrayed on Zapotec urns who wear bird helmets or bird masks (Caso and Bernal 1952:173, 199-205). The best known example comes from a Period II tomb found within a mound group on Terrace 453 at Monte Albán. This mound group is located directly upslope from one of the entry-ways through the defensive wall to the hilltop center, and, it apparently formed the focus of one of Monte Albán's subdivisions or *barrios* during the Late Formative period (Blanton 1978:45). The urn in question depicts a young man's head, whose face is painted and who wears an elaborate bird helmet characterized by a protruding beak (Caso and Bernal 1952: Fig. 341, 341bis). Other representations of men wearing bird masks and bird helmets are found at Monte Albán as well as at sites on the valley floor in Period II. Similar to the representations of men wearing jaguar costumes, these figures may denote another military order that was instituted precisely at the time of Monte Albán's military expansion into surrounding regions. These wide-beaked bird helmets and masks probably represent eagles or some other raptorial bird, another one of the wild beasts who may have served as patrons of the Zapotec warrior orders.

We would also expect to find archaeological indications of the early Zapotec military organization resulting from the body of activities performed by this new institution. Among the archaeological correlates of the militaristic activities that Burgoa described for the Postclassic Zapotec would be the permanent offensive and defensive military facilities erected by the military: hilltop outposts and garrisons with massive stone slab and boulder fortifications, defensive walls, and trenches. We would expect to find military installations such as these in regions where Zapotec military personnel carried out Monte Albán's expansionistic policies, as well as in strategic situations within the Valley of Oaxaca itself. As we saw in Chapter 4, the Zapotec established military outposts at the northern boundary of the Cuicatlán Cañada sometime during the Lomas phase in order to define and defend the Monte Albán state's expanded frontier there. I refer the reader to the detailed descriptions and maps of the frontier facilities at Quiotepec in that previous chapter.

Within the Valley of Oaxaca, the activities of such a burgeoning military order in the Late Formative period are clearly manifested, albeit in fewer facilities. It was at this time that a series of impressive defensive walls were built along the lower slopes of Monte Albán. As we saw in the introductory chapter, Blanton (1978:52-54) believes that the principal function of these walls was to defend the northern and western slopes of the hilltop center. Another edifice that was raised as a result of the Valley Zapotec's militaristic activities was the arrowhead-shaped Building J in the Main Plaza of Monte Albán. While perhaps not a military installation in and of itself, the function of Building J must certainly have been related to the military conquests that were recorded on stone slabs set into its outer walls. Indeed, Blanton refers to Building J as a "military showcase" (Blanton 1978:47). An arrowhead-shaped building similar in plan and orientation to Building J was erected at the site of Caballito Blanco, in the Tlacolula branch of the Valley. A comparable function might be attributed to this smaller replica of Building J (Paddock 1966: Fig. 89), despite the fact that it lacks any inscriptions.

With the emergence of a body of military specialists, and with the establishment of Zapotec military outposts in frontier regions during the Late Formative period, it is not surprising to find evidence of a drop in the population of Monte Albán and of the valley floor immediately adjoining it during the transition from the latter part of Period I to Period II. Blanton (1978:44) estimates the Period II population at Monte Albán to have been between 9,650 and 19,300 persons, down slightly from the population estimate of 10,200 to 20,400 persons for Period Late I. Additional surveys conducted by Blanton and his collaborators on the valley floor have also documented a drop in the population of the central valley floor at this time; in the rural part of the central valley floor where 154 Period Late I occupations were found, only 23 small Period II occupations occurred (Blanton et al. 1979:379, 1982: 74-77). Depopulation of Monte Albán and of surrounding communities in Period II might have resulted from the local manpower that joined the military effort to fight and to staff Monte Albán's frontier outposts.

Administration of a Tributary Network

Following the Zapotec conquest and pacification of outlying regions, Monte Albán would begin to implement its imperial policies in the subject regions. If we assume that each of the conquest slabs on Building J represents a separate region or place that was taken over by Monte Albán, the implementation of an imperial policy in these regions outside the Valley of Oaxaca would have enormous consequences for the polity centered at Monte Albán. Monte Albán's administrative apparatus would have increased greatly in size if, as I have suggested (Chapter 4), the Zapotec replaced the native ruling elites of conquered regions with Zapotec administrators for the purpose of enforcing the collection of tribute.

There seems to be little doubt that the Zapotec were exacting tribute in the Cuicatlán Cañada after that region's subjugation. In Chapter 4 we saw how the Zapotec expanded the Cañada's agricultural potential by introducing the irrigation facilities that were needed to cultivate the region's high alluvium. Communities were shifted off the high alluvial terraces and re-settled on piedmont ridges overlooking the canyon floor. But since the region's population remained far below the carrying capacity of the productive alluvium during the Lomas phase, it appears that the expansion of the Cañada's agricultural régime at this time was intended to meet the tribute demands imposed upon the region by the Zapotec. While part of this tribute might have been designed to provision the Zapotec personnel stationed there, the remaining due would have been sent to the Valley of Oaxaca, in a manner analogous to the Postclassic pattern of tribute mobilization reported in the ethnohistorical documents. Midden deposits at one of the Lomas phase communities in the Cañada included enormous densities of tropical fruit and palm nut remains, suggesting that at least part of the Cañada's tribute to Monte Albán was met in the form of these *tierra caliente* products, which cannot be grown in the cooler climate of the Oaxaca Valley.

How, then, did Monte Albán coordinate the flow of tribute from as many as 40 conquered places like the Cuicatlán Cañada to the Oaxaca Valley? We might expect to find administrative facilities established at critical nodes in the tributary network during the Late Formative period in order to coordinate the movement of tribute from the subject regions to Monte Albán. We would also expect to find evidence at Monte Albán for the eventual receipt of these tribute items.

I propose that one such administrative facility was established at the northwestern end of the Etla branch of the Oaxaca Valley, in a strategic position at the entry of natural communication routes from the Mixteca Alta and the Cuicatlán Cañada to the Oaxaca Valley. I am referring to the large Period II site of Suchilquitongo, which covers a hill rising 300-400 m at the northwestern end of the Etla branch, and below which pass both the modern highway and the railroad en route to Oaxaca (Fig.1). The site of Suchilquitongo was surveyed by Dudley Varner (1974) and more recently by Richard Blanton and Gary Feinman, who told me of the site's size and initial date of occupation (Feinman, personal communication, 1977). Feinman also mentioned mapping an impressive mound group and tracing a curious traffic pattern at the site.

Intrigued by Feinman's description of Suchilquitongo, Charles Spencer and I visited the site in 1978. Our inspection of the surface debris led us to agree with the initial Period II date assigned to it, an occupation which extends over an estimated 50 ha. In retracing the site's road pattern, we detected a major road that traversed Suchilquitongo in a north to south direction. A prehistoric traveler from the Cuicatlán Cañada, for example, would have entered the Oaxaca Valley near the present town of Telixtlahuaca. Immediately after passing by Telixtlahuaca, the traveler would have followed an ancient road that climbs to the hilltop site of Suchilquitongo by way of a long gradually sloping ridge. The road ascends the hillslope to a terrace just below the large pyramidal mound group on the highest point of the hill (Pl. 41). Proceeding beneath the massive public buildings, the traveler would have continued around to the site's southern ridge, where a series of gate-like structures would have interrupted his passage (Pl. 41). Having passed through the gateways, the road would have led the traveler down the southern ridge of Suchilquitongo to the valley floor, from whence the traveler could have proceeded on to Monte Albán. It seems clear that this Period II hilltop center was strategically positioned at the point where major communication routes from the Cuicatlán Cañada and the Mixteca Alta enter the Oaxaca Valley, and that its road pattern was designed to channel traffic directly beneath the group of large public buildings on the hilltop and through a series of gateways or checkpoints.

For these reasons alone, I would propose that Suchilquitongo was a specialized administrative facility that was established by the Monte Albán state during the Late Formative period in order to regulate the flow of traffic, tribute, and trade goods entering the Oaxaca Valley from regions to the north. In line with this interpretation of Suchilquitongo is the discovery of a large jaguar statue at the entrance to a tomb here (Fig. 60), similar to one found on the Main Plaza at Monte Albán (Caso and Bernal 1952:55, 62-63). If in fact the jaguar was a symbol of Monte Albán's imperial power, it is not surprising to find evidence of such a military contingent at this specialized facility of the state.

Upon reaching the northern slope of Monte Albán, a traveler would have been channeled through an opening in that center's defensive wall, at a point along the wall where a number of ancient roads converged (Blanton 1978:64-66). Blanton has suggested that the large, flat platform located at the opening in Monte Albán's defensive wall had gatelike functions, "indicating, perhaps, an interest among the community's administrators in regulating and/or taxing traffic flow" (Blanton 1978:52). As the principal point of entry to the Zapotec capital, this gateway was probably a final checkpoint through which all tribute cargos borne from subjugated regions entered Monte Albán.

Plate 41. Period II site of Suchilquitongo, Oaxaca Valley. *Above*, the large pyramidal mound group on the hilltop, facing north. *Below*, road passes below the mound group and through a series of gateways before proceeding southward onto valley floor and Monte Albán in the distance.

Plate 42. Building J conquest slab with "palm-fronds" place glyph.

Unfortunately, there is no direct evidence at Monte Albán for the receipt of tribute items from regions like the Cuicatlán Cañada. If lowland products such as black zapote fruits and coyol palm nuts were indeed sent as tribute to the Zapotec capital, their recovery from excavations at Monte Albán would have depended upon techniques of water flotation. Most of the excavations at Monte Albán, however, were carried out well before flotation techniques were introduced to archaeology (Struever

1968). Future research in other regions that were taken over by the Zapotec may some day reveal the sources of other exotic items that were sent as tribute to Monte Albán.

Although we lack the direct evidence needed to demonstrate Monte Albán's position at the center of a tributary network, we have some indirect evidence at Monte Albán that illustrates the Zapotec rulers' interest in subjugating places that cultivated tropical plants. The evidence comes from at least one of the carved stone slabs set into the outer face of Building J in the Main Plaza of the site. This particular slab (Pl. 42) contains the three basic elements that are commonly found on the Building J inscriptions: an upside-down head, signifying conquest; a "hill" glyph that means place; and, a combination of glyphs above the general place glyph that refers to the specific name of the conquered place (Chapter 1). The specific place glyph on this conquest slab consists of two outcurving leafy branches, which, in my opinion, represent palm fronds. Alfonso Caso also interpreted a similar place glyph on another conquest slab in this way (Caso 1947:27). The conquest slab shown in Plate 42 might therefore refer to a "Place of Palms" that was taken over by the Valley Zapotec in order to extract locally-produced items in the form of tribute. Because palm trees are characteristic of lowland regions, it is likely that the tribute items drawn from that conquered place consisted largely of lowland tropical products, not available in the Valley of Oaxaca.

I have suggested that the Zapotec state implemented its imperial policies by replacing the native ruling elites of subject regions with state-level administrators, whose duties included enforcing the collection of tribute and overseeing its mobilization to the Oaxaca Valley. Specialized administrative facilities were constructed at key nodes in the tributary network in order to regulate the movement of tribute bearers from hinterland regions. Entry to the Zapotec capital itself was by way of a final checkpoint located at an opening in the city's defensive wall. Clearly, the management of a tributary network would have placed considerable demands upon Monte Albán's decision-making organization. The administration of entire, new organizational units (i.e. tributary regions), including the collection and mobilization of tribute from those regions, would almost certainly have resulted in the differentiation and elaboration of Monte Albán's administrative apparatus. The successful implementation of the Zapotec's imperial policy would depend upon an increasing amount of horizontal specialization (Johnson 1978:87) in Monte Albán's decision-making organization in order to administer the added organizational units and tribute-related activities. The emergence of higher-order vertical control units in the decision-making apparatus—designated vertical specialization (Johnson 1978:87-88)—would also be required to integrate the new horizontally specialized components of the decision-making organization.

The elaboration of Monte Albán's decision-making organization by means of the addition of new horizontally specialized components and by the emergence of new higher-order vertical control units would result in an internally-specialized decision-making organization. As we saw in the introductory chapter, an internally-specialized administrative organization is a major characteristic of the state (Wright 1977:383). Only such an internally-specialized decision-making organization will be capable of performing central decision-making activities in different places and at different times. Consequently, the ability of the Zapotec rulers to delegate aspects of regional level decision-making to specialized administrators located at places other than the regional capital atop Monte Albán would have underlain the successful implementation of their imperial policies.

The ability of a central decision-maker to delegate partial authority to specialized administrators stationed at distant places is what Spencer has termed the capacity for decentralized decision-making (Spencer 1982:6, 250-251). According to Spencer, the development of effective decentralized decision-making was perhaps the most critical adjustment that the Zapotec faced when they embarked upon their interregional conquest strategy. That the Zapotec polity centered at Monte Albán developed an internally-specialized administrative organization, one that was capable of effective decentralized decision-making, is reflected in the establishment of frontier outposts and way stations to administer a vast tributary network. In this way, the administration of a tributary network was perhaps one of the important factors motivating Monte Albán's rise to statehood by the beginning of Period II.

New Interregional Exchange Mechanisms

In Chapter 4 we saw how Monte Albán's militaristic ventures into surrounding regions during the Late Formative period disrupted the interregional exchange relationships that had previously linked the Oaxaca Valley elite with elites in adjacent regions. Monte Albán's expansion into the Cuicatlán Cañada resulted in the establishment of a military frontier at the northern Quiotepec boundary of the region, which prevented the subject communities in the Cañada from interacting freely with the autonomous polities located beyond the frontier to the north in the Tehuacán Valley. Thus, in order for Monte Albán to have maintained its previous trade relations with polities located beyond its expanded frontiers, we expected to find evidence for the emergence of new interregional trade mechanisms at this time.

I have proposed that one of the possible new interregional exchange mechanisms that developed in response to Monte Albán's imperial expansion involved the establishment of neutral ports of trade beyond the borders of Zapotec-controlled territory. Ports of trade are usually established to facilitate trade between rulers of separate polities. Located as they are on the borders of separate regions, ports of trade provide a neutral meeting ground where representatives of the interacting polities may exchange.

Monte Albán maintained its previous trade relations with polities located in regions beyond the Cuicatlán Cañada by joining in the establishment of a port of trade at Llano de los Mogotes (Cs1-L), just north of the Quiotepec frontier at the southernmost end of the Tehuacán Valley. Located outside the border of Zapotec territory in an undefended position on the valley floor, Llano de los Mogotes probably served as a neutral meeting place for Zapotec traders to exchange with traders from independent polities beyond Monte Albán's northern frontier. Aside from its intermediary and undefended location, the Palo Blanco phase site of Llano de los Mogotes near the modern town of Tecomavaca exhibits a number of other unusual features that can perhaps be best understood in view of its possible role as a port of trade. I refer the reader to my detailed description of Llano de los Mogotes in Chapter 4, where I also discuss that settlement's port-of-trade functions.

We can view the establishment of ports of trade like the one at Llano de los Mogotes as more than simply a response to the disruptive effects that the Zapotec conquest strategy had upon previous interregional exchange relationships. The establishment of ports of trade was in the vital interests of the expansionistic Zapotec because it was by means of these facilities that the Zapotec procured certain raw materials such as obsidian that were needed to produce part of their military equipment. All the major obsidian sources of the central Mexican highlands lay beyond Monte Albán's frontiers and were controlled by independent polities. Ports of trade constituted a necessary vehicle for the supply of raw materials like obsidian to the Zapotec military forces, and hence, were critical for the very maintenance of Monte Albán's domination over its frontier regions. Another reason why Monte Albán might have sought to control the importation of raw materials used in the production of military equipment was that it provided a way for the Zapotec state to ensure greater command over the troops it stationed in frontier regions. By directly controlling the supply of raw materials needed to manufacture military equipment, Monte Albán would be in a favorable position to supervise the armament of its troops, thereby ensuring a greater degree of internal cohesion in its imperial network (Andrzejewski 1954:87). Thus, I consider the founding of ports of trade beyond Monte Albán's frontiers to have been closely related to the Zapotec imperial strategy.

The establishment of ports of trade beyond the expanded borders of the Zapotec state would have entailed a further elaboration of Monte Albán's administrative apparatus during the Late Formative period. I suggest that a body of specialized traders might have been instituted by the state at this time for the purpose of conducting this state-administered exchange at the distant ports of trade (cf. Chapman 1957:120-122; Dibble and Anderson 1959; Sanders 1977:405). A new state-level institution would have arisen, adding yet another specialized component to Monte Albán's decision-making organization. The emergence of such a trading institution would have contributed to the internally-specialized character of Monte Albán's administrative apparatus.

Moreover, because a large portion of the activities performed by this body of long-distance traders occurred at faraway ports of trade, the overall management of this specialized trading institution was contingent upon the Zapotec rulers' ability to delegate aspects of the centralized decision-making process to specialized administrators located at places other than the regional capital. For this reason, it is fitting that the trade conducted at most ethnographically documented ports of trade is considered "an affair of state" between the polities that are represented by their respective long-distance traders. The activities carried out by specialized Zapotec traders at the ports of trade that were established in regions beyond Monte Albán's frontiers—like the functions of the newly-instituted Zapotec military order and those involved in the administration of the vast tributary network—demanded the development of effective decentralized decision-making on the part of the Zapotec administration centered at Monte Albán.

Political Ascendance of the Military

Early in Monte Albán's campaign of interregional conquests, a permanent body of military specialists was probably instituted, consisting of ranked warrior orders. This military organization that was formed to carry out the expansionistic policies of Monte Albán's rulers would have constituted a special arm of the early Zapotec state, what can be referred to as a special-purpose institution (Flannery 1972:411). One of the effects of the conquest strategy, however, might have been to foster the emergence of a privileged group of warriors. In time, the conquest strategy might have nurtured the rise to political prominence of certain war leaders, who had been delegated the authority to carry out the state's imperial policies (Andrzejewski 1954:39, 134; Adams 1966:139-140, 152-153). As the privileged military leaders increased their status and authority in response to the demands and rewards of the Zapotec expansionistic strategies, they might have begun to assume many of the state's central decision-making functions. In the process, the military arm of the early Zapotec state might have become a more general-purpose institution (Flannery 1972:411-413), one that came to be identified with Monte Albán's decision-making organization.

Given the potential for a military institution like the one established by the emergent Zapotec state during the Late Formative period to promote itself to a higher position in the central decision-making hierarchy, we might expect to find evidence for the eventual growth in political prominence of the Zapotec military organization. The ascendance of Zapotec military leaders to prominent positions in Monte Albán's decision-making organization might have been reflected in the adoption of "martial attitudes . . . associated with kingship" (Adams 1966:146). We might expect to find representations of Zapotec rulers in military regalia, weaponry in royal tombs, historical inscriptions boasting of military victories, and the rise to prominence of militaristic supernatural beings (Adams 1966:135-136, 145-148) following Monte Albán's conquest strategy.

These are not idle speculations; our ethnohistorical sources on Postclassic Zapotec society allude to the social mobility of Zapotec warriors as well as to the close ties that existed between the Zapotec military and political institutions at that time (see Chapter 2). Privileged military leaders were entitled to many of the sumptuary privileges enjoyed by the Zapotec elite. Moreover, the Zapotec rulers outfitted themselves with military accouterments. I would contend that the social mobility of Zapotec warriors and the martial attitudes associated with Zapotec rulership during the Postclassic period originated much earlier in the history of the Zapotec state.

The evidence to document the political ascendance of the Zapotec military organization following Monte Albán's conquest strategy is admittedly limited; nevertheless, it is suggestive and entirely consistent with the previous discussion concerning the military's potential to promote itself under certain conditions. It is in the period following the Zapotec imperial strategy that inscribed stone monuments at Monte Albán begin to include the indigenous place name for that regional center, which according to historical documents from a nearby community on the valley floor was named "Hill of Twenty Jaguars" in Mixtec, and "Hill of the Jaguar" in Spanish (Marcus 1976:130; Blanton 1978:5). I am referring to the stone monuments (stelae) arranged at the four corners of the massive pyramidal platform that was erected on the southern end of the Main Plaza at Monte Albán in Period IIIa (ca. A.D 200-400), whose inscriptions include the portrayal of foreign emissaries arriving at a place named "Hill of 1 Jaguar" (Marcus 1980:57-59). Although "1 Jaguar" in these inscriptions might refer to the specific calendrical name of Monte Albán's ruler at that particular time, the historical documents suggest a more general place name—"Hill of the Jaguar"—for ancient Monte Albán. Furthermore, although Monte Albán might have been named "Hill of the Jaguar" long before Period IIIa, it is significant that the

SUMMARY AND CONCLUSION

earliest record of its name dates to the period following Monte Albán's conquest strategy. If I am correct in associating the jaguar with a Zapotec military order composed of privileged warriors, the Early Classic period name for Monte Albán might reflect the rise of such a military order to a prominent position of authority within the Zapotec state's decision-making body centered at Monte Albán. Such a military order that was instituted during the Late Formative period in order to implement the imperialistic policies of the Zapotec rulers, in time gained the "manpower, resources, and organization" (Rappaport 1974:65) that enabled it to assume control of the state's central decision-making organization.

The Lápida de Bazán (Fig. 61) is also significant in this regard. This inscribed travertine slab, which was discovered in a Period IIIa context atop Mound X at Monte Albán, records a meeting between two personages:

> One figure, on the left, is dressed in Teotihuacán style and holds a pouch of copal in one hand. The other is costumed as a jaguar in the style of the lords of Monte Albán.
> . . . I regard it tentatively as being a record of an agreement between representatives of the two cites. [Marcus 1980:58-59]

By Period IIIa, therefore, a person dressed in the military garb of the jaguar order—complete with a jaguar mask, jaguar paws, and a jaguar tail—occupied a high position of rulership within the Zapotec state centered at Monte Albán, such that he met with lords from foreign polities like Teotihuacán. I believe that the Lápida de Bazán provides an example of the powers assumed by the Zapotec military order of the jaguar in the period following Monte Albán's interregional conquest strategy. By the Early Classic period, the effects of the Valley Zapotec's militaristic expansion into surrounding regions like the Cuicatlán Cañada were complete with the political ascendance of this military order. There can be little doubt that the Zapotec state—in its inception and apparently right through its history to the arrival of the European *conquistadores* in the sixteenth century—was truly a militaristic state.

Appendix I

Neutron-Activation Analysis of Ceramics from the Valley of Oaxaca and the Cuicatlán Cañada

Elsa M. Redmond and Garman Harbottle

INTRODUCTION

Mesoamerican archaeologists often make inferences about the kinds of relationships that existed between neighboring regions in prehistoric Mesoamerica by plotting the distributions of stylistically similar ceramics in the pertinent regions. Redmond's investigation of the Cuicatlán Cañada's relationship to the Valley of Oaxaca during the Middle and Late Formative periods was to proceed accordingly. Her research design included a regional settlement pattern survey of the Cuicatlán Cañada, followed by a program of intensive mapping and surface collection at all Middle and Late Formative period sites found in the region. On the basis of the controlled surface collections she expected to plot the distribution of the Monte Albán ceramics in the Cañada for the two time periods in question. The resulting ceramic distributions were intended to constitute one line of evidence that could be used in conjunction with other independent archaeological data to evaluate the possibility that during the Late Formative period the Cuicatlán Cañada became a frontier region of the early Zapotec state centered at Monte Albán in the Oaxaca Valley. In Chapter 2 Redmond presented a model that outlines the determinants and consequences of the Cuicatlán Cañada's possible subjugation by Monte Albán in the Late Formative period, together with their potential archaeological manifestations.

Central to Redmond's plan for studying the regional distribution of Oaxaca ceramics in the Cuicatlán Cañada during the Middle and Late Formative periods was her ability to differentiate between true imported Monte Albán ceramics from the Valley of Oaxaca and any locally-produced imitations of Monte Albán wares in the Cañada. Her classification was to be based upon the common visual identification of differing paste types, surface finishes, and other ceramic attributes that characterize the pottery from the two regions. It was with the aim of corroborating the visual distinction of local Cañada wares from what she considered to be imported Oaxaca Valley ceramics that Redmond turned to techniques of trace-element analysis. It was hoped that the chemical characterization of a representative sample of local Cañada wares and imported wares from the Oaxaca Valley would confirm their apparent differences.

Dr. Garman Harbottle at Brookhaven National Laboratory agreed to carry out the trace-element analysis of a sample of Formative period ceramics from the Oaxaca Valley and the Cuicatlán Cañada. Having analyzed only a small sample of Oaxaca ceramics from later time periods, Harbottle was particularly interested in the opportunity to characterize by chemical means a representative sample of Formative period ceramics from Monte Albán.

Because no such analysis had ever been performed on Middle and Late Formative ceramics from either the Cuicatlán Cañada or the Oaxaca Valley, the task of selecting ceramics for the proposed trace-element analysis was guided by the following considerations: (1) the general need to examine a completely representative sample of Middle and Late Formative period ceramics from the two regions; (2) Redmond's specific interest in the chemical distinction between imported Oaxaca ceramics and any locally-produced imitations of Monte Albán ceramics in the Cuicatlán Cañada during the two Formative periods; and (3) the overall need to keep the number of chosen ceramic samples to a minimum due to the high cost of performing such analyses.

With these needs and constraints in mind, Redmond selected a total of 40 Formative sherds from each region. The sample of sherds from the Cuicatlán Cañada Project represented primarily the region's local ceramic wares during the Formative period: Perdido Gray, Lomas Gray, and Lomas Plain (see Chapter 2). Included in the sample, however, were a number of examples of what Redmond considered to be ceramics imported by the Cañada from the Oaxaca Valley during the Middle and Late Formative periods, namely Monte Albán I Crema ware, and Monte Albán Ic-II Crema ware described by Caso, Bernal, and Acosta (1967).

A similarly representative sample of 40 sherds from the Oaxaca Valley was selected from ceramic collections belonging to several related sub-projects of the Prehistory and Human Ecology of the Valley of Oaxaca Project, which are now under the care of the INAH Centro Regional de Oaxaca. The majority of the sherds came from the site of Monte Albán, both from the Monte Albán Survey Project directed by Richard Blanton (Blanton 1978), and from excavations carried out in a residential sector of Monte Albán by Marcus Winter (Winter 1974). The sample contained examples of the three major Monte Albán ceramic wares defined by Caso, Bernal, and Acosta (1967) for the corresponding Monte Albán Periods I and II: Rosario/Monte Albán Ia Gray ware, Monte Albán I Crema ware, Monte Albán I Café ware, Monte Albán Ic-II Gray ware, Monte Albán Ic-II Crema ware, and Monte Albán Ic-II Café ware. Two Monte Albán IIIb Gray ware sherds of the Classic period were added to the sample of Oaxaca Valley ceramics.

The total 82 sherds destined for trace-element analysis were labeled, described, and illustrated before being sent to Brookhaven National Laboratory. The following section includes a list of the sherds together with their provenience designations and a brief description of each sherd. The sample number designations CC, VO, and MA refer to Cuicatlán Cañada, Valley of Oaxaca, and Monte Albán, respectively. The provenience designations for the ceramics from the Cuicatlán Cañada Project bear a Cañada site number followed by a slash and the number of a specific surface collection or excavated provenience (for example, Cs25/913). The sample of Oaxaca Valley ceramics includes the following provenience designations: MAS-T. for a particular surface collection of the Monte Albán Survey; MA-72 or MA-73 for an excavated provenience from Monte Albán; B74 for the valley-floor site of Tierras Largas (Winter 1972); and B23 for the valley-floor site of Fábrica San José (Drennan 1976a).

CERAMICS SELECTED FOR NEUTRON-ACTIVATION ANALYSIS

I. Perdido Gray outleaned-wall bowl rims with distinctive incised decoration on rim (CC1-10) (Fig. 62)

These 10 gray ware sherds come from 9 Perdido phase sites the length of the Cuicatlán Cañada. This incised gray bowl is a dominant local ceramic in the Cañada during the Middle Formative period (see Chapter 2, Fig. 9). Although similar to the contemporaneous Rosario/Period Early I gray ware in the Valley of Oaxaca (samples VO41-44 and MA45-47), these Perdido Gray bowls are probably all of local manufacture in the Cañada.

Sample #	Provenience	Description
CC1	Cs25/913	Gray outleaned-wall bowl rim with incising
CC2	Cs19/123	Gray outleaned-wall bowl rim with incising
CC3	Cs17/117	Gray outleaned-wall bowl rim with incising
CC4	Cs15/100	Gray outleaned-wall bowl rim with incising
CC5	Cs10/009	Gray outleaned-wall bowl rim with incising
CC6	Cs9/089	Gray outleaned-wall bowl rim with incising
CC7	Cs4/037	Gray outleaned-wall bowl rim with incising
CC8	Cs4/030	Gray outleaned-wall bowl rim with incising
CC9	Cs27/217	Gray outleaned-wall bowl rim with incising
CC10	Cs1/058	Gray outleaned-wall bowl rim with incising

II. Monte Albán I Crema ware in the Cañada (CC11-13) (Fig. 63)

These 3 Crema paste sherds come from 2 Perdido phase sites in the Cañada and are considered to have been imported from the Valley of Oaxaca. They should belong to the group of equivalent Monte Albán I Cremas from Monte Albán (MA48-53). Descriptions of the precise Crema types are found in Caso, Bernal, and Acosta (1967: 45–46, Figs. 19, 21, Lám. II, VII).

Sample#	Provenience	Description
CC11	Cs25/1388	C.2 bowl rim, thick walled
CC12	Cs4/038	C.4 Suchilquitongo plate rim (see Drennan 1976a:26–27)
CC13	Cs25/1205	C.4 bottle rim

III. Lomas Gray outleaned-wall bowl rims and bases with distinctive decoration (CC14-22) (Fig. 64)

These 9 gray paste sherds come from 4 Lomas phase sites in the Cañada. Outleaned-wall bowls such as these with two parallel lines incised around the interior rim and a combed decoration on the interior base are diagnostic of this time period in the Valley of

Oaxaca; they correspond to types G.12 and G.21 in Caso, Bernal, and Acosta's classification (Caso, Bernal, and Acosta 1967: 25-26, 67, Fig. 4-6, 43). While the majority are probably of local manufacture in the Cuicatlán Cañada (see Chapter 2, Fig. 16), some of the examples may actually have been imported from the Valley of Oaxaca.

Sample #	Provenience	Description
CC14	Cs25/1312	Gray outleaned-wall bowl rim with parallel incised lines and a combed base
CC15	Cs25/1317	Gray outleaned-wall bowl rim with parallel incised lines
CC16	Cs25/1317	Gray outleaned-wall bowl rim with parallel incised lines, brown surface color
CC17	Cs25/1317	Gray outleaned-wall bowl base angle with combed decoration
CC18	Cs19/129	Gray outleaned-wall bowl rim with parallel incised lines
CC19	Cs19/129	Gray outleaned-wall bowl base angle with combed decoration
CC20	Cs13/274	Gray outleaned-wall bowl base angle with combed decoration
CC21	Cs13/294	Gray outleaned-wall bowl base with G.21-type decoration (Caso, Bernal, and Acosta 1967:62)
CC22	Cs11/075	Gray outleaned-wall base angle with G.21-type decoration

IV. Monte Albán Ic-II Crema ware in the Cañada (CC23-26) (Fig. 65)

These 4 sherds come from 4 Lomas phase sites in the Cañada and are considered to have been imported from the Valley of Oaxaca. They should belong to the group of equivalent Monte Albán Ic-II Cremas from Monte Albán (MA63-75). Descriptions of the precise Crema types are found in Caso, Bernal, and Acosta (1967:67-68, Lám X, Fig. 205, 208).

Sample #	Provenience	Description
CC23	Cs25/1312	C.7 outleaned-wall bowl rim with specular red paint on orange decoration
CC24	Cs2/168	C.11 outleaned-wall bowl body sherds with specular red paint on orange and post-firing scratched decoration
CC25	Cs3/196	C.7 outleaned-wall bowl rim with specular red paint on orange decoration
CC26	Cs27/216	C.11 outleaned-wall bowl rim with specular red paint on orange decoration

V. Lomas Plain ware imitations of Monte Albán Ic-II Cremas (CC27-34) (Fig. 66)

These 8 plain ware sherds come from 5 Lomas phase sites in the Cuicatlán Cañada and are considered to have been local imitations of Monte Albán Ic-II Cremas. They should belong to the paste group Lomas Plain (see Chapter 2, Fig. 18-19), of which other examples have been submitted for analysis (CC35-40). Redmond finds these Lomas Plain imitations of Monte Albán Cremas to be discretely distributed in the Cañada during the period of Zapotec subjugation of that region; their abundance at Lomas phase settlements on the region's northernmost alluvial fan leads her to suggest that these Monte Albán-style ceramics were being manufactured at the Quiotepec frontier in order to serve the needs of the military personnel stationed there (see Chapter 4).

Sample #	Provenience	Description
CC27	Cs25/1316	Plain outleaned-wall bowl rim with specular red on orange decoration
CC28	Cs19/128	Plain bowl body sherd with C.11-type post-firing scratched decoration
CC29	Cs6/015	Plain cylinder rim with specular red on orange decoration
CC30	Cs3/189	Plain outleaned-wall bowl rim with C.11-type post-firing scratched decoration
CC31	Cs3/193	Plain outleaned-wall bowl rim with C.11-type post-firing scratched decoration
CC32	Cs3/196	Plain bowl body sherd with C.11-type post-firing scratched decoration
CC33	Cs27/215	Plain outleaned-wall bowl base angle with C.11-type post-firing scratched decoration
CC34	Cs27/216	Plain outleaned-wall bowl base angle with C.11-type post-firing scratched decoration

VI. Lomas Plain ware (CC35-40) (Fig. 67)

These 6 plain paste sherds come from 4 Lomas phase sites in the Cañada and are representative of the Lomas Plain ware tradition (see Chapter 2, Fig. 17). Because they come from diverse communities located the length of the region, they should reflect the range of variation of locally available clays.

Sample #	Provenience	Description
CC35	Cs25/1312	Plain olla rim, tall and flared
CC36	Cs6/015	Plain olla rim, tall and flared
CC37	Cs3/189	Plain olla rim, tall and flared
CC38	Cs3/189	Plain comal rim
CC39	Cs27/215	Plain comal rim
CC40	Cs27/216	Plain olla rim, tall and flared

VII. Rosario Gray outleaned-wall bowl rims with distinctive incised decoration on rim (VO41-44) (Fig. 68).

These 4 examples of Rosario gray ware come from 2 Middle Formative period sites in the Etla branch of the Oaxaca Valley. Rosario gray ware, which is also known as Socorro Fine Gray (Drennan 1976a:22, 36-43), represents the immediate precursor of the Monte Albán gray ware tradition.

Sample #	Provenience	Description
VO41	B74A/F.10	Gray outleaned-wall bowl rim with incising
VO42	B74A/F.9	Gray outleaned-wall bowl rim with incising
VO43	B74A/F.9	Gray outleaned-wall bowl with eccentric rim and incising
VO44	B23A/99M/	

	Z.H/35-55	Gray outleaned-wall bowl rim with incising

VIII. Monte Albán I Gray ware (MA45-47) (Fig. 69)

These 3 gray ware sherds come from Monte Albán and are representative of the Monte Albán I gray ware described by Caso, Bernal, and Acosta (1967: 32-35, Fig. 8-12, Fig. 140-141).

Sample #	Provenience	Description
MA45	MA-73-1012	Gray everted rim bowl with incising
MA46	MA-73-1036	Gray outleaned-wall bowl rim with incising
MA47	MA-72-1	Gray composite silhouette bowl with an everted rim and incising.

IX. Monte Albán I Crema ware (MA48-53) (Fig. 70)

These 6 Crema ware sherds come from Monte Albán and are representative of the Monte Albán I Crema ware described by Caso, Bernal, and Acosta (1967:44-46, Fig. 19, 21, Lám. II, VII).

Sample #	Provenience	Description
MA48	MA-73-1022	C.2 olla rim
MA49	MA-72-1	C.2 bowl (*apaxtli*) rim
MA50	MA-73-1021	C.2 comal rim
MA51	MA-72-1	C.4 bowl rim (see Caso, Bernal, and Acosta 1967: Fig. 21)
MA52	MA-72-502	C.4 Suchilquitongo plate rim (see Drennan 1976a: 26-27)
MA53	MAS-T.28	C.4 bottle rim

X. Monte Albán Ic-II Gray outleaned-wall bowl rims and bases with distinctive decoration (MA54-62) (Fig. 71)

These 9 gray paste sherds come from Monte Albán and are examples of the G.12 and G.21 ceramic types described by Caso, Bernal, and Acosta (1967:25-26, 67, Fig. 4-6, 43, 130-132). Both ceramic types are diagnostic of Monte Albán Ic-II gray ware.

Sample #	Provenience	Description
MA54	MA-72-670	Gray outleaned-wall bowl rim with parallel incised lines
MA55	MA-72-60	Gray outleaned-wall bowl rim with parallel incised lines
MA56	MA-72-209	Gray outleaned-wall bowl rim with parallel incised lines
MA57	MA-72-525	Gray outleaned-wall bowl rim with parallel incised lines
MA58	MAS-T.24	Gray outleaned-wall bowl base with combed decoration
MA59	MAS-T.31	Gray outleaned-wall bowl base with combed decoration
MA60	MAS-T.391	Gray outleaned-wall bowl base with combed decoration
MA61	MA-72-214	Gray outleaned-wall bowl base angle with combed decoration
MA62	MA-72-377	Gray outleaned-wall bowl base angle with G.21-type decoration (Caso, Bernal, and Acosta 1967:62)

XI. Monte Albán Ic-II Crema ware (MA63-75) (Fig. 72)

These 13 Crema paste sherds come from Monte Albán and are diagnostic of Monte Albán Ic-II Crema ware (Caso, Bernal, and Acosta 1967:67-68). Redmond believes that these Cremas represent a Monte Albán ceramic ware that was being imitated by local potters in the Cañada and, to a lesser extent, that was being imported into the Cañada during the Late Formative period, when the region came under Zapotec control.

Sample #	Provenience	Description
MA63	MA-72-1	C.7 outleaned-wall bowl rim with specular red paint on orange decoration
MA64	MAS-T.123	C.7 outleaned-wall bowl rim with specular red paint on orange decoration
MA65	MAS-T.105	C.7 outleaned-wall bowl rim with specular red paint on orange decoration
MA66	MAS-T.51	C.7 outleaned-wall bowl rim with specular red paint on orange decoration
MA67	MAS-T.192	C.7 outleaned-wall bowl rim with specular red paint on orange decoration
MA68	MAS-T.27	C.7 comal rim with streaky red paint on orange decoration
MA69	MA-72-1	C.11 outleaned-wall bowl rim with red paint on orange and post-firing scratched decoration
MA70	MAS-T.51	C.11 outleaned-wall bowl rim with red paint on orange and post-firing scratched decoration
MA71	MAS-T.556	C.11 outleaned-wall bowl rim with specular red paint on orange and post-firing scratched decoration
MA72	MAS-T.165	C.11 outleaned-wall bowl rim with specular red paint on orange and post-firing scratched decoration
MA73	MAS-T.136	C.11 outleaned-wall bowl base angle with red paint on orange and post-firing scratched decoration
MA74	MA-73-1401	C.11 outleaned-wall bowl base angle with red paint on orange and post-firing scratched decoration
MA75	MAS-T.274	C.11 outleaned-wall bowl base angle with red paint on orange and post-firing scratched decoration

XII. Monte Albán I Café ware (MA76-78) (Fig. 73)

These 3 Café paste sherds come from Monte Albán and are representative of the Monte Albán I Café ware described by Caso, Bernal, and Acosta (1967:49-51, Fig. 27-29).

Sample #	Provenience	Description
MA76	MA-72-10	Café olla rim
MA77	MA-73-1311	Café bowl rim
MA78	MA-73-1298	Café bowl rim with red paint on rim.

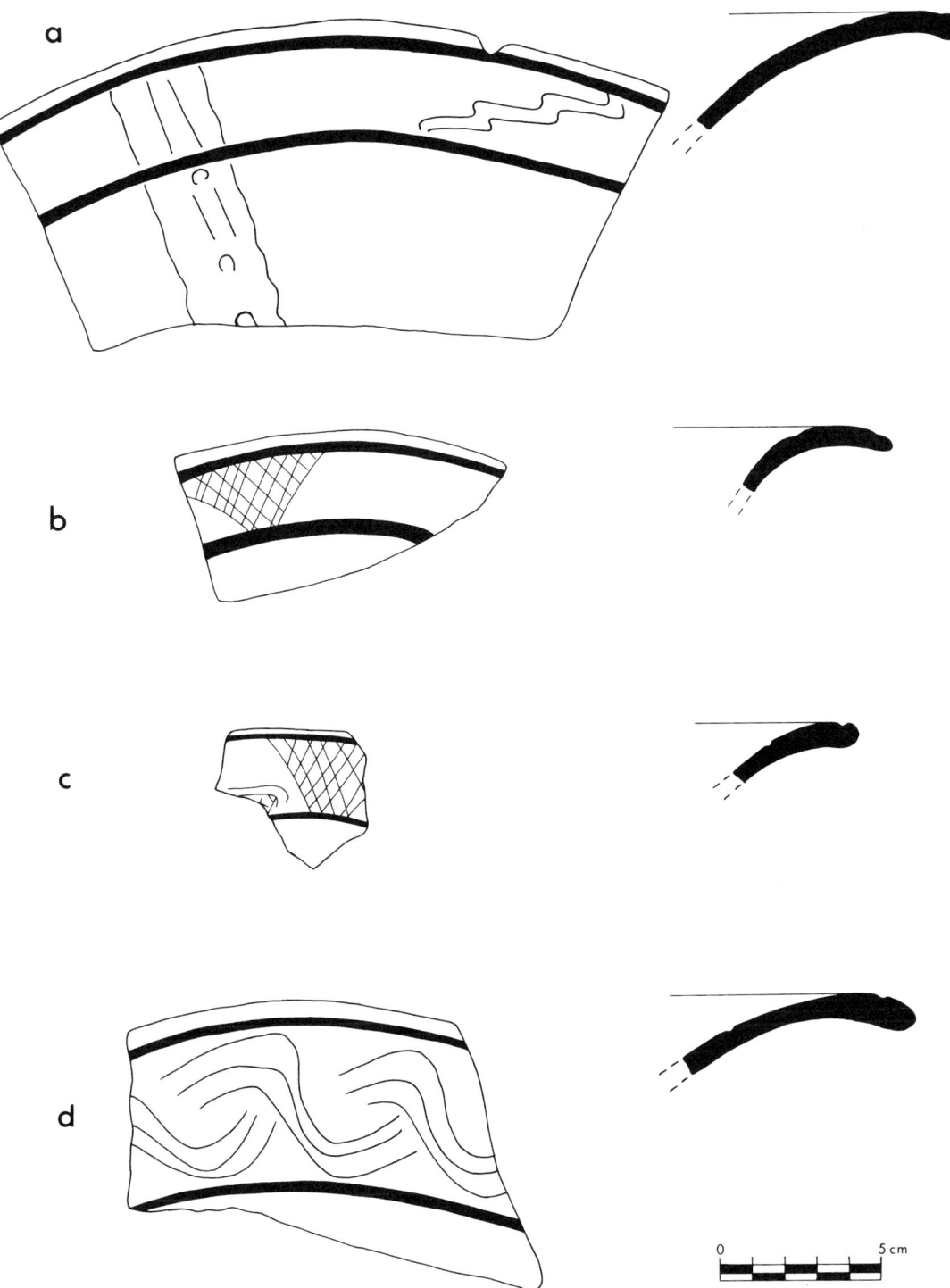

Figure 62. Perdido Gray outleaned-wall bowl rims. *a*, CC1; *b*, CC3; *c*, CC7; *d*, CC9.

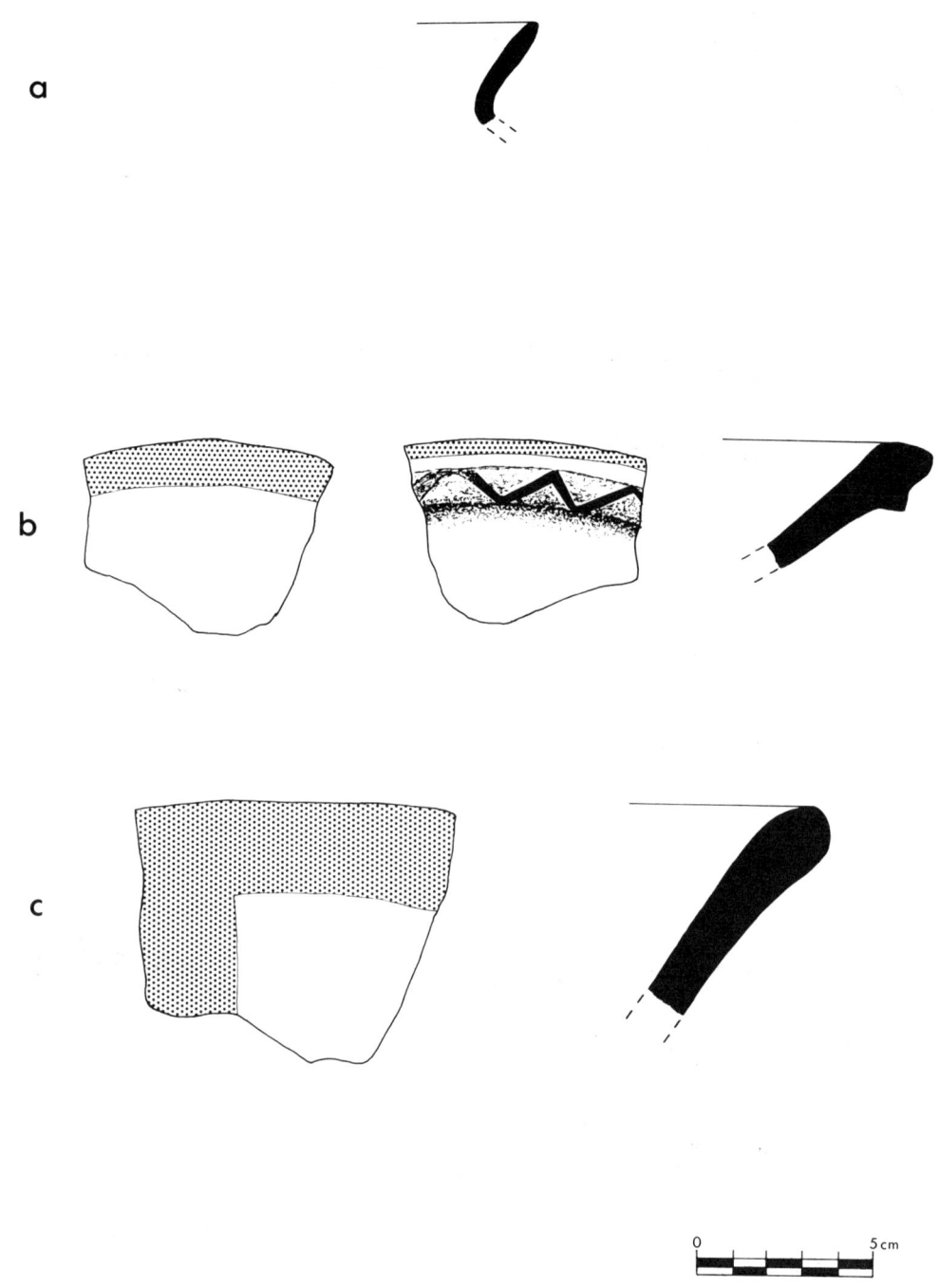

Figure 63. Monte Albán I Crema ware in the Cañada. *a*, CC13; *b*, CC12, interior surface (left), exterior surface (right); *c*, CC11, interior surface.

APPENDIX

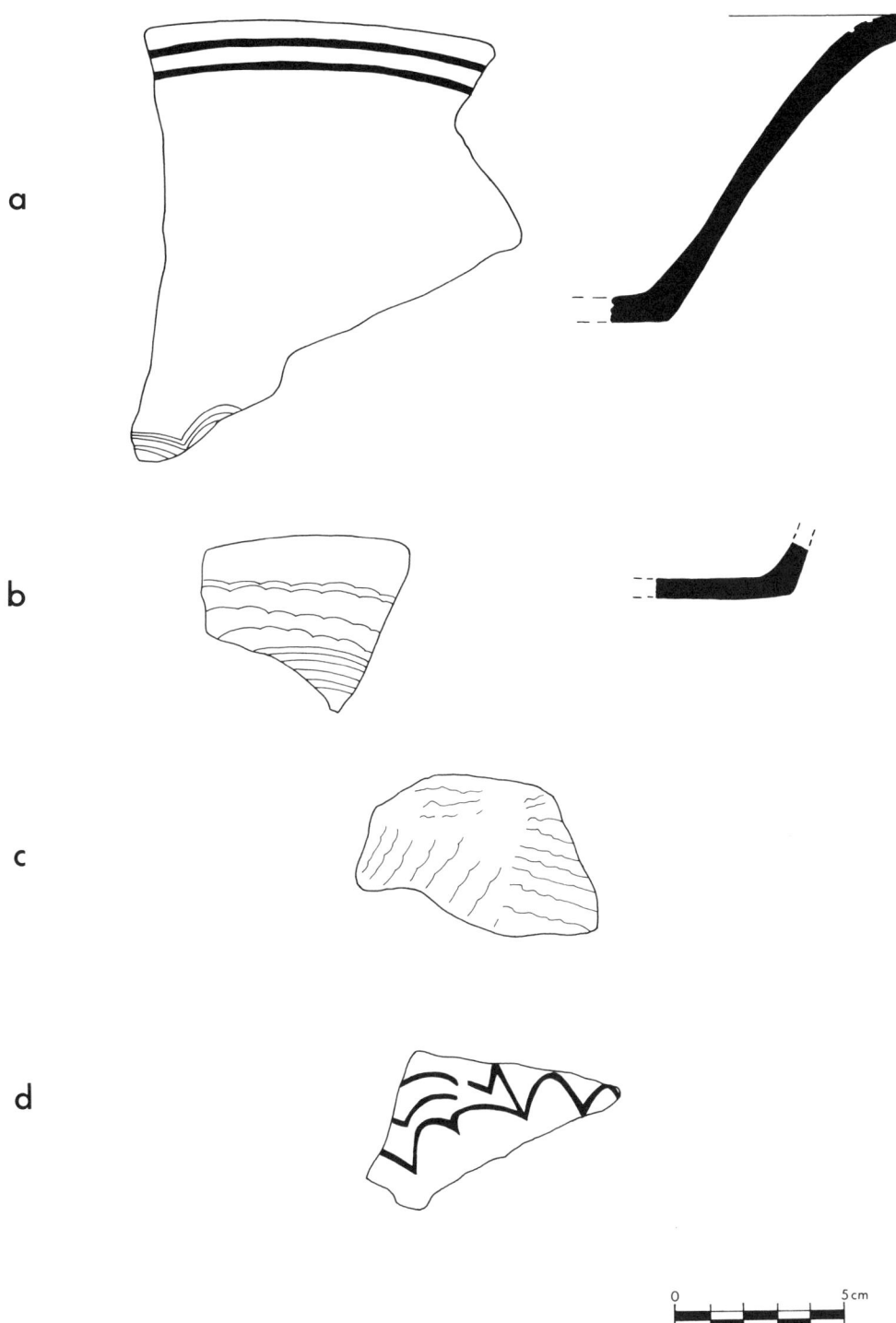

Figure 64. Lomas Gray outleaned-wall bowl rims and bases. *a*, CC14; *b*, CC17; *c*, CC19; *d*, CC21.

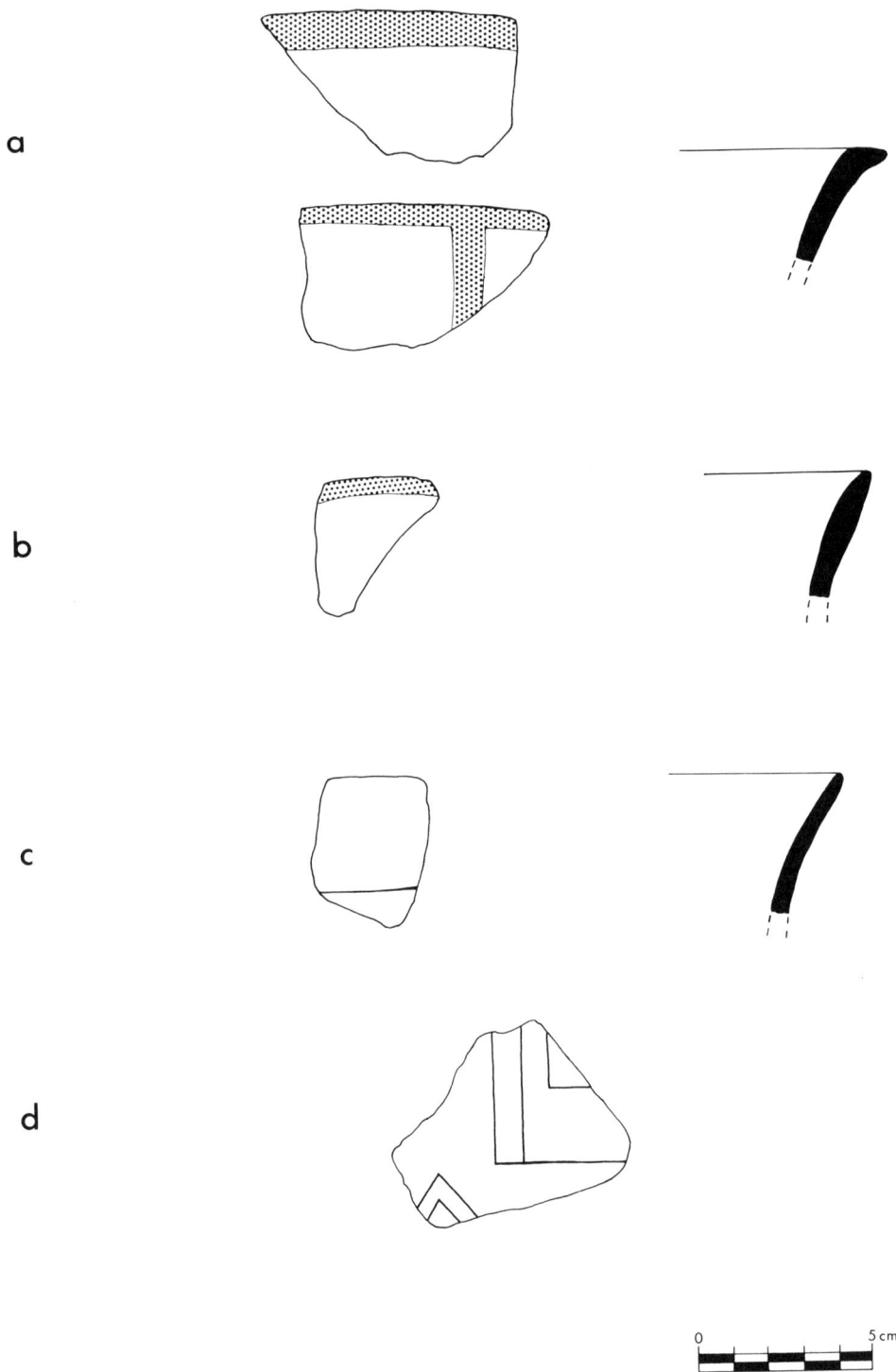

Figure 65. Monte Albán Ic-II Crema ware in the Cañada. *a*, CC23, interior surface (top), exterior surface (bottom); *b*, CC25, interior surface; *c*, CC26, exterior surface; *d*, CC24, exterior surface.

APPENDIX 193

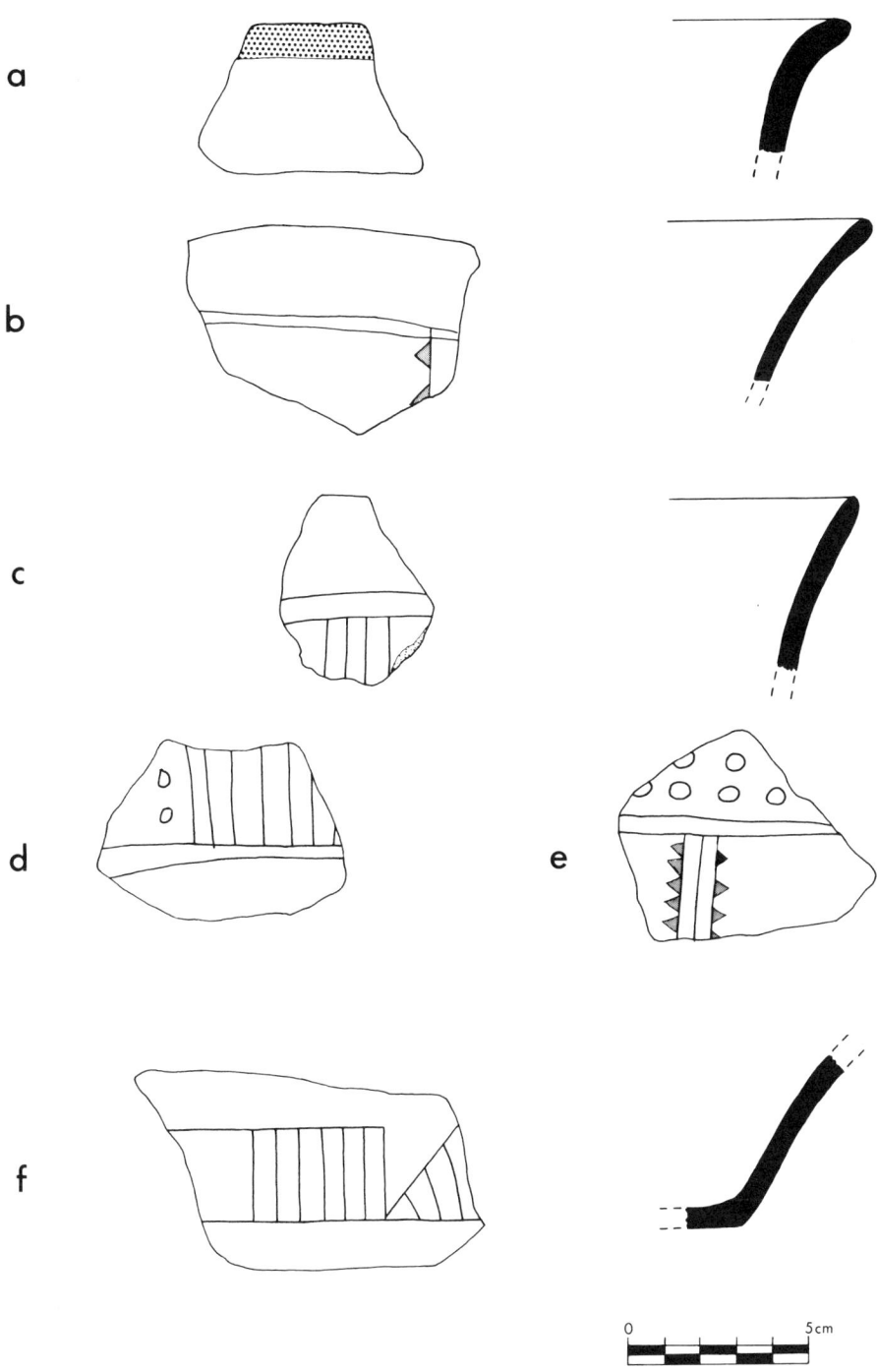

Figure 66. Lomas Plain ware imitations of Monte Albán Ic-II Cremas. *a*, CC27, interior surface; *b*, CC30, exterior surface; *c*, CC31, exterior surface; *d*, CC28, exterior surface; *e*, CC32, exterior surface; *f*, CC34, exterior surface.

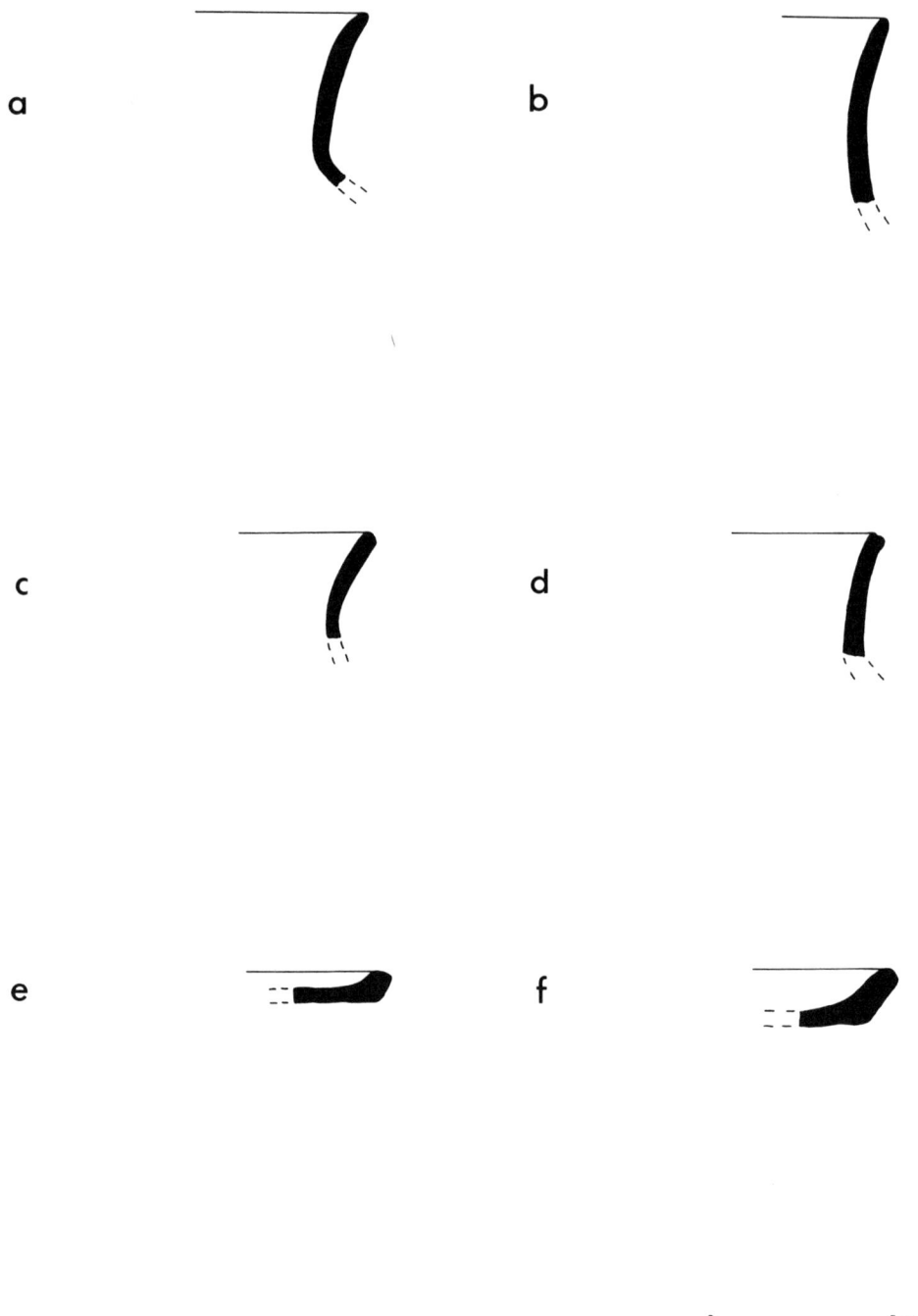

Figure 67. Lomas Plain ware. *a*, CC35; *b*, CC37; *c*, CC36; *d*, CC40; *e*, CC38; *f*, CC39.

APPENDIX

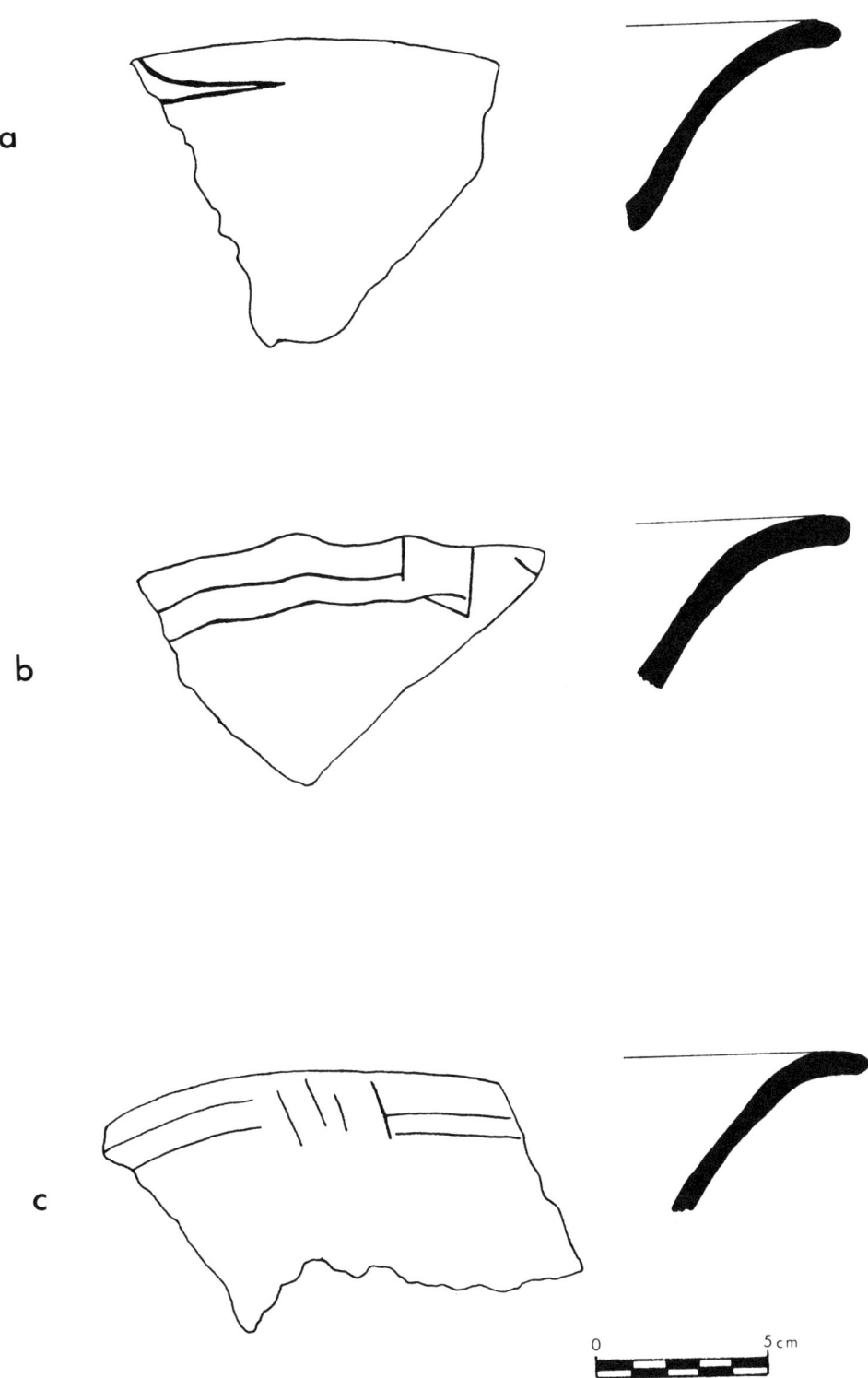

Figure 68. Rosario Gray outleaned-wall bowl rims. *a*, VO41; *b*, VO43; *c*, VO44.

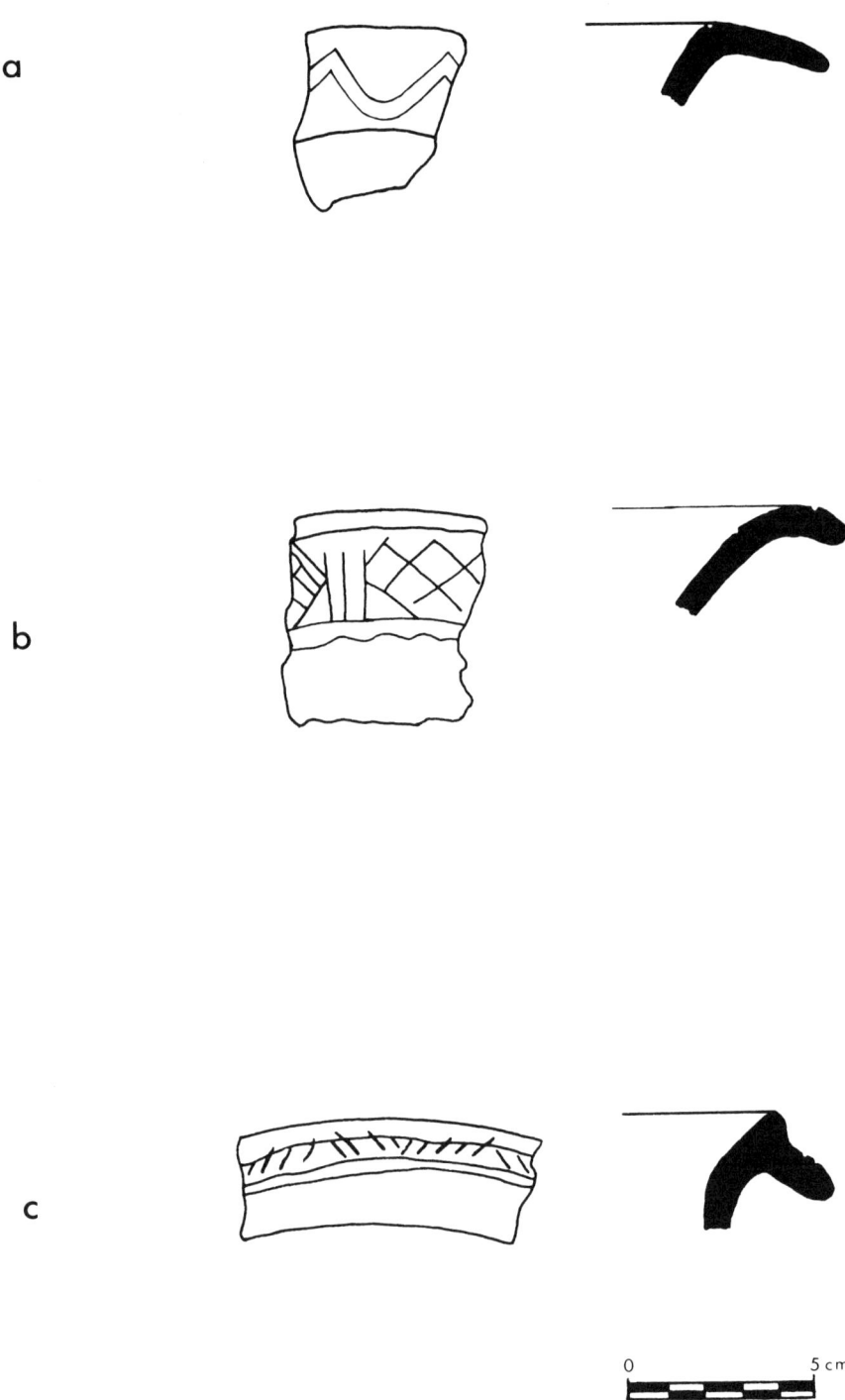

Figure 69. Monte Albán I Gray ware. *a*, MA45; *b*, MA46; *c*, MA47.

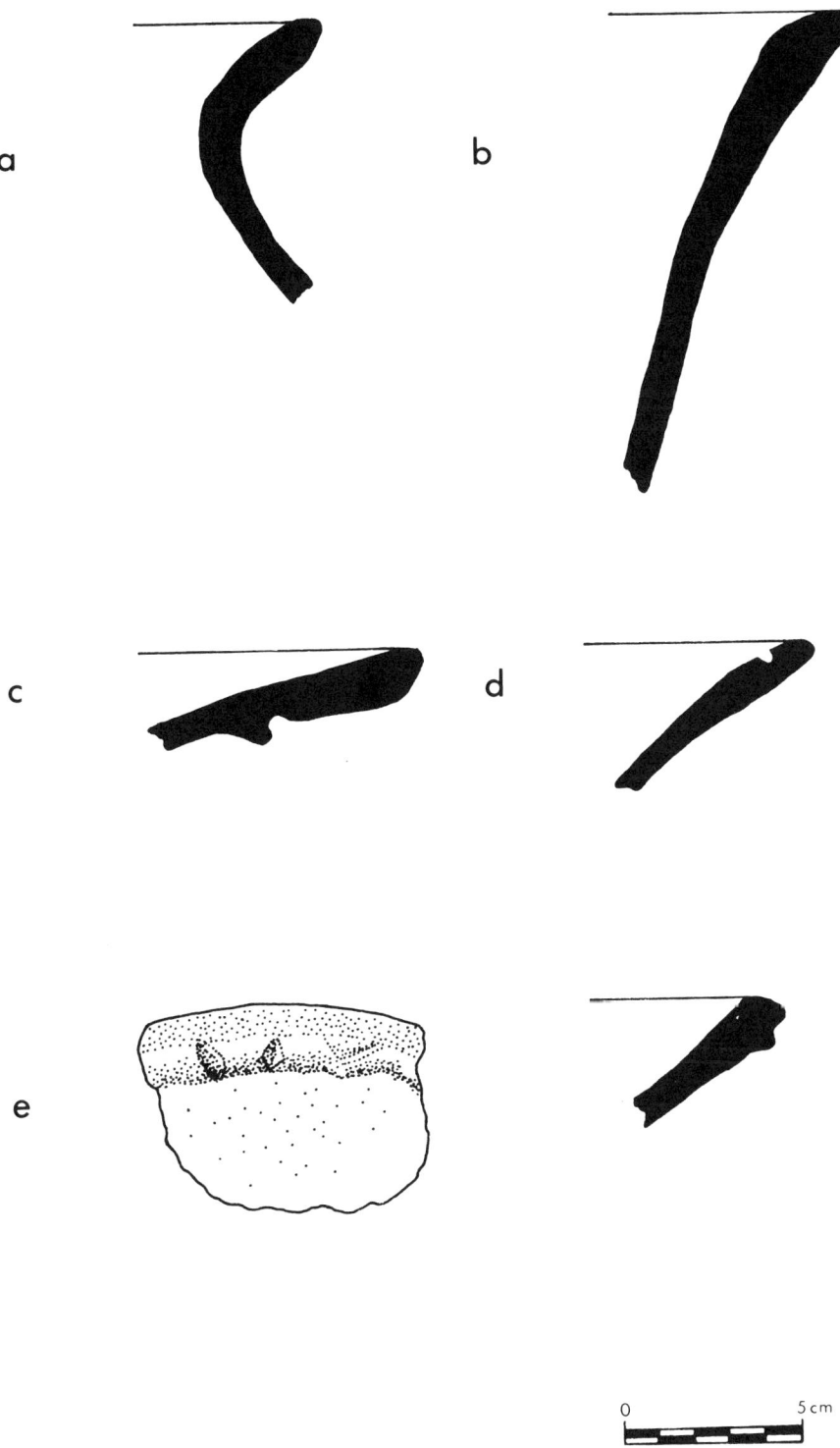

Figure 70. Monte Albán I Crema ware. *a*, MA48; *b*, MA49; *c*, MA50; *d*, MA51; *e*, MA52.

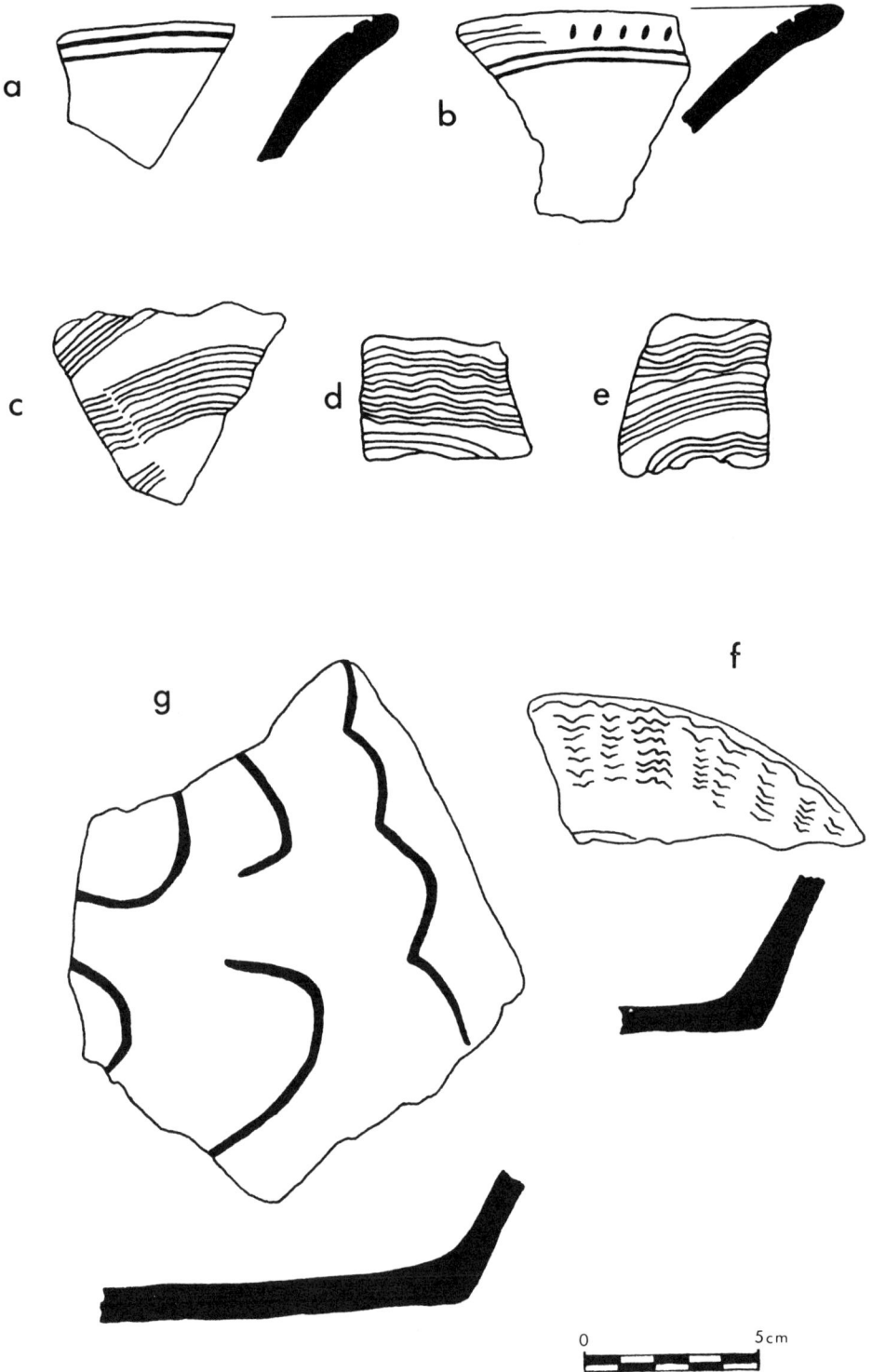

Figure 71. Monte Albán Ic-II Gray outleaned-wall bowl rims and bases. *a*, MA55; *b*, MA54; *c*, MA58; *d*, MA59; *e*, MA60; *f*, MA61; *g*, MA62.

APPENDIX

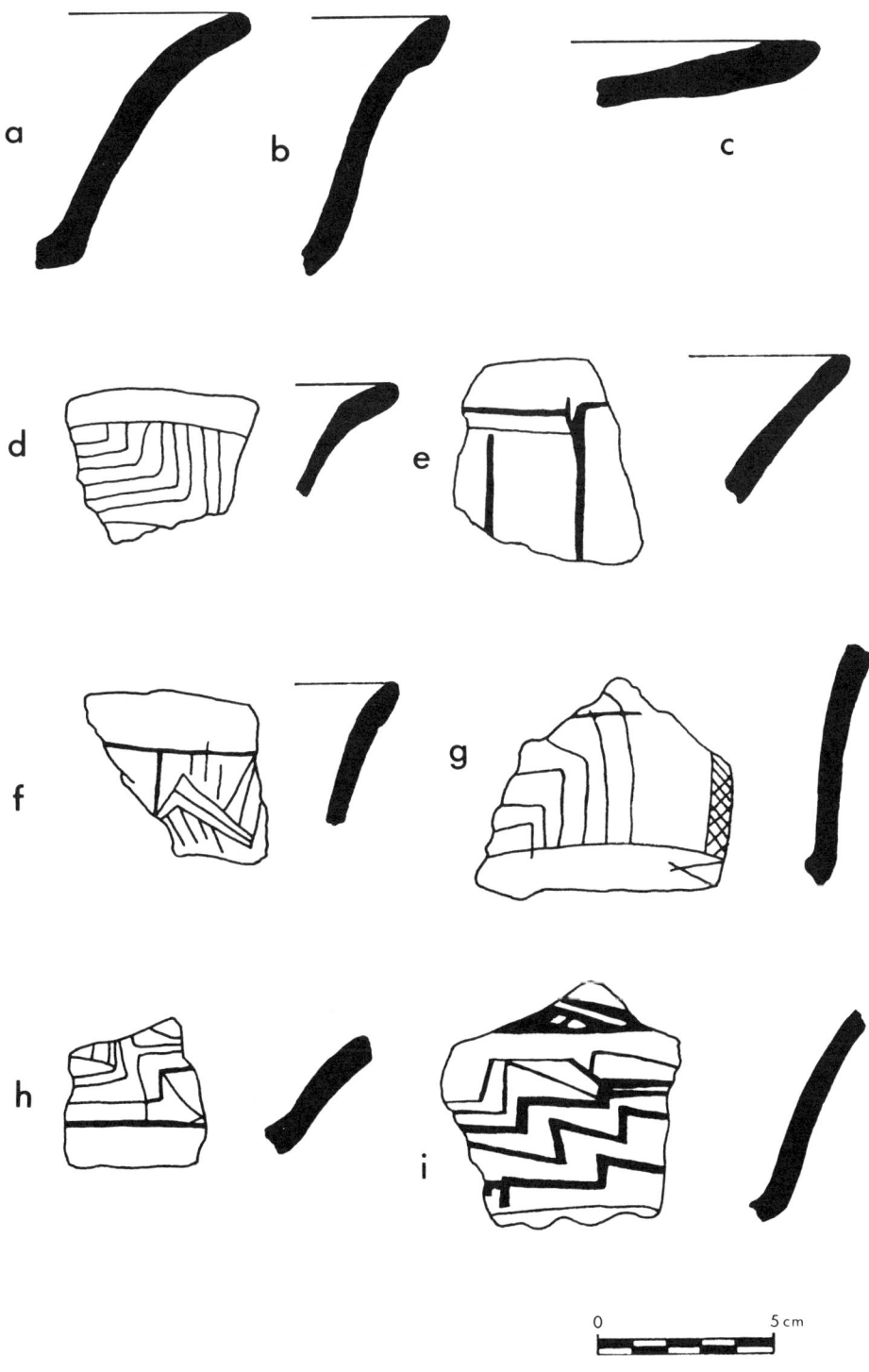

Figure 72. Monte Albán Ic-II Crema ware. *a*, MA63; *b*, MA66; *c*, MA68; *d*, MA71; *e*, MA69; *f*, MA70; *g*, MA74; *h*, MA73; *i*, MA75.

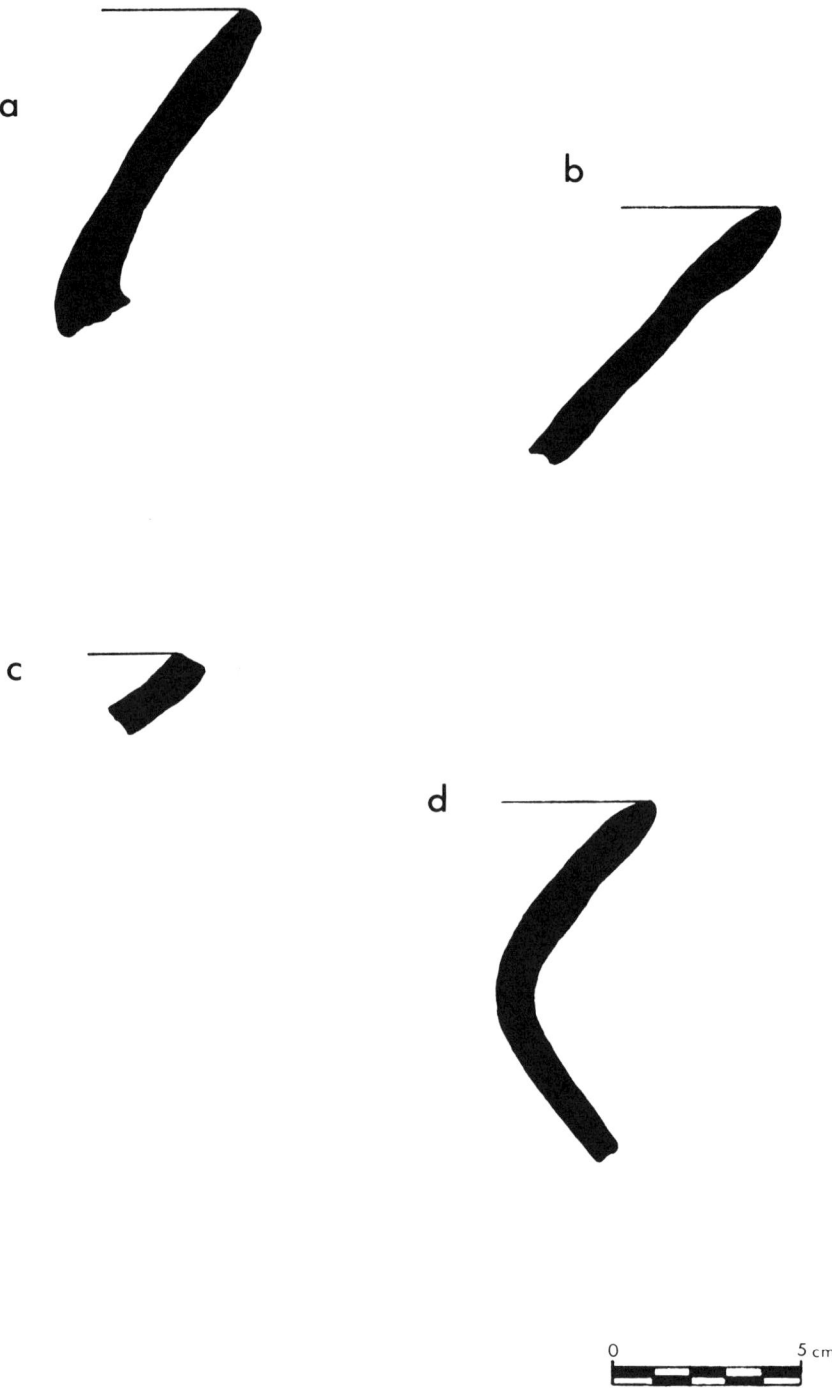

Figure 73. Monte Albán I-II Café ware. *a*, MA76; *b*, MA77; *c*, MA78; *d*, MA79.

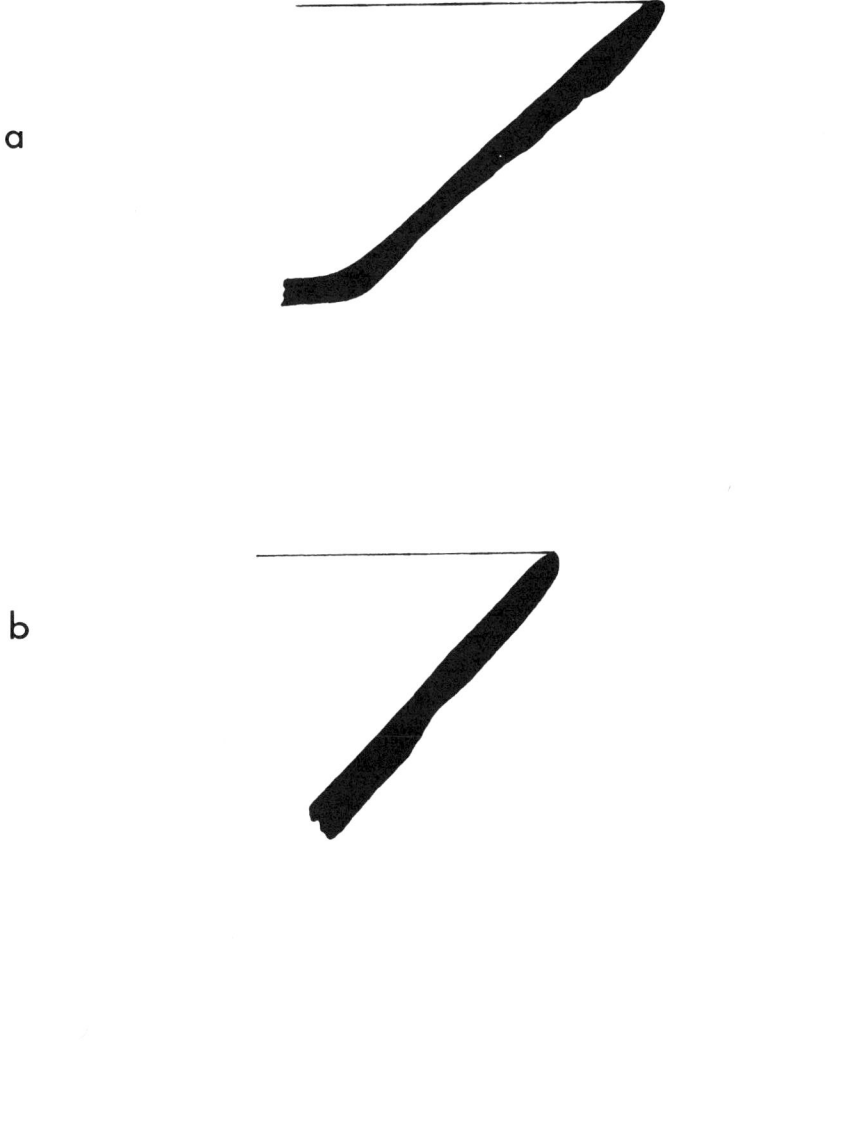

Figure 74. Monte Albán IIIb Gray ware. *a*, MA82; *b*, MA81.

202 A FUEGO Y SANGRE

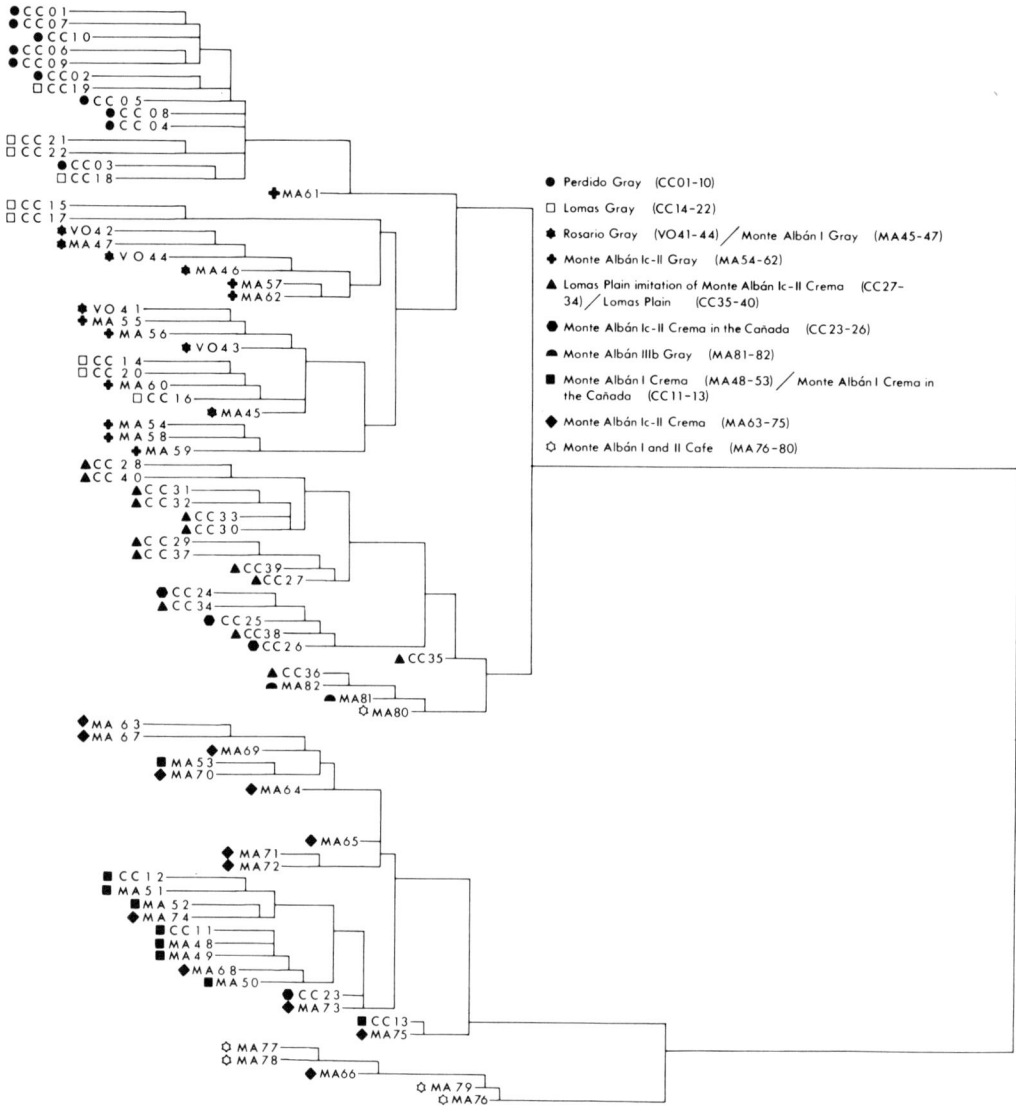

Figure 75. Dendrogram of ceramic samples submitted to neutron activation (from AGCLUS program).

XIII. Monte Albán Ic-II Café ware (MA79-80) (Fig. 73)

These 2 Café paste sherds come from Monte Albán and are examples of the Monte Albán Ic-II Café ware described by Caso, Bernal, and Acosta (1967:51-53, 69-70).

Sample #	Provenience	Description
MA79	MA-73-1703	Café olla rim
MA80	MAS-T.621	Café outleaned-wall bowl rim with incising

XIV. Monte Albán IIIb Gray ware (MA81-82) (Fig. 74)

These two gray paste sherds come from Monte Albán and are examples of the dominant gray ceramic type in the Valley of Oaxaca during the Classic period, designated G. 35 in the Caso, Bernal, and Acosta classification (1967: 80-82, 385-387).

Sample #	Provenience	Description
MA81	MA-73/ E.71/9	G.35 outleaned-wall bowl rim
MA82	MA-73/ E.71/5	G.35 outleaned-wall bowl rim

SOME RESULTS OF THE NEUTRON-ACTIVATION ANALYSIS

The actual analytical procedure was outlined in Chapter 2 and will be only briefly summarized here. Small samples of the 82 sherds were subjected to neutron activation in the Brookhaven High Flux Beam Reactor. The ensuing spectrum analysis determined the analytical values for the 23 elements being measured in the sampled sherds. The final stage of the analysis employed numerical taxonomic procedures in order to arrange the sampled sherds in groups according to the similarities in their chemical properties. The resulting groups of the cluster analysis are presented in the form of a dendrogram (Fig. 75).

The dendrogram reveals four broad groups or clusters of sherds, and a probable fifth group. At the top lies the group of Cañada gray wares (Perdido Gray and Lomas Gray), which Harbottle considers to be an extremely uniform group. Indeed, Harbottle suggests that either there is widespread regional uniformity in the composition of the clays that were used to make these gray ceramics, or that a single clay source is responsible for the unusually tight group.

The next group below consists of contemporaneous Middle and Late Formative period gray wares from the Oaxaca Valley. Thus, there is clear continuity between the gray ware tradition of the Rosario phase (Socorro Fine Gray) and the succeeding Monte Albán gray ware tradition. According to Harbottle, this Oaxaca gray ware tradition appears to be uniquely identified with the Valley of Oaxaca; rather than constituting a single clay source, it more likely represents an extended valley-wide composition.

The succeeding group in the dendrogram contains examples of the Cañada's plain ware tradition (Lomas Plain). Although the region's Perdido Plain ware was not represented in this analysis, it is probable that this earlier Cañada ware belongs to the same plain pottery tradition. Consistent with Redmond's expectations, those Late Formative period sherds classified as Lomas Plain imitations of Monte Albán ceramics fell firmly within this group, thereby confirming their local manufacture in the Cuicatlán Cañada and their classification within the region's plain ware tradition. Compared to the marked uniformity of the Cañada's gray wares, however, the region's plain ware tradition—as represented by Lomas Plain—appears more diverse.

A distinctive fourth cluster consists of the Oaxaca Cremas, which are notable for their very low iron content. Anna Shepard was the first to comment on the Crema paste's unusual petrographic composition, which she distinguished for its diorite temper (Shepard 1967: 478-479). Like Shepard, Harbottle suggests that the source of the Monte Albán Cremas lies in the Etla branch of the Oaxaca Valley, in the vicinity of the modern town of Santa María Atzompa where local potters today produce a similar diorite-tempered ware (Shepard 1967:478).

At the bottom of the dendrogram is a probable fifth group, which contains four of the five examples of Monte Albán Café ware (Caso, Bernal, and Acosta 1967:18, 49). Future analyses of additional Café paste sherds will likely confirm this tentative grouping.

The neutron-activation analysis clearly distinguished between the local Formative ceramic wares of the Cuicatlán Cañada and those of the Oaxaca Valley. For the Valley of Oaxaca, the chemical analysis recognized differences between the three major wares defined by Caso, Bernal, and Acosta in their classification of the ceramics from Monte Albán, as had Shepard's petrographic analysis of these wares (Shepard 1967:477-484). The dendrogram reveals the chemical distinctions between the Oaxaca Gray paste, the Crema paste, and the Café paste. The two Formative ceramic wares described for the Cuicatlán Cañada—a gray ware and a plain ware—also occupy separate positions in the dendrogram. Thus, the general goal of characterizing the chemical properties of a representative sample of Formative ceramics from the two regions was achieved in the current analysis.

While the neutron-activation analysis of the representative Middle Formative period ceramics from the two regions yielded no unexpected surprises, the chemical characterization of certain "Oaxaca imports" and local Cañada imitations of Monte Albán ceramics dating to the Late Formative period did produce some surprises. The neutron-activation analysis distinguished between the Middle Formative period gray ware of the Cañada (Perdido Gray CC1-10) and the contemporaneous Rosario/

Monte Albán I gray ware of the Oaxaca Valley (VO41-44, MA45-47). As expected, all the Perdido Gray outleaned-wall bowl rims submitted for chemical analysis constituted local Cañada products. This does not rule out the possibility, of course, that some gray ware from the Oaxaca Valley was imported to the Cañada during the Middle Formative period; Redmond suggests that the analysis of a greater variety of Perdido Gray ceramics—including rarer vessel forms such as composite silhouette bowls with mammiform feet and ovate pinched-rim bowls—would probably have revealed some imports from the Oaxaca Valley (see Spencer 1982: 106-110, 152-153).

Such was the case for the succeeding sample of Late Formative gray outleaned-wall bowls from the Cañada (Lomas Gray), three examples of which turned out to be actual G.12s (Caso, Bernal, and Acosta 1967:25-29) from the Oaxaca Valley. On the dendrogram, these three examples of imported gray ware—CC14, CC16, and CC20—fall firmly within the second cluster made up by the Formative Oaxaca gray ware. Two of the three specimens came from Loma de la Coyotera (Cs25) at the southernmost tip of the Cañada; the other Oaxaca import was found at Loma Grande (Cs13) on the region's central alluvial fan. Samples CC15 and CC17 also do not fall within the group of Cañada gray ware, but neither do they occupy central positions within the following cluster of Formative Oaxaca gray ware. It is due precisely to the difficulty of visually differentiating between the local Cañada gray ware and any gray ware imported from the Oaxaca Valley that Redmond chose not to perform distributional analyses on these gray Monte Albán-style ceramics in the Cuicatlán Cañada.

Instead, distributional analyses were carried out on a group of highly distinctive Oaxaca ceramics known as Cremas. Notable for their diorite temper and very low average iron content (ca. 2.6%), these light-colored paste ceramics form the fourth main cluster on the dendrogram. The trace-element analysis of three examples considered by Redmond to be Cremas traded to the Cuicatlán Cañada from the Oaxaca Valley during the Middle Formative period (CC11, CC12, and CC13) succeeded in positively identifying them as Oaxaca Cremas. The dendrogram shows their association with the fourth group of Monte Albán Cremas.

The same was not true in the case of the comparable sample of Cremas that Redmond believed to have been imported to the Cuicatlán Cañada during the following Late Formative period when the Valley Zapotec apparently incorporated the Cañada into their expanding realm. Redmond discovered a concentration of these Monte Albán-style ceramics at the Cañada's northern frontier, some of which she considered to be actual imported Cremas. The trace-element analysis of four of these possible Monte Albán Ic-II Cremas (CC23, CC24, CC25, CC26) revealed that only CC23 was a genuine imported Crema; the other three potential Cremas appeared instead to be closely related to the Cañada's local plain ware. The dendrogram shows the position of CC23 within the fourth grouping of Monte Albán Cremas, while it arranges CC24, CC25, and CC26 together with the third cluster of Lomas Plain ceramics from the Cañada. Instead of being real Cremas, these three sherds are extremely good locally-produced imitations of Monte Albán Ic-II Cremas; their average iron content of about 4.5% is lower than the mean value for Lomas Plain ceramics (ca. 6.7%), which is what gives their paste the lighter color characteristic of the Oaxaca Crema ware. The iron content of actual Monte Albán Cremas, however, is much lower (ca. 2.6%).

The results of the neutron-activation analysis point to a change in the nature of interregional exchange between the Oaxaca Valley and the Cuicatlán Cañada during the Late Formative period. With the Cuicatlán Cañada's transformation into a frontier region of the Monte Albán state, there appears to have been a drop in the amount of ceramics imported from the Valley of Oaxaca. One possible explanation might be that with the imposition of tribute demands upon the Cañada, the Valley Zapotec no longer maintained the reciprocal exchange relationship that bound the two regions previously during the Middle Formative period—which was manifested archaeologically by the distribution of Oaxaca ceramics (Monte Albán I Cremas) in the Cañada (Chapter 3). Instead, the Monte Albán state administered the Cañada directly and established a local ceramic ware in the region that deliberately imitated Monte Albán ceramics.

Finally, the position of the two Classic period gray sherds from Monte Albán on the dendrogram also constituted somewhat of a surprise. These two examples of the dominant gray ceramic type in the Valley of Oaxaca during the Classic period (MA81, MA82) do not relate closely to the stock of Formative Oaxaca gray ware. Harbottle suggests that their non-agreement with the previous Formative Oaxaca gray ware might be due to the use of new or different tempering agents, or perhaps to the introduction of new techniques of clay preparation. The neutron-activation analysis of additional Classic period ceramics will undoubtedly help to settle these questions and others.[1]

[1] The neutron-activation analysis was carried out under contract with the U.S. Department of Energy.

Bibliography

Abascal-M., Rafael, Garman Harbottle, and Edward V. Sayre
    1974   Correlation between Terra Cotta Figurines and Pottery from the Valley of Mexico and Source Clays by Activation Analysis. In *Archaeological Chemistry*, edited by Curt W. Beck. Washington, D.C.: American Chemical Society.

Acosta, Jorge R.
    1958   Exploraciones Arqueológicas en Monte Albán, XVIII Temporada. *Revista Mexicana de Estudios Antropológicos* 15:7-50.
    1965   Preclassic and Classic Architecture of Oaxaca. In *Handbook of Middle American Indians*, Vol. 3, edited by Gordon R. Willey, pp. 814-836. Austin: University of Texas Press.

Adams, Robert McC.
    1966   *The Evolution of Urban Society*. Chicago: Aldine Publishing Company.
    1974   The Mesopotamian Social Landscape: A View from the Frontier. In Reconstructing Complex Societies, edited by Charlotte B. Moore. *Supplement to the Bulletin of the American Schools of Oriental Research* 20:1-20.

Andrzejewski, Stanislaw
    1954   *Military Organization and Society*. London: Routledge and Kegan Paul Ltd.

Arnold, Rosemary
    1957a   A Port-of-Trade: Whydah on the Guinea Coast. In *Trade and Market in the Early Empires*, edited by Karl Polanyi, Conrad M. Arensberg, and Harry W. Pearson, pp. 154-176. Glencoe, Illinois: The Free Press.
    1957b   Separation of Trade and Market. Great Market of Whydah. In *Trade and Market in the Early Empires*, edited by Karl Polanyi, Conrad M. Arensberg, and Harry W. Pearson, pp. 177-187. Glencoe, Illinois: The Free Press.

Bazán, Martín
    1928   Informe sobre las Ruinas de Quiotepec y Zaachila en el Estado de Oaxaca. In *Estado Actual de los Principales Edificios Arqueológicos de México*. Contribución de México al XXIII Congreso de Americanistas. Secretaría de Educación Pública. México: Talleres Gráficos de la Nación.

Bernal, Ignacio
    1965   Archaeological Synthesis of Oaxaca. In *Handbook of Middle American Indians*, Vol. 3, edited by Gordon R. Willey, pp. 788-813. Austin: University of Texas Press.
    1966   Ruinas de Santo Domingo, Oaxaca. *Boletín del Instituto Nacional de Antropología e Historia* 24:8-12.

Bieber A.M., Jr., D.W. Brooks, G. Harbottle, and E.V. Sayre
    1976   Application of Multivariate Techniques to Analytical Data on Aegean Ceramics. *Archaeometry* 18(1):59-74.

Blanton, Richard E.
    1972   Prehispanic Settlement Patterns of the Ixtapalapa Peninsula Region, Mexico. Department of Anthropology, The Pennsylvania State University, *Occasional Papers in Anthropology* 6. University Park, Pennsylvania.
    1976a   The Origins of Monte Albán. In *Cultural Change and Continuity*, edited by Charles Cleland, pp. 223-232. New York: Academic Press.
    1976b   Anthropological Studies of Cities. *Annual Review of Anthropology* 5:249-264.
    1978   *Monte Albán: Settlement Patterns at the Ancient Zapotec Capital*. New York: Academic Press.
    1980   Cultural Ecology Reconsidered. *American Antiquity* 45:145-151.

Blanton, Richard E., Jill Appel, Laura Finsten, Stephen Kowalewski, Gary Feinman, and Eva Fisch
    1979   Regional Evolution in the Valley of Oaxaca, Mexico. *Journal of Field Archaeology* 6:369-390.

Blanton, Richard E., Stephen A. Kowalewski, Gary Feinman, and Jill Appel
    1981   *Ancient Mesoamerica. A Comparison of Change in Three Regions*. New York: Cambridge University Press.
    1982   Monte Albán's Hinterland, Part I: The Prehispanic Settlement Patterns of the Central and Southern Parts of the Valley of Oaxaca, Mexico. Prehistory and Human Ecology of the Valley of Oaxaca, Vol. 7. *Memoirs of the Museum of Anthropology, University of Michigan* No. 15. Ann Arbor.

Boletín
    1975   *Boletín del Centro Regional de Oaxaca*, No. 2. Mayo, 1975. Oaxaca, Mexico: Instituto Nacional de Antropología e Historia.

Borhegyi, Stephan F. de
    1980   The Precolumbian Ballgames: A Pan-Mesoamerican Tradition. *Milwaukee Public Museum, Contributions in Anthropology and History* 1.

Brown, Kenneth L.
    1977   The Valley of Guatemala: A Highland Port of Trade. In *Teotihuacán and Kaminaljuyú: A Study in Prehistoric Culture Contact*, edited by William T. Sanders and Joseph W. Michels, pp. 205-395. State College: The Pennsylvania State University Press.

Burgoa, Fray Francisco de
    1670   Palestra Historial de Virtudes y Ejemplares Apostólicas. Reprinted in *Publicaciones del Archivo General de la Nación* 24. México, D.F.: Talleres Gráficos de la Nación (1934).
    1674a   Geográfica Descripción, Vol. 1. Reprinted in *Publicaciones del Archivo General de la Nación* 25. México, D.F.: Talleres Gráficos de la Nación (1934).
    1674b   Geográfica Descripción, Vol. 2. Reprinted in *Publicaciones del Archivo General de la Nación* 26. México, D.F.: Talleres Gráficos de la Nación (1934).

Byers, Douglas (editor)
    1967   *The Prehistory of the Tehuacán Valley*, Vol. 1: Environ-

ment and Subsistence. Austin: University of Texas Press.

Carneiro, Robert L.
1970 A Theory of the Origin of the State. *Science* 169:733-738.

Caso, Alfonso
1928 Las Estelas Zapotecas. *Monografías del Museo Nacional de Arqueología, Historia y Etnología.* México D.F.: Secretaría de Educación Pública.
1932 Las Exploraciones en Monte Albán, Temporada 1931-2. *Instituto Panamericano de Geografía e Historia* 7.
1935 Las Exploraciones en Monte Albán, Temporada 1934-5. *Instituto Panamericano de Geografía e Historia* 18.
1938 Exploraciones en Oaxaca, Quinta y Sexta Temporadas, 1936-7. *Instituto Panamericano de Geografía e Historia* 34.
1942 Resumen del Informe de las Exploraciones en Oaxaca durante la 7a y la 8a Temporadas, 1937-1938 y 1938-1939. *Actas del XXVII Congreso Internacional de Americanistas*, 1939, II:159-187.
1947 Calendario y Escritura de las Antiguas Culturas de Monte Albán. In *Obras Completas de Miguel Othón de Mendizábal* I:115-143.
1965a Sculpture and Mural Painting of Oaxaca. In *Handbook of Middle American Indians*, Vol. 3, edited by Gordon R. Willey, pp. 849-870. Austin: University of Texas Press.
1965b Lapidary Work, Goldwork, and Copperwork from Oaxaca. In *Handbook of Middle American Indians*, Vol. 3, edited by Gordon R. Willey, pp. 896-930. Austin: University of Texas Press.
1970 El Tesoro de Monte Albán. *Memorias del Instituto Nacional de Antropología e Historia* III. México.

Caso, Alfonso, and Ignacio Bernal
1952 Urnas de Oaxaca. *Memorias del Instituto Nacional de Antropología e Historia* II. México.

Caso, Alfonso, Ignacio Bernal, and Jorge Acosta
1967 La Cerámica de Monte Albán. *Memorias del Instituto Nacional de Antropología e Historia* XIII. México.

Chapman, Anne C.
1957 Port of Trade Enclaves in Aztec and Maya Civilizations. In *Trade and Market in the Early Empires*, edited by Karl Polanyi, Conrad M. Arensberg, and Harry W. Pearson, pp. 114-153. Glencoe, Illinois: The Free Press.

Cheek, Charles D.
1977 Excavations at the Palangana and the Acropolis, Kaminaljuyú. In *Teotihuacán and Kaminaljuyú: A Study in Prehistoric Culture Contact*, edited by William T. Sanders and Joseph W. Michels, pp. 1-204. State College: The Pennsylvania State University Press.

Coe, Michael D.
1962 *Mexico*. New York: Praeger.

Coe, Michael D., and Richard A. Diehl
1980 *In the Land of the Olmec*, Vol. 1: *The Archaeology of San Lorenzo Tenochtitlán.* Austin: University of Texas Press.

Córdova, Fray Juan de
1578 Vocabulario en Lengua Zapoteca. México, D.F.: Pedro Charte y Antonio Ricardo. Reprinted in *Biblioteca Lingüística Mexicana* I. México, D.F.: Secretaría de Educación Pública (1942).

Davis, John C.
1973 *Statistics and Data Analysis in Geology*. New York: John Wiley & Sons, Inc.

Dibble, Charles E., and Arthur J. O. Anderson (editors)
1959 The Florentine Codex: Book 9—The Merchants. *Monographs of the School of American Research* No. 14, Part 10. Santa Fe, New Mexico: The School of American Research and the University of Utah.

Drennan, Robert D.
1976a Fábrica San José and Middle Formative Society in the Valley of Oaxaca. Prehistory and Human Ecology of the Valley of Oaxaca, Vol.4. *Memoirs of the Museum of Anthropology, University of Michigan* No. 8. Ann Arbor.
1976b Religion and Social Evolution in Formative Mesoamerica. In *The Early Mesoamerican Village*, edited by Kent V. Flannery, pp. 345-368. New York: Academic Press.
1978 Excavations at Quachilco: A Report on the 1977 Season of the Palo Blanco Project in the Tehuacán Valley. *Museum of Anthropology, University of Michigan, Technical Reports* No. 7. Ann Arbor.

Drennan, Robert D. (editor)
1977 The Palo Blanco Project: A Report on the 1975 and 1976 Seasons in the Tehuacán Valley. Andover: R.S. Peabody Foundation for Archaeology. Ann Arbor: University of Michigan Museum of Anthropology.
1979 Prehistoric Social, Political, and Economic Development in the Area of the Tehuacán Valley: Some Results of the Palo Blanco Project. *Museum of Anthropology, University of Michigan, Technical Reports* No. 11. Ann Arbor.

Drennan, Robert D., and Judith A. Nowack
1977 El Posible Papel de Teotihuacán en el Desarrollo Clásico del Valle de Tehuacán. Paper presented at the meetings of the Sociedad Mexicana de Antropología. Guanajuato, México.

Drennan, Robert D., and Rafael Vásquez
n.d. Reconocimiento Arqueológico al Norte del Valle de Oaxaca (mimeographed).

Earle, Timothy K.
1978 Economic and Social Organization of a Complex Chiefdom: The Halelea District, Kaua'i Hawaii. *Museum of Anthropology, University of Michigan, Anthropological Papers* No. 63. Ann Arbor.

Earle, Timothy K., and Jonathon E. Ericson (editors)
1977 *Exchange Systems in Prehistory*. New York: Academic Press.

Flannery, Kent V.
1968 The Olmec and the Valley of Oaxaca: A Model for Inter-Regional Interaction in Formative Times. In *Dumbarton Oaks Conference on the Olmec*, edited by Elizabeth P. Benson, pp. 79-110. Washington, D.C.: Dumbarton Oaks.
1972 The Cultural Evolution of Civilizations. *Annual Review of Ecology and Systematics* 3:399-426.
1973 The Origins of Agriculture. *Annual Review of Anthropology.* 2:271-310.
1976a *The Early Mesoamerican Village* (editor). New York: Academic Press.
1976b Evolution of Complex Settlement Systems. In *The Early Mesoamerican Village*, edited by Kent V. Flannery, pp. 162-173. New York: Academic Press.
1976c Linear Stream Patterns and Riverside Settlement Rules. In *The Early Mesoamerican Village*, edited by Kent V. Flannery, pp. 173-180. New York: Academic Press.
1976d Contextual Analysis of Ritual Paraphernalia from Formative Oaxaca. In *The Early Mesoamerican Village*, edited by Kent V. Flannery, pp. 333-345. New York: Academic Press.

Flannery, Kent V., and Joyce Marcus

1976a Evolution of the Public Building in Formative Oaxaca. In *Cultural Change and Continuity*, edited by Charles Cleland, pp. 205-221. New York: Academic Press.

1976b Formative Oaxaca and The Zapotec Cosmos. *American Scientist* 64(4): 374-383.

1983 San José Mogote in Monte Albán II: A Secondary Administrative Center. In *The Cloud People: Divergent Evolution of the Zapotec and Mixtec Civilizations*, edited by Kent V. Flannery and Joyce Marcus, pp. 111-113. New York: Academic Press.

Flannery, Kent V., Joyce Marcus, and Stephen A. Kowalewski
1981 The Preceramic and Formative of the Valley of Oaxaca. In *Supplement to the Handbook of Middle American Indians*, edited by Jeremy A. Sabloff (volume editor) and Victoria R. Bricker (general series editor), Vol. 1, Archaeology, pp. 48-93. Austin: University of Texas Press.

Flannery, Kent V., Anne V.T. Kirkby, Michael J. Kirkby, and Aubrey W. Williams, Jr.
1967 Farming Systems and Political Growth in Ancient Oaxaca. *Science* 158:445-454.

Flannery, Kent V., Marcus Winter, Susan Lees, James Neely, James Schoenwetter, Susan Kitchen, and Jane Wheeler
1970 Preliminary Archaeological Investigations in the Valley of Oaxaca, Mexico, 1966-1969: A Report to the National Science Foundation and the Instituto Nacional de Antropología e Historia. University of Michigan Museum of Anthropology. Ann Arbor (mimeographed).

Fox, John W.
1978 *Quiche Conquest: Centralism and Regionalism in Highland Guatemalan State Development*. Albuquerque: University of New Mexico Press.

Frere, Sheppard S.
1974 *Britannia: A History of Roman Britain*. 2nd ed. London: Sphere Books.

Fried, Morton H.
1961 Warfare, Military Organization, and the Evolution of Society. *Anthropologica* 3(2):134-147.
1967 *The Evolution of Political Society*. New York: Random House.

Gallego, Juan
1580 "Relación de Cuicatlán" in *Papeles de Nueva España: Segunda Serie, Geografía y Estadística*, Vol. 4, edited by Francisco del Paso y Troncoso, pp. 183-189. Madrid: Sucesores de Rivadeneyra.

Gearing, Fred
1958 The Structural Poses of Eighteenth Century Cherokee Villages. *American Anthropologist* 60(6):1148-1157.
1962 Priests and Warriors: Social Structures for Cherokee Politics in the Eighteenth Century. *American Anthropological Association Memoirs*, No. 93. Washington, D.C.: American Anthropological Association.

Gorenstein, Shirley
1973 Tepexi el Viejo: A Postclassic Fortified Site in the Mixteca-Puebla Region of Mexico. *Transactions of the American Philosophical Society*, Vol. 63, Part 1. Philadelphia: American Philosophical Society.

Hammond, Norman, Garman Harbottle, and Trevor Gazard
1976 Neutron Activation and Statistical Analysis of Maya Ceramics and Clays from Lubaantun, Belize. *Archaeometry* 18(2):147-168.

Harbottle, Garman
1976 Activation Analysis in Archaeology. *Chemical Society Specialist Periodical Report* 19, Vol. 3, Radiochemistry. London: Chemical Society.

Helms, Mary
1979 *Ancient Panama: Chiefs in Search of Power*. Austin: University of Texas Press.

Henderson, John S., Ilene Sterns, Anthony Wonderley, and Patricia A. Urban
1979 Archaeological Investigations in the Valle de Naco, Northwestern Honduras: A Preliminary Report. *Journal of Field Archaeology* 6(2):169-192.

Hill, James N. (editor)
1977 Systems Theory and the Explanation of Change. In *Explanation of Prehistoric Change*, edited by James N. Hill, pp. 59-103. Albuquerque: University of New Mexico Press.

Hirth, Kenneth
1978 Teotihuacán Regional Population Administration in Eastern Morelos. *World Archaeology* 9:320-333.

Hirth, Kenneth, and Jorge Angulo Villaseñor
1981 Early State Expansion in Central Mexico: Teotihuacán in Morelos. *Journal of Field Archaeology* 8:135-150.

Hodder, Ian R.
1972 Locational Models and the Study of Romano-British Settlement. In *Models in Archaeology*, edited by David L. Clark, pp. 887-909. London: Methuen & Co. Ltd.

Hopkins, Joseph
1973 Ceramics of La Cañada, Oaxaca, Mexico. *Vanderbilt University Publications in Anthropology* 6. Nashville.
1974 Irrigation and the Cuicatec Ecosystem: A Study of Agriculture and Civilization in North Central Oaxaca, Mexico. Ph.D. Dissertation, Department of Anthropology, University of Chicago.

Hunt, Eva
1972 Irrigation and the Socio-Political Organization of Cuicatec Cacicazgos. In *The Prehistory of the Tehuacán Valley*, Vol. 4: *Chronology and Irrigation*, edited by Frederick Johnson, pp. 162-259. Austin: University of Texas Press.

Hunt, Robert, and Eva Hunt
1974 Irrigation, Conflict, and Politics: A Mexican Case. In *Irrigation's Impact on Society*, edited by Theodore Downing and McGuire Gibson, pp. 129-157. Tucson: University of Arizona Press.
1976 Canal Irrigation and Local Social Organization. *Current Anthropology* 17:389-411.

Johnson, Frederick (editor)
1972 *The Prehistory of the Tehuacán Valley*, Vol. 4: *Chronology and Irrigation*. Austin: University of Texas Press

Johnson, Gregory A.
1973 Local Exchange and Early State Development in Southwestern Iran. *Museum of Anthropology, University of Michigan, Anthropological Papers* No. 51. Ann Arbor.
1978 Information Sources and the Development of Decision-Making Organizations. In *Social Archaeology: Beyond Subsistence and Dating*, edited by Charles Redman et al., pp. 87-112. New York: Academic Press.

Joralemon, David
1974 Ritual Blood-Sacrifice Among the Ancient Maya: Part I. In *Primera Mesa Redonda de Palenque* Part II, edited by Merle Greene Robertson, pp. 59-75. Pebble Beach, California: The Robert Louis Stevenson School, Pre-Columbian Art Research.

Kidder, Alfred V., Jesse D. Jennings, and Edwin M. Shook
1946 Excavations at Kaminaljuyú, Guatemala. *Carnegie Institution of Washington Publication* 561. Washington, D.C.: Carnegie Institution.

Kirkby, Anne V.T.
1973 The Use of Land and Water Resources in the Past and Present Valley of Oaxaca, Mexico. Prehistory and Human Ecology of the Valley of Oaxaca, Vol. 1.

Memoirs of the Museum of Anthropology, University of Michigan, No. 5. Ann Arbor.

Kowalewski, Stephen
- 1976 Prehispanic Settlement Patterns of the Central Part of the Valley of Oaxaca, Mexico. Ph.D. Dissertation, Department of Anthropology, University of Arizona.
- 1980 Population-Resource Balances in Period I of Oaxaca, Mexico. *American Antiquity* 45:151-165.

Lattimore, Owen
- 1962 *Studies in Frontier History 1928-1958.* London: Oxford University Press.

Leeds, Anthony
- 1961 The Port-of-Trade in Pre-European India as an Ecological and Evolutionary Type. In *Proceedings of the Annual Spring Meeting of the American Ethnological Society,* edited by V.E. Garfield, pp. 26-48. Seattle: University of Washington Press.

MacNeish, Richard S.
- 1964 Ancient Mesoamerican Civilization. *Science* 143:531-537.

MacNeish, Richard S., Antoinette Nelken-Terner, and Irmgard W. Johnson
- 1967 *The Prehistory of the Tehuacán Valley,* Vol. 2: *Non-Ceramic Artifacts.* Austin: University of Texas Press.

MacNeish, Richard S., Frederick Peterson, and Kent V. Flannery
- 1970 *The Prehistory of the Tehuacán Valley,* Vol. 3: *Ceramics.* Austin: University of Texas Press.

MacNeish, Richard S., Melvin Fowler, Angel García Cook, Frederick Peterson, Antoinette Nelken-Terner, and James Neely
- 1972 *The Prehistory of the Tehuacán Valley,* Vol. 5: *Excavations and Reconnaissance.* Austin: University of Texas Press.

Marcus, Joyce
- 1974 The Iconography of Power Among the Classic Maya. *World Archaeology* 6:83-94.
- 1976 The Iconography of Militarism at Monte Albán and Neighboring Sites in the Valley of Oaxaca. In *The Origins of Religious Art and Iconography in Preclassic Mesoamerica,* edited by H.B. Nicholson, pp. 123-139. Los Angeles: Latin American Center, University of California.
- 1978 Archaeology and Religion: A Comparison of the Zapotec and Maya. *World Archaeology* 10(2): 172-191.
- 1980 Zapotec Writing. *Scientific American* 242(2): 50-64.
- 1983a The Conquest Slabs of Building J, Monte Albán. In *The Cloud People: Divergent Evolution of the Zapotec and Mixtec Civilizations,* edited by Kent V. Flannery and Joyce Marcus, pp. 106-108. New York: Academic Press.
- 1983b Rethinking the Zapotec Urn. In *The Cloud People: Divergent Evolution of the Zapotec and Mixtec Civilizations,* edited by Kent V. Flannery and Joyce Marcus, pp. 144-148. New York: Academic Press.

Marcus, Joyce, and Kent V. Flannery
- 1978 Ethnoscience of the Sixteenth-Century Valley Zapotec. In: *The Nature and Status of Ethnobotany,* edited by Richard I. Ford. *Museum of Anthropology, University of Michigan, Anthropological Papers* 67:51-79.

Marquina, Ignacio
- 1964 Arquitectura Prehispánica. *Memorias del Instituto Nacional de Antropología e Historia* I. México.

Michels, Joseph W.
- 1973 *Dating Methods in Archaeology.* New York: Academic Press.

Millon, René
- 1973 *Urbanization at Teotihuacán, Mexico,* Vol. 1: *The Teotihuacán Map, Part One: Text.* Austin: University of Texas Press.
- 1981 Teotihuacán: City, State, and Civilization. In *Supplement to the Handbook of Middle American Indians,* edited by Jeremy A. Sabloff, (volume editor) and Victoria R. Bricker (general series editor). Vol. 1, Archaeology, pp. 198-243. Austin: University of Texas Press.

Morris, Craig
- 1972 State Settlements in Tawantisuyu: A Strategy of Compulsory Urbanism. In *Contemporary Archaeology,* edited by Mark P. Leone, pp. 393-401. Carbondale: Southern Illinois University Press.
- 1974 Reconstructing Patterns of Non-Agricultural Production in the Inca Economy: Archaeology and Documents in Institutional Analysis. In: Reconstructing Complex Societies, edited by Charlotte B. Moore. *Supplement to the Bulletin of the American Schools of Oriental Research* 20:49-68.

Moser, Chris L.
- 1969 La Tumba I del Barrio del Rosario, Huitzo, Oaxaca. *Boletín del Instituto Nacional de Antropología e Historia* 36:41-47.

Nowack, Judith A.
- 1977 Surface Survey at Major Palo Blanco Sites. In *The Palo Blanco Project: A Report on the 1975 and 1976 Seasons in the Tehuacán Valley,* edited by Robert D. Drennan, pp. 35-48. Andover: R.S. Peabody Foundation for Archaeology. Ann Arbor: University of Michigan Museum of Anthropology.

Olivier, D.C.
- 1973 AGCLUS, an Aggregative, Hierarchical Clustering Program. Department of Psychology and Social Relations, Harvard University, Cambridge, Massachusetts (mimeographed).

Paddock, John
- 1966 Oaxaca in Ancient Mesoamerica. In *Ancient Oaxaca,* edited by John Paddock, pp. 83-242. Stanford: Stanford University Press.

Pareyón, Eduardo
- 1960 Exploraciones Arqueológicas en la Ciudad Vieja de Quiotepec, Oaxaca. *Revista Mexicana de Estudios Antropológicos* 16:97-104.

Parsons, Jeffrey R.
- 1971 Prehistoric Settlement Patterns in the Texcoco Region, Mexico. *Memoirs of the Museum of Anthropology, University of Michigan* No. 3. Ann Arbor.
- 1976a The Role of Chinampa Agriculture in the Food Supply of Aztec Tenochtitlán. In *Cultural Change and Continuity,* edited by Charles Cleland, pp. 233-257. New York: Academic Press.
- 1976b Settlement and Population History of the Basin of Mexico. In *The Valley of Mexico: Studies in Pre-Hispanic Ecology and Society,* edited by Eric R. Wolf, pp. 69-100. Albuquerque: University of New Mexico Press.

Parsons, Mary H.
- 1972 Spindle Whorls from the Teotihuacán Valley, Mexico. In: Miscellaneous Studies in Mexican Prehistory, by M.W. Spence, J.R. Parsons, and M.H. Parsons. *Museum of Anthropology, University of Michigan, Anthropological Papers* 45:45-80.

Paso y Troncoso, Francisco del
- 1905 *Papeles de Nueva España: Segunda Serie, Geografía y Estadística,* Vol. 4. Madrid: Sucesores de Rivadeneyra.

Peebles, Christopher, and Susan Kus
- 1977 Some Archaeological Correlates of Rank Societies. *American Antiquity* 42: 421-448.

Peterson, David A., and Thomas B. MacDougall

BIBLIOGRAPHY

1974 Guiengola: A Fortified Site in the Isthmus of Tehuantepec. *Vanderbilt University Publications in Anthropology 10*. Nashville.

Pires-Ferreira, Jane W.
1975 Formative Mesoamerican Exchange Networks with Special Reference to the Valley of Oaxaca. Prehistory and Human Ecology of the Valley of Oaxaca, Vol. 3. *Memoirs of the Museum of Anthropology, University of Michigan*, No. 7. Ann Arbor.

Pires-Ferreira, Jane W., and Kent V. Flannery
1976 Ethnographic Models for Formative Exchange. In *The Early Mesoamerican Village*, edited by Kent V. Flannery, pp. 286-292. New York: Academic Press.

Rappaport, Roy A.
1971 The Sacred in Human Evolution. *Annual Review of Ecology and Systematics* 2:23-44.
1974 Sanctity and Adaptation. Paper prepared for Wenner-Gren Conference on the Moral and Aesthetic Structure of Adaptation. Reprinted in *Coevolution Quarterly* (Summer):54-68.

Rathje, William L., and Jeremy A., Sabloff
1973 Ancient Maya Commercial Systems: A Research Design for the Island of Cozumel, Mexico. *World Archaeology* 5:221-231.

Redman, Charles, and Patty Jo Watson
1970 Systematic, Intensive Surface Collection. *American Antiquity* 35:279-291.

Redmond, Elsa M.
1979 A Terminal Formative Ceramic Workshop in the Tehuacán Valley. In: Prehistoric Social, Political, and Economic Development in the Area of the Tehuacán Valley, edited by Robert D. Drennan. *Museum of Anthropology, University of Michigan, Technical Reports* No. 11:111-127. Ann Arbor.
n.d. Prehistoric Settlement Patterns on the Zapotec Frontier. Monograph in preparation. Museum of Anthropology, University of Michigan.

Renfrew, Colin
1972 *The Emergence of Civilisations: The Cyclades and the Aegean in the Third Millennium B.C.* London: Methuen & Co. Ltd.
1977 Alternative Models for Exchange and Spatial Distribution. In *Exchange Systems in Prehistory*, edited by Timothy K. Earle and Jonathon E. Ericson, pp. 71-90. New York: Academic Press.

Rickards, Constantine
1926 The Ruins of Quiotepec, District of Cuicatlán. *International Congress of Americanists* 22:625-631.

Roper, Donna C.
1979 The Method and Theory of Site Catchment Analysis: A Review. In *Advances in Archaeological Method and Theory*, Vol. 2, edited by Michael B. Schiffer, pp. 120-140. New York: Academic Press.

Rowlands, M.J.
1972 Defence: a Factor in the Organization of Settlements. In *Man, Settlement, and Urbanism*, edited by P.J. Ucko, R. Tringham, and G.W. Dimbleby, pp. 447-462. London: Duckworth.

Sabloff, Jeremy A., W.L. Rathje, D.A. Freidel, J.G. Connor, and P.L.W. Sabloff
1974 Trade and Power in Postclassic Yucatán: Initial Observations. In *Mesoamerican Archaeology: New Approaches*, edited by Norman Hammond, pp. 397-416. Austin: University of Texas Press.

Sabloff, Jeremy A. and D.A. Freidel
1975 A Model of a Pre-Columbian Trading Center. In *Ancient Civilization and Trade*, edited by Jeremy A. Sabloff and C.C. Lamberg-Karlovsky, pp. 369-408. Albuquerque: University of New Mexico Press.

Sabloff, Jeremy A. and William L. Rathje (editors)
1975 A Study of Changing Pre-Columbian Commercial Systems. *Monographs of the Peabody Museum of American Archaeology*, No. 3. Cambridge: Harvard University.

Sanders, William T.
1965 The Cultural Ecology of the Teotihuacán Valley. Department of Sociology and Anthropology, The Pennsylvania State University (mimeographed).
1974 Chiefdom to State: Political Evolution at Kaminaljuyú, Guatemala. In: Reconstructing Complex Societies, edited by Charlotte B. Moore, *Supplement to the Bulletin of the American Schools of Oriental Research* 20:97-121.
1976 The Agricultural History of the Basin of Mexico. In *The Valley of Mexico: Studies in Pre-Hispanic Ecology and Society*, edited by Eric R. Wolf, pp. 101-159. Albuquerque: University of New Mexico Press.
1977 Ethnographic Analogy and the Teotihuacán Horizon Style. In *Teotihuacán and Kaminaljuyú: A Study in Prehistoric Culture Contact*, edited by William T. Sanders and Joseph W. Michels, pp. 397-410. State College: The Pennsylvania State University Press.

Sanders, William T., and Barbara J. Price
1968 *Mesoamerica: The Evolution of a Civilization*. New York: Random House.

Sanders, William T., and Joseph W. Michels (editors)
1977 *Teotihuacán and Kaminaljuyú: A Study in Prehistoric Culture Contact*. State College: The Pennsylvania State University Press.

Sanders, William T., Jeffrey R. Parsons, and Robert S. Santley
1979 *The Basin of Mexico: Ecological Processes in the Evolution of a Civilization*. New York: Academic Press.

Sayre, Edward V.
1976 Brookhaven Procedures for Statistical Analyses of Multivariate Archaeometric Data. Brookhaven National Laboratory Report, BNL-21693.

Scholes, France V. and Ralph L. Roys
1948 The Maya Chontal Indians of Acalan Tixchel. *Carnegie Institution of Washington Publication 560*. Washington, D.C.: Carnegie Institution.

Séjourné, Laurette
1966 *Arqueología de Teotihuacán: La Cerámica*. México: Fondo de Cultura Económica.

Service, Elman R.
1962 *Primitive Social Organization*. New York: Random House.
1975 *Origins of the State and Civilization*. New York: W.W. Norton and Company.

Shepard, Anna
1967 Preliminary Notes on the Paste Composition of Monte Albán Pottery. Appendix in: La Cerámica de Monte Albán, by Alfonso Caso, Ignacio Bernal, and Jorge Acosta. *Memorias del Instituto Nacional de Antropología e Historia* 13:475-484. México.

Sisson, Edward
1973 First Annual Report of the Coxcatlán Project. Andover: R.S. Peabody Foundation for Archaeology.

Smith, Bruce D.
1977 Archaeological Inference and Inductive Confirmation. *American Anthropologist* 79:598-617.

Smith, Judith
1979 Carbonized Botanical Remains from Quachilco, Cuayucatepec, and La Coyotera: A Preliminary Report. In: Prehistoric Social, Political, and Economic Development in the Area of the Tehuacán Valley, edited by Robert D. Drennan. *Museum of Anthropology,*

University of Michigan, Technical Reports No. 11:217-250. Ann Arbor.

Smith, Mary Elizabeth
   1973 *Picture Writing from Ancient Southern Mexico: Mixtec Place Signs and Maps*. Norman: University of Oklahoma Press.

Sneath, Peter H.A. and Robert R. Sokal
   1973 *Numerical Taxonomy*. San Francisco: Freeman.

Spencer, Charles S.
   1979 Irrigation, Administration, and Society in Formative Tehuacán. In: Prehistoric Social, Political, and Economic Development in the Area of the Tehuacán Valley, edited by Robert D. Drennan. *Museum of Anthropology, University of Michigan Technical Reports* No. 11:13-109. Ann Arbor.
   1982 *The Cuicatlán Cañada and Monte Albán: A Study of Primary State Formation*. New York: Academic Press.

Spencer, Charles S., and Elsa M. Redmond
   1979 Formative and Classic Developments in the Cuicatlán Cañada: A Preliminary Report. In: Prehistoric Social, Political, and Economic Development in the Area of the Tehuacán Valley, edited by Robert D. Drennan. *Museum of Anthropology, University of Michigan, Technical Reports* No. 11:201-215.
   1982 Ceramic Chronology for the Cuicatlán Cañada. Appendix in *The Cuicatlán Cañada and Monte Albán: A Study of Primary State Formation*, by Charles S. Spencer, pp. 261-307. New York: Academic Press.

Spencer, Herbert
   1967 *The Evolution of Society*, edited by Robert L. Carneiro. Chicago: University of Chicago Press.

Spores, Ronald
   1965 The Zapotec and Mixtec at Spanish Contact. In *Handbook of Middle American Indians*, Vol. 3, edited by Gordon R. Willey, pp. 962-987. Austin: University of Texas Press.
   1972 An Archaeological Settlement Survey of the Nochixtlán Valley, Oaxaca. *Vanderbilt University Publications in Anthropology* 1. Nashville.

Struever, Stuart
   1968 Flotation techniques for the recovery of small-scale archaeological remains. *American Antiquity* 33:353-362.

Taylor, Donna
   1975 Some Locational Aspects of Middle-Range Hierarchical Societies. Ph.D. Dissertation, Department of Anthropology, City University of New York.

Varner, Dudley M.
   1974 Prehispanic Settlement Patterns in the Valley of Oaxaca, Mexico. Ph.D. Dissertation, Department of Anthropology, University of Arizona.

Vita-Finzi, Claudio and E.S. Higgs
   1970 Prehistoric economy in the Mt. Carmel area of Palestine: A Site Catchment Analysis. *Proceedings of the Prehistoric Society* 36:1-37.

Webb, Malcolm C.
   1975 The Flag Follows Trade: An Essay on the Necessary Interaction of Military and Commercial Factors in State Formation. In *Ancient Civilization and Trade*, edited by Jeremy A. Sabloff and C. C. Lamberg-Karlovsky, pp. 155-209. Albuquerque: University of New Mexico Press.

Webster, David L.
   1975 Warfare and the Evolution of the State: A Reconsideration. *American Antiquity* 40:464-470.
   1977 Warfare and the Evolution of Maya Civilization. In *The Origins of Maya Civilization*, edited by Richard E. W. Adams, pp. 335-372. Albuquerque: University of New Mexico Press.

Whitecotton, Joseph W.
   1977 *The Zapotecs: Princes, Priests, and Peasants*. Norman: University of Oklahoma Press.

Winter, Marcus C.
   1972 Tierras Largas: A Formative Community in the Valley of Oaxaca, Mexico. Ph.D. Dissertation, Department of Anthropology, University of Arizona.
   1974 Residential Patterns at Monte Albán, Oaxaca, Mexico. *Science* 186:981-987.

Winter, Marcus C., and Jane W. Pires-Ferreira
   1976 Distribution of Obsidian among Households in Two Oaxacan Villages. In *The Early Mesoamerican Village*, edited by Kent V. Flannery, pp. 306-311. New York: Academic Press.

Winter, Marcus C., Margarita Gaxiola, and Gilberto Hernández
   1977 Comparaciones Arqueológicas de La Cañada, La Mixteca Alta, El Valle de Oaxaca y El Valle de Tehuacán. Centro Regional de Oaxaca, Instituto Nacional de Antropología e Historia, *Estudios de Antropología e Historia* No. 1. Oaxaca.

Wright, Henry T.
   1977 Recent Research on the Origin of the State. *Annual Review of Anthropology* 6:379-397.

Wright, Henry T., and Gregory A. Johnson
   1975 Population, Exchange, and Early State Formation in Southwestern Iran. *American Anthropologist* 77:267-289.

Zeitlin, Robert N.
   1979 Prehistoric Long-Distance Exchange on the Southern Isthmus of Tehuantepec, Mexico. Ph.D. Dissertation, Department of Anthropology, Yale University.

Resumen en Español

Capítulo I. Introducción

El objetivo principal del presente volumen es el de investigar cómo factores militares hayan contribuido al surgimiento del estado zapoteco en el Valle de Oaxaca hacia el comienzo de la fase Monte Albán II (ca. 100 a.C.-200 d.C.) (Fig. 8). Este importante desarrollo está atestiguado en el gran centro arqueológico que llamamos hoy Monte Albán, el cual llegó a ser la capital de la nación zapoteca. Es aquí donde cambios en el patrón de asentamiento, tanto como la construcción de una cantidad de edificios públicos por todos lados de la Plaza Central—inclusive plataformas, templos, y un juego de pelota—señalan el establecimiento de un sistema de administración regional bastante más complejo a principios de la fase Monte Albán II.

La posibilidad de que estos cambios administrativos hayan sido concurrentes con campañas montadas por tropas zapotecas en regiones cercanas surge de una serie de 40 lápidas que están colocadas en las paredes del curioso Montículo J (Fig. 2,3, Lámina 2), otro de los edificios construidos en la Plaza Central de Monte Albán durante la fase Monte Albán II. Las inscripciones del Montículo J han sido descifradas e interpretadas como memorias de conquistas de lugares como Cuicatlán. En vista de esta información concerniente a las circunstancias posiblemente bélicas que pueden haber sido importantes en el surgimiento del estado zapoteco, la introducción concluye con un repaso general sobre este tema. Se concluye que ciertas condiciones de movilización militar pueden efectuar cambios perdurables en la administración regional de una sociedad compleja respectiva.

Capítulo II. La Cañada de Cuicatlán: Un modelo explicativo de su conquista por Monte Albán

La presente investigación del imperialismo zapoteco antiguo está basada en la Cañada de Cuicatlán, uno de los 40 lugares que posiblemente fueron conquistados e incorporados a la nación zapoteca a fines del período Formativo. La Cañada de Cuicatlán constituye un corredor angosto entre el Valle de Oaxaca hacia el sur y el Valle de Tehuacán hacia el norte (Fig. 5). Debido a que se extiende a alturas entre 500-700 m sobre el nivel del mar, la región posee un clima tropical. Aunque la poca lluvia que cae en la Cañada no permite que se practique la agricultura de secano, los habitantes de la región cultivan sus terrenos en los suelos aluviales del Río Grande por medio de varios métodos de riego. La tierra de aluvión baja se riega por inundación, utilizando presas sencillas de desviación hechas de ramas y piedras que se colocan en pleno río. La tierra de aluvión alta se cultiva por medio de canales de irrigación que utilizan el agua que mana de diversas fuentes o tomas de agua. Estas técnicas de riego rinden cosechas abundantes en la Cañada, con rendiciones de maíz que comparan muy favorablemente con las que se producen en los valles montañosos cercanos (Cuadro 1). Además, esta región calurosa produce una serie de frutas tropicales que no pueden ser cultivadas en los valles adyacentes.

En vista del enorme potencial agrícola en la Cañada de Cuicatlán, gran parte del capítulo sirve para formular un modelo explicativo de su posible conquista por Monte Albán en el período Formativo Tardío. El modelo utiliza datos sobre las tácticas militares que aprovechaban los zapotecos durante el período Postclásico, según las crónicas de Fr. Juan de Córdova (1578) y Fr. Francisco de Burgoa (1670, 1674a, 1674b).

Comenzando con el período Formativo Medio, es decir durante el período anterior a la supuesta conquista, el modelo versa con los aspectos de la Cañada que pudieron haber atraído a los zapotecos y que pudieron haber sido entre los objetivos de tal conquista. El modelo considera después las consecuencias de una conquista dirigida contra la Cañada, la cual hubiera sido convertida en una provincia tributaria del estado zapoteco. Por último, el modelo considera cómo la sucesión de campañas y conquistas en territorios lejanos, por sus requisitos burocráticos, hayan contribuido al surgimiento del estado zapoteco en el Valle de Oaxaca.

Las expectativas del ya dicho modelo de conquista fueron puestas a prueba frente a los descubrimientos de un programa arqueológico de reconocimiento superficial que Redmond realizó en la Cañada de Cuicatlán en 1977. Se discuten los diferentes métodos de campo que se emplearon: el reconocimiento extensivo de la región con el uso de aerofotos para precisar las ubicaciones de todos los sitios arqueológicos que fueron encontrados, y el reconocimiento intensivo de todos los sitios pertenecientes a los períodos Formativo y Clásico por medio del levantamiento de planos topográficos y de recolecciones sistemáticas en forma de cuadrados colocados junto a diversas clases de elementos superficiales. También se describen los métodos empleados en los siguientes análisis que fueron llevados a cabo con los datos y artefactos recolectados: el análisis de la relación entre la población prehistórica de la región (calculada para cada una de las fases cronológicas) y la población que hubiera podido ser sostenida dada la producción del maíz bajo diferentes regímenes agrícolas, el establecimiento de una cronología cerámica para las fases de los períodos Formativo y Clásico, la asignación de los artefactos recolectados en los cuadrados de recolección a diferentes fases de ocupación, y la caracterización química de muestras cerámicas provenientes de la Cañada y del Valle de Oaxaca por medio de la activación de neutrones (cuyos resultados están presentados en el Apéndice I).

Capítulo III. Desarrollos en la Cañada de Cuicatlán durante la fase Perdido del período Formativo Medio (ca. 650-300 a.C.)

La Cañada de Cuicatlán fué testigo del crecimiento de 12 comunidades a lo largo de la zona de aluvión alta (Fig. 24). Todas menos dos medían menos de 5 hectáreas y carecían de montículos piramidales. Sin embargo, dos asentamientos eran considerablemente más grandes, las cuales también tenían complejos de arquitectura pública que consistían de plazas centrales y montículos piramidales de hasta 4 m de altura (Figs. 27, 28). Por consiguiente, se propone que estas dos comunidades correspondían a los centros de cacicazgos autónomos que florecieron en la Cañada durante el período Formativo Medio.

Esta hipótesis está apoyada por la distribución de varios artículos exóticos (cerámica del Valle de Oaxaca, obsidiana, y concha marítima) entre las comunidades pertenecientes a la fase Perdido. Estos artículos, que por cierto fueron importados a la Cañada, se encuentran en mayor cantidad en los dos centros cacicales (Fig. 32). La distribución de estos artículos exóticos indica un tipo de intercambio que no es simplemente una función de distancia de la fuente o el yacimiento, sino que por su asociación con los centros cacicales, representa un vehículo de intercambio que sirve para establecer y mantener alianzas entre los élites de muchas regiones. Este tipo de intercambio es muy característico de sociedades distinguidas en la literatura etnográfica por sus mandos cacicales.

Capítulo IV. Desarrollos en la Cañada de Cuicatlán durante la fase Lomas del período Formativo Tardío (ca. 300 a.C.-200 d.C.)

La fase Lomas introdujo cambios significativos en el patrón de asentamiento de la Cañada. Todos los asentamientos del período Formativo Medio fueron abandonados, y un total de 21 poblados fueron establecidos encima de colinas que tienen vista a los suelos aluvionales del Río Grande (Fig. 34). Mientras que los asentamientos ubicados en la parte central y sur de la Cañada permanecieron menos de 5 hectáreas en tamaño, los que fueron establecidos al límite norte de la región fueron bastante más grandes.

Ahí en la confluencia de los Ríos Grande y Salado, frente al pueblo de Quiotepec, se levanta un macizo de cerros que se desprende de la sierra como península, obstruyendo el paso por la Cañada (Lámina 13). Un pasadizo a través del macizo—donde corre actualmente el ferrocarril—constituye el único medio natural de comunicación entre la Cañada y el Valle de Tehuacán. Durante la fase Lomas 7 asentamientos fueron fundados en las cercanías de Quiotepec. Entre ellos se encuentra una fortaleza compuesta de dos complejos de plataformas monumentales, un juego de pelota, y unos 30 domicilios, limitada por enormes muros de retención (Fig. 43), una plaza aislada que sostiene un montículo de 10 m de altura, la cual pudo haber servido como atalaya (Cs74-L), y otro poblado fortificado que atraviesa ambos lados del paso mencionado, el cual contiene un conjunto de plataformas, un juego de pelota, y numerosos domicilios (Fig. 41). Atravesando el Río Grande por un vado mayor se halla una plaza en la ribera opuesta al paso montañoso—extendida sobre casi 10 hectáreas de los terrenos cultivados por habitantes de Quiotepec—la cual está rodeada por montículos largos y estrechos (Fig. 44).

Juntos, estos asentamientos establecidos en Quiotepec durante la fase Lomas comprenden un total de 44.34 hectáreas de ocupación. Se estima que hasta cuatro veces más gente residían aquí de la que pudiera haber sido sostenida por medio del cultivo de los terrenos disponibles. Estos asentamientos también marcan el límite norte de la distribución de cerámica parecida a la de la fase Monte Albán II en el Valle de Oaxaca, en vista de que solo 7 kilómetros más al norte, cerca de Tecomavaca, se encuentra un sitio contemporáneo (Cs1), cuya superficie está cubierta de cerámica caraterística de la fase Palo Blanco en el Valle de Tehuacán.

Por lo tanto, se propone que Quiotepec constituyó la frontera del imperio zapoteco durante el período Formativo Tardío, y que sus poblados fortificados fueron establecidos por los zapotecos para resguardar el límite de su dominio. Esta hipótesis está apoyada por las actividades que se documentan arqueológicamente en los sitios fronterizos, muchas de las cuales concuerdan con los datos proporcionados por las fuentes etnohistóricas sobre las guarniciones que establecían los zapotecos a lo largo de sus fronteras en el período Postclásico.

Atrás de la frontera, en la parte central y sur de la Cañada de Cuicatlán, vemos evidencia de la política que impusieron los zapotecos dentro del territorio anexado. El objetivo principal parece haber sido la extracción de tributo de la región en la forma de sus recursos indígenas. Facilidades para la irrigación con canales fueron introducidas a la Cañada con el propósito de aumentar las rendiciones agrícolas por medio del cultivo de la tierra de aluvión alta. Mientras que parte del tributo exigido se pagaba con provisiones y servicios prestados a la guarnición zapoteca en Quiotepec, se demuestra cómo gran parte del tributo extraido de los pueblos sujetos en la Cañada de Cuicatlán consistió en frutas indígenas, entre ellas el zapote negro y el coyol.

También se demuestra como el asentamiento contemporáneo en Tecomavaca (Cs1) (Fig. 50), ubicado fuera del territorio aparentemente conquistado por los zapotecos, pudo haber servido como importante centro comercial para el intercambio de bienes entre el estado zapoteco y otras "naciones" de Mesoamérica.

Se concluye que durante la fase Lomas la Cañada cayó efectivamente bajo el dominio zapoteco y se convirtió en una provincia tributaria al estado zapoteco. No cabe duda de que Quiotepec constituyó la frontera norte del estado zapoteco a la vez que los pueblos en la parte principal de la Cañada fueron obligados a intensificar la producción agrícola regional con el fin de satisfacer las demandas de tributo exigidas por Monte Albán. Para obtener recursos no disponibles dentro de los confines de su territorio, los zapotecos pudieron haberse aprovechado de centros comerciales como el que se fundó justamente fuera de su frontera en Quiotepec.

Capítulo V. Desarrollos en la Cañada de Cuicatlán durante la fase Trujano del período Clásico (ca. 200-1000 d.C.).

Hasta cierto punto, el patrón de asentamiento en la Cañada de Cuicatlán durante la fase Trujano se revirtió al estado alcanzado en la fase Perdido del Formativo Medio (Fig. 51). Los asentamientos que marcaron la frontera en Quiotepec durante la fase Lomas fueron abandonados en gran parte: sólo tres poblados permanecieron ahí, ocupando un total de 9.7 hectáreas (Cuadro 33). En cambio, la parte central y sur de la Cañada fué testigo de un resurgimiento y crecimiento de población. De los 23 sitios hallados en la cumbre de colinas aquí, la mayoría permaneció menos de 4 hectáreas en tamaño, pero tres sitios llegaron a ser centros de grado superior, en virtud de sus tamaños considerables y sus complejos de arquitectura pública (Fig. 52, Cuadro 38). Esparcidos a lo largo de la región, cada uno de estos centros nucleares (Cs14-T, Cs18-T, Cs25-T), junto con sus pueblos subsidiarios, hubiera correspondido a territorios distintos. Además de los tres centros nucleares en la parte central y sur de la Cañada, se identifica un cuarto centro semejante (Cs2-T) en Quiotepec.

Por lo tanto, se propone que por algún motivo las fuerzas zapotecas se retiraron de la Cañada de Cuicatlán hacia el comienzo del período Clásico. Ante la evidente expansión del poderío mexicano de Teotihuacán en esta época, es posible que Monte Albán haya necesitado adoptar una política defensiva. Tal política pudo haber resultado en el retiro de las fuerzas zapotecas de territorios lejanos como la Cañada. Y en el vacío político dejado por los zapotecos, surgieron los cuatro centros nucleares ya mencionados.

Según las fuentes etnohistóricas, los habitantes de la Cañada de Cuicatlán en la última época prehispánica pertenecían a tres cacicazgos autónomos (Hunt 1972). Cada uno de estos cacicazgos consistía de un centro nuclear, el cual servía como cabecera, junto con sus aldeas subsidiarias. En la cabecera residía el cacique, quien presidía su cacicazgo y en cambio recibía tributo de sus sujetos. Se comprueban estos datos concernientes a la organización sociopolítica de la Cañada poco antes de la Conquista con el patrón de asentamiento obtenido ahí durante la fase Iglesia Vieja del período Postclásico (Fig. 57). El patrón de asentamiento en cuestión demuestra una concordancia sorprendente con los datos proporcionados por las crónicas.

En cuanto al período Clásico, se propone que los cacicazgos autónomos del siglo XVI tuvieron su origen hacia el comienzo de la fase Trujano debido al semejante patrón de asentamiento obtenido en esta época. Los cuatro centros que surgieron a lo largo de la Cañada después del retiro de las fuerzas zapotecas hubieran constituido las cabeceras de tales cacicazgos nacientes. Esta hipótesis está apoyada por los resultados del análisis de la distribución de población relativa a la distribución de terrenos cultivables durante la fase Trujano, los cuales indican la auto-suficiencia económica de tales cacicazgos. Las distribuciones de ciertos tipos de artefactos (obsidiana, cerámica anaranjada delgada, y urnas antropomórficas) entre las comunidades pertenecientes a la fase Trujano también concuerdan con otras expectaciones derivadas de la hipótesis acerca del origen de los cacicazgos autónomos.

Se concluye que el patrón de cacicazgos autónomos caracterizó la organización sociopolítica de la Cañada de Cuicatlán en el transcurso de la mayor parte de la época prehistórica, en vista de los cacicazgos que florecieron ahí durante el período Formativo Medio. La única interrupción sucedió durante el período Formativo Tardío, cuando la Cañada cayó bajo el dominio zapoteco.

Capítulo VI. Sumario y conclusión

Después de resumir los resultados del presente estudio de la Cañada de Cuicatlán y de su propuesta conquista por Monte Albán, el capítulo versa con el componente final del modelo de conquista, es decir, con las consecuencias del imperialismo zapoteco para el estado zapoteco mismo. Se consideran las siguientes consecuencias de la expansión zapoteca: (1) el establecimiento de fuerzas militares permanentes; (2) la administración del imperio; (3) el surgimiento de nuevos vehículos de intercambio de larga distancia; y (4) la ascensión eventual del cuerpo militar a una posición predominante dentro del gobierno zapoteco. Se demuestra cómo las tres primeras consecuencias hubieran efectuado cambios perdurables en la organización administrativa de Monte Albán, debido a sus requisitos burocráticos. De este modo, los requisitos burocráticos del imperialismo zapoteco pudieron haber contribuido a la formación del estado zapoteco en el período Formativo Tardío. Por último, se demuestra cómo las fuerzas militares que llevaron a cabo la sucesión de campañas y conquistas en territorios lejanos se elevaron al fin y al cabo a una posición superior dentro del gobierno zapoteco. Así se concluye que el estado zapoteco constituyó un poderío militar desde su principio hasta la llegada de los conquistadores españoles en el siglo XVI.